TABLE OF CONTENTS

Academic Vocabulary for the Unit

Academic vocabulary is the language you use to talk and write about the subjects you are studying, including math, science, social studies, and language arts. Understanding and using academic vocabulary will help you succeed in school and on assessments.

Each unit in this book introduces five academic vocabulary words. You will have the opportunity to practice using these words after each selection.

Academic Vocabulary for Unit 1

Preview the following Academic Vocabulary words. You will encounter these words as you work through this book and will use them as you write and talk about the selections in this unit.

analyze (ăn'ə-līz) *v.* to separate or break into parts and examine
*After reading a story I like to **analyze** the plot.*

element (ĕl'ə-mənt) *n.* one necessary or basic part of a whole
*An interesting setting is just one **element** of a good story.*

infer (ĭn fər') *v.* to decide based on evidence or knowledge; to draw a conclusion
*Based on the character's statement I can **infer** that she doesn't approve of her friend's actions.*

sequence (sē'kwəns) *n.* the chronological, causal, or logical order in which one thing follows another
*The **sequence** of events are out of order.*

structure (strŭk'chər) *n.* something constructed or built, such as a building
*How does the **structure** of the story add to its suspense?*

Think of a book you've read or movie you've seen recently. Write a few sentences about the **elements** that made the story enjoyable for you, using at least two Academic Vocabulary words in your response.

_____

_____

_____

ACADEMIC VOCABULARY   3

Before Reading

The Before Reading pages introduce you to the literary and reading skills you will practice as you read. Vocabulary words for the selection are introduced here as well.

Before Reading

The Gift of the Magi
Short Story by O. Henry

What are you willing to **SACRIFICE?**

Have you ever made a sacrifice in order to help others or make someone happy? In "The Gift of the Magi," a young couple have to decide what each is willing to do to show love for the other.

DISCUSS Work with a partner to make a list of things that people sacrifice for those they love. Think about examples in real life as well as those in books, movies, and television shows. Circle the sacrifice that was hardest to make. Put a check next to the sacrifice that shows the greatest love.

Sacrifices for Someone You Love

1. *Spending a week's allowance to buy a gift*
2. _____
3. _____
4. _____

Text Analysis: Irony

Irony is a contrast between what is expected to happen and what actually occurs. There are three types of irony commonly used in literature. The chart below provides definitions and examples of each type.

Irony	Definition	Example
Situational Irony	when a character or the readers expects one thing to happen but something else happens instead	You stay up all night cramming for a test only to find out the next day it has been moved to the following week.
Verbal Irony	when what is said is the opposite of what is meant	It's a rainy, dark day and you say "What a gorgeous day!"
Dramatic Irony	when what a character knows contrasts with what the audience knows	In a stunning upset, a champion boxer loses a big fight—the reader knows the boxer has been paid to lose.

O. Henry is well-known for writing stories in which the plot twists due to situational irony. As you read "The Gift of the Magi," think about what you expect to happen next.

Big Question

This activity gets you thinking about the real-life questions that literature addresses. Sometimes you'll work in a group or with a partner to complete this activity. After reading, you'll return to this activity. Don't be surprised if you have a different perspective.

Text Analysis

This section presents a brief, easy-to-understand lesson that introduces an important literary element and explains what to look for in the selection you are about to read.

Reading Skill or Strategy

This lesson presents a reading skill or strategy that will help your reading comprehension. Opportunities to practice these skills will be provided as you read the selection.

Vocabulary in Context

Vocabulary words for the selection are introduced before reading. Each entry gives the pronunciation and definition of the word as well as a context sentence. Occasional **Vocabulary Practice** activities will give you a chance to practice using selection vocabulary.

Reading Strategy: Predict

A well-written story will keep you wondering what happens next. Successful readers ask questions and predict possible answers. To make a prediction:

• Look for **clues** in the story to suggest what might happen next.

• Make a **prediction** about future events based on clues in the story and what you know from your own experience.

• Read on to confirm your prediction and see if it is correct.

Vocabulary in Context

Note: Words are listed in the order in which they appear in the story.

instigate (ĭn'stĭ-gāt') v. to stir up; provoke
When Jim and Della fight, it is usually money that **instigates** the argument.

vestibule (vĕs'tə-byōōl') n. a small entryway within a building
Della had the visitor wait in the **vestibule** while she went downstairs to meet him.

agile (ăj'əl) adj. able to move quickly and easily
Della appeared **agile** as she danced around the apartment.

falter (fôl'tər) v. to hesitate from lack of courage or confidence
Although Della was nervous, she did not **falter**.

ransack (răn'săk') v. to search or examine vigorously
Della **ransacked** her purse looking for change to pay the jeweler.

prudence (prōōd'ns) n. the use of good judgment and common sense
Jim used **prudence** when deciding how much to spend on a gift for Della.

ravage (răv'ĭj) n. serious damage
The old house showed the **ravage** cause by many years of neglect.

assertion (ə-sûr'shən) n. a statement
Jim's **assertion** came as a surprise to Della.

coveted (kŭv'ĭ-tĭd) adj. greedily desired or wished for
Other women **coveted** Della's silky hair.

chronicle (krŏn'ĭ-kəl) n. a record of events
The Christmas ornaments served as a **chronicle** for the many holidays they had spent together.

Reading the Selection

Notes in the side columns guide your interaction with the selection. Many notes ask you to underline or circle in the text itself. Others provide lines on which you can write your answers.

Set a Purpose for Reading

This feature gives you a reason for reading the selection.

Background

This paragraph gives you important information about the selection you are about to read. The background helps you understand the context of the literature by providing additional information about the author, the subject, or the time period during which the selection was written.

Monitor Your Comprehension

SET A PURPOSE FOR READING

Read this story to find out what sacrifices a young couple make for each other one Christmas many years ago.

The Gift of the Magi

Short Story by **O. HENRY**

BACKGROUND In this story, O. Henry makes an **allusion**, or reference, to the Magi. According to Christian tradition, the Magi were three wise men or kings who traveled to Bethlehem, guided by a miraculous star, to present gifts of frankincense, myrrh (substances prized for their fragrance), and gold to the infant Jesus. These gifts were prized possessions, having monetary, medical, and ceremonial value.

One dollar and eighty-seven cents. That was all. And 60 cents of it was in pennies. Pennies saved one and two at a time by bulldozing the grocer and the vegetable man and the butcher until one's cheeks burned with the silent imputation of parsimony[1] that such close dealing implied. Three times Della counted it. One dollar and eighty-seven cents. And the next day would be Christmas.

---

1. **imputation** (ĭm'pyŏō-tā'shən) **of parsimony** (pär'sə-mō'nē): suggestion of stinginess.

How to Use This Book

There was clearly nothing to do but flop down on the shabby
little couch and howl. So Della did it. Which instigates the moral
reflection that life is made up of sobs, sniffles, and smiles, with
sniffles predominating. **PAUSE & REFLECT**

While the mistress of the home is gradually subsiding from
the first stage to the second, take a look at the home. A furnished
flat at $8 per week. It did not exactly beggar description, but
it certainly had that word on the lookout for the mendicancy
squad.[2]

In the vestibule below belonged to this flat a letterbox into
which no letter would go and an electric button from which no
mortal finger could coax a ring. Also appertaining thereunto was
a card bearing the name "Mr. James Dillingham Young."

The "Dillingham" had been flung to the breeze during a
former period of prosperity when its possessor was being paid
$30 per week. Now, when the income was shrunk to $20, the
letters of "Dillingham" looked blurred, as though they were
thinking seriously of contracting to a modest and unassuming
D. But whenever Mr. James Dillingham Young came home and
reached his flat above, he was called "Jim" and greatly hugged
by Mrs. James Dillingham Young, already introduced to you as
Della. Which is all very good.

Della finished her cry and attended to her cheeks with the
powder rag. She stood by the window and looked out dully at a
gray cat walking a gray fence in a gray backyard. Tomorrow would
be Christmas Day, and she had only $1.87 with which to buy Jim
a present. She had been saving every penny she could for months,
with this result. Twenty dollars a week doesn't go far. Expenses
had been greater than she had calculated. They always are. Only
$1.87 to buy a present for Jim. Her Jim. Many a happy hour she
had spent planning for something nice for him. Something fine
and rare and sterling—something just a little bit near to being
worthy of the honor of being owned by Jim.

Monitor Your Comprehension

instigate (ĭn'stĭ-gāt') v. to stir
up; provoke

PAUSE & REFLECT
Reread the first two paragraphs.
Why does Della flop down on the
couch and howl?

vestibule (věs'tə-byōōl') n. a
small entryway within a building

IRONY
Irony is the difference between
what you expect to happen and
what actually happens. You
might expect someone named
Mr. James Dillingham Young to
be rich. Cite details from the text
that tell you he is not.

2. **mendicancy** (měn'dĭ-kan-sē) **squad:** a police unit assigned to arrest beggars.

THE GIFT OF THE MAGI   37

Side notes provide a variety of activities for you to
complete as you read the selection.

Pause & Reflect
Notes in the side column allow you a chance to
pause from your reading and think about what you
have read.

Vocabulary words
Definitions for vocabulary words are provided in
the side margin at point of use. Occasional
activities offer opportunities for you to use the
vocabulary words.

Text Analysis or Reading Skill
These notes help you identify and analyze the
literary element or reading skill you learned about
on the Before Reading page.

After Reading

Text Analysis: Irony
"The Gift of the Magi" is famous for its situational irony. Fill in the Irony Map
below to understand how the story's events create situational irony.

IRONY MAP	
Della	Jim
What Della Sells:	What Jim Sells:
What Della Buys:	What Jim Buys:
What Della Receives:	What Jim Receives:
Why the Gift is Useless:	Why the Gift is Useless:

Review your notes for "Gift of the Magi" and your completed Irony Map. Then,
write a brief explanation of what O. Henry's use of irony tells us about Della
and Jim's relationship.

THE GIFT OF THE MAGI   43

After Reading
The After Reading pages help you assess the skills
you have practiced throughout the selection.

Text Analysis
Demonstrate your knowledge of the literary skill by
filling out the organizer on this page and answering
the question that follows.

After Reading

Reading Skill: Predict

Look back at the predictions you made as you read. Which predictions proved true and which did not? For the predictions that did not prove true, write a sentence explaining the outcome in the chart below.

Clue	

↓

Prediction	

↓

Outcome	

What are you willing to SACRIFICE?

What material possessions could you live without?

_____

_____

Vocabulary Practice

Circle the word that is most different in meaning from the others.

1. (a) destruction, (b) ravage, (c) ruin, (d) creation
2. (a) stop, (b) stir, (c) urge, (d) instigate
3. (a) desired, (b) coveted, (c) craved, (d) unwanted
4. (a) cellar, (b) vestibule, (c) foyer, (d) entryway
5. (a) waver, (b) proceed, (c) falter, (d) hesitate
6. (a) questions, (b) assertion, (c) statement, (d) explanation
7. (a) limber, (b) clumsy, (c) flexible, (d) agile
8. (a) loot, (b) plunder, (c) organize, (d) ransack
9. (a) history, (b) record, (c) chronicle, (d) prediction
10. (a) carelessness, (b) caution, (c) prudence, (d) wisdom

Reading Skill

The Reading Skill activity follows up on the skill you used as you read the text.

Big Question

The Big Question is followed up here with an opportunity for you to think about what you learned about life as you read.

Vocabulary Practice

Your knowledge of the vocabulary words is assessed with a variety of activities.

Academic Vocabulary in Speaking

analyze	element	infer	sequence	structure

An **element** is one necessary or basic part of a whole thing. A short story has various **elements**, including a plot, characters, setting, narrator, and conflict. What elements in "The Gift of the Magi" help create the suspense? Think about what the narrator tells you and what the narrator leaves out. Use at least one Academic Vocabulary word in your response. Definitions for these words can be found on page 3.

_____

_____

_____

Assessment Practice

DIRECTIONS Use "The Gift of the Magi" to answer questions 1–6.

1 Della buys a watch fob for Jim because —
   (A) he lost his watch
   (B) he treasures his watch
   (C) he doesn't know how to tell time
   (D) it's his birthday

2 When Jim sees Della's short hair, he realizes —
   (A) she has been to a beauty parlor
   (B) he likes her hair short
   (C) his gift for her will be useless
   (D) she couldn't always have long hair

3 Which statement best describes the situational irony in the story?
   (A) The watch fob is as useless to Jim as the combs are to Della.
   (B) Jim and Della bought each other expensive gifts.
   (C) Della's combs were bought with the money she received for her hair.
   (D) Jim and Della are as wise as the Magi.

4 O. Henry suggests that Della and Jim's "greatest treasure" is —
   (A) a watch fob and a comb
   (B) their foolishness
   (C) their sacrifices
   (D) their love for each other

5 To create a surprise ending, O. Henry —
   (A) does not introduce Jim until the end of the story
   (B) withholds information about Jim's plan
   (C) explains right away what the characters know
   (D) does not reveal Della's motivation for cutting her hair

6 What does the story reveal about Della and Jim?
   (A) They are greedy and selfish.
   (B) The put each other's happiness above their own.
   (C) They don't know each other as well as they thought.
   (D) They have fallen out of love.

Academic Vocabulary

The academic vocabulary words are followed up here. You will be asked to use at least one of the words in a speaking or writing activity about the selection.

Assessment Practice

To help you on your state tests, each selection is followed up by multiple-choice questions that test your comprehension of the selection.

UNIT 1

The Plot Thickens

NARRATIVE STRUCTURE

Be sure to read the Text Analysis Workshop
on pp. 28–35 in *Holt McDougal Literature.*

Academic Vocabulary for Unit 1

Preview the following Academic Vocabulary words. You will encounter these words as you work through this book and will use them as you write and talk about the selections in this unit.

analyze (ăn´ə-līz) *v.* to separate or break into parts and examine

*After reading a story I like to **analyze** the plot.*

●

element (el´ə mənt) *n.* one necessary or basic part of a whole

*An interesting setting is just one **element** of a good story.*

●

infer (in fər´) *v.* to decide based on evidence or knowledge; to draw a conclusion

*Based on the character's statement I can **infer** that she doesn't approve of her friend's actions.*

●

sequence (sē´kwəns) *n.* the chronological, causal, or logical order in which one thing follows another

*The **sequence** of events are out of order.*

●

structure (strŭk´chər) *n.* something constructed or built, such as a building

*How does the **structure** of the story add to its suspense?*

Think of a book you've read or movie you've seen recently. Write a few sentences about the **elements** that made the story enjoyable for you, using at least two Academic Vocabulary words in your response.

_____

_____

_____

The Most Dangerous Game

Short Story by **Richard Connell**

What does it take to be a **SURVIVOR?**

You probably know that water, food, and shelter are necessary to live. But when it comes to survival, what **traits**, or qualities, help a person succeed? That's the question posed in "The Most Dangerous Game," the story you are about to read.

QUICKWRITE Think about movies you've seen or books you've read in which one person survives against the odds. What qualities or abilities do survivors share? Write down a list like the one on the left of qualities a person needs to survive. Then, discuss with a partner which traits you think are the most important.

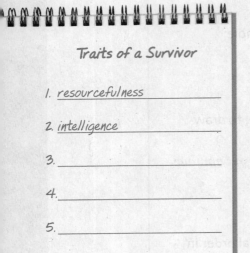

Traits of a Survivor

1. resourcefulness

2. intelligence

3. _____

4. _____

5. _____

6. _____

Text Analysis: Conflict

Plot is the series of events that make up a story. At the heart of any plot, is a **conflict,** or struggle, between opposing forces. A plot usually follows a pattern like the one shown in the diagram below.

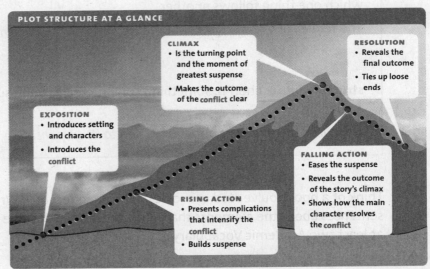

PLOT STRUCTURE AT A GLANCE

CLIMAX
- Is the turning point and the moment of greatest suspense
- Makes the outcome of the conflict clear

RESOLUTION
- Reveals the final outcome
- Ties up loose ends

EXPOSITION
- Introduces setting and characters
- Introduces the conflict

RISING ACTION
- Presents complications that intensify the conflict
- Builds suspense

FALLING ACTION
- Eases the suspense
- Reveals the outcome of the story's climax
- Shows how the main character resolves the conflict

Sometimes, however, writers may play with the sequence of events creating a plot that is **non-linear.** A writer may use **flashbacks,** or interruptions in the action of the story to tell about events that happen in the past. To create **suspense**, a feeling of anxiety or dread, writers may use **foreshadowing,** dropping clues in the text to hint at complications that will happen later in the story. As you read, look out for the use of these techniques and how they influence the conflicts the main character faces.

Reading Strategy: Visualize

Good readers use a writer's words to **visualize**, or form images of the story's setting and characters. To visualize a story:

- pay special attention to descriptions and word choices
- look for **sensory details**, ones that appeal to one or more of your senses
- reread lengthy descriptions to catch details you might have missed

Vocabulary in Context

Note: Words are listed in the order they appear in the story.

tangible (tăn′jə-bəl) *adj.* capable of being touched having form and substance
*Rainsford didn't believe Ship-Trap Island was a real, **tangible** place*

quarry (kwôr′ē) *n.* the object of a hunt; prey
*The hunters followed their **quarry** for hours before taking the fatal shot.*

disarming (dĭs-är′mĭng) *adj.* removing suspicion; inspiring confidence
*Rainsford's fears were put at ease by the general's **disarming** smile.*

cultivated (kŭl′tə-vā′tĭd) *adj.* refined or cultured in manner
*One could tell from the many collectibles that he was a **cultivated** gentleman.*

amenity (ə-mĕn′ĭ-tē) *n.* something that adds to one's comfort or convenience
*The ship offered every **amenity** a traveler would desire.*

condone (kən-dōn′) *v.* to forgive or overlook
*Rainsford would not **condone** the general's actions.*

droll (drōl) *adj.* amusingly odd or comical
*Rainsford enjoyed the general's **droll** sense of humor.*

scruple (skrōō′pəl) *n.* a feeling of uneasiness
*Most sailors had **scruples** about traveling to the abandoned island.*

solicitously (sə-lĭs′ĭ-təs-lē) *adv.* in a manner expressing care or concern
*"Are you feeling alright," the general asked **solicitously**.*

imperative (ĭm-pĕr′ə-tĭv) *adj.* absolutely necessary
*It is **imperative** that Rainsford follow the rules set by the general.*

zealous (zĕl′əs) *adj.* intensely enthusiastic
*The men were **zealous** about beginning the hunt.*

uncanny (ŭn-kăn′ē) *adj.* so remarkable as to seem supernatural
*The general's skills as a hunter are **uncanny**.*

Reading Strategy: Visuali ze

Good readers use a wo...

setting and character...

reread lengthy descri...

Vocabulary in Cont...

Note: Words in blue...

tangible (t n' jə bəl)...

Rainsford didn't belie...

...

amenity...

The ship offers e...

scruple...

Rainsford would...

diabol...

Reading...

scruple...

scrupulously...

Are you sure of it...

restore...

The doctors...

...

uncanny...

The general skill...

SET A PURPOSE FOR READING

Read this story to find out what one hunter thinks is the most dangerous game.

The Most Dangerous Game

Short Story by

RICHARD CONNELL

BACKGROUND Hunting for big game, such as lions, rhinos, and leopards, was a popular sport among wealthy people in the early 20th century, when Connell was writing. These people had time and money to spend on travel and on satisfying their thirst for conquest, danger, and excitement. The two main characters in "The Most Dangerous Game" are experienced hunters in search of a greater challenge.

Ⓐ CONFLICT

Foreshadowing occurs when the author plants clues in the text to hint at what's to come. Circle the words in lines 1–6 that hint at possible conflict.

"Off there to the right—somewhere—is a large island," said Whitney. "It's rather a mystery—"

"What island is it?" Rainsford asked.

"The old charts call it 'Ship-Trap Island,'" Whitney replied. "A suggestive name, isn't it? Sailors have a curious dread of the place. I don't know why. Some superstition—" Ⓐ

"Can't see it," remarked Rainsford, trying to peer through the dank tropical night that was palpable as it pressed its thick warm blackness in upon the yacht.

10 "You've good eyes," said Whitney, with a laugh, "and I've seen you pick off a moose moving in the brown fall bush at four hundred yards, but even you can't see four miles or so through a moonless Caribbean night."

"Nor four yards," admitted Rainsford. "Ugh! It's like moist black velvet."

"It will be light enough in Rio,"[1] promised Whitney. "We should make it in a few days. I hope the jaguar guns have come from Purdey's. We should have some good hunting up the Amazon. Great sport, hunting."

20   "The best sport in the world," agreed Rainsford.

"For the hunter," amended Whitney. "Not for the jaguar."

"Don't talk rot, Whitney," said Rainsford. "You're a big-game hunter, not a philosopher. Who cares how a jaguar feels?"

"Perhaps the jaguar does," observed Whitney.

"Bah! They've no understanding." **B**

"Even so, I rather think they understand one thing—fear. The fear of pain and the fear of death."

"Nonsense," laughed Rainsford. "This hot weather is making you soft, Whitney. Be a realist. The world is made up of two 30 classes—the hunters and the huntees. Luckily, you and I are hunters. Do you think we've passed that island yet?"

"I can't tell in the dark. I hope so."

"Why?" asked Rainsford.

"The place has a reputation—a bad one."

"Cannibals?" suggested Rainsford.

"Hardly. Even cannibals wouldn't live in such a Godforsaken place. But it's gotten into sailor lore, somehow. Didn't you notice that the crew's nerves seemed a bit jumpy today?"

"They were a bit strange, now you mention it. Even Captain 40 Nielsen—"

"Yes, even that tough-minded old Swede, who'd go up to the devil himself and ask him for a light. Those fishy blue eyes held a look I never saw there before. All I could get out of him was: 'This place has an evil name among seafaring men, sir.' Then he said to me, very gravely: 'Don't you feel anything?'—as if the air about us was actually poisonous. Now, you mustn't laugh when I tell you this—I did feel something like a sudden chill. **PAUSE & REFLECT**

"There was no breeze. The sea was as flat as a plate-glass window. We were drawing near the island then. What I felt was 50 a—a mental chill; a sort of sudden dread."

---

1. **Rio:** Rio de Janeiro (rē′ō dā zhə-nâr′ō): a city on the coast of Brazil.

B CONFLICT
Reread lines 20–25. In your own words, describe the conflict between Rainsford and Whitney.

Whitney cares about the Animal while Rainsford does Not.

PAUSE & REFLECT
The author has just provided you with important information about the setting. What happens to Captain Nielsen and the crew when they get near Ship-Trap Island?

This place gave everyone a chilling vibe.

tangible (tăn'jə-bəl) *adj.* capable of being touched; having form and substance

C VISUALIZE
Reread lines 66–69. Circle the words that describe the night. To which sense or senses do these descriptions appeal?

The eyes "it shows" that it so dark that [illegible] eyes were usless to see.

"Pure imagination," said Rainsford. "One superstitious sailor can taint the whole ship's company with his fear."

"Maybe. But sometimes I think sailors have an extra sense that tells them when they are in danger. Sometimes I think evil is a **tangible** thing—with wavelengths, just as sound and light have. An evil place can, so to speak, broadcast vibrations of evil. Anyhow, I'm glad we're getting out of this zone. Well, I think I'll turn in now, Rainsford."

"I'm not sleepy," said Rainsford. "I'm going to smoke another
60 pipe up on the afterdeck."

"Good night, then, Rainsford. See you at breakfast."

"Right. Good night, Whitney."

There was no sound in the night as Rainsford sat there but the muffled throb of the engine that drove the yacht swiftly through the darkness, and the swish and ripple of the wash of the propeller.

Rainsford, reclining in a steamer chair, indolently puffed on his favorite brier.[2] The sensuous drowsiness of the night was on him. "It's so dark," he thought, "that I could sleep without closing my eyes; the night would be my eyelids—" **C**
70 An abrupt sound startled him. Off to the right he heard it, and his ears, expert in such matters, could not be mistaken. Again he heard the sound, and again. Somewhere, off in the blackness, someone had fired a gun three times.

Rainsford sprang up and moved quickly to the rail, mystified. He strained his eyes in the direction from which the reports had come, but it was like trying to see through a blanket. He leaped upon the rail and balanced himself there, to get greater elevation; his pipe, striking a rope, was knocked from his mouth. He lunged for it; a short, hoarse cry came from his lips as he realized he had
80 reached too far and had lost his balance. The cry was pinched off short as the blood-warm waters of the Caribbean Sea closed over his head.

He struggled up to the surface and tried to cry out, but the wash from the speeding yacht slapped him in the face, and the salt water in his open mouth made him gag and strangle. Desperately he struck out with strong strokes after the receding lights of the

2. **brier** (brī'ər): a tobacco pipe.

yacht, but he stopped before he had swum fifty feet. A certain cool-headedness had come to him; it was not the first time he had been in a tight place. There was a chance that his cries could be
90 heard by someone aboard the yacht, but that chance was slender and grew more slender as the yacht raced on. He wrestled himself out of his clothes and shouted with all his power. The lights of the yacht became faint and ever-vanishing fireflies; then they were blotted out entirely by the night. ❶

Rainsford remembered the shots. They had come from the right, and doggedly he swam in that direction, swimming with slow, deliberate strokes, conserving his strength. For a seemingly endless time he fought the sea. He began to count his strokes; he could do possibly a hundred more and then—

100 Rainsford heard a sound. It came out of the darkness, a high, screaming sound, the sound of an animal in an extremity of anguish and terror.

He did not recognize the animal that made the sound; he did not try to; with fresh vitality he swam toward the sound. He heard it again; then it was cut short by another noise, crisp, staccato.

"Pistol shot," muttered Rainsford, swimming on.

Ten minutes of determined effort brought another sound to his ears—the most welcome he had ever heard—the muttering
110 and growling of the sea breaking on a rocky shore. He was almost on the rocks before he saw them; on a night less calm he would have been shattered against them. With his remaining strength he dragged himself from the swirling waters. Jagged crags appeared to jut up into the opaqueness; he forced himself upward, hand over hand. Gasping, his hands raw, he reached a flat place at the top. Dense jungle came down to the very edge of the cliffs. What perils that tangle of trees and underbrush might hold for him did not concern Rainsford just then. All he knew was that he was safe from his enemy, the sea, and
120 that utter weariness was on him. He flung himself down at the jungle edge and tumbled headlong into the deepest sleep of his life. ❷

❶ **CONFLICT**
An **internal conflict** is created when a character struggles with his or her own heart or mind. An **external conflict** occurs when an outside force prevents the character from reaching a goal. Describe the conflict that Rainsford confronts now. Is the conflict internal or external?

external He was knocked out of the Boat and Now He is lost to the sea

❷ **VISUALIZE**
Underline the details in this paragraph that help you visualize the scene.

THE MOST DANGEROUS GAME 9

When he opened his eyes, he knew from the position of the sun that it was late in the afternoon. Sleep had given him new vigor; a sharp hunger was picking at him. He looked about him, almost cheerfully.

"Where there are pistol shots, there are men. Where there are men, there is food," he thought. But what kind of men, he wondered, in so forbidding a place? An unbroken front of snarled 130 and ragged jungle fringed the shore. PAUSE & REFLECT

He saw no sign of a trail through the closely knit web of weeds and trees; it was easier to go along the shore, and Rainsford floundered along by the water. Not far from where he had landed, he stopped.

Some wounded thing, by the evidence a large animal, had thrashed about in the underbrush; the jungle weeds were crushed down, and the moss was lacerated; one patch of weeds was stained crimson. A small, glittering object not far away caught Rainsford's eye, and he picked it up. It was an empty cartridge.

140 "A twenty-two," he remarked. "That's odd. It must have been a fairly large animal, too. The hunter had his nerve with him to tackle it with a light gun. It's clear that the brute put up a fight. I suppose the first three shots I heard was when the hunter flushed his **quarry** and wounded it. The last shot was when he trailed it here and finished it."

He examined the ground closely and found what he had hoped to find—the print of hunting boots. They pointed along the cliff in the direction he had been going. Eagerly he hurried along, now slipping on a rotten log or a loose stone, but making headway; 150 night was beginning to settle down on the island.

Bleak darkness was blacking out the sea and jungle when Rainsford sighted the lights. He came upon them as he turned a crook in the coastline, and his first thought was that he had come upon a village, for there were many lights. But as he forged along, he saw to his great astonishment that all the lights were in one enormous building—a lofty structure with pointed towers

PAUSE & REFLECT

Why does Rainsford ask himself "what kind of men" live on the island?

becuse its complesy under developed

---

quarry (kwôr′ē) *n.* the object of a hunt; prey

What kind of animal do you think might have been the quarry?

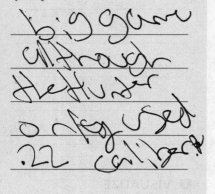
big game although the hunter only used a .22 caliber

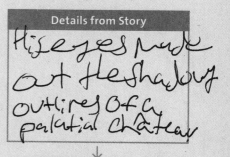
plunging upward into the gloom. His eyes made out the shadowy outlines of a palatial château; it was set on a high bluff, and on three sides of it cliffs dived down to where the sea licked greedy lips in the shadows.

160   "Mirage," thought Rainsford. But it was no mirage, he found, when he opened the tall spiked iron gate. The stone steps were real enough; the massive door with a leering gargoyle for a knocker was real enough; yet about it all hung an air of unreality. **F**

He lifted the knocker, and it creaked up stiffly as if it had never before been used. He let it fall, and it startled him with its booming loudness. He thought he heard steps within; the door remained closed. Again Rainsford lifted the heavy knocker and let it fall. The door opened then, opened as suddenly as if it were on a spring, and Rainsford stood blinking in the river of glaring gold

170 light that poured out. The first thing Rainsford's eyes discerned was the largest man Rainsford had ever seen—a gigantic creature, solidly made and black-bearded to the waist. In his hand the man held a long-barreled revolver, and he was pointing it straight at Rainsford's heart.

Out of the snarl of beard two small eyes regarded Rainsford.

"Don't be alarmed," said Rainsford, with a smile which he hoped was **disarming**. "I'm no robber. I fell off a yacht. My name is Sanger Rainsford of New York City."

F VISUALIZE
Reread the description of the castle in lines 151–163 and fill out the graphic organizer below.

Details from Story
His eyes made out the shadowy outlines of a palatial château

↓

What I Visualize
a large castle that is built on a hill

disarming (dĭs-är′mĭng) *adj.* removing suspicion; inspiring confidence

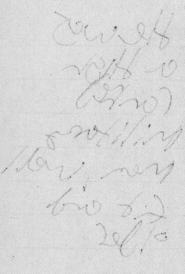

The menacing look in the eyes did not change. The revolver
180 pointed as rigidly as if the giant were a statue. He gave no sign
that he understood Rainsford's words, or that he had even heard
them. He was dressed in uniform, a black uniform trimmed with
gray astrakhan.[3]

"I'm Sanger Rainsford of New York," Rainsford began again.
"I fell off a yacht. I am hungry."

The man's only answer was to raise with his thumb the
hammer of his revolver. Then Rainsford saw the man's free
hand go to his forehead in a military salute, and he saw him
click his heels together and stand at attention. Another man
190 was coming down the broad marble steps, an erect, slender man
in evening clothes. He advanced to Rainsford and held out
his hand.

In a **cultivated** voice marked by a slight accent that gave it
added precision and deliberateness, he said: "It is a very great
pleasure and honor to welcome Mr. Sanger Rainsford, the
celebrated hunter, to my home."

Automatically Rainsford shook the man's hand.

"I've read your book about hunting snow leopards in Tibet,[4]
you see," explained the man. "I am General Zaroff."

200 Rainsford's first impression was that the man was singularly
handsome; his second was that there was an original, almost
bizarre quality about the general's face. He was a tall man
past middle age, for his hair was a vivid white; but his thick
eyebrows and pointed military moustache were as black as
the night from which Rainsford had come. His eyes, too,
were black and very bright. He had high cheekbones, a
sharp-cut nose, a spare, dark face, the face of a man used to
giving orders, the face of an aristocrat. Turning to the giant
in uniform, the general made a sign. The giant put away his
210 pistol, saluted, withdrew. **G**

"Ivan is an incredibly strong fellow," remarked the general, "but
he has the misfortune to be deaf and dumb. A simple fellow, but,
I'm afraid, like all his race, a bit of a savage."

---

3. **astrakhan** (ăs′trə-kăn′): a fur made from the curly, wavy wool of young lambs
   from Astrakhan (a city of southwest Russia).
4. **Tibet** (tə-bĕt′): a region in central Asia.

cultivated (kŭl′tə-vā′tĭd) *adj.*
refined or cultured in manner

G VISUALIZE
You've just read a detailed
description of General Zaroff.
Circle the words or phrases that
describe him. What do these
details lead you to believe about
him?

He was
a High
ranky
military
men well
fit and
order

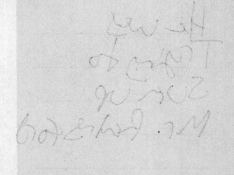

"Is he Russian?"

"He is a Cossack,"[5] said the general, and his smile showed red lips and pointed teeth. "So am I.

"Come," he said, "we shouldn't be chatting here. We can talk later. Now you want clothes, food, rest. You shall have them. This is a most restful spot."

220 Ivan had reappeared, and the general spoke to him with lips that moved but gave forth no sound.

"Follow Ivan, if you please, Mr. Rainsford," said the general. "I was about to have my dinner when you came. I'll wait for you. You'll find that my clothes will fit you, I think."

It was to a huge, beam-ceilinged bedroom with a canopied bed big enough for six men that Rainsford followed the silent giant. Ivan laid out an evening suit, and Rainsford, as he put it on, noticed that it came from a London tailor who ordinarily cut and sewed for none below the rank of duke.

230 The dining room to which Ivan conducted him was in many ways remarkable. There was a medieval magnificence about it; it suggested a baronial hall of feudal times with its oaken panels, its high ceiling, its vast refectory table where two score men could sit down to eat. About the hall were the mounted heads of many animals—lions, tigers, elephants, moose, bears; larger or more perfect specimens Rainsford had never seen. At the great table the general was sitting, alone.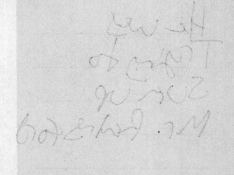

"You'll have a cocktail, Mr. Rainsford," he suggested. The cocktail was surpassingly good; and, Rainsford noted, the table

240 appointments were of the finest—the linen, the crystal, the silver, the china.

They were eating *borsch*, the rich red soup with whipped cream so dear to Russian palates. Half apologetically General Zaroff said: "We do our best to preserve the **amenities** of civilization here. Please forgive any lapses. We are well off the beaten track, you know. Do you think the champagne has suffered from its long ocean trip?"

---

5. **Cossack** (kŏs′ăk): a member of a southern Russian people, many of whom served as fierce cavalrymen under the Russian tsars.

H VISUALIZE
Underline the words and phrases that help you visualize this "remarkable" room.

amenity (ə-mĕn′ĭ-tē) *n.* something that adds to one's comfort or convenience

PAUSE & REFLECT

Rainsford is uncomfortable with the general's judging him. What do you think the general is trying to do here?

He was
Trying to
Sum up
Mr. Rainsford

"Not in the least," declared Rainsford. He was finding the general a most thoughtful and affable host, a true cosmopolite.[6] But there was one small trait of the general's that made Rainsford uncomfortable. Whenever he looked up from his plate, he found the general studying him, appraising him narrowly. **PAUSE & REFLECT**

"Perhaps," said General Zaroff, "you were surprised that I recognized your name. You see, I read all books on hunting published in English, French, and Russian. I have but one passion in my life, Mr. Rainsford, and it is the hunt."

"You have some wonderful heads here," said Rainsford as he ate a particularly well cooked filet mignon. "That Cape buffalo is the largest I ever saw."

"Oh, that fellow. Yes, he was a monster."

"Did he charge you?"

"Hurled me against a tree," said the general. "Fractured my skull. But I got the brute."

"I've always thought," said Rainsford, "that the Cape buffalo is the most dangerous of all big game."

For a moment the general did not reply; he was smiling his curious red-lipped smile. Then he said slowly: "No. You are wrong, sir. The Cape buffalo is not the most dangerous big game." He sipped his wine. "Here in my preserve on this island," he said, in the same slow tone, "I hunt more dangerous game."

Rainsford expressed his surprise. "Is there big game on this island?"

The general nodded. "The biggest."

"Really?"

"Oh, it isn't here naturally, of course. I have to stock the island."

"What have you imported, General?" Rainsford asked. "Tigers?"

The general smiled. "No," he said. "Hunting tigers ceased to interest me some years ago. I exhausted their possibilities, you

---

6. **cosmopolite** (kŏz-mŏp′ə-līt′): a sophisticated person who can handle any situation well.

see. No thrill left in tigers, no real danger. I live for danger, Mr. Rainsford."

The general took from his pocket a gold cigarette case and offered his guest a long black cigarette with a silver tip; it was perfumed and gave off a smell like incense.

"We will have some capital hunting, you and I," said the general. "I shall be most glad to have your society."

"But what game—" began Rainsford.

"I'll tell you," said the general. "You will be amused, I know. 290 I think I may say, in all modesty, that I have done a rare thing. I have invented a new sensation. May I pour you another glass of port, Mr. Rainsford?"

"Thank you, General." ❶

The general filled both glasses and said: "God makes some men poets. Some he makes kings, some beggars. Me he made a hunter. My hand was made for the trigger, my father said. He was a very rich man with a quarter of a million acres in the Crimea, and he was an ardent sportsman. When I was only five years old, he gave me a little gun, specially made in Moscow 300 for me, to shoot sparrows with. When I shot some of his prize turkeys with it, he did not punish me; he complimented me on my marksmanship. I killed my first bear in the Caucasus[7] when I was ten. My whole life has been one prolonged hunt. I went into the army—it was expected of noblemen's sons—and for a time commanded a division of Cossack cavalry, but my real interest was always the hunt. I have hunted every kind of game in every land. It would be impossible for me to tell you how many animals I have killed."

The general puffed at his cigarette.

310 "After the debacle in Russia I left the country, for it was imprudent for an officer of the Tsar[8] to stay there. Many noble Russians lost everything. I, luckily, had invested heavily in American securities, so I shall never have to open a tearoom in Monte Carlo or drive a taxi in Paris. Naturally, I continued

___

7. **Crimea** (krī-mē′ə) . . . **Caucasus** (kô′kə-səs): regions in the southern part of the former Russian Empire, near the Black Sea.

8. **debacle in Russia . . . Tsar** (zär): a reference to the 1917 Russian Revolution, in which the emperor, Tsar Nicholas II, was violently overthrown.

❶ **CONFLICT**
Rainsford and Zaroff are having a conversation about hunting. Review the dialogue in lines 260–293. Circle what Rainsford thinks of as the most dangerous game. What clues in this conversation hint that there is more conflict to come?

He seems to be willing or avoiding what he stocks the Island w.

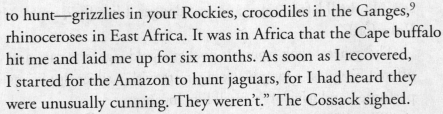

to hunt—grizzlies in your Rockies, crocodiles in the Ganges,[9] rhinoceroses in East Africa. It was in Africa that the Cape buffalo hit me and laid me up for six months. As soon as I recovered, I started for the Amazon to hunt jaguars, for I had heard they were unusually cunning. They weren't." The Cossack sighed.

320 "They were no match at all for a hunter with his wits about him, and a high-powered rifle. I was bitterly disappointed. I was lying in my tent with a splitting headache one night when a terrible thought pushed its way into my mind. Hunting was beginning to bore me! And hunting, remember, had been my life. I have heard that in America businessmen often go to pieces when they give up the business that has been their life." ❿

"Yes, that's so," said Rainsford.

The general smiled. "I had no wish to go to pieces," he said. "I must do something. Now, mine is an analytical mind,

330 Mr. Rainsford. Doubtless that is why I enjoy the problems of the chase."

"No doubt, General Zaroff."

"So," continued the general, "I asked myself why the hunt no longer fascinated me. You are much younger than I am, Mr. Rainsford, and have not hunted as much, but you perhaps can guess the answer."

"What was it?"

"Simply this: hunting had ceased to be what you call 'a sporting proposition.' It had become too easy. I always got my

340 quarry. Always. There is no greater bore than perfection."

The general lit a fresh cigarette.

"No animal had a chance with me any more. That is no boast; it is a mathematical certainty. The animal had nothing but his legs and his instinct. Instinct is no match for reason. When I thought of this, it was a tragic moment for me, I can tell you."

Rainsford leaned across the table, absorbed in what his host was saying.

"It came to me as an inspiration what I must do," the general

350 went on.

---

9. **Ganges** (găn'jēz'): a river in northern India.

Ⓙ **CONFLICT**
Underline the sentence in this paragraph that states the conflict the general faced in his past.

"And that was?"

The general smiled the quiet smile of one who has faced an obstacle and surmounted it with success. "I had to invent a new animal to hunt," he said.

"A new animal? You're joking."

"Not at all," said the general. "I never joke about hunting. I needed a new animal. I found one. So I bought this island, built this house, and here I do my hunting. The island is perfect for my purposes—there are jungles with a maze of trails in them, hills, 360 swamps—"

"But the animal, General Zaroff?" **K**

"Oh," said the general, "it supplies me with the most exciting hunting in the world. No other hunting compares with it for an instant. Every day I hunt, and I never grow bored now, for I have a quarry with which I can match my wits."

Rainsford's bewilderment showed in his face.

"I wanted the ideal animal to hunt," explained the general. "So I said: 'What are the attributes of an ideal quarry?' And the answer was, of course: 'It must have courage, cunning, and, above 370 all, it must be able to reason.'"

"But no animal can reason," objected Rainsford.

"My dear fellow," said the general, "there is one that can."

"But you can't mean—" gasped Rainsford.

"And why not?"

"I can't believe you are serious, General Zaroff. This is a grisly joke."

"Why should I not be serious? I am speaking of hunting."

"Hunting? Good God, General Zaroff, what you speak of is murder." PAUSE & REFLECT

380 The general laughed with entire good nature. He regarded Rainsford quizzically. "I refuse to believe that so modern and civilized a young man as you seem to be harbors romantic ideas about the value of human life. Surely your experiences in the war—"

K PLOT DEVELOPMENT

In order to create suspense, the author has used **foreshadowing**, planting clues in the text to hint at what's to come. Circle the places in the text where Rainsford asks question of Zaroff.

What does Rainsford want to know?

What he hunts.

What animal do you think Zaroff "invented"?

None I think it's Humans.

PAUSE & REFLECT

Rainsford's question is finally answered. What is Zaroff speaking of?

Humans.

condone (kən-dōn′) *v.* to forgive or overlook

droll (drōl) *adj.* amusingly odd or comical

scruple (skrōō′pəl) *n.* a feeling of uneasiness that keeps a person from doing something

What does Rainsford feel uneasy about?

How the General is Hunting Humans.

PAUSE & REFLECT

Reread lines 408–410. The general says he enjoys hunting men because unlike other animals they can reason—they have feelings, ideas, and beliefs of their own. Why does this fact make them interesting prey?

Because They can be dangerous.

"Did not make me **condone** cold-blooded murder," finished Rainsford, stiffly.

Laughter shook the general. "How extraordinarily **droll** you are!" he said. "One does not expect nowadays to find a young man of the educated class, even in America, with such a naïve,
390 and, if I may say so, mid-Victorian point of view. It's like finding a snuffbox in a limousine. Ah, well, doubtless you had Puritan ancestors. So many Americans appear to have had. I'll wager you'll forget your notions when you go hunting with me. You've a genuine new thrill in store for you, Mr. Rainsford."

"Thank you, I'm a hunter, not a murderer."

"Dear me," said the general, quite unruffled, "again that unpleasant word. But I think I can show you that your **scruples** are quite ill-founded."

"Yes?"

400 "Life is for the strong, to be lived by the strong, and, if needs be, taken by the strong. The weak of the world were put here to give the strong pleasure. I am strong. Why should I not use my gift? If I wish to hunt, why should I not? I hunt the scum of the earth—sailors from tramp ships—lascars,[10] blacks, Chinese, whites, mongrels—a thoroughbred horse or hound is worth more than a score of them."

"But they are men," said Rainsford, hotly.

"Precisely," said the general. "That is why I use them. It gives me pleasure. They can reason, after a fashion. So they are
410 dangerous." **PAUSE & REFLECT**

"But where do you get them?"

The general's left eyelid fluttered down in a wink. "This island is called Ship Trap," he answered. "Sometimes an angry god of the high seas sends them to me. Sometimes, when Providence is not so kind, I help Providence a bit. Come to the window with me."

Rainsford went to the window and looked out toward the sea.

---

10. **lascars** (lăs′kərz): sailors from India.

"Watch! Out there!" exclaimed the general, pointing into the night. Rainsford's eyes saw only blackness, and then, as the
420 general pressed a button, far out to sea Rainsford saw the flash of lights.

The general chuckled. "They indicate a channel," he said, "where there's none: giant rocks with razor edges crouch like a sea monster with wide-open jaws. They can crush a ship as easily as I crush this nut." He dropped a walnut on the hardwood floor and brought his heel grinding down on it. "Oh, yes," he said, casually, as if in answer to a question, "I have electricity. We try to be civilized here."

"Civilized? And you shoot down men?"

430 A trace of anger was in the general's black eyes, but it was there for but a second, and he said, in his most pleasant manner: "Dear me, what a righteous young man you are! I assure you I do not do the thing you suggest. That would be barbarous. I treat these visitors with every consideration. They get plenty of good food and exercise. They get into splendid physical condition. You shall see for yourself tomorrow."

"What do you mean?"

"We'll visit my training school," smiled the general. "It's in the cellar. I have about a dozen pupils down there now. They're
440 from the Spanish bark *Sanlúcar* that had the bad luck to go on the rocks out there. A very inferior lot, I regret to say. Poor specimens and more accustomed to the deck than to the jungle."

He raised his hand, and Ivan, who served as waiter, brought thick Turkish coffee. Rainsford, with an effort, held his tongue in check.

"It's a game, you see," pursued the general, blandly. "I suggest to one of them that we go hunting. I give him a supply of food and an excellent hunting knife. I give him three hours' start. I am to follow, armed only with a pistol of the smallest caliber and
450 range. If my quarry eludes me for three whole days, he wins the game. If I find him"—the general smiled—"he loses." **L**

"Suppose he refuses to be hunted?"

L CONFLICT
Reread lines 438–451. In your own words, describe the game that Zaroff plays with his "pupils."

They get Them in Shape and Then He Hunts Them with 3 days either are wins or they die.

"Oh," said the general, "I give him his option, of course. He need not play that game if he doesn't wish to. If he does not wish to hunt, I turn him over to Ivan. Ivan once had the honor of serving as official knouter[11] to the Great White Tsar, and he has his own ideas of sport. Invariably, Mr. Rainsford, invariably they choose the hunt."

"And if they win?"

460 The smile on the general's face widened.

"To date I have not lost," he said.

Then he added, hastily: "I don't wish you to think me a braggart, Mr. Rainsford. Many of them afford only the most elementary sort of problem. Occasionally I strike a tartar.[12] One almost did win. I eventually had to use the dogs."

"The dogs?"

"This way, please. I'll show you."

The general steered Rainsford to a window. The lights from the windows sent a flickering illumination that made grotesque

470 patterns on the courtyard below, and Rainsford could see moving about there a dozen or so huge black shapes; as they turned toward him, their eyes glittered greenly.

"A rather good lot, I think," observed the general. "They are let out at seven every night. If anyone should try to get into my house—or out of it—something extremely regrettable would occur to him." He hummed a snatch of song from the Folies Bergère.[13]

"And now," said the general, "I want to show you my new collection of heads. Will you come with me to the library?"

"I hope," said Rainsford, "that you will excuse me tonight,

480 General Zaroff. I'm really not feeling at all well." Ⓜ

"Ah, indeed?" the general inquired, solicitously. "Well, I suppose that's only natural, after your long swim. You need a good, restful night's sleep. Tomorrow you'll feel like a new man, I'll wager. Then we'll hunt, eh? I've one rather promising prospect—"

Rainsford was hurrying from the room.

Ⓜ **CONFLICT**
Why do you think Rainsford dismisses himself? What might he suspect?

because He is tired and needs time to think.

solicitously (sə-lĭs′ĭ-təs-lē) *adv.* in a manner expressing care or concern

---

11. **knouter** (nou′tər): a person who whipped criminals in Russia.
12. **strike a tartar:** encounter a fierce opponent.
13. **Folies Bergère** (fô-lē′ bĕr-zhĕr′): a music hall in Paris, famous for its variety shows.

"Sorry you can't go with me tonight," called the general. "I expect rather fair sport—a big, strong black. He looks resourceful— Well, good night, Mr. Rainsford; I hope you have a
490 good night's rest."

The bed was good, and the pajamas of the softest silk, and he was tired in every fiber of his being, but nevertheless Rainsford could not quiet his brain with the opiate of sleep. He lay, eyes wide open. Once he thought he heard stealthy steps in the corridor outside his room. He sought to throw open the door; it would not open. He went to the window and looked out. His room was high up in one of the towers. The lights of the château were out now, and it was dark and silent, but there was a fragment of sallow moon, and by its wan light he could see, dimly, the
500 courtyard; there, weaving in and out in the pattern of shadow, were black, noiseless forms; the hounds heard him at the window and looked up, expectantly, with their green eyes. Rainsford went back to the bed and lay down. By many methods he tried to put himself to sleep. He had achieved a doze when, just as morning began to come, he heard, far off in the jungle, the faint report of a pistol. **N**

General Zaroff did not appear until luncheon. He was dressed faultlessly in the tweeds of a country squire. He was solicitous about the state of Rainsford's health.

510 "As for me," sighed the general, "I do not feel so well. I am worried, Mr. Rainsford. Last night I detected traces of my old complaint."

To Rainsford's questioning glance the general said: "Ennui. Boredom."

Then, taking a second helping of crêpes suzettes, the general explained: "The hunting was not good last night. The fellow lost his head. He made a straight trail that offered no problems at all. That's the trouble with these sailors; they have dull brains to begin with, and they do not know how to get about
520 in the woods. They do excessively stupid and obvious things.

N VISUALIZE

Underline the words and phrases in this paragraph that help you visualize the scene. How do these details affect the mood of the scene?

I shows the sketchy situation He is in

Reread lines 513–522. Why was the general bored by the hunt last night?

_____

_____

_____

_____

_____

_____

_____

_____

_____

○ CONFLICT

The main conflict in the story has become clear. What is it?

The General always to hunt Rainsford Therefore He Hunter will become Hunter.

It's most annoying. Will you have another glass of Chablis,[14] Mr. Rainsford?" PAUSE & REFLECT

"General," said Rainsford, firmly, "I wish to leave this island at once."

The general raised his thickets of eyebrows; he seemed hurt. "But, my dear fellow," the general protested, "you've only just come. You've had no hunting—"

"I wish to go today," said Rainsford. He saw the dead black eyes of the general on him, studying him. General Zaroff's face 530 suddenly brightened.

He filled Rainsford's glass with venerable Chablis from a dusty bottle.

"Tonight," said the general, "we will hunt—you and I."

Rainsford shook his head. "No, General," he said. "I will not hunt."

The general shrugged his shoulders and delicately ate a hothouse grape. "As you wish, my friend," he said. "The choice rests entirely with you. But may I not venture to suggest that you will find my idea of sport more diverting than Ivan's?"

540 He nodded toward the corner to where the giant stood, scowling, his thick arms crossed on his hogshead of chest.

"You don't mean—" cried Rainsford.

"My dear fellow," said the general, "have I not told you I always mean what I say about hunting? This is really an inspiration. I drink to a foeman worthy of my steel—at last." ○

The general raised his glass, but Rainsford sat staring at him.

"You'll find this game worth playing," the general said, enthusiastically. "Your brain against mine. Your woodcraft against mine. Your strength and stamina against mine. Outdoor chess! 550 And the stake is not without value, eh?"

"And if I win—" began Rainsford, huskily.

"I'll cheerfully acknowledge myself defeated if I do not find you by midnight of the third day," said General Zaroff. "My sloop will place you on the mainland near a town."

The general read what Rainsford was thinking.

---

14. **Chablis** (shă-blē´): a type of white French wine.

"Oh, you can trust me," said the Cossack. "I will give you my word as a gentleman and a sportsman. Of course, you, in turn, must agree to say nothing of your visit here."

"I'll agree to nothing of the kind," said Rainsford.

560 "Oh," said the general, "in that case— But why discuss that now? Three days hence we can discuss it over a bottle of Veuve Clicquot,[15] unless—"

The general sipped his wine.

Then a businesslike air animated him. "Ivan," he said to Rainsford, "will supply you with hunting clothes, food, a knife. I suggest you wear moccasins; they leave a poorer trail. I suggest, too, that you avoid the big swamp in the southeast corner of the island. We call it Death Swamp. There's quicksand there. One foolish fellow tried it. The deplorable part of it was that Lazarus

570 followed him. You can imagine my feelings, Mr. Rainsford. I loved Lazarus; he was the finest hound in my pack. Well, I must beg you to excuse me now. I always take a siesta after lunch. You'll hardly have time for a nap, I fear. You'll want to start, no doubt. I shall not follow till dusk. Hunting at night is so much more exciting than by day, don't you think? Au revoir,[16] Mr. Rainsford, au revoir." **PAUSE & REFLECT**

General Zaroff, with a deep, courtly bow, strolled from the room.

From another door came Ivan. Under one arm he carried khaki

580 hunting clothes, a haversack of food, a leather sheath containing a long-bladed hunting knife; his right hand rested on a cocked revolver thrust in the crimson sash about his waist. . . .

Rainsford had fought his way through the bush for two hours. "I must keep my nerve. I must keep my nerve," he said, through tight teeth.

He had not been entirely clear-headed when the château gates snapped shut behind him. His whole idea at first was to put distance between himself and General Zaroff, and, to this end, he

---

15. **Veuve Clicquot** (vœv′ klĭ-kō′): a French champagne.
16. **au revoir** (ō′ rə-vwär′): goodbye; farewell till we meet again.

PAUSE & REFLECT
Now the rules of the game have been established. What do you think will happen?

_____

_____

_____

_____

_____

_____

_____

had plunged along, spurred on by the sharp rowels of something
590 very like panic. Now he had got a grip on himself, had stopped,
and was taking stock of himself and the situation.

He saw that straight flight was futile; inevitably it would
bring him face to face with the sea. He was in a picture with a
frame of water, and his operations, clearly, must take place within
that frame.

"I'll give him a trail to follow," muttered Rainsford, and he
struck off from the rude path he had been following into the
trackless wilderness. He executed a series of intricate loops; he
doubled on his trail again and again, recalling all the lore of
600 the fox hunt, and all the dodges of the fox. Night found him
leg-weary, with hands and face lashed by the branches, on a
thickly wooded ridge. He knew it would be insane to blunder
on through the dark, even if he had the strength. His need for
rest was **imperative**, and he thought, "I have played the fox;
now I must play the cat of the fable."[17] A big tree with a thick
trunk and outspread branches was nearby, and, taking care to
leave not the slightest mark, he climbed up into the crotch and,
stretching out on one of the broad limbs, after a fashion, rested.
Rest brought him new confidence and almost a feeling of security.
610 Even so **zealous** a hunter as General Zaroff could not trace him
there, he told himself; only the devil himself could follow that
complicated trail through the jungle after dark. But perhaps the
general was a devil—

An apprehensive night crawled slowly by like a wounded
snake, and sleep did not visit Rainsford, although the silence of
a dead world was on the jungle. Toward morning, when a dingy
gray was varnishing the sky, the cry of some startled bird focused
Rainsford's attention in that direction. Something was coming
through the bush, coming slowly, carefully, coming by the same
620 winding way Rainsford had come. He flattened himself down
on the limb, and through a screen of leaves almost as thick as
tapestry, he watched. The thing that was approaching was a man.

imperative (ĭm-pĕr′ə-tĭv) *adj.*
absolutely necessary

zealous (zĕl′əs) *adj.* intensely
enthusiastic

---

17. **I have played the fox . . . fable:** In Aesop's fable "The Cat and the Fox," the fox
brags of knowing many ways to escape an enemy. The cat knows only one,
but is successful with it.

It was General Zaroff. He made his way along with his eyes fixed in utmost concentration on the ground before him. He paused, almost beneath the tree, dropped to his knees, and studied the ground. Rainsford's impulse was to hurl himself down like a panther, but he saw that the general's right hand held something metallic—a small automatic pistol. **PAUSE & REFLECT**

The hunter shook his head several times, as if he were puzzled.
630 Then he straightened up and took from his case one of his black cigarettes; its pungent, incenselike smoke floated up to Rainsford's nostrils.

Rainsford held his breath. The general's eyes had left the ground and were traveling inch by inch up the tree. Rainsford froze there, every muscle tensed for a spring. But the sharp eyes of the hunter stopped before they reached the limb where Rainsford lay; a smile spread over his brown face. Very deliberately he blew a smoke ring into the air; then he turned his back on the tree and walked carelessly away, back along the trail he had come. The
640 swish of the underbrush against his hunting boots grew fainter and fainter.

The pent-up air burst hotly from Rainsford's lungs. His first thought made him feel sick and numb. The general could follow a trail through the woods at night; he could follow an extremely difficult trail; he must have **uncanny** powers; only by the merest chance had the Cossack failed to see his quarry.

Rainsford's second thought was even more terrible. It sent a shudder of cold horror through his whole being. Why had the general smiled? Why had he turned back?
650 Rainsford did not want to believe what his reason told him was true, but the truth was as evident as the sun that had by now pushed through the morning mists. The general was playing with him! The general was saving him for another day's sport! The Cossack was the cat; he was the mouse. Then it was that Rainsford knew the full meaning of terror. **P**

PAUSE & REFLECT
What do you think will happen next?

uncanny (ŭn-kăn′ē) adj. so remarkable as to seem supernatural

P CONFLICT
The author adds to the suspense by having Rainsford ask himself questions and then answer them. Circle the questions Rainsford asks in lines 647–649. How do the answers to these questions add to the conflict?

This shows/reveals that the General had seen him and is playing w/ Rainsford.

"I will not lose my nerve. I will not."

He slid down from the tree and struck off again into the woods. His face was set, and he forced the machinery of his mind to function. Three hundred yards from his hiding place he stopped where a huge dead tree leaned precariously on a smaller, living one. Throwing off his sack of food, Rainsford took his knife from its sheath and began to work with all his energy.

The job was finished at last, and he threw himself down behind a fallen log a hundred feet away. He did not have to wait long. The cat was coming again to play with the mouse.

Following the trail with the sureness of a bloodhound came General Zaroff. Nothing escaped those searching black eyes, no crushed blade of grass, no bent twig, no mark, no matter how faint, in the moss. So intent was the Cossack on his stalking that he was upon the thing Rainsford had made before he saw it. His foot touched the protruding bough[18] that was the trigger. Even as he touched it, the general sensed his danger and leaped back with the agility of an ape. But he was not quite quick enough; the dead tree, delicately adjusted to rest on the cut living one, crashed down and struck the general a glancing blow on the shoulder as it fell; but for his alertness, he must have been smashed beneath it. He staggered, but he did not fall; nor did he drop his revolver. He stood there, rubbing his injured shoulder, and Rainsford, with fear again gripping his heart, heard the general's mocking laugh ring through the jungle.

"Rainsford," called the general, "if you are within sound of my voice, as I suppose you are, let me congratulate you. Not many men know how to make a Malay man-catcher. Luckily for me I, too, have hunted in Malacca.[19] You are proving interesting, Mr. Rainsford. I am going now to have my wound dressed; it's only a slight one. But I shall be back. I shall be back."

When the general, nursing his bruised shoulder, had gone, Rainsford took up his flight again. It was flight now, a desperate, hopeless flight, that carried him on for some hours. Dusk came,

⊙ CONFLICT
How is Rainsford proving to be interesting prey for the general?

He managed to ~~kill~~ wound the general by using an interesting trap.

---

18. **protruding bough** (bou): a tree branch that extends or juts out.

19. **Malay** (mə-lā′) . . . **Malacca** (mə-lăk′ə): The Malays are a people of southeast Asia. Malacca is a region they inhabit, just south of Thailand.

then darkness, and still he pressed on. The ground grew softer under his moccasins; the vegetation grew ranker, denser; insects bit him savagely. Then, as he stepped forward, his foot sank into the ooze. He tried to wrench it back, but the muck sucked viciously at his foot as if it were a giant leech. With a violent effort he tore his foot loose. He knew where he was now. Death Swamp and its quicksand.

His hands were tight closed as if his nerve were something tangible that someone in the darkness was trying to tear from his

700 grip. The softness of the earth had given him an idea. He stepped back from the quicksand a dozen feet or so, and like some huge prehistoric beaver, he began to dig.

Rainsford had dug himself in in France when a second's delay meant death. That had been a placid pastime compared to his digging now. The pit grew deeper; when it was above his shoulders, he climbed out and from some hard saplings cut stakes and sharpened them to a fine point. These stakes he planted in the bottom of the pit with the points sticking up. With flying fingers he wove a rough carpet of weeds and branches, and with it

710 he covered the mouth of the pit. Then, wet with sweat and aching with tiredness, he crouched behind the stump of a lightning-charred tree.

He knew his pursuer was coming; he heard the padding sound of feet on the soft earth, and the night breeze brought him the perfume of the general's cigarette. It seemed to Rainsford that the general was coming with unusual swiftness; he was not feeling his way along, foot by foot. Rainsford, crouching there, could not see

® VISUALIZE
Reread this paragraph and record the words and phrases that appeal to your senses.

Details from Story

↓

What I Visualize

the general, nor could he see the pit. He lived a year in a minute.
Then he felt an impulse to cry aloud with joy, for he heard the
720 sharp crackle of the breaking branches as the cover of the pit
gave way; he heard the sharp scream of pain as the pointed stakes
found their mark. He leaped up from his place of concealment.
Then he cowered back. Three feet from the pit a man was
standing, with an electric torch in his hand.

"You've done well, Rainsford," the voice of the general called.
"Your Burmese tiger pit[20] has claimed one of my best dogs. Again
you score. I think, Mr. Rainsford, I'll see what you can do against
my whole pack. I'm going home for a rest now. Thank you for a
most amusing evening."

730 At daybreak Rainsford, lying near the swamp, was awakened
by a sound that made him know that he had new things to learn
about fear. It was a distant sound, faint and wavering, but he
knew it. It was the baying of a pack of hounds. **S**

Rainsford knew he could do one of two things. He could stay
where he was and wait. That was suicide. He could flee. That was
postponing the inevitable. For a moment he stood there, thinking.
An idea that held a wild chance came to him, and, tightening his
belt, he headed away from the swamp.

The baying of the hounds grew nearer, then still nearer,
740 nearer, ever nearer. On a ridge Rainsford climbed a tree. Down a
watercourse, not a quarter of a mile away, he could see the bush
moving. Straining his eyes, he saw the lean figure of General
Zaroff; just ahead of him, Rainsford made out another figure
whose wide shoulders surged through the tall jungle weeds;
it was the giant Ivan, and he seemed pulled forward by some
unseen force; Rainsford knew that Ivan must be holding the
pack in leash.

They would be on him any minute now. His mind worked
frantically. He thought of a native trick he had learned in
750 Uganda.[21] He slid down the tree. He caught hold of a springy
young sapling, and to it he fastened his hunting knife, with the

---

S CONFLICT

What additional complication has been added to the game?

The General released hounds and Rainsford has entered the forbidden Swamp.

---

20. **Burmese** (bər-mēz') **tiger pit:** a trap used for catching tigers in Myanmar, a
    country in Southeast Asia formerly called Burma.
21. **Uganda** (yōo-găn'də): a country in central Africa.

blade pointing down the trail; with a bit of wild grapevine he tied back the sapling. Then he ran for his life. The hounds raised their voices as they hit the fresh scent. Rainsford knew now how an animal at bay feels.

He had to stop to get his breath. The baying of the hounds stopped abruptly, and Rainsford's heart stopped, too. They must have reached the knife.

He shinned excitedly up a tree and looked back. His pursuers 760 had stopped. But the hope that was in Rainsford's brain when he climbed died, for he saw in the shallow valley that General Zaroff was still on his feet. But Ivan was not. The knife, driven by the recoil of the springing tree, had not wholly failed.

Rainsford had hardly tumbled to the ground when the pack took up the cry again.

"Nerve, nerve, nerve!" he panted, as he dashed along. A blue gap showed between the trees dead ahead. Ever nearer drew the hounds. Rainsford forced himself on toward that gap. He reached it. It was the shore of the sea. Across a cove he could see the 770 gloomy gray stone of the château. Twenty feet below him the sea rumbled and hissed. Rainsford hesitated. He heard the hounds. Then he leaped far out into the sea. . . . **PAUSE & REFLECT**

When the general and his pack reached the place by the sea, the Cossack stopped. For some minutes he stood regarding the blue-green expanse of water. He shrugged his shoulders. Then he sat down, took a drink of brandy from a silver flask, lit a perfumed cigarette, and hummed a bit from *Madama Butterfly*.[22] **T**

General Zaroff had an exceedingly good dinner in his great paneled dining hall that evening. With it he had a bottle of Pol 780 Roger and half a bottle of Chambertin.[23] Two slight annoyances kept him from perfect enjoyment. One was the thought that it would be difficult to replace Ivan; the other was that his quarry had escaped him; of course the American hadn't played

---

22. *Madama Butterfly:* a famous opera by the Italian composer Giacomo Puccini.
23. **Pol Roger** (pôl′ rô-zhā′) **. . . Chambertin** (shăm-bĕr-tăN′): Pol Roger is a French champagne. Chambertin is a red French wine.

PAUSE & REFLECT
Describe what just happened in your own words.

Rainsford had killed Ivan with a knife, while later the pack of dogs chased him to the sea and Rainsford leapt out to the sea.

T VISUALIZE
What is Zaroff's reaction when he reaches the water?

_____

_____

_____

the game—so thought the general as he tasted his after-dinner liqueur. In his library he read, to soothe himself, from the works of Marcus Aurelius.[24] At ten he went up to his bedroom. He was deliciously tired, he said to himself, as he locked himself in. There was a little moonlight, so before turning on his light he went to the window and looked down at the courtyard. He could see the

790 great hounds, and he called "Better luck another time" to them. Then he switched on the light.

A man, who had been hiding in the curtains of the bed, was standing there.

"Rainsford!" screamed the general. "How in God's name did you get here?"

"Swam," said Rainsford. "I found it quicker than walking through the jungle."

The general sucked in his breath and smiled. "I congratulate you," he said. "You have won the game."

800 Rainsford did not smile. "I am still a beast at bay," he said, in a low, hoarse voice. "Get ready, General Zaroff."

The general made one of his deepest bows.

"I see," he said. "Splendid! One of us is to furnish a repast[25] for the hounds. The other will sleep in this very excellent bed. On guard, Rainsford. . . ."

He had never slept in a better bed, Rainsford decided.

PAUSE & REFLECT

PAUSE & REFLECT
Who has won "the most dangerous game?" Circle the winner's name.

---

24. **Marcus Aurelius** (mär′kəs ô-rē′lē-əs): an ancient Roman emperor and philosopher.
25. **furnish a repast**: serve as a meal.

Text Analysis: Conflict

Remember that most stories are built around a central conflict, or struggle.
An **external conflict** involves a character pitted against an outside force. An
internal conflict occurs when the struggle takes place within a character's
own mind. List examples of each kind of conflict in the story.

Internal Conflict	
Zaroff	*bored with hunting and looking for a new "thrill"*
Rainsford	

External Conflict	
Person vs. Person	
Person vs. Nature	
Person vs. Obstacle	

Go back to the story and find three examples of foreshadowing. What clues
does the author drop that hint at future events? Do you think this technique
added suspense to the story? Why or why not?

_____

_____

_____

_____

Reading Skill: Visualize

Choose at least two descriptions from the story that evoked the most striking sensory images in your mind. List the words and phrases that helped create this image and note the sense to which they appeal.

Image #1	
Image #2	

What does it take to be a SURVIVOR?

What characteristics help people survive dangerous situations?

_____

_____

Vocabulary Practice

For each vocabulary word at the left write down the letter of the word at the right that's closest to its meaning.

1. tangible _____	a. carefully
2. quarry _____	b. charming
3. disarming _____	c. comfort
4. cultivated _____	d. enthusiastic
5. amenity _____	e. funny
6. condone _____	f. necessary
7. droll _____	g. overlook
8. scruples _____	h. prey
9. solicitously _____	i. refined
10. imperative _____	j. touchable
11. zealous _____	k. uneasiness
12. uncanny _____	l. unusual

Academic Vocabulary in Writing

analyze	element	infer	sequence	structure

A **structure** can refer to a building or the way in which something is built. Write a few sentences about the structure of the plot in "The Most Dangerous Game." How does the author build the plot? Use at least two Academic Vocabulary words in your response. Definitions for these terms are listed on page 3.

_____

_____

_____

Assessment Practice

DIRECTIONS Use "The Most Dangerous Game" to answer questions 1–6.

1 Why does Zaroff "invent" a new kind of game?

- **A** He wants to impress Rainsford.
- **B** Rainsford suggests a new kind of game.
- **C** He is bored with the animals he has already hunted.
- **D** He wants to hunt animals without killing them.

2 Which of the following passages foreshadows danger?

- **A** "You've good eyes" Whitney said.
- **B** "It will be light in Rio," promised Whitney.
- **C** "What island is it?" Rainsford asked.
- **D** "The old charts call it Ship-Trap Island," Whitney replied.

3 The main conflict Rainsford faces in this story is —

- **A** to protect himself from wild animals
- **B** to survive as Zaroff hunts him
- **C** to swim to shore after falling off the boat
- **D** to change Zaroff's mind

4 What causes Rainsford to know "the full meaning of terror"?

- **A** Rainsford finds out Zaroff is a better hunter than he is.
- **B** Zaroff has followed Rainsford all night.
- **C** Zaroff sees Rainsford in the tree.
- **D** Rainsford realizes that Zaroff is just playing with him.

5 Which of the following events happens first?

- **A** Rainsford kills Ivan.
- **B** Rainsford kills one of Zaroff's dogs.
- **C** Rainsford wounds Zaroff.
- **D** Rainsford dives into the sea.

6 Which of the following events happens last?

- **A** Rainsford and Zaroff fight in the bedroom.
- **B** Rainsford builds a Burmese tiger pit.
- **C** Rainsford builds a Malay mancatcher.
- **D** Rainsford falls in quicksand.

The Gift of the Magi

Short Story by O.Henry

What are you willing to SACRIFICE?

Have you ever made a sacrifice in order to help others or make someone happy? In "The Gift of the Magi," a young couple have to decide what each is willing to do to show love for the other.

DISCUSS Work with a partner to make a list of things that people sacrifice for those they love. Think about examples in real life as well as those in books, movies, and television shows. Circle the sacrifice that was hardest to make. Put a check next to the sacrifice that shows the greatest love.

Sacrifices for Someone You Love

1. Spending a week's allowance to buy a gift

2. _____

   _____

3. _____

   _____

4. _____

   _____

Text Analysis: Irony

Irony is a contrast between what is expected to happen and what actually occurs. There are three types of irony commonly used in literature. The chart below provides definitions and examples of each type.

Irony	Definition	Example
Situational Irony	when a character or the readers expects one thing to happen but something else happens instead	You stay up all night cramming for a test only to find out the next day it has been moved to the following week.
Verbal Irony	when what is said is the opposite of what is meant	It's a rainy, dark day and you say "What a gorgeous day!"
Dramatic Irony	when what a character knows contrasts with what the audience knows	In a stunning upset, a champion boxer loses a big fight—the reader knows the boxer has been paid to lose.

O. Henry is well-known for writing stories in which the plot twists due to situational irony. As you read "The Gift of the Magi," think about what you expect to happen next.

Reading Strategy: Predict

A well-written story will keep you wondering what happens next. Successful readers ask questions and predict possible answers. To make a prediction:

- Look for **clues** in the story to suggest what might happen next.

- Make a **prediction** about future events based on clues in the story and what you know from your own experience.

- Read on to confirm your prediction and see if it is correct.

Vocabulary in Context

Note: Words are listed in the order in which they appear in the story.

instigate (ĭn'stĭ-gāt') *v.* to stir up; provoke
*When Jim and Della fight, it is usually money that **instigates** the argument.*

vestibule (vĕs'tə-byōōl') *n.* a small entryway within a building
*Della had the visitor wait in the **vestibule** while she went downstairs to meet him.*

agile (ăj'əl) *adj.* able to move quickly and easily
*Della appeared **agile** as she danced around the apartment.*

falter (fôl'tər) *v.* to hesitate from lack of courage or confidence
*Although Della was nervous, she did not **falter**.*

ransack (răn'săk') *v.* to search or examine vigorously
*Della **ransacked** her purse looking for change to pay the jeweler.*

prudence (prōōd'ns) *n.* the use of good judgment and common sense
*Jim used **prudence** when deciding how much to spend on a gift for Della.*

ravage (răv'ĭj) *n.* serious damage
*The old house showed the **ravage** cause by many years of neglect.*

assertion (ə-sûr'shən) *n.* a statement
*Jim's **assertion** came as a surprise to Della.*

coveted (kŭv'ĭ-tĭd) *adj.* greedily desired or wished for
*Other women **coveted** Della's silky hair.*

chronicle (krŏn'ĭ-kəl) *n.* a record of events
*The Christmas ornaments served as a **chronicle** for the many holidays they had spent together.*

SET A PURPOSE FOR READING

Read this story to find out what sacrifices a young couple make for each other one Christmas many years ago.

The Gift of the Magi

Short Story by **O. HENRY**

BACKGROUND In this story, O. Henry makes an **allusion,** or reference, to the Magi. According to Christian tradition, the Magi were three wise men or kings who traveled to Bethlehem, guided by a miraculous star, to present gifts of frankincense, myrrh (substances prized for their fragrance), and gold to the infant Jesus. These gifts were prized possessions, having monetary, medical, and ceremonial value.

One dollar and eighty-seven cents. That was all. And 60 cents of it was in pennies. Pennies saved one and two at a time by bulldozing the grocer and the vegetable man and the butcher until one's cheeks burned with the silent imputation of parsimony[1] that such close dealing implied. Three times Della counted it. One dollar and eighty-seven cents. And the next day would be Christmas.

---

1. **imputation** (ĭm′pyŏŏ-tā′shən) **of parsimony** (pär′sə-mō′nē): suggestion of stinginess.

There was clearly nothing to do but flop down on the shabby little couch and howl. So Della did it. Which <u>instigates</u> the moral reflection that life is made up of sobs, sniffles, and smiles, with sniffles predominating. **PAUSE & REFLECT**

While the mistress of the home is gradually subsiding from the first stage to the second, take a look at the home. A furnished flat at $8 per week. It did not exactly beggar description, but it certainly had that word on the lookout for the mendicancy squad.[2]

In the <u>vestibule</u> below belonged to this flat a letterbox into which no letter would go and an electric button from which no mortal finger could coax a ring. Also appertaining thereunto was a card bearing the name "Mr. James Dillingham Young."

The "Dillingham" had been flung to the breeze during a former period of prosperity when its possessor was being paid $30 per week. Now, when the income was shrunk to $20, the letters of "Dillingham" looked blurred, as though they were thinking seriously of contracting to a modest and unassuming D. But whenever Mr. James Dillingham Young came home and a reached his flat above, he was called "Jim" and greatly hugged by Mrs. James Dillingham Young, already introduced to you as Della. Which is all very good. **A**

Della finished her cry and attended to her cheeks with the powder rag. She stood by the window and looked out dully at a gray cat walking a gray fence in a gray backyard. Tomorrow would be Christmas Day, and she had only $1.87 with which to buy Jim a present. She had been saving every penny she could for months, with this result. Twenty dollars a week doesn't go far. Expenses had been greater than she had calculated. They always are. Only $1.87 to buy a present for Jim. Her Jim. Many a happy hour she had spent planning for something nice for him. Something fine and rare and sterling—something just a little bit near to being worthy of the honor of being owned by Jim.

instigate (ĭn'stĭ-gāt') *v.* to stir up; provoke

PAUSE & REFLECT
Reread the first two paragraphs. Why does Della flop down on the couch and howl?

_____

_____

_____

vestibule (vĕs'tə-byōōl') *n.* a small entryway within a building

A IRONY
Irony is the difference between what you expect to happen and what actually happens. You might expect someone named Mr. James Dillingham Young to be rich. Cite details from the text that tell you he is not.

_____

_____

_____

_____

_____

_____

---

2. **mendicancy** (mĕn'dĭ-kən-sē) **squad:** a police unit assigned to arrest beggars.

agile (ăj'əl) *adj.* able to move quickly and easily

Underline words in lines 41–44 that hint at Della's **agility**.

B PREDICT
Circle the two prized possessions described in this paragraph. What do you think Della might do with her prized possession?

_____

_____

_____

falter (fôl'tər) *v.* to hesitate from lack of courage or confidence

There was a pier glass[3] between the windows of the room. Perhaps you have seen a pier glass in an $8 flat. A very thin and very **agile** person may, by observing his reflection in a rapid sequence of longitudinal strips, obtain a fairly accurate conception of his looks. Della, being slender, had mastered the art.

Suddenly she whirled from the window and stood before the glass. Her eyes were shining brilliantly, but her face had lost its color within twenty seconds. Rapidly she pulled down her hair and let it fall to its full length.

50 Now, there were two possessions of the James Dillingham Youngs in which they both took a mighty pride. One was Jim's gold watch that had been his father's and his grandfather's. The other was Della's hair. Had the Queen of Sheba[4] lived in the flat across the air shaft, Della would have let her hair hang out the window some day to dry and mocked at Her Majesty's jewels and gifts. Had King Solomon[5] been the janitor, with all his treasures piled up in the basement, Jim would have pulled out his watch every time he passed, just to see him pluck at his beard from envy. **B**

60 So now Della's beautiful hair fell about her, rippling and shining like a cascade of brown waters. It reached below her knee and made itself almost a garment for her. And then she did it up again nervously and quickly. Once she **faltered** for a minute and stood still while a tear or two splashed on the worn red carpet.

On went her old brown jacket; on went her old brown hat. With a whirl of skirts and with the brilliant sparkle still in her eyes, she fluttered out the door and down the stairs to the street.

Where she stopped, the sign read "Mme. Sofronie. Hair Goods of All Kinds." One flight up Della ran and collected herself, 70 panting, before Madame, large, too white, chilly, and hardly looking the "Sofronie."

"Will you buy my hair?" asked Della.

"I buy hair," said Madame. "Take yer hat off and let's have a sight at the looks of it."

---

3. **pier glass:** a large mirror set in a wall section between windows.
4. **Queen of Sheba:** in the Bible, a rich Arabian queen.
5. **King Solomon:** a Biblical king of Israel, known for his wisdom and wealth.

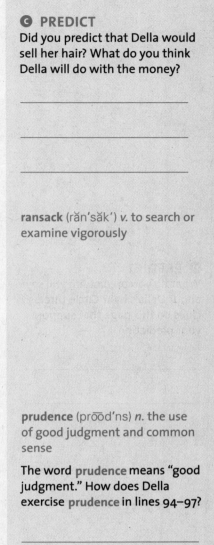

Down rippled the brown cascade. "Twenty dollars," said Madame, lifting the mass with a practiced hand.

"Give it to me quick," said Della. **C**

Oh, and the next two hours tripped by on rosy wings. Forget the hashed metaphor. She was <u>ransacking</u> the stores for Jim's
80 present.

She found it at last. It surely had been made for Jim and no one else. There was none other like it in any of the stores, and she had turned all of them inside out. It was a platinum fob chain[6] simple and chaste in design, properly proclaiming its value by substance alone and not by meretricious ornamentation[7]—as all good things should do. It was even worthy of The Watch. As soon as she saw it, she knew that it must be Jim's. It was like him. Quietness and value—the description applied to both. Twenty-one dollars they took from her for it, and she hurried home with
90 the 87 cents. With that chain on his watch Jim might be properly anxious about the time in any company. Grand as the watch was, he sometimes looked at it on the sly on account of the old leather strap that he used in place of a chain.

When Della reached home, her intoxication gave way a little to <u>prudence</u> and reason. She got out her curling irons and lighted the gas and went to work repairing the <u>ravages</u> made by generosity added to love. Which is always a tremendous task, dear friends—a mammoth task.

Within forty minutes her head was covered with tiny, close-
100 lying curls that made her look wonderfully like a truant schoolboy. She looked at her reflection in the mirror long, carefully, and critically.

"If Jim doesn't kill me," she said to herself, "before he takes a second look at me, he'll say I look like a Coney Island[8] chorus girl. But what could I do—oh, what could I do with a dollar and eighty-seven cents!"

At 7 o'clock the coffee was made, and the frying pan was on the back of the stove hot and ready to cook the chops.

---

6. **fob chain:** a short chain for a pocket watch.
7. **meretricious** (mĕr′ĭ-trĭsh′əs) **ornamentation:** cheap, gaudy decoration.
8. **Coney Island:** a resort district of Brooklyn, New York, famous for its amusement park.

C PREDICT
Did you predict that Della would sell her hair? What do you think Della will do with the money?

_____

_____

_____

ransack (răn′săk′) *v.* to search or examine vigorously

prudence (prōōd′ns) *n.* the use of good judgment and common sense

The word **prudence** means "good judgment." How does Della exercise **prudence** in lines 94–97?

_____

_____

_____

ravage (răv′ĭj) *n.* serious damage

Jim was never late. Della doubled the fob chain in her hand
110 and sat on the corner of the table near the door that he always
entered. Then she heard his step on the stair away down on the
first flight, and she turned white for just a moment. She had a
habit of saying little silent prayers about the simplest everyday
things, and now she whispered: "Please, God, make him think
I am still pretty."

The door opened, and Jim stepped in and closed it. He looked
thin and very serious. Poor fellow, he was only twenty-two—and
to be burdened with a family! He needed a new overcoat, and he
was without gloves.

120 Jim stopped inside the door, as immovable as a setter at the
scent of a quail. His eyes were fixed upon Della, and there was an
expression in them that she could not read, and it terrified her.
It was not anger, nor surprise, nor disapproval, nor horror, nor any
of the sentiments that she had been prepared for. He simply stared
at her fixedly with that peculiar expression on his face. **D**

Della wriggled off the table and went for him.

"Jim, darling," she cried, "don't look at me that way. I had
my hair cut off and sold it because I couldn't have lived through
Christmas without giving you a present. It'll grow again—you
130 won't mind, will you? I just had to do it. My hair grows awfully
fast. Say 'Merry Christmas!' Jim, and let's be happy. You don't
know what a nice—what a beautiful, nice gift I've got for you."

"You've cut off your hair?" asked Jim, laboriously, as if he
had not arrived at that patent fact yet even after the hardest
mental labor.

"Cut it off and sold it," said Della. "Don't you like me just as
well, anyhow? I'm me without my hair, ain't I?"

Jim looked about the room curiously.

"You say your hair is gone?" he said, with an air almost of
140 idiocy. **PAUSE & REFLECT**

D PREDICT

What do you predict Jim will say
about Della's hair? Circle three
clues on this page that support
your prediction.

_____

_____

_____

_____

PAUSE & REFLECT

Think back to the beginning of
the story. What are the couple's
most prized possessions? How
do you think Jim feels now
that he knows one of those
possessions is gone?

_____

_____

_____

_____

"You needn't look for it," said Della. "It's sold, I tell you—sold and gone too. It's Christmas Eve, boy. Be good to me, for it went for you. Maybe the hairs of my head were numbered," she went on with a sudden serious sweetness, "but nobody could ever count my love for you. Shall I put the chops on, Jim?"

Out of his trance Jim seemed to quickly wake. He enfolded his Della. For ten seconds let us regard with discreet scrutiny[9] some inconsequential object in the other direction. Eight dollars a week or a million a year—what is the difference? A mathematician or a wit would give you the wrong answer. The magi brought valuable gifts, but that was not among them. This dark **assertion** will be illuminated later on.

Jim drew a package from his overcoat pocket and threw it upon the table.

"Don't make any mistake, Dell," he said, "about me. I don't think there's anything in the way of a haircut or a shave or a shampoo that could make me like my girl any less. But if you'll unwrap that package, you may see why you had me going awhile at first." **E**

White fingers and nimble tore at the string and paper. And then an ecstatic scream of joy, and then, alas! a quick feminine change to hysterical tears and wails, necessitating the immediate employment of all the comforting powers of the lord of the flat.

For there lay The Combs—the set of combs, side and back, that Della had worshiped for long in a Broadway window. Beautiful combs, pure tortoise shell, with jeweled rims—just the shade to wear in the beautiful vanished hair. They were expensive combs, she knew, and her heart had simply craved and yearned over them without the least hope of possession. And now, they were hers, but the tresses that should have adorned the **coveted** adornments were gone.

But she hugged them to her bosom, and at length she was able to look up with dim eyes and a smile and say, "My hair grows so fast, Jim!"

assertion (ə-sûr′shən) *n.* a statement

E PREDICT
What do you think Jim has bought for Della? What clue from the text helped you make this prediction?

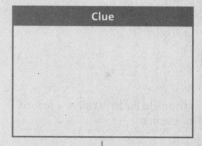

Clue

↓

Prediction

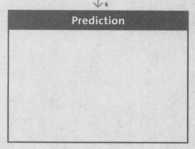

coveted (kŭv′ĭ-tĭd) *adj.* greedily desired or wished for

---

9. **discreet scrutiny:** cautious observation.

⒡ IRONY
Explain the **situational irony** in the resolution of the plot. What is ironic about each person's choice of gift?

_____

_____

_____

chronicle (krŏn′ĭ-kəl) *n.* a record of events

And then Della leaped up like a little singed cat and cried, "Oh, oh!"

Jim had not yet seen his beautiful present. She held it out to him eagerly upon her open palm. The dull, precious metal seemed to flash with a reflection of her bright and ardent spirit.

180 "Isn't it a dandy, Jim? I hunted all over town to find it. You'll have to look at the time a hundred times a day now. Give me your watch. I want to see how it looks on it." Instead of obeying, Jim tumbled down on the couch and put his hands under the back of his head and smiled.

"Dell," said he, "let's put our Christmas presents away and keep 'em a while. They're too nice to use just at present. I sold the watch to get the money to buy your combs. And now suppose you put the chops on." ⒡

The magi, as you know, were wise men—wonderfully wise 190 men—who brought gifts to the Babe in the manger. They invented the art of giving Christmas gifts. Being wise, their gifts were no doubt wise ones, possibly bearing the privilege of exchange in case of duplication. And here I have lamely related to you the uneventful **chronicle** of two foolish children in a flat who most unwisely sacrificed for each other the greatest treasures of their house. But in a last word to the wise of these days let it be said that of all who give gifts these two were of the wisest. Of all who give and receive gifts, such as they are the wisest. Everywhere they are the wisest. They are the magi.

Text Analysis: Irony

"The Gift of the Magi" is famous for its situational irony. Fill in the Irony Map below to understand how the story's events create situational irony.

IRONY MAP	
Della	**Jim**
What Della Sells:	What Jim Sells:
What Della Buys:	What Jim Buys:
What Della Receives:	What Jim Receives:
Why the Gift is Useless:	Why the Gift is Useless:

Review your notes for "Gift of the Magi" and your completed Irony Map. Then, write a brief explanation of what O. Henry's use of irony tells us about Della and Jim's relationship.

_____

_____

_____

_____

Reading Skill: Predict

Look back at the predictions you made as you read. Which predictions proved true and which did not? For the predictions that did not prove true, write a sentence explaining the outcome in the chart below.

Clue	

↓

Prediction	

↓

Outcome	

What are you willing to **SACRIFICE?**

What material possessions could you live without?

_____

_____

Vocabulary Practice

Circle the word that is most different in meaning from the others.

1. (a) destruction, (b) ravage, (c) ruin, (d) creation
2. (a) stop, (b) stir, (c) urge, (d) instigate
3. (a) desired, (b) coveted, (c) craved, (d) unwanted
4. (a) cellar, (b) vestibule, (c) foyer, (d) entryway
5. (a) waver, (b) proceed, (c) falter, (d) hesitate
6. (a) questions, (b) assertion, (c) statement, (d) explanation
7. (a) limber, (b) clumsy, (c) flexible, (d) agile
8. (a) loot, (b) plunder, (c) organize, (d) ransack
9. (a) history, (b) record, (c) chronicle, (d) prediction
10. (a) carelessness, (b) caution, (c) prudence, (d) wisdom

Academic Vocabulary in Speaking

analyze	element	infer	sequence	structure

An **element** is one necessary or basic part of a whole thing. A short story has various **elements**, including a plot, characters, setting, narrator, and conflict. What elements in "The Gift of the Magi" help create the suspense? Think about what the narrator tells you and what the narrator leaves out. Use at least one Academic Vocabulary word in your response. Definitions for these words can be found on page 3.

_____

_____

_____

Assessment Practice

DIRECTIONS Use "The Gift of the Magi" to answer questions 1–6.

1 Della buys a watch fob for Jim because —

- **A** he lost his watch
- **B** he treasures his watch
- **C** he doesn't know how to tell time
- **D** it's his birthday

2 When Jim sees Della's short hair, he realizes —

- **A** she has been to a beauty parlor
- **B** he likes her hair short
- **C** his gift for her will be useless
- **D** she couldn't always have long hair

3 Which statement best describes the situational irony in the story?

- **A** The watch fob is as useless to Jim as the combs are to Della.
- **B** Jim and Della bought each other expensive gifts.
- **C** Della's combs were bought with the money she received for her hair.
- **D** Jim and Della are as wise as the Magi.

4 O. Henry suggests that Della and Jim's "greatest treasure" is —

- **A** a watch fob and a comb
- **B** their foolishness
- **C** their sacrifices
- **D** their love for each other

5 To create a surprise ending, O. Henry —

- **A** does not introduce Jim until the end of the story
- **B** withholds information about Jim's plan
- **C** explains right away what the characters know
- **D** does not reveal Della's motivation for cutting her hair

6 What does the story reveal about Della and Jim?

- **A** They are greedy and selfish.
- **B** The put each other's happiness above their own.
- **C** They don't know each other as well as they thought.
- **D** They have fallen out of love.

Horse of the Century

- Magazine Article, page 47
- Timeline, page 49
- Radio Transcript, page 51

Background

During the Great Depression, an American racehorse named Seabiscuit became an unlikely hero. Despite early losses and a crooked leg, Seabiscuit managed to win Horse of the Year honors in 1938 after defeating War Admiral in a race that almost 40 million people listened to on the radio. The following informational texts will help you get a sense of what it was like to be at a horserace and why Seabiscuit became so popular.

Standards Focus: Synthesize

To get the most information on a topic, it helps to read more than one source. When you **synthesize** information, you put together the facts and ideas from each source to come to a greater understanding of your topic. These steps will help you synthesize the information from the following pieces about Seabiscuit.

1. Summarize the main ideas in each piece.

2. Jot down any questions you have as you read.

3. Note if information from one text conflicts with information in another.

4. Look for **textual evidence**—facts and details from the selections—to help you make logical connections and to support your conclusions.

Use a chart like the one below to keep track of your notes and questions as you read.

Source	Main Ideas	Questions
from "Four Good Legs Between Us"	Even though Seabiscuit lost this race, he was fast becoming a celebrity.	Howard made him popular by racing him all over the country. What was going on in Europe?
Timeline: Seabiscuit		
"Races on the Radio"		

SET A PURPOSE
FOR READING
Read the following informational
texts to find out why Seabiscuit
became such a popular celebrity.

from
Four Good Legs Between Us
Laura Hillenbrand

Though Seabiscuit had lost [the Santa Anita Handicap], he was rapidly becoming a phenomenal celebrity. Two factors converged to create and nourish this. The first was Charles Howard. A born adman, Howard courted the nation on behalf of his horse much as he had hawked his first Buicks, undertaking exhaustive promotion that presaged the modern marketing of athletes. Crafting daring, unprecedented coast-to-coast racing campaigns, he shipped Seabiscuit over fifty thousand railroad miles to showcase

10 his talent at eighteen tracks in seven states and Mexico. The second factor was timing. The nation was sliding from economic ruin into the whirling eddy of Europe's cataclysm.

Ⓐ **SYNTHESIZE**
Underline the two causes of
Seabiscuit's popularity presented
in lines 1–16.

PAUSE & REFLECT
Why do you think people at the
time were so impressed with
Seabiscuit? How do you think
they felt when they heard about
his success?

Seabiscuit, Howard, Pollard, and Smith, whose fortunes
swung in epic parabolas, would have resonated in any
age, but in cruel years the peculiar union among the four
transcended the racetrack. Ⓐ

The result was stupendous popularity. In one year
Seabiscuit garnered more newspaper column inches than
Roosevelt, Hitler, or Mussolini. *Life* even ran a pictorial on
20 his facial expressions. Cities had to route special trains to
accommodate the invariably record-shattering crowds that
came to see him run. Smith, fearing Seabiscuit wouldn't get
any rest, hoodwinked the press by trotting out a look-alike.
Such fame fueled the immediate, immense success of
Howard's Santa Anita and California's new racing industry,
today a four-billion-dollar business. **PAUSE & REFLECT**

Timeline: Seabiscuit

1937

○ *February 27:* In his first try at the Santa Anita Handicap, Seabiscuit loses to Rosemont by a nose, in a photo finish.

○ *March 6:* Seabiscuit draws a crowd of 45,000 excited fans and wins the San Juan Capistrano Handicap by seven lengths, smashing the track record.

○ *May 6:* The German airship *Hindenburg* bursts into flames as it is about to land in Lakehurst, New Jersey.

○ *June 5:* War Admiral captures the Triple Crown after a win at the Belmont Stakes.

○ *June 26:* Seabiscuit runs in the Brooklyn Handicap, beating rival Rosemont and local horse Aneroid.

○ *July:* Seabiscuit wins the Butler Handicap and the Yonkers Handicap easily, despite carrying far more weight than his competitors in both races.

○ *September 11:* At the Narragansett Special in Rhode Island, Seabiscuit finishes third due to muddy track conditions.

○ *October 12:* Seabiscuit wins the Continental Handicap in New York, gaining the top spot in the 1937 winnings race with $152,780 earned, $8,000 ahead of War Admiral.

○ *October 30:* Seabiscuit and War Admiral are slated to meet on the track, but Seabiscuit is scratched from the Washington Handicap due to muddy track conditions, allowing an easy victory for his rival.

Ⓑ SYNTHESIZE

Look back at the magazine article on pages 47–48. According to this timeline, in what year did the events in that article take place?

_____

_____

G SYNTHESIZE

Circle one or two new ideas or pieces of information presented in this timeline that adds to your knowledge of Seabiscuit. In the organizer below, rephrase this information in your own words and record any questions you have.

Main Idea

↓

Questions

○ *December 7:* War Admiral is named horse of the year by *Turf and Sport Digest*.

1938

○ *October 30:* Orson Welles's radio broadcast of *The War of the Worlds*, the tale of a Martian invasion on Earth, creates panic among listeners who mistake it for news.

○ *November 1:* With 40 million listeners tuned in across the country, Seabiscuit beats War Admiral by four lengths in just over a minute fifty-six for the mile and three-sixteenths, a new Pimlico record.

1939

○ *February 14:* Seabiscuit injures his suspensory ligament in a prep race for Santa Anita.

○ *September 3:* Britain and France declare war on Germany.

1940

○ *March 2:* Seabiscuit wins in his third try at the $100,000 Santa Anita Handicap. He clocks the fastest mile and a quarter in Santa Anita's history, the second fastest ever run in the United States. The most people ever to attend an American horse race—75,000—watch as Pollard leads Seabiscuit from behind to victory.

○ *April 10:* Seabiscuit retires to Charles Howard's Ridgewood Ranch. **G**

Races on the Radio
Santa Anita Handicap (1937)
with Clem McCarthy and Buddy Twist

CLEM McCARTHY:

Eddy Thomas won't take the start until he's on his toes and the jockey is ready. Then he'll push that button, the bell will ring, and they'll be on their way. We don't have any starting barriers now, as you know. Here they go. And they're on their way down the stretch. The break was good; every horse got a chance just as they left there.

As they come down here to the eighth pole, it is Time Supply and Special Agent. Special Agent is trying to force his way to the front and he's going to do a good job of it as they
10 pass the stands. Here on the outside comes Rosemont in a good position. And as they go by me it is Special Agent on the lead by one length. Special Agent has the lead and then comes Time Supply in second place right along beside him. Going to the first turn is Special Agent by a length. Time Supply is second and on the outside of him is Accolade. And Boxthorn is close up. Far back in the crowd, on the inside, in about twelfth place is Red Rain. Up there close is Rosemont in about sixth place. ❶

They're going into the stretch; they've gone half a mile.
20 And the time for the first quarter over this track was 22 and

❶ **SYNTHESIZE**
This radio transcript includes the names of other horses who raced in the Santa Anita Handicap. Underline the names of the other horses as you read.

E SYNTHESIZE
Knowing the meanings of some horse racing terms will help you visualize the race. The "stretch" refers to the final straight portion of the racetrack to the finish. What do you think a "photograph finish" refers to?

_____

_____

_____

F SYNTHESIZE
Reread lines 35–52. Then, look at the arrows below and put the names Rosemont, Special Agent, and Seabiscuit on the appropriate arrow to show where each horse finished.

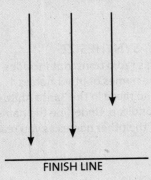

FINISH LINE

two fifths seconds, the half in 45 and four. They're turning into the backstretch with Special Agent on the lead. Special Agent has a lead now of one length and a half. Right behind him comes Time Supply. And in there, slipping through on the inside is . . . Indian Broom is going up on the inside now in a good position. Around that far turn, there's still no change in the positions. Rosemont is having a hard time working his way through, he's now in sixth position going around on the inside, he's saving ground, he's got plenty left.
30 If he's enough horse, he may get home. And on the outside, here comes the other one, Indian Broom. And Goldeneye is moving up from the rear. Here comes Accolade in second position. And Seabiscuit is now moving up and is challenging as they turn for home. **E**

It's Special Agent and Seabiscuit challenging head-and-head as they swing into the stretch. And they've only got a quarter of a mile to come. They've stepped the first mile in 1:36 and four-fifths—and that shows you what this pace is. He can't live at it. Seabiscuit has got the lead half way
40 down the stretch. But here comes one of the Baroni entries challenging on the outside, challenging boldly. And the battle is on. Indian Broom is coming fast and here comes Rosemont between horses. And Rosemont may take it all. It's gonna be a photograph finish. And it's anybody's race right to the end.

I think Rosemont got the money. I think Rosemont was first. It was an eyebrow finish. And Seabiscuit was the second horse. Seabiscuit was second and one of the Taylor entries; I think Indian Broom, was third. It was very close. That was an eyelash finish. Rosemont was closing strong,
50 but Seabiscuit hung on. The time of the race was 2:02 and four-fifths, which makes the track almost identically like the track of two years ago . . . **F**

BUDDY TWIST:

Oh boy, one of the most thrilling finishes I think that
I've ever seen in a horse race in my life, Clem. The crowd
down here has gone completely mad. The photographers
are outside the charm circle, which is a white circle here,
where the winner will come up in just a moment. Newsreel
photographers are setting up on every hand. The horses are
just coming back now. And everybody, depending on who
60   was their favorite, was shouting "Rosemont," "Seabiscuit"—
one would call Rosemont, one Seabiscuit. There were
half-a-dozen here who were just as sure Rosemont won as
Seabiscuit, they don't know what to think of it. One of the
most beautiful driving finishes I think I've ever seen.

CLEM McCARTHY:

Here's the photograph finish. Hold it now. Get ready for it.
Just a few seconds and we'll know the winner of this race.
I think Rosemont won it, but that's only my guess from
where I stand. The photograph will tell us the actual winner.
The naked eye is not as good as the photograph, we'll have
70   it in a second. They're looking at it down there. I know it
was an eyelash finish. Either horse won by a whisker and
that's all. Just about a quarter of an inch, I can't see any
more between them. I really shouldn't express an opinion
on a finish that close. And they're still waiting. That shows
you what a difficult . . . There it is, Rosemont is the winner.
Rosemont by a nose. Seabiscuit is second. Just a minute
Buddy until I get it. Rosemont is the winner—I want you
to get that jockey if you got him—Seabiscuit is second. And
the Taylor entry finished third and fourth. They haven't
80   put up the distinguishing numbers and they finished very
close together. **G**

G SYNTHESIZE
Reread lines 59–76. What
information does this transcript
reveal about the end of the race
that the other texts do not?

_____

_____

_____

_____

_____

_____

_____

_____

Practicing Your Skills

Now that you have completed the three readings about Seabiscuit, fill out the following chart with the information you've learned. In the last row, synthesize the information to come up with one or two main ideas about Seabiscuit's popularity.

Source	Main Ideas	Supporting Details
from "Four Good Legs Between Us"		
Timeline: Seabiscuit		
"Races on the Radio"		
SYNTHESIS:		

Academic Vocabulary in Writing

| analyze | element | infer | sequence | structure |

Which of the informational texts do you think provided the most useful information about Seabiscuit? Consider the way each article is **structured,** or built, as well as the purpose of each text. Definitions for these terms are listed on page 3.

_____

_____

_____

Assessment Practice

DIRECTIONS Use the texts entitled "Horse of the Century" to answer questions 1–4.

1 What happened during the Santa Anita Handicap in 1937?

  (A) Seabiscuit came from behind to win the race.

  (B) Seabiscuit injured his leg.

  (C) Most people wanted Seabiscuit to win the race.

  (D) Rosemont beat Seabiscuit by a nose.

2 How does the information in the first article differ from the information presented in the timeline?

  (A) The first article was written by Seabiscuit's owner.

  (B) The first article tells what happened during the Santa Anita Handicap in 1940.

  (C) The timeline tells what happened during the Santa Anita Handicap in 1940.

  (D) The timeline explains the reasons for Seabiscuit's popularity.

3 The radio transcript is an important source because it —

  (A) offers a play-by-play commentary of the race as it happened

  (B) provides background on Seabiscuit's jockey and owner

  (C) shows that the announcers knew which horse won

  (D) gives facts about the number of people watching the race

4 In the commentary from Buddy Twist in the radio transcript, the reader can conclude that —

  (A) Seabiscuit was cheated at the finish line

  (B) the race had one of the most exciting finishes Buddy Twist had seen

  (C) Buddy Twist wanted Rosemont to win the race

  (D) Buddy Twist was new at announcing horse races

The Raven
Poem by Edgar Allan Poe

Incident in a Rose Garden
Poem by Donald Justice

Why are we fascinated by the UNKNOWN?

Our fascination with weird events make us part of a long tradition of writers and readers who enjoy speculating on the unknown. The writers of the poems you are about to read relied on that universal fascination when they introduced us to two strange, and perhaps imaginary, visitors.

LIST IT With a partner, list three events from movies, television shows, or urban legends that you find fascinating or unbelievable.

Text Analysis: Narrative Poetry

Like fiction, **narrative poetry** contains the elements of plot, conflict, character, and setting that combine to create a story. In poetry, these elements are often condensed into images and compact descriptions. In each of the following narrative poems, the **speaker,** or voice that talks to the reader, is also the main character in the story. As you read, note what events each speaker describes and how these create a compelling story in verse.

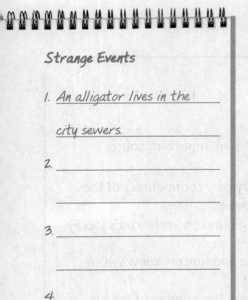

Strange Events

1. An alligator lives in the city sewers.

2. _____

3. _____

4. _____

	"The Raven"	"Incident in a Rose Garden"
Speaker	a man who has lost his love Lenore	
Setting	dreary night in December in the man's bedroom	
Conflict	he hears knocking on his door	
Event 1		
Event 2		
Resolution		

Reading Skill: Reading Poetry

To help you understand the events in a narrative poem, use the following strategies:

1. Read the poem silently to get an idea of the basic story line.

2. Keep an eye out for examples of **irony**—when the outcome of an event is different than you expected.

3. Read the poem aloud twice. Pay attention to sound devices such as **rhyme, rhythm, repetition,** and **alliteration** (the repetition of consonants in words). Circle or underline any instances you find of sound devices as you read.

4. Look for clues that reveal something about the speaker. How does the speaker feel about the events in the poem?

As you read each poem, record the most striking examples of sound devices in the chart below.

Sound Devices	"The Raven"	"Incident in a Rose Garden"
alliteration (repetition of consonant sounds)	"nodded, nearly napping"	
repetition (repeating words, phrases or lines)		
rhyme (similar sounds at the end of two or more words)		
rhythm (pattern of stressed and unstressed syllables in a line of poetry)		

SET A PURPOSE FOR READING

Read "The Raven" several times to enjoy the sound effects Poe has created in this poem—one of his most famous works.

The RAVEN

Narrative Poem by

EDGAR ALLAN POE

BACKGROUND An obsession is an idea that we cannot get out of our minds. "The Raven" is about a man obsessed by the memory of Lenore, a woman he loved who is now dead. As he is thinking about her, a strange bird flies into his study and keeps croaking one word, making the speaker feel even worse.

A READING POETRY

Circle the rhyming words in lines 1–6. What is happening at the beginning of this poem?

_____

_____

_____

_____

_____

_____

Once upon a midnight dreary, while I pondered, weak and weary,
Over many a quaint and curious volume of forgotten lore—
While I nodded, nearly napping, suddenly there came a tapping,
As of someone gently rapping, rapping at my chamber door.
5 "'Tis some visitor," I muttered, "tapping at my chamber door—
Only this and nothing more." **A**

Ah, distinctly I remember it was in the bleak December;
And each separate dying ember wrought its ghost upon the floor.
Eagerly I wished the morrow;—vainly I had sought to borrow
10 From my books surcease of sorrow[1]—sorrow for the lost Lenore—
For the rare and radiant maiden whom the angels name Lenore—
     Nameless *here* forevermore. **B**

And the silken, sad, uncertain rustling of each purple curtain
Thrilled me—filled me with fantastic terrors never felt before;
15 So that now, to still the beating of my heart, I stood repeating
"'Tis some visitor entreating entrance at my chamber door;—
Some late visitor entreating entrance at my chamber door;—
     That it is and nothing more."

Presently my soul grew stronger; hesitating then no longer,
20 "Sir," said I, "or Madam, truly your forgiveness I implore;
But the fact is I was napping, and so gently you came rapping,
And so faintly you came tapping, tapping at my chamber door,
That I scarce was sure I heard you"—here I opened wide
    the door;—
     Darkness there and nothing more.

25 Deep into that darkness peering, long I stood there wondering,
    fearing,
Doubting, dreaming dreams no mortal ever dared to dream
    before;
But the silence was unbroken, and the stillness gave no token,
And the only word there spoken was the whispered word,
    "Lenore!"
This I whispered, and an echo murmured back the word "Lenore!"
30   Merely this and nothing more. **C**

B NARRATIVE POETRY
With what **internal conflict** does the speaker struggle? Who has he lost?

_____

_____

_____

_____

_____

C READING POETRY
Reread lines 25–30. Underline any examples of **alliteration,** the repetition of consonant sounds at the beginning of words. What is the effect of this sound device?

_____

_____

_____

_____

_____

_____

_____

---

1. **from my books surcease of sorrow:** from reading, an end to sorrow.

Back into the chamber turning, all my soul within me burning,
Soon again I heard a tapping somewhat louder than before.
"Surely," said I, "surely that is something at my window lattice;
Let me see, then, what thereat is, and this mystery explore—
35 Let my heart be still a moment and this mystery explore;—
       'Tis the wind and nothing more!"

Open here I flung the shutter, when, with many a flirt and flutter,
In there stepped a stately Raven of the saintly days of yore.[2]
Not the least obeisance made he;[3] not a minute stopped or
      stayed he;
40 But, with mien of lord or lady,[4] perched above my chamber
      door—
Perched upon a bust of Pallas[5] just above my chamber door—
      Perched, and sat, and nothing more. **D**

Then this ebony bird beguiling[6] my sad fancy into smiling,
By the grave and stern decorum of the countenance[7] it wore,
45 "Though thy crest be shorn and shaven, thou," I said, "art sure
      no craven,[8]
Ghastly grim and ancient Raven wandering from the Nightly
      shore—
Tell me what thy lordly name is on the Night's Plutonian[9] shore!"
      Quoth the Raven, "Nevermore."

Much I marveled this ungainly fowl to hear discourse so plainly,
50 Though its answer little meaning—little relevancy bore;
For we cannot help agreeing that no living human being

D NARRATIVE POETRY
What can you conclude about the **speaker** from the way he reacts to the raven's entrance?

_____
_____
_____
_____
_____
_____
_____
_____
_____
_____
_____
_____
_____
_____
_____
_____

2. **saintly days of yore:** sacred days of the past.
3. **not the least obeisance** (ō-bā'səns) **made he:** he did not bow or make any other gesture of respect.
4. **with mien of lord or lady:** with the appearance of a noble person.
5. **bust of Pallas:** statue of the head and shoulders of Athena, Greek goddess of war and wisdom.
6. **this ebony bird beguiling** (bǐ-gī'lǐng): this black bird that is charming or delighting.
7. **grave and stern decorum . . . countenance** (koun'tə-nəns): serious and dignified expression on the face.
8. **art sure no craven:** are surely not cowardly.
9. **Plutonian:** having to do with Pluto, Roman god of the dead and ruler of the underworld.

Ever yet was blessed with seeing bird above his chamber door—
Bird or beast upon the sculptured bust above his chamber door,
      With such name as "Nevermore."

55 But the Raven, sitting lonely on the placid bust, spoke only
That one word, as if his soul in that one word he did outpour.
Nothing farther then he uttered—not a feather then he
    fluttered—
Till I scarcely more than muttered, "Other friends have flown
    before—
On the morrow *he* will leave me, as my hopes have flown before."
60   Then the bird said, "Nevermore."

Startled at the stillness broken by reply so aptly spoken,
"Doubtless," said I, "what it utters is its only stock and store
Caught from some unhappy master whom unmerciful Disaster 🅔
Followed fast and followed faster till his songs one burden bore—
65 Till the dirges of his Hope[10] that melancholy burden bore
      Of 'Never—nevermore.'"

But the Raven still beguiling all my fancy into smiling,
Straight I wheeled a cushioned seat in front of bird and bust and
    door;
Then, upon the velvet sinking, I betook myself to linking
70 Fancy unto fancy, thinking what this ominous bird of yore—
What this grim, ungainly, ghastly, gaunt, and ominous bird
    of yore
      Meant in croaking, "Nevermore." **PAUSE & REFLECT**

This I sat engaged in guessing, but no syllable expressing
To the fowl whose fiery eyes now burned into my bosom's core;
75 This and more I sat divining,[11] with my head at ease reclining
On the cushion's velvet lining that the lamp-light gloated o'er,
But whose velvet violet lining with the lamp-light gloating o'er,
      She shall press, ah, nevermore!

🅔 **READING POETRY**
Internal rhyme occurs when a line of poetry contains similar or identical sounds. Reread this stanza and circle all the internal rhymes you can find.

PAUSE & REFLECT
At this point in the poem, what is the speaker doing?

_____

_____

_____

_____

_____

_____

_____

---

10. **dirges** (dûr′jĭz) **of his Hope:** funeral hymns mourning the loss of hope.
11. **divining** (dĭ-vī′nĭng): guessing or speculating.

Then, methought, the air grew denser, perfumed from an unseen censer

80 Swung by Seraphim[12] whose foot-falls tinkled on the tufted floor.

"Wretch," I cried, "thy God hath lent thee—by these angels he hath sent thee

Respite—respite and nepenthe[13] from thy memories of Lenore;

Quaff, oh quaff this kind nepenthe[14] and forget this lost Lenore!"

Quoth the Raven, "Nevermore."

85 "Prophet!" said I, "thing of evil!—prophet still, if bird or devil!—

Whether Tempter sent, or whether tempest tossed[15] thee here ashore,

Desolate yet all undaunted,[16] on this desert land enchanted—

On this home by Horror haunted—tell me truly, I implore—

Is there—*is* there balm in Gilead?[17]—tell me—tell me, I implore!"

90   Quoth the Raven, "Nevermore." **F**

"Prophet!" said I, "thing of evil!—prophet still, if bird or devil!

By that Heaven that bends above us—by that God we both adore—

Tell this soul with sorrow laden if, within the distant Aidenn,[18]

It shall clasp a sainted maiden whom the angels name Lenore—

95 Clasp a rare and radiant maiden whom the angels name Lenore."

            Quoth the Raven, "Nevermore."

F   READING POETRY
Underline the **repetition** in lines 88–89. What does this repetition tell you about the poem's speaker?

_____

_____

_____

_____

_____

_____

_____

_____

_____

_____

12. **censer swung by Seraphim** (sĕr'ə-fĭm): container of burning incense swung by angels of the highest rank.

13. **he hath sent thee respite** (rĕs'pĭt) . . . **nepenthe** (nĭ-pĕn'thē): God has sent you relief and forgetfulness of sorrow.

14. **quaff, oh quaff this kind nepenthe:** drink this beverage that eases pain.

15. **whether Tempter sent . . . tempest tossed:** whether the devil sent or a violent storm carried.

16. **desolate yet all undaunted:** alone and yet unafraid.

17. **balm in Gilead** (gĭl'ē-əd): relief from suffering.

18. **Aidenn** (ād'n): heaven.

"Be that word our sign of parting, bird or fiend!" I shrieked,
    upstarting—
"Get thee back into the tempest and the Night's Plutonian shore!
Leave no black plume as a token of that lie thy soul hath spoken!
100 Leave my loneliness unbroken!—quit the bust above my door!
Take thy beak from out my heart, and take thy form from off my
    door!"
        Quoth the Raven, "Nevermore."

And the Raven, never flitting, still is sitting, *still* is sitting
On the pallid bust of Pallas just above my chamber door;
105 And his eyes have all the seeming of a demon's that is dreaming,
And the lamp-light o'er him streaming throws his shadow on
    the floor;
And my soul from out that shadow that lies floating on the floor
        Shall be lifted—nevermore! **G**

G NARRATIVE POETRY
Think about whether the speaker's **conflict** is resolved at the end of the poem. What do you think will happen to him? Explain.

_____

_____

_____

_____

_____

_____

_____

_____

_____

_____

SET A PURPOSE FOR READING

Read this poem to find out what "incident" happens in the speaker's rose garden.

Incident *in a* Rose Garden

Narrative Poem by
DONALD JUSTICE

BACKGROUND In this poem, the text in italics represents the voices of the different characters.

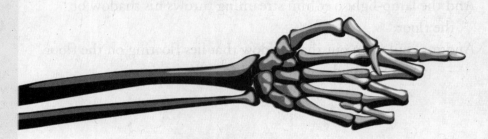

The gardener came running,
An old man, out of breath.
Fear had given him legs.
    Sir, I encountered Death
5   *Just now among the roses.*
    Thin as a scythe he stood there.
    I knew him by his pictures.
    He had his black coat on,
    Black gloves, a broad black hat.
10   *I think he would have spoken,*
    Seeing his mouth stood open.
    Big it was, with white teeth.
    As soon as he beckoned, I ran.
    I ran until I found you.
15   *Sir, I am quitting my job.*
    I want to see my sons
    Once more before I die.
    I want to see California. **H**

H NARRATIVE POETRY
In lines 4–18, the gardener describes the character of Death. What do these lines suggest the **conflict** of the poem will be?

_____

_____

_____

_____

_____

_____

We shook hands; he was off.
20 And there stood Death in the garden,
Dressed like a Spanish waiter.
He had the air of someone
Who because he likes arriving
At all appointments early
25 Learns to think himself patient.
I watched him pinch one bloom off
And hold it to his nose—
A connoisseur of roses—
One bloom and then another. **I**
30 They strewed the earth around him.
Sir, you must be that stranger
Who threatened my gardener.
This is my property, sir.
I welcome only friends here. **J**

35 Death grinned, and his eyes lit up
With the pale glow of those lanterns
That workmen carry sometimes
To light their way through the dusk.
Now with great care he slid
40 The glove from his right hand
And held that out in greeting,
A little cage of bone.
Sir, I knew your father,
And we were friends at the end.
45 As for your gardener,
I did not threaten him.
Old men mistake my gestures.
I only meant to ask him
To show me to his master.
50 I take it you are he? **PAUSE & REFLECT**

for Mark Strand

I READING POETRY
Read aloud lines 26–29 and note the **rhythm** created by the shorter lines. What effect does this add to the image presented?

J READING POETRY
What conflict is the speaker trying to resolve here?

PAUSE & REFLECT
What is the surprise ending revealed in lines 48–50?

Text Analysis: Narrative Poetry

Narrative poems like "The Raven" and "Incident in a Rose Garden" contain most of the same elements found in short stories. Fill in the chart below with a brief explanation of each element.

Narrative Element	"The Raven"	"Incident in a Rose Garden"
Characters		
Setting / Atmosphere		
Conflict		
Resolution (How does it end?)		

Reading Skill: Reading Poetry

Which of the sound devices used in these poems do you think had the most profound effect? Explain.

_____

_____

_____

Why are we so fascinated with the **UNKNOWN?**

What is it about unexplained events or occurrences that people find intriguing?

_____

_____

_____

Academic Vocabulary in Writing

analyze	element	infer	sequence	structure

When you **analyze** something, you examine it closely. Go back to "The Raven" and think about how Poe creates an atmosphere, or mood, of mystery and dread. What **elements** of the setting help create this atmosphere? Use at least one Academic Vocabulary word in your response. Definitions for these terms are listed on page 3.

Assessment Practice

DIRECTIONS Use "The Raven" and "Incident in a Rose Garden" to answer questions 1–4.

1 In "The Raven" the speaker is trying to forget the loss of —
- **A** his life
- **B** his child
- **C** the raven
- **D** his lover Lenore

2 In "Incident in a Rose Garden," for whom has Death really come?
- **A** the speaker
- **B** the gardener
- **C** the speaker's father
- **D** no one

3 A poem's rhyme scheme can be written in letters with repeating letters indicating end-rhyming lines. The rhyme scheme of "The Raven" can be written as —
- **A** ABABBB
- **B** ABCBBB
- **C** ABBCBA
- **D** ABABB

4 The ending of "Incident in a Rose Garden" is ironic because —
- **A** the gardener is already dead
- **B** the speaker is already dead
- **C** Death has come for the speaker
- **D** Death has come for the speaker's father

UNIT 2

People Watching

CHARACTERIZATION AND POINT OF VIEW

Be sure to read the Text Analysis Workshop on pp. 202–207 in *Holt McDougal Literature*.

Academic Vocabulary for Unit 2

Preview the following Academic Vocabulary words. You will encounter these words as you work through this book and will use them as you write and talk about the selections in this unit.

complex (käm pleks′) *adj.* made up of two or more parts; hard to understand or analyze

*The story characters are **complex,** just like real people.*

device (di vīs′) *n.* a thing created; a mechanical invention or creation

*There are many **devices** a writer can use to introduce the audience to a character.*

evaluate (ĭ-văl′yōō-āt) *v.* to find out the value or worth of something; to judge or examine

*My teacher thoroughly **evaluates** each draft of my paper.*

interact (in′tər akt′) *v.* to act or work with someone or something; to act with one another

*The writer used dialogue to show the reader how the characters **interact.***

perspective (pər spek′tiv) *adj.* point of view or mental view

*The story is told from the **perspective** of a young boy.*

Which type of character do you prefer: simple or **complex?** Choose a character from a book, TV show, or movie that you find interesting and explain whether he or she is simple or complex. What was it about the character that kept you wanting to know more?

_____

_____

_____

The Necklace

Short Story by **Guy de Maupassant**

How important is **STATUS?**

What happens to people who place too much importance on status, or the standing they have in a group? In "The Necklace," you'll meet Madame Loisel, an unforgettable character whose pursuit of status costs her more than she could have imagined.

QUICKWRITE List five factors that determine a person's status, or social standing, in your school. Add or delete from the list shown. Then write a few sentences explaining whether you think status should be determined by these factors.

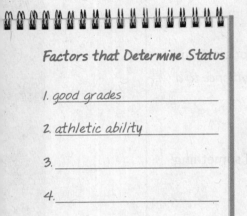

Factors that Determine Status

1. good grades

2. athletic ability

3. _____

4. _____

5. _____

Text Analysis: Character Motivation

A writer creates a believable character by describing not only his or her physical appearance but also by describing the way a character acts, speaks, and behaves. **Motivation** is the reason behind a character's action—what makes him or her act in a certain way. In the chart below, the description of the character's action in the left column reveals his or her motivation in the right column. In the last row, give a reason for Kyle's behavior in the empty box. What do his actions tell you about him?

ACTION	MOTIVATION
The toddler stomps her feet and points to candy counter.	The girl wants candy.
Monique brushes her hair with her fingers and tucks it behind her ear. She glances quickly at James, trying not to look too interested.	Monique has a crush on James.
Kyle cancels plans to go skateboarding with his friends in order to work on his science project.	

As you read "The Necklace," pay attention to the author's descriptions of Madame Loisel. What do her actions and motivations tell you about her character?

Reading Skill: Make Inferences

Instead of directly telling readers what a character is like, a writer often includes details that are clues to the character's personality. Readers can use these details, along with their own knowledge, to **make inferences,** or guesses, about the character's motivations, values, and feelings. As you read "The Necklace," notes in the side column will prompt you to record your inferences.

Vocabulary in Context

Note: Words are listed in the order in which they appear in the story.

prospects (prŏs′pĕkts′) *n.* chances or possibilities, especially for financial success
*Janet's **prospects** for success would be better with a recommendation from her boss.*

incessantly (ĭn-sĕs′ənt-lē) *adv.* without interruption; continuously
*Jeremy worked on the painting **incessantly,** trying to make it perfect for the exhibit.*

vexation (vĕk-sā′shən) *n.* irritation; annoyance
*The teacher felt great **vexation** at the sight of her students' incomplete assignments.*

pauper (pô′pər) *n.* a poor person, especially one who depends on public charity
*The **pauper** asked passersby for spare change.*

adulation (ăj′ə-lā′shən) *n.* excessive praise or flattery
*The young dancer's performance was met with **adulation** from her encouraging instructor.*

disconsolate (dĭs-kŏn′sə-lĭt) *adj.* extremely depressed or dejected
*The man was **disconsolate** after loosing his job.*

aghast (ə-găst′) *adj.* filled with shock or horror
*I was **aghast** when I saw that the famous theatre had burned to the ground.*

gamut (găm′ət) *n.* an entire range or series
*The teenager's musical interest ran the **gamut** from classic rock to rap.*

privation (prī-vā′shən) *n.* the lack of a basic necessity or a comfort of life
*With no milk, the infant fell ill from **privation.***

askew (ə-skyōō′) *adj.* crooked; to one side
*The painting was **askew,** tilting slightly to the left.*

SET A PURPOSE FOR READING

Read this story to find out how a borrowed necklace changes a woman's life.

The Necklace

Short Story by

GUY DE MAUPASSANT

BACKGROUND Guy de Maupassant is considered by many to be the greatest French short story writer. His specialty was creating precise characters and showing what made them tick. "The Necklace" takes place in Paris during the late 1800s. At the time, European societies were divided into upper, middle, and lower classes. Usually, a person was born into his or her social class, although sometimes a man could move up by making money. A woman could improve her class by marrying into a higher class. To do this she had to have a dowry—money or property that a bride's family was expected to give her new husband, but poorer families were unable to provide.

prospects (prŏs′pĕkts′) *n.* chances or possibilities, especially for financial success

She was one of those pretty and charming girls, born, as if by an accident of fate, into a family of clerks. With no dowry, no **prospects**, no way of any kind of being met, understood, loved, and married by a man both prosperous and famous, she was finally married to a minor clerk in the Ministry of Education.

She dressed plainly because she could not afford fine clothes, but was as unhappy as a woman who has come down in the world; for women have no family rank or social class. With them, beauty, grace, and charm take the place of birth and breeding.
10 Their natural poise, their instinctive good taste, and their mental cleverness are the sole guiding principles which make daughters of the common people the equals of ladies in high society.

She grieved **incessantly**, feeling that she had been born for all the little niceties and luxuries of living. She grieved over the shabbiness of her apartment, the dinginess of the walls, the worn-out appearance of the chairs, the ugliness of the draperies. All these things, which another woman of her class would not even have noticed, gnawed at her and made her furious. The sight of the little Breton[1] girl who did her
20 humble housework roused in her disconsolate regrets and wild daydreams. She would dream of silent chambers, draped with Oriental tapestries and lighted by tall bronze floor lamps, and of two handsome butlers in knee breeches, who, drowsy from the heavy warmth cast by the central stove, dozed in large overstuffed armchairs. **A**

She would dream of great reception halls hung with old silks, of fine furniture filled with priceless curios, and of small, stylish, scented sitting rooms just right for the four o'clock chat with intimate friends, with distinguished and sought-after men whose
30 attention every woman envies and longs to attract.

When dining at the round table, covered for the third day with the same cloth, opposite her husband, who would raise the cover of the soup tureen, declaring delightedly, "Ah! A good stew! There's nothing I like better . . ." she would dream of fashionable dinner parties, of gleaming silverware, of tapestries making the walls alive with characters out of history and strange birds in a fairyland forest; she would dream of delicious dishes served on wonderful china, of gallant compliments whispered and listened to with a sphinxlike[2] smile as one eats the rosy flesh of a trout or
40 nibbles at the wings of a grouse.

She had no evening clothes, no jewels, nothing. But those were the things she wanted; she felt that was the kind of life for her. She so much longed to please, be envied, be fascinating and sought after. **B**

She had a well-to-do friend, a classmate of convent-school days whom she would no longer go to see, simply because

---

1. **Breton** (brĕt'n): from Brittany, a region in northwestern France.
2. **sphinxlike:** mysterious (from the Greek myth of the sphinx, a winged creature that killed those who could not answer its riddle).

incessantly (ĭn-sĕs'ənt-lē)
adv. without interruption; continuously

A MAKE INFERENCES
Underline words and phrases in the first two paragraphs of the story that describe Madame Loisel's physical appearance. Circle words and phrases in the third paragraph that describe her emotional state.

B MAKE INFERENCES
Think about Madame Loisel's dreams and desires. Have you ever wanted something you couldn't have? Record an inference about Madame Loisel on the chart below.

DETAIL ABOUT CHARACTER
wants things she cannot have

↓

PERSONAL EXPERIENCE

↓

MY INFERENCE

vexation (vĕk-sā'shən) *n.*
irritation; annoyance

Why does seeing her old friend fill Madame Loisel fill with vexation?

_____

_____

_____

_____

_____

_____

_____

PAUSE & REFLECT

Monsieur and Madame Loisel respond differently to the invitation. Underline a word or phrase in the text that shows each character's response. What do these reactions reveal about each character?

_____

_____

_____

_____

_____

_____

_____

she would feel so distressed on returning home. And she would weep for days on end from **vexation**, regret, despair, and anguish.

50 Then one evening, her husband came home proudly holding out a large envelope.

"Look," he said, "I've got something for you."

She excitedly tore open the envelope and pulled out a printed card bearing these words:

"The Minister of Education and Mme. Georges Ramponneau[3] beg M. and Mme. Loisel[4] to do them the honor of attending an evening reception at the Ministerial Mansion on Friday, January 18."

Instead of being delighted, as her husband had hoped, she
60 scornfully tossed the invitation on the table, murmuring, "What good is that to me?"

"But, my dear, I thought you'd be thrilled to death. You never get a chance to go out, and this is a real affair, a wonderful one! I had an awful time getting a card. Everybody wants one; it's much sought after, and not many clerks have a chance at one. You'll see all the most important people there."

She gave him an irritated glance and burst out impatiently, "What do you think I have to go in?"

He hadn't given that a thought. He stammered, "Why, the
70 dress you wear when we go to the theater. That looks quite nice, I think."

He stopped talking, dazed and distracted to see his wife burst out weeping. Two large tears slowly rolled from the corners of her eyes to the corners of her mouth; he gasped, "Why, what's the matter? What's the trouble?" **PAUSE & REFLECT**

By sheer will power she overcame her outburst and answered in a calm voice while wiping the tears from her wet cheeks:

3. **Mme. Georges Ramponneau** (zhôrzh' rän-pô-nō'): *Mme.* is an abbreviation for *Madame* (mə-däm'), a title of courtesy for a French married woman.
4. **M. and Mme. Loisel** (lwä-zĕl'): *M.* is an abbreviation for *Monsieur* (mə-syœ'), a title of courtesy for a Frenchman.

"Oh, nothing. Only I don't have an evening dress and therefore I can't go to that affair. Give the card to some friend at the office
80 whose wife can dress better than I can."

He was stunned. He resumed. "Let's see, Mathilde.[5] How much would a suitable outfit cost—one you could wear for other affairs too—something very simple?"

She thought it over for several seconds, going over her allowance and thinking also of the amount she could ask for without bringing an immediate refusal and an exclamation of dismay from the thrifty clerk.

Finally, she answered hesitatingly, "I'm not sure exactly, but I think with four hundred francs[6] I could manage it."

90 He turned a bit pale, for he had set aside just that amount to buy a rifle so that, the following summer, he could join some friends who were getting up a group to shoot larks on the plain near Nanterre.[7]

However, he said, "All right. I'll give you four hundred francs. But try to get a nice dress." **C**

As the day of the party approached, Mme. Loisel seemed sad, moody, and ill at ease. Her outfit was ready, however. Her husband said to her one evening, "What's the matter? You've been all out of sorts for three days."

100 And she answered, "It's embarrassing not to have a jewel or a gem—nothing to wear on my dress. I'll look like a **pauper**: I'd almost rather not go to that party."

He answered, "Why not wear some flowers? They're very fashionable this season. For ten francs you can get two or three gorgeous roses."

She wasn't at all convinced. "No. . . . There's nothing more humiliating than to look poor among a lot of rich women."

C CHARACTER MOTIVATION
What do you think is Monsieur Loisel's motivation for giving the money to his wife?

_____

_____

_____

_____

pauper (pô′pər) *n.* a poor person, especially one who depends on public charity

---

5. **Mathilde** (mä-tēld′).
6. **francs** (frăngks): The franc was the basic monetary unit of France.
7. **Nanterre** (näN-tĕr′): a city of north central France.

But her husband exclaimed, "My, but you're silly! Go see your friend Mme. Forestier[8] and ask her to lend you some jewelry. You and she know each other well enough for you to do that."

She gave a cry of joy, "Why, that's so! I hadn't thought of it."

The next day she paid her friend a visit and told her of her predicament.

Mme. Forestier went toward a large closet with mirrored doors, took out a large jewel box, brought it over, opened it, and said to Mme. Loisel, "Pick something out, my dear."

At first her eyes noted some bracelets, then a pearl necklace, then a Venetian cross, gold and gems, of marvelous workmanship. She tried on these adornments in front of the mirror, but hesitated, unable to decide which to part with and put back. She kept on asking, "Haven't you something else?"

"Oh, yes, keep on looking. I don't know just what you'd like."

All at once she found, in a black satin box, a superb diamond necklace; and her pulse beat faster with longing. Her hands trembled as she took it up. Clasping it around her throat, outside her high-necked dress, she stood in ecstasy looking at her reflection.

Then she asked, hesitatingly, pleading, "Could I borrow that, just that and nothing else?"

"Why, of course."

She threw her arms around her friend, kissed her warmly, and fled with her treasure. **D**

The day of the party arrived. Mme. Loisel was a sensation. She was the prettiest one there, fashionable, gracious, smiling, and wild with joy. All the men turned to look at her, asked who she was, begged to be introduced. All the Cabinet officials wanted to waltz with her. The minister took notice of her.

She danced madly, wildly, drunk with pleasure, giving no thought to anything in the triumph of her beauty, the pride of her success, in a kind of happy cloud composed of all the

D CHARACTER MOTIVATION

Of all the pieces in the closet, why do you think Madame Loisel chooses the diamond necklace?

_____

_____

_____

_____

_____

_____

_____

---

8. **Forestier** (fô-rĕs-tyā′).

adulation (ăj'ə-lā'shən) n.
excessive praise or flattery

adulation, of all the admiring glances, of all the awakened longings, of a sense of complete victory that is so sweet to a woman's heart.

She left around four o'clock in the morning. Her husband, since midnight,
150 had been dozing in a small empty sitting room with three other gentlemen whose wives were having too good a time.

He threw over her shoulders the wraps he had brought for going home, modest garments of everyday life whose shabbiness clashed with the stylishness of her evening clothes. She felt this and longed to escape, unseen by the other women who
160 were draped in expensive furs.

Loisel held her back.

"Hold on! You'll catch cold outside. I'll call a cab."

But she wouldn't listen to him and went rapidly down the stairs. When they were on the street, they didn't find a carriage; and they set out to hunt for one, hailing drivers whom they saw going by at a distance.

They walked toward the Seine,[9] **disconsolate** and shivering. Finally on the docks they found one of those carriages that one sees in Paris only after nightfall, as if they were ashamed to show
170 their drabness during daylight hours.

It dropped them at their door in the Rue des Martyrs,[10] and they climbed wearily up to their apartment. For her, it was all

disconsolate (dĭs-kŏn'sə-lĭt)
adj. extremely depressed or dejected

9. **Seine** (sĕn): the principal river of Paris.
10. **Rue des Martyrs** (rü' dā mär-tēr'): a street in Paris.

over. For him, there was the thought that he would have to be at the Ministry at ten o'clock.

Before the mirror, she let the wraps fall from her shoulders to see herself once again in all her glory. Suddenly she gave a cry. The necklace was gone.

Her husband, already half-undressed, said, "What's the trouble?"

180 She turned toward him despairingly, "I . . . I . . . I don't have Mme. Forestier's necklace."

"What! You can't mean it! It's impossible!"

They hunted everywhere, through the folds of the dress, through the folds of the coat, in the pockets. They found nothing.

He asked, "Are you sure you had it when leaving the dance?"

"Yes, I felt it when I was in the hall of the Ministry."

"But if you had lost it on the street, we'd have heard it drop. It must be in the cab."

"Yes. Quite likely. Did you get its number?"

190 "No. Didn't you notice it either?"

"No."

They looked at each other **aghast**. Finally Loisel got dressed again.

"I'll retrace our steps on foot," he said, "to see if I can find it."

And he went out. She remained in her evening clothes, without the strength to go to bed, slumped in a chair in the unheated room, her mind a blank.

Her husband came in about seven o'clock. He had had no luck.

He went to the police station, to the newspapers to post a
200 reward, to the cab companies, everywhere the slightest hope drove him.

That evening Loisel returned, pale, his face lined; still he had learned nothing.

"We'll have to write your friend," he said, "to tell her you have broken the catch and are having it repaired. That will give us a little time to turn around." **PAUSE & REFLECT**

She wrote to his dictation.

---

aghast (ə-găst′) *adj.* filled with shock or horror

Why is the couple aghast? What consequences might they face if they can't find the missing necklace?

_____

_____

_____

_____

_____

PAUSE & REFLECT

Why does Monsieur Loisel suggest lying to the friend, rather than telling her the truth about the lost necklace? What do you think will happen?

_____

_____

_____

_____

At the end of a week, they had given up all hope.

And Loisel, looking five years older, declared, "We must take
210 steps to replace that piece of jewelry."

The next day they took the case to the jeweler whose name
they found inside. He consulted his records. "I didn't sell that
necklace, madame," he said. "I only supplied the case."

Then they went from one jeweler to another hunting for a
similar necklace, going over their recollections, both sick with
despair and anxiety.

They found, in a shop in Palais Royal, a string of diamonds
which seemed exactly like the one they were seeking. It was priced
at forty thousand francs. They could get it for thirty-six.

220 They asked the jeweler to hold it for them for three days.
And they reached an agreement that he would take it back for
thirty-four thousand if the lost one was found before the end
of February.

Loisel had eighteen thousand francs he had inherited from his
father. He would borrow the rest.

He went about raising the money, asking a thousand francs
from one, four hundred from another, a hundred here, sixty
there. He signed notes, made ruinous deals, did business
with loan sharks, ran the whole **gamut** of moneylenders. He
230 compromised the rest of his life, risked his signature without
knowing if he'd be able to honor it, and then, terrified by the
outlook for the future, by the blackness of despair about to close
around him, by the prospect of all the **privations** of the body
and tortures of the spirit, he went to claim the new necklace with
the thirty-six thousand francs which he placed on the counter of
the shopkeeper. **E**

When Mme. Loisel took the necklace back, Mme. Forestier
said to her frostily, "You should have brought it back sooner;
I might have needed it."

gamut (găm′ət) *n.* an entire
range or series

privation (prī-vā′shən) *n.* the
lack of a basic necessity or a
comfort of life

**E CHARACTER
MOTIVATION**
Why do you think the Loisels
lie to Madame Forestier? What
motivates them to go into such
debt?

_____

_____

_____

_____

_____

_____

240   She didn't open the case, an action her friend was afraid of. If she had noticed the substitution, what would she have thought? What would she have said? Would she have thought her a thief?

    Mme. Loisel experienced the horrible life the needy live. She played her part, however, with sudden heroism. That frightful debt had to be paid. She would pay it. She dismissed her maid; they rented a garret under the eaves.

    She learned to do the heavy housework, to perform the hateful duties of cooking. She washed dishes, wearing down her shell-pink 250 nails scouring the grease from pots and pans; she scrubbed dirty linen, shirts, and cleaning rags which she hung on a line to dry; she took the garbage down to the street each morning and brought up water, stopping on each landing to get her breath. And, clad like a peasant woman, basket on arm, guarding sou[11] by sou her scanty allowance, she bargained with the fruit dealers, the grocer, the butcher, and was insulted by them.

    Each month notes had to be paid, and others renewed to give more time.

    Her husband labored evenings to balance a tradesman's 260 accounts, and at night, often, he copied documents at five sous a page.

    And this went on for ten years.

    Finally, all was paid back, everything including the exorbitant rates of the loan sharks and accumulated compound interest.

    Mme. Loisel appeared an old woman, now. She became heavy, rough, harsh, like one of the poor. Her hair untended, her skirts <u>askew</u>, her hands red, her voice shrill, she even slopped water on her floors and scrubbed them herself. But, sometimes, while her husband was at work, she would sit near the window and think 270 of that long-ago evening when, at the dance, she had been so beautiful and admired.

    What would have happened if she had not lost that necklace? Who knows? Who can say? How strange and unpredictable life is! How little there is between happiness and misery!

---

askew (ə-skyōō′) *adj.* crooked; to one side

How would a young Madame Loisel feel about this image of herself with her skirt **askew**?

_____

_____

_____

_____

_____

_____

---

11. **sou** (sōō): a French coin of small value.

Then one Sunday when she had gone for a walk on the Champs Élysées[12] to relax a bit from the week's labors, she suddenly noticed a woman strolling with a child. It was Mme. Forestier, still young-looking; still beautiful, still charming.

Mme. Loisel felt a rush of emotion. Should she speak to her? 280 Of course. And now that everything was paid off, she would tell her the whole story. Why not? PAUSE & REFLECT

She went toward her. "Hello, Jeanne."

The other, not recognizing her, showed astonishment at being spoken to so familiarly by this common person. She stammered. "But . . . madame . . . I don't recognize . . . You must be mistaken."

"No, I'm Mathilde Loisel."

Her friend gave a cry, "Oh, my poor Mathilde, how you've changed!"

290 "Yes, I've had a hard time since last seeing you. And plenty of misfortunes—and all on account of you!" **F**

"Of me . . . How do you mean?"

"Do you remember that diamond necklace you loaned me to wear to the dance at the Ministry?"

12. **Champs Élysées** (shän zā-lē-zā'): a famous wide street in Paris.

PAUSE & REFLECT

Do you think it's worthwhile for Madame Loisel to tell her friend the truth about the necklace now? Why or why not?

_____

_____

_____

_____

_____

_____

F CHARACTER MOTIVATION

What motivates Madame Loisel to approach Madame Forestier? Do you think she is justified in blaming her "misfortunes" on her friend? Explain.

_____

_____

_____

_____

_____

_____

_____

_____

_____

PAUSE & REFLECT

What realization has Madame Loisel come to?

_____

_____

_____

_____

_____

_____

"Yes, but what about it?"

"Well, I lost it."

"You lost it! But you returned it."

"I brought you another just like it. And we've been paying for it for ten years now. You can imagine that wasn't easy for us who had nothing. Well, it's over now, and I am glad of it."

Mme. Forestier stopped short, "You mean to say you bought a diamond necklace to replace mine?"

"Yes. You never noticed, then? They were quite alike."

And she smiled with proud and simple joy.

Mme. Forestier, quite overcome, clasped her by the hands. "Oh, my poor Mathilde. But mine was only paste.[13] Why, at most it was worth only five hundred francs!" **PAUSE & REFLECT**

---

13. **paste:** a hard, glassy material used in making imitation gems.

Text Analysis: Character Motivation

Consider what you know about each of the character's feelings and goals.
Review the actions listed in the left column of the chart below. In the right
column, write down the motivation for each action.

ACTION	MOTIVATION
Mme. Loisel weeps when she receives the invitation. (line 72)	
Mme. Loisel borrows jewelry rather than wear flowers. (line 128)	
Monsieur Loisel advises his wife not to tell her friend about the lost necklace. (204–206)	
Mme. Loisel approaches Mme. Forestier on the street and tells her about the lost necklace. (279–281)	

Before Madame Loisel realizes the necklace was a fake, she "smiled with
proud and simple joy." Why do you think Madame Loisel felt pride about the
hard work she did to replace the necklace? How do you think she felt after she
found out the truth? Write a few sentences.

_____

_____

_____

_____

_____

Reading Skill: Make Inferences

In the story, we learn a lot about Madame and Monsieur Loisel, but we don't know very much about Madame Forestier. Look back through the story to find two details about Madame Forestier and record them in the chart below. Then use the clues and your own knowledge to make an inference about her.

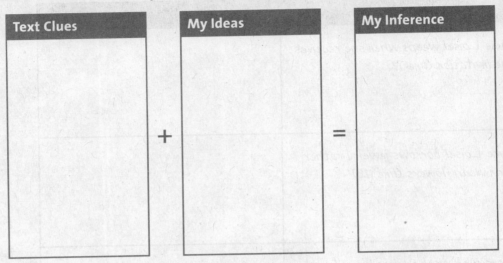

Text Clues	My Ideas	My Inference
	+	=

How important is STATUS?

Are there things you would be willing to give up in order to pursue popularity? Explain.

_____

_____

Vocabulary Practice

Use the vocabulary words at the right to fill in the blanks.

The girl had many _____ for college. They ran the

_____ from colleges in the Ivy League to state schools.

She obsessed _____ about which was the best choice

until finally her parents were filled with such _____

that they made the choice for her. She was _____

when she realized her parents had picked her least favorite

school and became _____.

WORD LIST

adulation

aghast

askew

disconsolate

gamut

incessantly

pauper

privation

prospects

vexation

Academic Vocabulary in Speaking

| complex | device | evaluate | interact | perspective |

Madame Loisel and Madame Forestier **interact,** or communicate, with each other three times in the story. With a partner **evaluate** their interactions. If either woman had acted or responded differently, how would the story have changed? Use at least one Academic Vocabulary word in your response. Definitions for these terms are listed on page 69.

_____

_____

_____

Assessment Practice

DIRECTIONS Use "The Necklace" to answer questions 1–6.

1 Madame Loisel is unhappy at the beginning of the story because —

- (A) she wishes she were pretty and charming
- (B) she doesn't like her husband
- (C) she wishes she had wealth and luxury
- (D) she does not like housework

2 Madame Loisel doesn't want to wear flowers to the party because they —

- (A) might stain her dress and make her feel out of place
- (B) look cheap and would make her look inferior
- (C) smell too strong and would embarrass her
- (D) wilt and make her feel unattractive

3 What is Madame Loisel's motivation for borrowing the necklace from her friend?

- (A) She wants to appear elegant and well dressed at the reception.
- (B) She wants to add some glamour to the dull dress she has to wear.
- (C) She likes her friend's jewelry better than her own.
- (D) She does not want to appear too dressed up at the reception.

4 What inference can you make about Monsieur Loisel's character?

- (A) He wants others to be impressed by his wealth.
- (B) He cares little about material things.
- (C) He often gives his wife extravagant gifts.
- (D) He was born into the upper class.

5 What inference can you make about the Loisels' motivation for lying about the lost necklace?

- (A) They are embarrassed by the situation.
- (B) They are in the habit of telling lies.
- (C) They are trying to trick Madame Forestier.
- (D) They are trying to keep the necklace for themselves.

6 What unexpected plot twist occurs at the end of the story?

- (A) Madame Forestier learns that the Loisels have been paying off debt.
- (B) Monsieur Loisel goes into debt to pay off the necklace.
- (C) Madame Loisel learns that the necklace is fake.
- (D) Madame Forestier doesn't recognize Madame Loisel.

from I Know Why the Caged Bird Sings
Autobiography by Maya Angelou

What is a TEACHER?

Your teachers at school are dedicated to helping you acquire knowledge, but are there individuals outside the classroom who teach you important things as well? In this selection, you'll meet Mrs. Flowers, a woman who acted as a mentor—a trusted counselor or teacher—to a young Maya Angelou.

DISCUSS Think of people who have shared wisdom with you, helped you see things in a new way, or pushed you when you needed encouragement. What traits, or qualities, did these people have? Write them down in the notebook page to the left.

Qualities of a Mentor

1. generosity _____

2. patience _____

3. _____

4. _____

5. _____

Text Analysis: Characterization in Autobiography

In an **autobiography,** the author writes about his or her own life. When describing individuals they have known, writers of autobiographies use the same methods of characterization as fiction writers. Sometimes the author might directly tell you what a character is like. More often a character's **traits,** or qualities, are revealed indirectly, as shown in the following chart.

METHODS OF CHARACTERIZATION	EXAMPLES
1. PHYSICAL APPEARANCE Descriptions of the character's • clothing • physical characteristics • body language and facial expressions • gestures or mannerisms	• A character who usually wears unmatched socks and stained shirts might be described as **slovenly.** • If a character is always smiling and making eye contact with others, you might infer that she is **warm** or **friendly.**
2. SPEECH, THOUGHTS, AND ACTIONS Presentation of the character's • speech patterns • habits and tastes • talents and abilities • interaction with others	• A character who speaks so quietly that others can't hear him might be described as **timid.** • You might infer that a character who repeatedly misses softball practice without telling the coach is **irresponsible** or **unreliable.**
3. OTHER CHARACTERS Presentation of other characters' • reactions to the character • relationships with the character • impression of the character's reputation • traits that contrast with the character's traits	• If a character's girlfriend describes him as a "no-good lying jerk," you might infer that he is **insensitive** and **dishonest.** • If people often confide their troubles to a character, you might conclude that she is **trustworthy.**

Reading Skill: Analyze Perspectives

Autobiographies often reflect two different **perspectives,** or viewpoints:

- that of a writer as he or she experiences events
- that of the writer looking back on these events years later

As you read, use a chart like the one shown to record Angelou's thoughts and observations from both her childhood and adult perspectives.

Child's Viewpoint	Adult's Viewpoint
"Why on earth did she insist on calling her Sister Flowers?" (lines 29–30)	"She was one of the few gentlewoman I have ever known . . ." (line 21)

Vocabulary in Context

taut (tôt) *adj.* pulled or drawn tight
*I pulled my shoelaces **taut** so they would not come untied again.*

sacrilegious (săk′rə-lĭj′əs) *adj.* disrespectful toward a sacred person, place, or thing
*It was considered **sacrilegious** to keep your hat on inside the church.*

clarity (klăr′ĭ-tē) *n.* clearness
*The author wrote with **clarity,** making his ideas easily understandable.*

infuse (ĭn-fyo͞oz′) *v.* to fill, as if by pouring
*The speaker **infused** her speech with humorous remarks.*

leer (lîr) *v.* to give a sly, evil glance
*Rebecca **leered** at me from the corner of her eye.*

illiteracy (ĭ-lĭt′ər-ə-sē) *n.* a lack of ability to read and write
*Mother tried to hide her **illiteracy** from us, but we knew she could not read.*

homely (hōm′lē) *adj.* characteristic of home life; simple; everyday
*In contrast to my aunt's elaborate costume, I looked quite **homely.***

cascade (kă-skād′) *v.* to fall or flow like a waterfall
*We watched the water **cascade** over the cliff's edge.*

Reading Skill Analyze Perspective

As you read, use a chart like the one shown to record Angelou's thoughts and observations from both her childhood and adult perspectives.

SET A PURPOSE FOR READING

Read the excerpt from this autobiography to discover how a neighbor helps a young girl in need.

I KNOW WHY THE
Caged Bird SINGS

Autobiography by

MAYA ANGELOU

BACKGROUND In this excerpt from her autobiography, Maya Angelou (born Marguerite Johnson) describes her childhood in the 1930s in Stamps, Arkansas, a small segregated town. She and her brother Bailey lived with their grandmother, called Momma, who ran the general store. A year before this selection begins, Marguerite was abused by a family friend. As a result she became depressed and withdrawn, and she stopped speaking.

taut (tôt) *adj.* pulled or drawn tight

Ⓐ CHARACTERIZATION

Circle the words and phrases in lines 4–15 that describe Mrs. Flowers's appearance. What do these details suggest about the kind of person she is?

_____

_____

_____

_____

_____

_____

For nearly a year, I sopped around the house, the Store, the school and the church, like an old biscuit, dirty and inedible. Then I met, or rather got to know, the lady who threw me my first life line.

Mrs. Bertha Flowers was the aristocrat of Black Stamps. She had the grace of control to appear warm in the coldest weather, and on the Arkansas summer days it seemed she had a private breeze which swirled around, cooling her. She was thin without the **taut** look of wiry people, and her printed voile dresses and flowered hats were as right for her as denim overalls for a
10 farmer. She was our side's answer to the richest white woman in town.

Her skin was a rich black that would have peeled like a plum if snagged, but then no one would have thought of getting close enough to Mrs. Flowers to ruffle her dress, let alone snag her skin. She didn't encourage familiarity. She wore gloves too. Ⓐ

I don't think I ever saw Mrs. Flowers laugh, but she smiled often. A slow widening of her thin black lips to show even, small white teeth, then the slow, effortless closing. When she chose to smile on me, I always wanted to thank her. The action was so
20 graceful and inclusively benign.

She was one of the few gentlewomen I have ever known, and has remained throughout my life the measure of what a human being can be.

Momma had a strange relationship with her. Most often when she passed on the road in front of the Store, she spoke to Momma in that soft yet carrying voice, "Good day, Mrs. Henderson." Momma responded with "How you, Sister Flowers?"

Mrs. Flowers didn't belong to our church, nor was she Momma's familiar.[1] Why on earth did she insist on calling
30 her Sister Flowers? Shame made me want to hide my face. Mrs. Flowers deserved better than to be called Sister. Then, Momma left out the verb. Why not ask, "How *are* you, *Mrs.* Flowers?" With the unbalanced passion of the young, I hated her for showing her ignorance to Mrs. Flowers. It didn't occur to me for many years that they were as alike as sisters, separated only by formal education. **B**

Although I was upset, neither of the women was in the least shaken by what I thought an unceremonious greeting. Mrs. Flowers would continue her easy gait up the hill to her little
40 bungalow, and Momma kept on shelling peas or doing whatever had brought her to the front porch.

Occasionally, though, Mrs. Flowers would drift off the road and down to the Store and Momma would say to me, "Sister, you go on and play." As I left I would hear the beginning of an intimate conversation, Momma persistently using the wrong verb, or none at all.

"Brother and Sister Wilcox is sho'ly the meanest—" "Is," Momma? "Is"? Oh, please, not "is," Momma, for two or more. But they talked, and from the side of the building where I waited
50 for the ground to open up and swallow me, I heard the soft-voiced Mrs. Flowers and the textured voice of my grandmother merging

---

1. **familiar:** a close friend or associate.

B ANALYZE PERSPECTIVES
Reread lines 28–36. What does the adult Angelou see looking back on this situation that the younger Angelou does not? Write your answers in the chart below.

Child's Perspective

↓

Adult's Perspective

C ANALYZE PERSPECTIVES
Reread lines 47–56. Why is Angelou upset with Momma in lines 47–48? What should Momma say?

_____

_____

_____

_____

_____

_____

_____

_____

_____

_____

_____

_____

PAUSE & REFLECT
What is Angelou saying about "powhitefolks" here? How does the name _Bertha_ contrast with the images Angelou associates with Mrs. Flowers in lines 59–67?

_____

_____

_____

_____

_____

_____

_____

and melting. They were interrupted from time to time by giggles that must have come from Mrs. Flowers (Momma never giggled in her life). Then she was gone. **C**

She appealed to me because she was like people I had never met personally. Like women in
60 English novels who walked the moors[2] (whatever they were) with their loyal dogs racing at a respectful distance. Like the women who sat in front of roaring fireplaces, drinking tea incessantly from silver trays full of scones and crumpets.[3] Women who walked over the "heath"[4] and read morocco-bound[5] books and had two last names divided by a hyphen. It would be safe to say that she made me proud to be Negro, just by being herself.

She acted just as refined as whitefolks in the movies and books and she was more beautiful, for none of them could have come
70 near that warm color without looking gray by comparison.

It was fortunate that I never saw her in the company of powhitefolks. For since they tend to think of their whiteness as an evenizer, I'm certain that I would have had to hear her spoken to commonly as Bertha, and my image of her would have been shattered like the unmendable Humpty-Dumpty. **PAUSE & REFLECT**

One summer afternoon, sweet-milk fresh in my memory, she stopped at the Store to buy provisions. Another Negro woman of her health and age would have been expected to carry the paper sacks home in one hand, but Momma said, "Sister Flowers, I'll
80 send Bailey up to your house with these things."

2. **moors:** broad open areas of countryside with marshes and patches of low shrubs.
3. **scones** (skōnz) **and crumpets** (krŭm'pĭts): Scones are small, biscuitlike pastries; crumpets are rolls similar to English muffins.
4. **heath** (hēth): another word for a moor.
5. **morocco-bound:** Morocco is a soft leather sometimes used for expensive book covers.

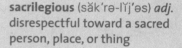

She smiled that slow dragging smile, "Thank you, Mrs. Henderson. I'd prefer Marguerite, though." My name was beautiful when she said it. "I've been meaning to talk to her, anyway." They gave each other age-group looks.

Momma said, "Well, that's all right then. Sister, go and change your dress. You going to Sister Flowers's."

The chifforobe[6] was a maze. What on earth did one put on to go to Mrs. Flowers's house? I knew I shouldn't put on a Sunday dress. It might be <u>sacrilegious</u>. Certainly not a house dress, since 90 I was already wearing a fresh one. I chose a school dress, naturally. It was formal without suggesting that going to Mrs. Flowers's house was equivalent to attending church.

I trusted myself back into the Store.

"Now, don't you look nice." I had chosen the right thing, for once.

"Mrs. Henderson, you make most of the children's clothes, don't you?"

"Yes, ma'am. Sure do. Store-bought clothes ain't hardly worth the thread it take to stitch them."

100 "I'll say you do a lovely job, though, so neat. That dress looks professional."

Momma was enjoying the seldom-received compliments. Since everyone we knew (except Mrs. Flowers, of course) could sew competently, praise was rarely handed out for the commonly practiced craft.

"I try, with the help of the Lord, Sister Flowers, to finish the inside just like I does the outside. Come here, Sister."

I had buttoned up the collar and tied the belt, apronlike, in back. Momma told me to turn around. With one hand she pulled 110 the strings and the belt fell free at both sides of my waist. Then her large hands were at my neck, opening the button loops. I was terrified. What was happening?

sacrilegious (săk′rə-lĭj′əs) *adj.* disrespectful toward a sacred person, place, or thing

Why might wearing a Sunday dress be considered **sacrilegious**? Underline the words that tell you so.

---

6. **chifforobe** (shĭf′ə-rōb′): a chest of drawers combined with a small closet for hanging clothes.

"Take it off, Sister." She had her hands on the hem of the dress.

"I don't need to see the inside, Mrs. Henderson, I can tell . . ." But the dress was over my head and my arms were stuck in the sleeves. Momma said, "That'll do. See here, Sister Flowers, I French-seams[7] around the armholes." Through the cloth film, I saw the shadow approach. "That makes it last 120 longer. Children these days would bust out of sheet-metal clothes. They so rough."

"That is a very good job, Mrs. Henderson. You should be proud. You can put your dress back on, Marguerite."

"No ma'am. Pride is a sin. And 'cording to the Good Book, it goeth before a fall."

"That's right. So the Bible says. It's a good thing to keep in mind."

I wouldn't look at either of them. Momma hadn't thought that taking off my dress in front of Mrs. Flowers would kill me stone 130 dead. If I had refused, she would have thought I was trying to be "womanish" and might have remembered St. Louis. Mrs. Flowers had known that I would be embarrassed and that was even worse. I picked up the groceries and went out to wait in the hot sunshine. It would be fitting if I got a sunstroke and died before they came outside. Just dropped dead on the slanting porch. **D**

There was a little path beside the rocky road, and Mrs. Flowers walked in front swinging her arms and picking her way over the stones.

She said, without turning her head, to me, "I hear you're doing 140 very good school work, Marguerite, but that it's all written. The teachers report that they have trouble getting you to talk in class." We passed the triangular farm on our left and the path widened to allow us to walk together. I hung back in the separate unasked and unanswerable questions.

"Come and walk along with me, Marguerite." I couldn't have refused even if I wanted to. She pronounced my name so nicely. Or more correctly, she spoke each word with such **clarity**

D CHARACTERIZATION
Reread lines 106–135. What does this episode tell you about Angelou's character? List three traits that Marguerite exhibits.

_____

_____

_____

_____

clarity (klăr′ĭ-tē) *n.* clearness

---

7. **French-seams:** sew seams that are turned in and stitched on the wrong side so that the unfinished edges of the cloth are not visible.

that I was certain a foreigner who didn't understand English could have understood her.

150   "Now no one is going to make you talk—possibly no one can. But bear in mind, language is man's way of communicating with his fellow man and it is language alone which separates him from the lower animals." That was a totally new idea to me, and I would need time to think about it.

    "Your grandmother says you read a lot. Every chance you get. That's good, but not good enough. Words mean more than what is set down on paper. It takes the human voice to **infuse** them with the shades of deeper meaning." ⓔ

    I memorized the part about the human voice infusing words.
160 It seemed so valid and poetic.

    She said she was going to give me some books and that I not only must read them, I must read them aloud. She suggested that I try to make a sentence sound in as many different ways as possible.

    "I'll accept no excuse if you return a book to me that has been badly handled." My imagination boggled at the punishment I would deserve if in fact I did abuse a book of Mrs. Flowers'. Death would be too kind and brief.

    The odors in the house surprised me. Somehow I had never connected Mrs. Flowers with food or eating or any other
170 common experience of common people. There must have been an outhouse, too, but my mind never recorded it.

    The sweet scent of vanilla had met us as she opened the door.

infuse (ĭn-fyōōz´) v. to fill, as if by pouring

ⓔ **CHARACTERIZATION**
Underline Mrs. Flowers's words in lines 139–158. What is Mrs. Flowers trying to get Marguerite to do? Why?

_____
_____
_____
_____
_____
_____
_____
_____
_____
_____
_____
_____
_____
_____

leer (lĭr) *v.* to give a sly, evil glance

PAUSE & REFLECT

Why is Marguerite surprised that Mrs. Flowers has an icebox? What does this tell you about Mrs. Flowers?

_____

_____

_____

_____

_____

_____

_____

_____

_____

illiteracy (ĭ-lĭt′ər-ə-sē) *n.* a lack of ability to read and write

What is the difference between **illiteracy** and ignorance?

_____

_____

_____

_____

"I made tea cookies this morning. You see, I had planned to invite you for cookies and lemonade so we could have this little chat. The lemonade is in the icebox."

It followed that Mrs. Flowers would have ice on an ordinary day, when most families in our town bought ice late on Saturdays only a few times during the summer to be used in the wooden ice-cream freezers. **PAUSE & REFLECT**

180 She took the bags from me and disappeared through the kitchen door. I looked around the room that I had never in my wildest fantasies imagined I would see. Browned photographs <u>leered</u> or threatened from the walls and the white, freshly done curtains pushed against themselves and against the wind. I wanted to gobble up the room entire and take it to Bailey, who would help me analyze and enjoy it.

"Have a seat, Marguerite. Over there by the table." She carried a platter covered with a tea towel. Although she warned that she hadn't tried her hand at baking sweets for some time, I was certain 190 that like everything else about her the cookies would be perfect.

They were flat round wafers, slightly browned on the edges and butter-yellow in the center. With the cold lemonade they were sufficient for childhood's lifelong diet. Remembering my manners, I took nice little lady like bites off the edges. She said she had made them expressly for me and that she had a few in the kitchen that I could take home to my brother. So I jammed one whole cake in my mouth and the rough crumbs scratched the insides of my jaws, and if I hadn't had to swallow, it would have been a dream come true.

200 As I ate she began the first of what we later called "my lessons in living." She said that I must always be intolerant of ignorance but understanding of <u>illiteracy</u>. That some people, unable to go to school, were more educated and even more intelligent than college professors. She encouraged me to listen carefully to what

country people called mother wit. That in those <u>homely</u> sayings was couched the collective wisdom of generations.

When I finished the cookies she brushed off the table and brought a thick, small book from the bookcase. I had read *A Tale of Two Cities*[8] and found it up to my standards as a romantic
210 novel. She opened the first page and I heard poetry for the first time in my life.

"It was the best of times and the worst of times . . ."[9] Her voice slid in and curved down through and over the words. She was nearly singing. I wanted to look at the pages. Were they the same that I had read? Or were there notes, music, lined on the pages, as in a hymn book? Her sounds began <u>cascading</u> gently. I knew from listening to a thousand preachers that she was nearing the end of her reading, and I hadn't really heard, heard to understand, a single word.

220 "How do you like that?"

It occurred to me that she expected a response. The sweet vanilla flavor was still on my tongue and her reading was a wonder in my ears. I had to speak.

I said, "Yes, ma'am." It was the least I could do, but it was the most also. **F**

"There's one more thing. Take this book of poems and memorize one for me. Next time you pay me a visit, I want you to recite."

I have tried often to search behind the sophistication of years
230 for the enchantment I so easily found in those gifts. The essence escapes but its aura remains.[10] To be allowed, no, invited, into the private lives of strangers, and to share their joys and fears,

homely (hōm′lē) *adj.* characteristic of home life; simple; everyday

cascade (kă-skād′) *v.* to fall or flow like a waterfall

F CHARACTERIZATION
What has Marguerite just done? Why was it both the least and the most she could do?

_____

_____

_____

_____

_____

_____

_____

---

8. *A Tale of Two Cities:* a novel by Charles Dickens, set in Paris and London during the French Revolution (1789–1799).

9. **"It was . . . the worst of times . . .":** the famous opening sentence of *A Tale of Two Cities*.

10. **The essence . . . remains:** The basic quality of a thing or event escapes, but the feelings or atmosphere that it creates remains.

was a chance to exchange the Southern bitter wormwood for a cup of mead with Beowulf or a hot cup of tea and milk with Oliver Twist.[11] When I said aloud, "It is a far, far better thing that I do, than I have ever done . . ."[12] tears of love filled my eyes at my selflessness.

On that first day, I ran down the hill and into the road (few cars ever came along it) and had the good sense to stop 240 running before I reached the Store.

I was liked, and what a difference it made. I was respected not as Mrs. Henderson's grandchild or Bailey's sister but for just being Marguerite Johnson.

Childhood's logic never asks to be proved (all conclusions are absolute). I didn't question why Mrs. Flowers had singled me out for attention, nor did it occur to me that Momma might have asked her to give me a little talking to. All I cared about was that she had made tea cookies for me and read to me from her favorite book. It was enough to prove that she liked me. **G**

G ANALYZE PERSPECTIVES
Underline the words in lines 229–249 in which Angelou is narrating her experience as a child. Circle the lines in which she shares her insights as an adult.

---

11. **a chance to exchange . . . with Oliver Twist:** Angelou compares her existence as a black child in the bigoted South to wormwood, a bitter herb. Mead (a liquor made from honey) and tea with milk were common drinks in the respective eras of Beowulf and Oliver Twist, two characters from English literature. Angelou suggests that reading about such characters provided an escape from her racist Southern surroundings.

12. **"It is a far . . . than I have ever done . . .":** the final line of *A Tale of Two Cities*, spoken by a man who sacrifices his own life to save that of another.

Text Analysis: Characterization in Autobiography

Skim the selection and find examples of the various methods of
characterization used by Angelou in her autobiography to describe
Mrs. Flowers. Write them in the chart below.

METHODS OF CHARACTERIZATION	EXAMPLES
1. Physical Appearance	
2. Speech, Thoughts, and Actions	
3. Other Characters	

Which method of characterization was the most useful in describing
Mrs. Flowers? Explain.

_____

_____

_____

_____

_____

Reading Skill: Analyze Perspectives

In her autobiography, Angelou presents her experiences as a child and also as an adult looking back on her childhood. Find an example of each perspective and enter it into the chart below.

Child's Perspective	Adult Perspective

How does Angelou's adult perspective help you understand the effect that Mrs. Flowers had on her life?

_____

_____

What is a **TEACHER**?

What does it take for a person to be considered a teacher?

_____

_____

Vocabulary Practice

Determine the relationship between the first pair of words in each analogy below. Then write the vocabulary word that best completes the second pair. The first example has been done for you.

1. *Drift* is to *snow* as <u>*cascade*</u> is to *water*.

2. *Smile* is to *sweetness* as _____ is to *wickedness*.

3. *Disease* is to *medicine* as _____ is to *education*.

4. *Fancy* is to *special* as _____ is to *everyday*.

5. *Toxic* is to *environment* as _____ is to *religion*.

6. *Bewilderment* is to *confusion* as *understanding* is to _____.

7. *Untied* is to *tied* as *loose* is to _____.

8. *Help* is to *assist* as _____ is to *inject*.

> **WORD LIST**
> cascade
> clarity
> homely
> illiteracy
> infuse
> leer
> sacrilegious
> taut

Academic Vocabulary in Writing

complex	device	evaluate	interact	perspective

Why do you think Maya Angelou decided to call her autobiography *I Know Why the Caged Bird Sings?* **Evaluate** her choice of the title. Do you think the image is effective or not? Explain. Use at least one Academic Vocabulary word in your response. Definitions for these terms are listed on page 69.

_____

_____

_____

Assessment Practice

DIRECTIONS Use "I Know Why the Caged Bird Sings" to answer questions 1–4.

1 Mrs. Flowers gives Marguerite an assignment to —

   (A) memorize a poem
   (B) talk in class
   (C) sweep the porch
   (D) read from *A Tale of Two Cities*

2 Which of the following is an example of Angelou's adult perspective?

   (A) *When she chose to smile on me, I always wanted to thank her.*
   (B) *For nearly a year, I sopped around the house, the Store, the school and the church, like an old biscuit, dirty and inedible.*
   (C) *Mrs. Flowers didn't belong to our church, nor was she Momma's familiar.*
   (D) *What on earth did one put on to go to Mrs. Flowers's house?*

3 Which of the following is an example of characterization by description?

   (A) *She didn't encourage familiarity.*
   (B) *Mrs. Flowers would continue her easy gait up the hill to her little bungalow . . .*
   (C) *She took the bags from me and disappeared through the kitchen door.*
   (D) *Her skin was a rich black that would have pulled like a plum if snagged . . .*

4 Which words *best* describe Mrs. Flowers?

   (A) aristocratic, gentle
   (B) polite, strained
   (C) common, ignorant
   (D) dignified, gracious

from Rosa Parks

Biography by **Douglas Brinkley**

Rosa

Poem by **Rita Dove**

What is DIGNITY?

What is dignity but a quiet strength and an air of self worth? Rosa Parks is one historical figure who had dignity—so much that she refused to give up her seat to a white passenger on a segregated bus in Montgomery, Alabama. You are about to read two selections about Rosa Parks—a biography and a poem. Both pieces portray her as a dignified and courageous woman.

DISCUSS With a partner, list five people, living or dead, real or fictional, whom you consider to have dignity. Then discuss whether dignity comes mainly from within or from the approval of others.

Text Analysis: Characterization Across Genres

Writers of fiction use various methods of **characterization** to develop the made-up characters in their stories. Fiction writers might provide descriptions of the character's appearance, examples of the person's speech, thoughts and feelings, and ideas and comments about the character. However, when writers of other **genres,** such as nonfiction and poetry, write about real people, they cannot make up facts and details. Instead, writers shape readers' ideas about the person by combining facts about the person with elements that are unique to the genres in which they are working.

The biography and poem that you are about to read tell about Rosa Parks. Below are some of the techniques each writer uses to characterize her. As you read, look out for examples of these techniques.

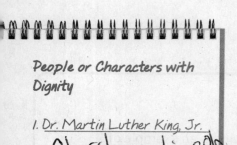

People or Characters with Dignity

1. Dr. Martin Luther King, Jr.
2. Abraham Lincoln
3. _____
4. _____
5. _____

Techniques Used in the Biography	Techniques Used in the Poem
• facts and details about Rosa Parks's actions, thoughts, and appearance	• word choice to describe Rosa Parks's actions and appearance
• quotations from Rosa Parks	• images to depict Rosa Parks's traits
• quotations from others who knew Rosa Parks	

Reading Strategy: Set a Purpose for Reading

When you **set a purpose for reading,** you find specific reasons for reading a work. Your purpose for reading the selections that follow is to **compare and contrast** the ways in which Rosa Park is portrayed. Use the chart below to compare the biography and poem.

Points of Comparison: Rosa Parks	In the Biography	In the Poem
Her appearance	appears tired, has swollen feet (lines 37–40)	wears a sensible coat (line 6)
Her daily life		
Her personality, thoughts, and feelings		
Her values and the things she thought were important		

Vocabulary in Context

Note: Words are listed in the order they appear in the story.

frenetically (frə-nĕt'ĭk-lē) *adv.* in a frenzied or frantic way
*The crowd cheered **frenetically** during the suspenseful competition.*

protégé (prō'tə-zhā') *n.* a person who is guided or supported by an older or more influential person
*The chef's **protégé** asked if he could design a menu for the restaurant.*

reverie (rĕv'ə-rē) *n.* a state of daydreaming
*During class I let my mind wander in a pleasant **reverie.***

exhortation (ĕg'zôr-tā'shən) *n.* a communication strongly urging that something be done
*After we lost the game, our coach gave us an **exhortation** to try harder.*

serene (sə-rēn') *adj.* calm; peaceful
*The water on the lake is as **serene** as a summer day.*

retrieve (rĭ-trēv') *v.* to find and return safely
*The nice young lady helped me **retrieve** the lost scarf.*

**SET A PURPOSE
FOR READING**

Read this biography to find out how Rosa Parks made history.

Rosa Parks

Biography by
DOUGLAS BRINKLEY

BACKGROUND Southern states once had laws that enforced racial segregation, or separation. Among other injustices, African Americans were forced to sit in separate sections of busses. In 1955, Rosa Parks's refusal to give up her seat for a white passenger on a bus triggered a 382-day bus boycott by African Americans in Montgomery, Alabama. The boycott brought Rosa Parks, Dr. Martin Luther King, Jr., and their cause to the attention of the nation. In 1956, the Supreme Court ruled that segregation on buses and other transportation was unconstitutional.

PAUSE & REFLECT

Look back at the background and consider what you already know about Rosa Parks. Why does she "see little of the holiday glitter" (lines 9–10) at the tailor shop?

_____

_____

_____

_____

_____

Rosa Parks headed to work on December 1, 1955, on the Cleveland Avenue bus to Court Square. It was a typical prewinter morning in the Alabama capital, chilly and raw, topcoat weather. Outside the Montgomery Fair Department Store a Salvation Army Santa rang his bell for coins in front of window displays of toy trains and mannequins modeling reindeer sweaters. Every afternoon when school let out, hordes of children would invade the store to gawk at the giant Christmas tree draped with blinking lights, a mid-1950s electrical marvel. But Rosa Parks saw
10 little of the holiday glitter down in the small tailor shop in the basement next to the huge steam presses, where the only hint of Yuletide cheer came from a sagging, water-stained banner reading "Merry Christmas and a Happy New Year." **PAUSE & REFLECT**

Not that many of Montgomery Fair's lower-level employees had the time to let the faded decoration make them sad. The department store rang up nearly half of its sales between Thanksgiving and New Year's Day, which turned the tailor shop into a beehive of activity every December. But even on days spent <u>frenetically</u> hemming, ironing, and steam-pressing, Parks's mind

20 was more with the NAACP[1] than her workday duties. She was in the midst of organizing a workshop to be held at Alabama State University on December 3–4 and spent the morning during her coffee break telephoning H. Council Trenholm, president of the university, applying enough quiet persuasion to be granted the use of a classroom over the weekend. "I was also getting the notices in the mail for the election of officers of the senior branch of the NAACP, which would be [the] next week," Parks recalled. That afternoon, she lunched with Fred Gray, the lawyer who defended Claudette Colvin and was serving as Clifford Durr's[2] <u>protégé</u> at

30 his law office above the Sears Auto Tire Store.

"When 1:00 P.M. came and the lunch hour ended, Mrs. Parks went back to her work as a seamstress," Gray would write in his civil rights memoir, *Bus Ride to Justice*. "I continued my work and left the office in the early afternoon for an out-of-town engagement." Ⓐ

Shortly after 5:00 P.M., Rosa Parks clocked out of work and walked the block to Court Square to wait for her bus home. It had been a hard day, and her body ached, from her feet swollen from the constant standing to her shoulders throbbing from the strain

40 and her chronic bursitis. But the bus stand was packed, so Parks, disinclined to jockey for a rush-hour seat, crossed Dexter Avenue to do a little shopping at Lee's Cut-Rate Drug. She had decided to treat herself to a heating pad but found them too pricey. Instead, she bought some Christmas gifts, along with aspirin, toothpaste, and a few other sundries, and headed back to the bus stop wondering how her husband's day had been at the Maxwell

---

1. **NAACP:** a civil rights organization. The initials stand for National Association for the Advancement of Colored People.
2. **Claudette Colvin . . . Clifford Durr's:** Claudette Colvin was an African-American teenager who had refused to give up her seat on a Montgomery city bus earlier in 1955. Clifford Durr was a white lawyer who worked for civil rights.

frenetically (frə-nĕt′ĭk-lē) *adv.* in a frenzied or frantic way

protégé (prō′tə-zhā′) *n.* a person who is guided or supported by an older or more influential person

Why is the meeting with Clifford Durr's **protégé** significant?

_____

_____

_____

_____

Ⓐ **CHARACTERIZATION**
What do you learn about Rosa Parks's daily life from the last three paragraphs? What was she interested in outside of her job as a seamstress? Add this information to the chart you started page 101.

_____

_____

_____

_____

_____

_____

reverie (rĕv′ə-rē) *n.* a state of daydreaming

PAUSE & REFLECT
Why is it significant that there was one white passenger left standing? What does everyone on the bus expect Rosa Parks and the other black passengers to do?

_____

_____

_____

_____

_____

_____

B CHARACTERIZATION
Reread lines 62–79. How does Rosa Parks react to the bus driver's commands? Based on this reaction, what can you guess about her values and what she thinks is important?

_____

_____

_____

_____

_____

_____

Air Force Base Barber Shop and thinking about what her mother would cook for dinner.

It was in this late-day **reverie** that Rosa Parks dropped her
50 dime in the box and boarded the yellow-olive city bus. She took an aisle seat in the racially neutral middle section,[3] behind the movable sign which read "colored." She was not expecting any problems, as there were several empty spaces at the whites-only front of the bus. A black man was sitting next to her on her right and staring out the window; across the aisle sat two black women deep in conversation. At the next two stops enough white passengers got on to nearly fill up the front section. At the third stop, in front of the Empire Theater, a famous shrine to country-music fans as the stage where the legendary Hank Williams
60 got his start, the last front seats were taken, with one man left standing. **PAUSE & REFLECT**

The bus driver twisted around and locked his eyes on Rosa Parks. Her heart almost stopped when she saw it was James F. Blake, the bully who had put her off his bus twelve years earlier. She didn't know his name, but since that incident in 1943, she had never boarded a bus that Blake was driving. This day, however, she had absentmindedly stepped in. "Move y'all, I want those two seats," the driver barked on behalf of Jim Crow,[4] which dictated that all four blacks in that row of the middle section
70 would have to surrender their seats to accommodate a single white man, as no "colored" could be allowed to sit parallel with him. A stony silence fell over the bus as nobody moved. "Y'all better make it light on yourselves and let me have those seats," Blake sputtered, more impatiently than before. Quietly and in unison, the two black women sitting across from Parks rose and moved to the back. Her seatmate quickly followed suit, and she swung her legs to the side to let him out. Then Parks slid over to the window and gazed out at the Empire Theater marquee promoting *A Man Alone*, a new Western starring Ray Milland. **B**

---

3. **racially neutral middle section:** a section of the bus where African Americans could sit, as long as no whites needed or wanted seats there.

4. **Jim Crow:** a term referring to the segregation of African Americans.

80   The next ten seconds seemed like an eternity to Rosa Parks.
As Blake made his way toward her, all she could think about were
her forebears, who, Maya Angelou would put it, took the lash, the
branding iron, and untold humiliations while only praying that
their children would someday "flesh out" the dream of equality.
But unlike the poet, it was not Africa in the days of the slave trade
that Parks was thinking about; it was racist Alabama in the here
and now. She shuddered with the memory of her grandfather
back in Pine Level keeping watch for the KKK[5] every night with
a loaded shotgun in his lap, echoing abolitionist John Brown's[6]
90 **exhortation**: "Talk! Talk! Talk! That didn't free the slaves. . . .
What is needed is action! Action!" So when Parks looked up at
Blake, his hard, thoughtless scowl filled her with pity. She felt
fearless, bold, and **serene**. "Are you going to stand up?" the driver
demanded. Rosa Parks looked straight at him and said: "No."
Flustered and not quite sure what to do, Blake retorted, "Well,
I'm going to have you arrested." And Parks, still sitting next to
the window, replied softly, "You may do that."

      Her majestic use of "may" rather than "can" put Parks on
the high ground, establishing her as a protester, not a victim.
100 "When I made that decision," Parks stated later, "I knew I had
the strength of my ancestors with me," and obviously their dignity
as well. And her formal dignified "No," uttered on a suppertime
bus in the cradle of the Confederacy as darkness fell, ignited the
collective "no" of black history in America, a defiance as liberating
as John Brown's on the gallows in Harpers Ferry. **C**

exhortation (ĕg'zôr-tā'shən) *n.* a communication strongly urging that something be done

serene (sə-rēn') *adj.* calm; peaceful

C CHARACTERIZATION
Reread lines 80–105. Underline examples of the following genre techniques in the last few paragraphs of his biography of Rosa Parks:
• facts and details about Rosa Parks's actions, thoughts, and appearance
• quotations from Rosa Parks

---

5. **back in Pine Level . . . KKK:** Pine Level is a town about 100 miles southeast of Birmingham. The KKK was the Ku Klux Klan, an extremist secret society that often violently terrorized blacks in the South.

6. **abolitionist John Brown's:** Brown, a white militant, performed radical acts to force the abolition of slavery, including a failed attempt to steal guns from the U.S. arsenal at Harpers Ferry, Virginia.

SET A PURPOSE FOR READING

Read this poem to compare and contrast the characterization of Rosa Parks in the biography and in the poem.

D PARADOX

A **paradox** is a statement that seems to say the opposite of what it means and that reveals some insight or truth. For example, the statement "I always lie" is a paradox. If a man says he always lies, he is admitting that he is a liar, which is a truthful statement. Therefore, the man sometimes tells the truth. How is the thought expressed in line 7 a paradox?

_____

_____

_____

_____

_____

_____

retrieve (rĭ-trēv′) *v.* to find and return safely

E CHARACTERIZATION

Underline an image in the poem that portrays Rosa Parks as a modest person.

Rosa

Poem by
RITA DOVE

BACKGROUND When Rosa Parks made her momentous decision not to give up her seat on the bus in Montgomery, Alabama, she joined a tradition of nonviolent resistance that spans many cultures.

How she sat there,
the time right inside a place
so wrong it was ready.

That trim name with
5 its dream of a bench
to rest on. Her sensible coat.

Doing nothing was the doing: **D**
the clean flame of her gaze
carved by a camera flash.

10 How she stood up
when they bent down to **retrieve**
her purse. That courtesy. **E**

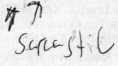

Text Analysis: Characterization Across Genres

You just read works by two different authors describing Rosa Parks. Now, use the chart below to help you analyze the characterization methods used by each writer. List at least one example from the texts for each technique.

BIOGRAPHY	POEM
Details about her actions, thoughts, and appearance *Example:* Doing nothing was the doing He body acted and was swollen	Words used to describe Rosa's actions and appearance *Example:* The clean flame of her gaze.
Quotations from Rosa Parks *Example:* Thinking about her grandfather and his actions.	Images to depict Rosa's traits *Example:* How She Sat there.
Quotations about Rosa Parks *Example:* She replied softly, "You may do that."	"Doing Nothing was the doing."

In both the biography and the poem, what words and actions convey Rosa Parks's dignity?

She was composed and calm even though she was probably frightened on the inside.

Reading Skill: Set a Purpose for Reading

Review the notes you took as you read. Then write a comparison statement for each point about Parks based on what you learned from reading the biography and the poem.

Points of Comparison: Rosa Parks	Comparison Statement
Her appearance	Parks was a sensible, hard-working woman.
Her daily life	She was calm and in a reverie but she also felt pain. very involved in the NAACP fought for civil rights for AAs.
Her personality, thoughts, and feelings	
Her values and the things she thought were important	to do the right thing to have dignity. civil rights for AA's

What is **DIGNITY?**

Is dignity something you have or would like to have? Explain.

Dignity shows maturity and confidence in oneself so, yes I would like to have it.

Vocabulary Practice

Use the vocabulary words to fill in the blanks.

1. Boarding the bus, Rosa Parks was lost in a private ___Reverie___ of memories.

2. She had been working ___Frenetically___ all day because it was the busy season.

3. She lunched with a lawyer who was a ___protégé___ of a famous civil rights attorney.

4. She recalled her grandfather's ___exhortation___ to act.

5. Her belief in her refusal made her calm and ___Serene___

6. If she lost her self-respect now, she might never ___retrieve___ it.

WORD LIST
~~exhortation~~
~~frenetically~~
~~protégé~~
~~retrieve~~
~~reverie~~
~~serene~~

Academic Vocabulary in Writing

complex	device	evaluate	interact	perspective

A new **perspective** is a fresh outlook or view on something. What did
you know about Rosa Parks before you read these selections? What new
perspective about civil rights have you gained from reading these selections?
Use at least one Academic Vocabulary word in your response. Definitions for
these terms are listed on page 69.

*Before reading this I knew
she stood her grand ma ups
but I know learned that she believed
in Dignity and she had it while this
event took place*

Assessment Practice

DIRECTIONS Use "Rosa Parks" and "Rosa" to answer questions 1–4.

1 What decision did Rosa Parks make on the bus?

A She decided not to give up her seat even if it meant getting arrested.

B She decided to move to the back of a bus.

C She decided to obey the laws of segregation.

D She decided to quit her job at the department store.

2 Which words describe the way Rosa Parks is characterized in both selections?

A aggressive, irritable

B sweet, kind

C dignified, noble

D uncaring, selfish

3 In the biography the writer reveals Parks's internal thoughts on the day she boarded the bus in Alabama. What did you learn from those thoughts?

A She refused to change seats simply because she disliked the driver.

B She was unaware of the sacrifices of her forbearers.

C She decided many days earlier that she would refuse to obey the driver.

D She felt fearless in the moments after the driver approached her.

4 Which of the following phrases from the poem best expresses the dignity that Rosa Parks possessed?

A How she sat there "the time right inside a place"

B That trim name with "its dream of a bench"

C Doing nothing was the doing "the clean flame of her gaze"

D How she stood up "when they bent down to retrieve" her purse.

UNIT 3

A Sense of Place

SETTING, MOOD, AND IMAGERY

Be sure to read the Text Analysis Workshop on pp. 330–335 in *Holt McDougal Literature*.

Academic Vocabulary for Unit 3

Preview the following Academic Vocabulary words. You will encounter these words as you work through this book and will use them as you write and talk about the selections in this unit.

aspect (as'pekt') *n.* a quality, part, or element

One important aspect of a good story is mood.

•

circumstance (sur kem' stans') *n.* a happening, event, or fact occurring near or in company with another

There were many circumstances that led to the murder of the main character.

•

contribute (kən trib'yōōt) *v.* to provide or give ideas, knowledge, material goods, etc.

The writer's use of imagery contributes to the eerie mood of the story.

•

distinct (di stinkt') *adj.* separate or different; defined clearly

Many writers have a distinct style that sets them apart from others.

•

perceive (pər sēv') *v.* to observe or become aware of

Different readers may perceive the same story in very different ways.

Think of a time when you **perceived** a story or circumstance differently than someone else. What do you think **contributed** to this difference? Use at least one Academic Vocabulary word in your response.

_____

_____

_____

_____

A Christmas Memory

Short Story by **Truman Capote**

What do you look for in a FRIEND?

Think about your friends. What draws you to someone and creates that bond of friendship? Does a friend have to be someone your own age? Do you always share the same interests and values? "A Christmas Memory" shows how important friendship can be to two very different individuals.

QUICKWRITE Make a "top five" list of the key qualities you look for in a friend. Then compare your list with those of your classmates. Does everyone's list have similar qualities?

Top 5 Qualities of a Good Friend

1. *sense of humor*

2. *similar interests*

3. _____

4. _____

5. _____

Text Analysis: Details of Setting

The **setting** of a story is more than just the time and place in which the action occurs. Through the **details of setting,** writers can also reveal information about the character's lives and their values, as well as the historical era—the buildings, people, and customs that existed at the time the story takes place. In some stories, the setting may even create conflicts for the characters and influence the choices they make.

ROLE OF SETTING	EXAMPLE SETTING
Setting can influence characters by • determining the living conditions and jobs available • shaping their personalities, their dreams, and their values	*A poor, drought-stricken Midwestern farm town in the 1930s* Despite months of grueling work, Joe's crops are failing again. Realizing that life may never improve, he becomes bitter and angry.
Setting can create conflicts by • exposing the characters to dangerous weather, such as a storm • making characters endure a difficult time period, such as the Great Depression	The drought has lasted seven years, and most of the farms are failing. People have begun to sell their most prized possessions because they need money.

Reading Skill: Analyze Imagery

Good writing is usually filled with **imagery**—words and phrases that appeal to the senses (sight, smell, hearing, taste, and touch). Capote gives readers a lasting impression of a holiday memory by using language that appeals to one or more senses. For example, read this phrase aloud and note how it appeals to your sense of hearing:

> *Lovely dimes, the liveliest coin, the one that really jingles.*

As you read, you will be prompted to record words and phrases that appeal to your senses.

Vocabulary in Context

Note: Words are listed in the order they appear in the story.

inaugurate (ĭn-ô′gyə-rāt′) *v.* to make a formal beginning of
*Each January the family hosts a party to **inaugurate** the New Year.*

exhilarate (ĭg-zĭl′ə-rāt′) *v.* to make merry or lively
*The holiday celebrations **exhilarate** me.*

paraphernalia (păr′ə-fər-nāl′yə) *n.* the articles needed for a particular event or activity
*After Christmas we take down the tree and all of the holiday **paraphernalia**.*

squander (skwŏn′dər) *v.* to spend or use wastefully
*It is best not to **squander** your allowance on candy and other useless items.*

prosaic (prō-zā′ĭk) *adj.* dull; commonplace
*At first the yearly trip was exciting, but after several years of doing the same thing it became **prosaic**.*

suffuse (sə-fyōōz′) *v.* to gradually spread through or over
*She waited for the smell of cookies to **suffuse** through the house.*

potent (pōt′nt) *adj.* powerful
*He found the flavor of the drink to be too **potent** for his liking.*

goad (gōd) *v.* to drive or urge
*I tried to **goad** her into action by promising her a reward.*

cavort (kə-vôrt′) *v.* to leap or romp about
*The children love to **cavort** in the playground.*

sever (sĕv′ər) *v.* to cut off
*I was so angry at my friend that I **severed** all ties to him.*

**SET A PURPOSE
FOR READING**
Read this story to discover why a young boy and his elderly cousin are best friends.

A Christmas Memory

Short Story by

TRUMAN CAPOTE

BACKGROUND This story is based on Truman Capote's childhood during the Great Depression of the 1930s. Set in an old house in rural Alabama, the narrator recalls the last Christmas season he shared with his "best friend," an elderly female cousin. Writing in the voice of an adult, Capote condenses years of experiences with his cousin into one memorable Christmas.

Imagine a morning in late November. A coming of winter morning more than twenty years ago. Consider the kitchen of a spreading old house in a country town. A great black stove is its main feature; but there is also a big round table and a fireplace with two rocking chairs placed in front of it. Just today the fireplace commenced its seasonal roar. **PAUSE & REFLECT**

A woman with shorn white hair is standing at the kitchen window. She is wearing tennis shoes and a shapeless gray sweater over a summery calico dress. She is small and sprightly, like a
10 bantam hen; but, due to a long youthful illness, her shoulders are pitifully hunched. Her face is remarkable—not unlike Lincoln's,

PAUSE & REFLECT
The adult narrator is telling a story about his childhood. Circle the details in lines 1–6 that tell you the narrator is an adult thinking back to an earlier time.

craggy like that, and tinted by sun and wind; but it is delicate too, finely boned, and her eyes are sherry-colored and timid. "Oh my," she exclaims, her breath smoking the windowpane, "it's fruitcake weather!"

The person to whom she is speaking is myself. I am seven; she is sixty-something. We are cousins, very distant ones, and we have lived together—well, as long as I can remember. Other people inhabit the house, relatives; and though they have power
20 over us, and frequently make us cry, we are not, on the whole, too much aware of them. We are each other's best friend. She calls me Buddy, in memory of a boy who was formerly her best friend. The other Buddy died in the 1880's, when she was still a child. She is still a child.

"I knew it before I got out of bed," she says, turning away from the window with a purposeful excitement in her eyes. "The courthouse bell sounded so cold and clear. And there were no birds singing; they've gone to warmer country, yes indeed. Oh, Buddy, stop stuffing biscuit and fetch our buggy. Help me find
30 my hat. We've thirty cakes to bake."

It's always the same: a morning arrives in November, and my friend, as though officially **inaugurating** the Christmas time of year that **exhilarates** her imagination and fuels the blaze of her heart, announces: "It's fruitcake weather! Fetch our buggy. Help me find my hat." Ⓐ

The hat is found, a straw cartwheel corsaged with velvet roses out-of-doors has faded: it once belonged to a more fashionable relative. Together, we guide our buggy, a dilapidated baby carriage, out to the garden and into a grove of pecan trees. The
40 buggy is mine; that is, it was bought for me when I was born. It is made of wicker, rather unraveled, and the wheels wobble like a drunkard's legs. But it is a faithful object; springtimes, we take it to the woods and fill it with flowers, herbs, wild fern for our porch pots; in the summer, we pile it with picnic **paraphernalia** and sugar-cane fishing poles and roll it down to the edge of a creek; it has its winter uses, too: as a truck for hauling firewood from the yard to the kitchen, as a warm bed

inaugurate (ĭn-ô′gyə-rāt′) *v.* to make a formal beginning of

exhilarate (ĭg-zĭl′ə-rāt′) *v.* to make merry or lively

Ⓐ **DETAILS OF SETTING**
Circle three details of the setting that are introduced on this page.

paraphernalia (păr′ə-fər-nāl′yə) *n.* the articles needed for a particular event or activity

B **DETAILS OF SETTING**
This story is set during the Great Depression, a time when most Americans had little, if any, money to spare. What do the details about the buggy tell you about the lives of those who push it?

_____

_____

_____

_____

_____

_____

_____

C **ANALYZE IMAGERY**
Which senses does the author appeal to in the description of the kitchen? Add an example of imagery to the chart below and note the sense to which each appeals.

Imagery
"Caarackle!" A cheery crunch."

↓

Sense

for Queenie, our tough little orange and white rat terrier who has survived distemper and two rattlesnake bites. Queenie is trotting
50 beside it now. **B**

Three hours later we are back in the kitchen hulling a heaping buggyload of windfall pecans. Our backs hurt from gathering them: how hard they were to find (the main crop having been shaken off the trees and sold by the orchard's owners, who are not us) among the concealing leaves, the frosted, deceiving grass. Caarackle! A cheery crunch, scraps of miniature thunder sound as the shells collapse and the golden mound of sweet oily ivory meat mounts in the milk-glass bowl. Queenie begs to taste, and now and again my friend sneaks
60 her a mite, though insisting we deprive ourselves. "We mustn't, Buddy. If we start, we won't stop. And there's scarcely enough as there is. For thirty cakes." The kitchen is growing dark. Dusk turns the window into a mirror: our reflections mingle with the rising moon as we work by the fireside in the firelight. At last, when the moon is quite high, we toss the final hull into the fire and, with joined sighs, watch it catch flame. The buggy is empty, the bowl is brimful. **C**

We eat our supper (cold biscuits, bacon, blackberry jam) and discuss tomorrow. Tomorrow the kind of work I like best begins:
70 buying. Cherries and citron, ginger and vanilla and canned Hawaiian pineapple, rinds and raisins and walnuts and whiskey and oh, so much flour, butter, so many eggs, spices, flavorings: why, we'll need a pony to pull the buggy home.

But before these purchases can be made, there is the question of money. Neither of us has any. Except for skinflint sums persons in the house occasionally provide (a dime is considered very big money); or what we earn ourselves from various activities: holding rummage sales, selling buckets of hand-picked blackberries, jars of homemade jam and apple jelly and peach preserves, rounding
80 up flowers for funerals and weddings. Once we won seventy-ninth prize, five dollars, in a national football contest. Not that we

know a fool thing about football. It's just that we enter any contest we hear about: at the moment our hopes are centered on the fifty-thousand-dollar Grand Prize being offered to name a new brand of coffee (we suggested "A.M."; and, after some hesitation, for my friend thought it perhaps sacrilegious, the slogan "A.M.! Amen!"). To tell the truth, our only *really* profitable enterprise was the Fun and Freak Museum we conducted in a back-yard woodshed two summers ago. The Fun was a stereopticon[1] with slide views of
90 Washington and New York lent us by a relative who had been to those places (she was furious when she discovered why we'd borrowed it); the Freak was a three-legged biddy chicken hatched by one of our own hens. Everybody hereabouts wanted to see that biddy: we charged grownups a nickel, kids two cents. And took in a good twenty dollars before the museum shut down due to the decease of the main attraction. **D**

But one way and another we do each year accumulate Christmas savings, a Fruitcake Fund. These moneys we keep hidden in an ancient bead purse under a loose board under the
100 floor under a chamber pot under my friend's bed. The purse is seldom removed from this safe location except to make a deposit or, as happens every Saturday, a withdrawal; for on Saturdays I am allowed ten cents to go to the picture show. My friend has never been to a picture show, nor does she intend to: "I'd rather hear you tell the story, Buddy. That way I can imagine it more. Besides, a person my age shouldn't **squander** their eyes. When the Lord comes, let me see him clear." In addition to never having seen a movie, she has never: eaten in a restaurant, traveled more than five miles from home, received or sent a telegram, read
110 anything except funny papers and the Bible, worn cosmetics, cursed, wished someone harm, told a lie on purpose, let a hungry dog go hungry. Here are a few things she has done, does do: killed with a hoe the biggest rattlesnake ever seen in this county (sixteen rattles), dip snuff[2] (secretly), tame hummingbirds (just try it) till they balance on her finger, tell ghost stories (we both believe

---

1. **stereopticon** (stĕr′ē-ŏp′tĭ-kŏn′): an early slide projector that could merge two images of the same scene on a screen, resulting in a 3-D effect.

2. **dip snuff:** to place a small amount of finely ground tobacco (snuff) in one's mouth.

D DETAILS OF SETTING
In lines 74–96, what do the details about the activities of the narrator and his friend tell you about the story's time and place?

squander (skwŏn′dər) *v.* to spend or use wastefully

The friend is much older than Buddy. What guess can you make about Buddy's friend based on the fact that she tells him not to **squander** his eyes?

in ghosts) so tingling they chill you in July, talk to herself, take walks in the rain, grow the prettiest japonicas in town, know the recipe for every sort of old-time Indian cure, including a magical wart remover.

120   Now, with supper finished, we retire to the room in a faraway part of the house where my friend sleeps in a scrap-quilt-covered iron bed painted rose pink, her favorite color. Silently, wallowing in the pleasures of conspiracy, we take the bead purse from its secret place and spill its contents on the scrap quilt. Dollar bills, tightly rolled and green as May buds. Somber fifty-cent pieces, heavy enough to weight a dead man's eyes.[3] Lovely dimes, the liveliest coin, the one that really jingles. Nickels and quarters, worn smooth as creek pebbles. But mostly a hateful heap of bitter-odored pennies. Last summer others in the house contracted

130 to pay us a penny for every twenty-five flies we killed. Oh, the carnage of August: the flies that flew to heaven! Yet it was not work in which we took pride. And, as we sit counting pennies, it is as though we were back tabulating dead flies. Neither of us has a head for figures; we count slowly, lose track, start again. According to her calculations, we have $12.73. According to mine, exactly $13. "I do hope you're wrong, Buddy. We can't mess around with thirteen. The cakes will fall. Or put somebody in the cemetery. Why, I wouldn't dream of getting out of bed on the thirteenth." This is true: she always spends thirteenths

140 in bed. So, to be on the safe side, we subtract a penny and toss it out the window.   **PAUSE & REFLECT**

Of the ingredients that go into our fruitcakes, whiskey is the most expensive, as well as the hardest to obtain: State laws forbid its sale. But everybody knows you can buy a bottle from Mr. Haha Jones. And the next day, having completed our more **prosaic** shopping, we set out for Mr. Haha's business address, a

PAUSE & REFLECT
What do the details in lines 97–141 reveal about Buddy's friend?

prosaic (prō-zā′ĭk) *adj.* dull; commonplace

3. **heavy enough to weight a dead man's eyes:** from the custom of putting coins on the closed eyes of corpses to keep the eyelids from opening.

"sinful" (to quote public opinion) fish-fry and dancing café down by the river. We've been there before, and on the same errand; but in previous years our dealings have been with Haha's wife,

150 an iodine-dark Indian woman with brassy peroxided hair and a dead-tired disposition. Actually, we've never laid eyes on her husband, though we've heard that he's an Indian too. A giant with razor scars across his cheeks. They call him Haha because he's so gloomy, a man who never laughs. As we approach his café (a large log cabin festooned inside and out with chains of garish-gay naked light bulbs and standing by the river's muddy edge under the shade of river trees where moss drifts through the branches like gray mist) our steps slow down. Even Queenie stops prancing and sticks close by. People have been murdered in Haha's café.

160 Cut to pieces. Hit on the head. There's a case coming up in court next month. **E**

Naturally these goings-on happen at night when the colored lights cast crazy patterns and the Victrola⁴ wails. In the daytime Haha's is shabby and deserted. I knock at the door, Queenie barks, my friend calls: "Mrs. Haha, ma'am? Anyone to home?"

Footsteps. The door opens. Our hearts overturn. It's Mr. Haha Jones himself! And he *is* a giant; he *does* have scars; he *doesn't* smile. No, he glowers at us through Satan-tilted eyes and demands to know: "What you want with Haha?"

170 For a moment we are too paralyzed to tell. Presently my friend half-finds her voice, a whispery voice at best: "If you please, Mr. Haha, we'd like a quart of your finest whiskey."

His eyes tilt more. Would you believe it? Haha is smiling! Laughing, too. "Which one of you is a drinkin' man?"

"It's for making fruitcakes, Mr. Haha. Cooking."

This sobers him. He frowns. "That's no way to waste good whiskey." Nevertheless, he retreats into the shadowed café and seconds later appears carrying a bottle of daisy-yellow unlabeled liquor. He demonstrates its sparkle in the sunlight and says:

180 "Two dollars."

---

4. **Victrola:** a trademark for a brand of old record player.

E DETAILS OF SETTING
From 1919–1933 the Unites States government enforced Prohibition, a ban on the manufacture, sale, and transportation of alcohol. What do you think Buddy means when he calls Mr. Haha's cafe a "sinful" place?

_____

_____

_____

Circle the details in lines 142–161 that tell you the café is a dangerous and "sinful" place.

We pay him with nickels and dimes and pennies. Suddenly, as he jangles the coins in his hand like a fistful of dice, his face softens. "Tell you what," he proposes, pouring the money back into our bead purse, "just send me one of them fruitcakes instead."

"Well," my friend remarks on our way home, "there's a lovely man. We'll put an extra cup of raisins in *his* cake."

The black stove, stoked with coal and firewood, glows like a lighted pumpkin. Eggbeaters whirl, spoons spin round in bowls of
190 butter and sugar, vanilla sweetens the air, ginger spices it; melting, nose-tingling odors saturate the kitchen, **suffuse** the house, drift out to the world on puffs of chimney smoke. In four days our work is done. Thirty-one cakes, dampened with whiskey, bask on windowsills and shelves.

Who are they for?

Friends. Not necessarily neighbor friends: indeed, the larger share is intended for persons we've met maybe once, perhaps not at all. People who've struck our fancy. Like President Roosevelt. Like the Reverend and Mrs. J. C. Lucey, Baptist missionaries to
200 Borneo[5] who lectured here last winter. Or the little knife grinder who comes through town twice a year. Or Abner Packer, the driver of the six o'clock bus from Mobile, who exchanges waves with us every day as he passes in a dust-cloud whoosh. Or the young Wistons, a California couple whose car one afternoon broke down outside the house and who spent a pleasant hour chatting with us on the porch (young Mr. Wiston snapped our picture, the only one we've ever had taken). Is it because my friend is shy with everyone *except* strangers that these strangers, and merest acquaintances, seem to us our truest friends? I think
210 yes. Also, the scrapbooks we keep of thank-you's on White House stationery, time-to-time communications from California and Borneo, the knife grinder's penny post cards, make us feel

suffuse (sə-fyo͞oz′) *v.* to gradually spread through or over

---

5. **Borneo** (bôr′nē-o′): a large island in the South China Sea, southwest of the Philippines.

connected to eventful worlds beyond the kitchen with its view of a sky that stops. PAUSE & REFLECT

Now a nude December fig branch grates against the window. The kitchen is empty, the cakes are gone; yesterday we carted the last of them to the post office, where the cost of stamps turned our purse inside out. We're broke. That rather depresses me, but my friend insists on celebrating—with two inches of
220 whiskey left in Haha's bottle. Queenie has a spoonful in a bowl of coffee (she likes her coffee chicory-flavored and strong). The rest we divide between a pair of jelly glasses. We're both quite awed at the prospect of drinking straight whiskey; the taste of it brings screwed-up expressions and sour shudders. But by and by we begin to sing, the two of us singing different songs simultaneously. I don't know the words to mine, just: *Come on along, come on along, to the dark-town strutters' ball.* But I can dance: that's what I mean to be, a tap dancer in the movies. My dancing shadow rollicks on the walls; our
230 voices rock the chinaware; we giggle: as if unseen hands were tickling us. Queenie rolls on her back, her paws plow the air, something like a grin stretches her black lips. Inside myself, I feel warm and sparky as those crumbling logs, carefree as the wind in the chimney. My friend waltzes round the stove, the hem of her poor calico skirt pinched between her fingers as though it were a party dress: *Show me the way to go home,* she sings, her tennis shoes squeaking on the floor. *Show me the way to go home.* **F**

Enter: two relatives. Very angry. **Potent** with eyes that scold,
240 tongues that scald. Listen to what they have to say, the words tumbling together into a wrathful tune: "A child of seven! whiskey on his breath! are you out of your mind? feeding a child

Monitor Your Comprehension

PAUSE & REFLECT
Why do you think Buddy and his friend send their fruitcakes to strangers?

_____

_____

_____

_____

_____

_____

_____

_____

F ANALYZE IMAGERY
In lines 215–238, Capote uses imagery to appeal to four out of five of our senses. Circle the imagery in these lines. What senses does Capote appeal to in this paragraph?

_____

_____

_____

potent (pōt'nt) *adj.* powerful

PAUSE & REFLECT
Reread lines 239–248. What impression do you get of the relatives?

of seven! must be loony! road to ruination! remember Cousin Kate? Uncle Charlie? Uncle Charlie's brother-in-law? shame! scandal! humiliation! kneel, pray, beg the Lord!"

Queenie sneaks under the stove. My friend gazes at her shoes, her chin quivers, she lifts her skirt and blows her nose and runs to her room. **PAUSE & REFLECT**

250 Long after the town has gone to sleep and the house is silent except for the chimings of clocks and the sputter of fading fires, she is weeping into a pillow already as wet as a widow's handkerchief.

"Don't cry," I say, sitting at the bottom of her bed and shivering despite my flannel nightgown that smells of last winter's cough syrup, "don't cry," I beg, teasing her toes, tickling her feet, "you're too old for that."

"It's because," she hiccups, "I *am* too old. Old and funny."

"Not funny. Fun. More fun than anybody. Listen. If you don't stop crying you'll be so tired tomorrow we can't go cut a tree."

260 She straightens up. Queenie jumps on the bed (where Queenie is not allowed) to lick her cheeks. "I know where we'll find real pretty trees, Buddy. And holly, too. With berries big as your eyes. It's way off in the woods. Farther than we've ever been. Papa used to bring us Christmas trees from there: carry them on his shoulder. That's fifty years ago. Well, now: I can't wait for morning."

Morning. Frozen rime[6] lusters the grass; the sun, round as an orange and orange as hot-weather moons, balances on the horizon, burnishes the silvered winter woods. A wild turkey calls.

270 A renegade hog grunts in the undergrowth. Soon, by the edge of knee-deep, rapid-running water, we have to abandon the buggy. Queenie wades the stream first, paddles across barking complaints at the swiftness of the current, the pneumonia-making coldness of it. We follow, holding our shoes and equipment (a hatchet, a

---

6. **rime:** a white frost.

burlap sack) above our heads. A mile more: of chastising thorns,
burrs and briers that catch at our clothes; of rusty pine needles
brilliant with gaudy fungus and molted feathers. Here, there,
a flash, a flutter, an ecstasy of shrillings remind us that not all
the birds have flown south. Always, the path unwinds through
280 lemony sun pools and pitch-black vine tunnels. Another creek
to cross: a disturbed armada of speckled trout froths the water
round us, and frogs the size of plates practice belly flops; beaver
workmen are building a dam. On the farther shore, Queenie
shakes herself and trembles. My friend shivers, too: not with cold
but enthusiasm. One of her hat's ragged roses sheds a petal as
she lifts her head and inhales the pine-heavy air. "We're almost
there; can you smell it, Buddy?" she says, as though we were
approaching an ocean. **G**

And, indeed, it is a kind of ocean. Scented acres of holiday
290 trees, prickly-leafed holly. Red berries shiny as Chinese bells:
black crows swoop upon them screaming. Having stuffed our
burlap sacks with enough greenery and crimson to garland a
dozen windows, we set about choosing a tree. "It should be,"
muses my friend, "twice as tall as a boy. So a boy can't steal the
star." The one we pick is twice as tall as me. A brave handsome
brute that survives thirty hatchet strokes before it keels with a
creaking rending cry. Lugging it like a kill, we commence the
long trek out. Every few yards we abandon the struggle, sit down
and pant. But we have the strength of triumphant huntsmen;
300 that and the tree's virile, icy perfume revive us, **goad** us on.
Many compliments accompany our sunset return along the red
clay road to town; but my friend is sly and noncommittal when
passers-by praise the treasure perched in our buggy: what a fine
tree, and where did it come from? "Yonderways," she murmurs
vaguely. Once a car stops, and the rich mill owner's lazy wife
leans out and whines: "Giveya two-bits⁷ cash for that ol tree."
Ordinarily my friend is afraid of saying no; but on this occasion

G ANALYZE IMAGERY
Circle two examples of imagery
in this paragraph. Add them to
your chart.

goad (gōd) *v.* to drive or urge

7. **two-bits:** 25 cents.

PAUSE & REFLECT

What do you learn about the narrator's friend based on her words and actions in lines 305–312?

_____

_____

_____

_____

_____

_____

_____

she promptly shakes her head: "We wouldn't take a dollar." The mill owner's wife persists. "A dollar, my foot! Fifty cents. That's my last offer. Goodness, woman, you can get another one." In answer, my friend gently reflects: "I doubt it. There's never two of anything." **PAUSE & REFLECT**

Home: Queenie slumps by the fire and sleeps till tomorrow, snoring loud as a human.

A trunk in the attic contains: a shoebox of ermine tails (off the opera cape of a curious lady who once rented a room in the house), coils of frazzled tinsel gone gold with age, one silver star, a brief rope of dilapidated, undoubtedly dangerous candylike light bulbs. Excellent decorations, as far as they go, which isn't far enough: my friend wants our tree to blaze "like a Baptist window," droop with weighty snows of ornament. But we can't afford the made-in-Japan splendors at the five-and-dime. So we do what we've always done: sit for days at the kitchen table with scissors and crayons and stacks of colored paper. I make sketches and my friend cuts them out: lots of cats, fish too (because they're easy to draw), some apples, some watermelons, a few winged angels devised from saved-up sheets of Hershey-bar tin foil. We use safety pins to attach these creations to the tree; as a final touch, we sprinkle the branches with shredded cotton (picked in August for this purpose). My friend, surveying the effect, clasps her hands together. "Now honest, Buddy. Doesn't it look good enough to eat?" Queenie tries to eat an angel.

After weaving and ribboning holly wreaths for all the front windows, our next project is the fashioning of family gifts. Tie-dye scarves for the ladies, for the men a home-brewed lemon and licorice and aspirin syrup to be taken "at the first Symptoms of a Cold and after Hunting." But when it comes time for making each other's gift, my friend and I separate to work secretly. I would

like to buy her a pearl-handled knife, a radio, a whole pound of
340 chocolate-covered cherries (we tasted some once, and she always
swears: "I could live on them, Buddy, Lord yes I could—and
that's not taking his name in vain"). Instead, I am building her a
kite. She would like to give me a bicycle (she's said so on several
million occasions: "If only I could, Buddy. It's bad enough in life
to do without something *you* want; but confound it, what gets
my goat is not being able to give somebody something you want
them to have. Only one of these days I will, Buddy. Locate you a
bike. Don't ask how. Steal it, maybe"). Instead, I'm fairly certain
that she is building me a kite—the same as last year and the year
350 before: the year before that we exchanged slingshots. All of which
is fine by me. For we are champion kite fliers who study the wind
like sailors; my friend, more accomplished than I, can get a kite
aloft when there isn't enough breeze to carry clouds. **H**

Christmas Eve afternoon we scrape together a nickel and go to
the butcher's to buy Queenie's traditional gift, a good gnawable
beef bone. The bone, wrapped in funny paper, is placed high in
the tree near the silver star. Queenie knows it's there. She squats at
the foot of the tree staring up in a trance of greed: when bedtime
arrives she refuses to budge. Her excitement is equaled by my
360 own. I kick the covers and turn my pillow as though it were a
scorching summer's night. Somewhere a rooster crows: falsely, for
the sun is still on the other side of the world.

"Buddy, are you awake?" It is my friend, calling from her
room, which is next to mine; and an instant later she is sitting on
my bed holding a candle. "Well, I can't sleep a hoot," she declares.
"My mind's jumping like a jack rabbit. Buddy, do you think
Mrs. Roosevelt will serve our cake at dinner?" We huddle in the
bed, and she squeezes my hand I-love-you. "Seems like your hand
used to be so much smaller. I guess I hate to see you grow up.
370 When you're grown up, will we still be friends?" I say always. "But
I feel so bad, Buddy. I wanted so bad to give you a bike. I tried to

H DETAILS OF SETTING
Buddy and his friend are making ornaments, wreaths, scarves, and kites. How do these details relate to the time and place of the story? How might this scene be different if the story were set during a different time period?

_____

_____

_____

_____

_____

_____

_____

sell my cameo Papa gave me. Buddy"—she hesitates, as though embarrassed—"I made you another kite." Then I confess that I made her one, too; and we laugh. The candle burns too short to hold. Out it goes, exposing the starlight, the stars spinning at the window like a visible caroling that slowly, slowly daybreak silences. Possibly we doze; but the beginnings of dawn splash us like cold water: we're up, wide-eyed and wandering while we wait for others to waken. Quite deliberately my friend drops a kettle 380 on the kitchen floor. I tap dance in front of closed doors. One by one the household emerges, looking as though they'd like to kill us both; but it's Christmas, so they can't. First, a gorgeous breakfast: just everything you can imagine—from flapjacks and fried squirrel to hominy grits and honey-in-the-comb. Which puts everyone in a good humor except my friend and me. Frankly, we're so impatient to get at the presents we can't eat a mouthful.

Well, I'm disappointed. Who wouldn't be? With socks, a Sunday school shirt, some handkerchiefs, a hand-me-down sweater, and a year's subscription to a religious magazine for 390 children. *The Little Shepherd*. It makes me boil. It really does. **PAUSE & REFLECT**

PAUSE & REFLECT
Why do the presents make Buddy "boil"?

My friend has a better haul. A sack of satsumas,[8] that's her best present. She is proudest, however, of a white wool shawl knitted by her married sister. But she *says* her favorite gift is the kite I built her. And it *is* very beautiful; though not as beautiful as the one she made me, which is blue and scattered with gold and green Good Conduct stars;[9] moreover, my name is painted on it, "Buddy."

"Buddy, the wind is blowing."

400 The wind is blowing, and nothing will do till we've run to a pasture below the house where Queenie has scooted to bury her bone (and where, a winter hence, Queenie will be buried, too). There, plunging through the healthy waist-high grass, we unreel

---

8. **satsumas** (săt-soo'məz): fruit similar to tangerines.
9. **Good Conduct stars:** small, shiny, glued paper stars often awarded to children for good behavior or perfect attendance in school.

our kites, feel them twitching at the string like sky fish as they swim into the wind. Satisfied, sun-warmed, we sprawl in the grass and peel satsumas and watch our kites **cavort**. Soon I forget the socks and hand-me-down sweater. I'm as happy as if we'd already won the fifty-thousand-dollar Grand Prize in that coffee-naming contest.

410 "My, how foolish I am!" my friend cries, suddenly alert, like a woman remembering too late she has biscuits in the oven. "You know what I've always thought?" she asks in a tone of discovery and not smiling at me but a point beyond. "I've always thought a body would have to be sick and dying before they saw the Lord. And I imagined that when he came it would be like looking at the Baptist window: pretty as colored glass with the sun pouring through, such a shine you don't know it's getting dark. And it's been a comfort: to think of that shine taking away all the spooky feeling. But I'll wager it never happens. I'll wager at the very end

420 a body realizes the Lord has already shown himself. That things as they are"—her hand circles in a gesture that gathers clouds and kites and grass and Queenie pawing earth over her bone—"just what they've always seen, was seeing him. As for me, I could leave the world with today in my eyes."

This is our last Christmas together.

Life separates us. Those who Know Best decide that I belong in a military school. And so follows a miserable succession of bugle-blowing prisons, grim reveille-ridden[10] summer camps. I have a new home too. But it doesn't count. Home is where my friend is,

430 and there I never go. ❶

And there she remains, puttering around the kitchen. Alone with Queenie. Then alone. ("Buddy dear," she writes in her wild hard-to-read script, "yesterday Jim Macy's horse kicked Queenie bad. Be thankful she didn't feel much. I wrapped her in a Fine Linen sheet and rode her in the buggy down to Simpson's pasture where she can be with all her Bones . . ."). For a few Novembers she continues to bake her fruitcakes single-handed; not as many,

cavort (kə-vôrt′) v. to leap or romp about

What does this image of the kites **cavorting** tell you about how the writer remembers this moment with his cousin?

_____

_____

_____

_____

_____

_____

❶ **DETAILS OF SETTING**
In line 425, the setting of the story changes and Buddy is looking back at his childhood from the perspective of an adult. How has Buddy's life changed since the last Christmas with his friend?

_____

_____

_____

_____

_____

_____

10. **reveille-ridden** (rĕv′ə-lē-rĭd′n): dominated by an early-morning signal, as on a bugle, to wake soldiers or campers.

sever (sĕv′ər) *v.* to cut off

Why does Buddy feel severed from his friend?

_____

_____

_____

_____

_____

_____

but some: and, of course, she always sends me "the best of the batch." Also, in every letter she encloses a dime wadded in toilet
440 paper: "See a picture show and write me the story." But gradually in her letters she tends to confuse me with her other friend, the Buddy who died in the 1880's; more and more, thirteenths are not the only days she stays in bed: a morning arrives in November, a leafless birdless coming of winter morning, when she cannot rouse herself to exclaim: "Oh my, it's fruitcake weather!"

And when that happens, I know it. A message saying so merely confirms a piece of news some secret vein had already received, **severing** from me an irreplaceable part of myself, letting it loose like a kite on a broken string. That is why, walking across a school
450 campus on this particular December morning, I keep searching the sky. As if I expected to see, rather like hearts, a lost pair of kites hurrying toward heaven.

Text Analysis: Details of Setting

Locate a passage in the story in which the description of the setting influences the characters' living conditions, personalities, dreams, or values. Then locate a passage where the details of setting create a conflict for the characters. Record this information in the chart below.

ROLE OF SETTING	EXAMPLE SETTING
Setting can influence characters by  • determining the living conditions and jobs available to them • shaping their personalities, their dreams, and their values	
Setting can create conflicts by  • exposing the characters to dangerous weather, such as a storm or a drought • making characters endure a difficult time period, such as the Great Depression	

How would "A Christmas Memory" change if it were set in a city instead of the country, or in contemporary times instead of the past? Choose one detail from the story and explain how the story would be different if the setting were changed.

_____

_____

_____

_____

_____

_____

Reading Skill: Evaluate Imagery

Review the description of Mr. Haha's café in lines 145–161. In the chart below, record examples of imagery from the passage and explain how each appeals to your senses. The first example has been done for you.

SENSORY IMAGES	
"fish-fry and dancing café" (line 147)	**Smell:** *oil, fish* **Hearing:** *music, feet stomping on the floor*

What do you look for in a **FRIEND?**

Look back at your list of the qualities of a good friend. Do you know someone who fulfills all or most of those qualities? What have you learned about yourself from being close with that person?

_____

Vocabulary Practice

Circle the letter of the word that is not related in meaning to the other words in the set.

1. **(a)** gear, **(b)** paraphernalia, **(c)** materials, **(d)** notice

2. **(a)** strong, **(b)** powerful, **(c)** prosaic, **(d)** forceful

3. **(a)** start, **(b)** finish, **(c)** begin, **(d)** inaugurate

4. **(a)** destroy, **(b)** suffuse, **(c)** demolish, **(d)** consume

5. **(a)** depress, **(b)** excite, **(c)** energize, **(d)** exhilarate

6. **(a)** squander, **(b)** waste, **(c)** save, **(d)** misuse

7. **(a)** return, **(b)** urge, **(c)** encourage, **(d)** goad

8. **(a)** potent, **(b)** mighty, **(c)** possible, **(d)** strong

9. **(a)** cavort, **(b)** prance, **(c)** dance, **(d)** fight

10. **(a)** cut, **(b)** separate, **(c)** join, **(d)** sever

Academic Vocabulary in Writing

aspect	circumstance	contribute	distinct	perceive

Buddy and his friend have a wonderful relationship because they each **contribute** to their friendship. Write two sentences: one about what Buddy contributes to the friendship and another about what his friend contributes. Use at least one Academic Vocabulary word in your response. Definitions for these terms are listed on page 111.

_____

_____

_____

Assessment Practice

DIRECTIONS Use "A Christmas Memory" to answer questions 1–4.

1 How is Buddy's friend different from most people her age?

　Ⓐ She still enjoys the Christmas holiday.
　Ⓑ She is childlike in her attitudes and actions.
　Ⓒ She has fewer friends than most.
　Ⓓ She takes care of someone younger than herself.

2 The following excerpt from "A Christmas Memory" describes the task of baking fruitcakes. To which sense does it appeal?

　Eggbeaters whirl, spoons spin round in bowls of butter and sugar, vanilla sweetens the air, ginger spices it; melting, nose-tingling odors saturate the kitchen, suffuse the house, drift out to the world on puffs of chimney smoke.

　Ⓐ touch and smell
　Ⓑ sight and smell
　Ⓒ hearing and sight
　Ⓓ taste and touch

3 What happens to the two friends after this particular Christmas?

　Ⓐ They separate and never see each other again
　Ⓑ They separate but visit each other often
　Ⓒ They continue their yearly holiday traditions
　Ⓓ They both move away from the relatives in the house

4 The setting complicates this story because at the time —

　Ⓐ there were few ways to entertain oneself
　Ⓑ there weren't many stores where the friends live
　Ⓒ there was little money to spare due to the depression
　Ⓓ there weren't many children where the friends live

Through the Tunnel

Short Story by **Doris Lessing**

When is a **RISK** worth taking?

Sometimes people take risks to prove something to themselves or others. These risks can be physical, emotional, or social. But when is an action too risky?

DISCUSS Think about a time when you or someone you know took a risk to prove something. Then fill in the chart in the notebook at the left. First list the activity. Then, list the risks and the benefits of taking that risk. Finally, discuss your chart with a partner. Do the possible benefits outweigh the risks?

Text Analysis: Setting as Symbol

A **symbol** is a person, place, object, or activity that stands for something beyond itself. For example, a car is a means of transportation, but in a story a car may come to symbolize independence or freedom. As you read "Through the Tunnel," think about how the **setting**—the time and place in which the story takes place—symbolizes important ideas. Use a chart like the one below to record passages that clue you in as to what various aspects of the setting might symbolize.

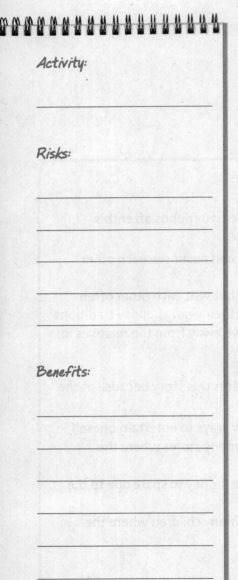

Activity:

_____

Risks:

_____

_____

_____

_____

Benefits:

_____

_____

_____

_____

Passage from Story	Possible Symbol
"It was a wild-looking place, and there was no one there; but she said, 'Of course, Jerry. When you've had enough, come to the big beach.'" (lines 26–28)	other beach could represent Jerry's independence

Reading Skill: Analyze Details

In order to understand the symbolic importance of each setting in "Through the Tunnel," you must analyze the **descriptive details** in each and think about the larger meanings they imply. For example, the big beach is a familiar place where Jerry's mother goes, so it might symbolize safety to Jerry. As you read, keep track of words and phrases from the text that describe each setting. Then, you can try to draw conclusions about what each setting symbolizes for the main character.

Big Beach	Bay	Tunnel
crowded familiar	wild and rocky	

Vocabulary in Context

Note: Words are listed in the order in which they appear in the story.

contrition (kən-trĭsh′ən) *n.* a feeling of regret for doing wrong
Jerry felt contrition whenever he disappointed his mother.

promontory (prŏm′ən-tôr′ē) *n.* a high ridge of land or rock jutting out into a body of water
He watched the other boys jump off the promontory into the water.

supplication (sŭp′lĭ-kā′shən) *n.* a humble request or prayer
He gave the other boys a look of supplication that showed how much he wanted to be a part of their group.

inquisitive (ĭn-kwĭz′ĭ-tĭv) *adj.* curious; inquiring
At the sound of his name, the dog cocked his ears and tilted his head in an inquisitive manner.

persistence (pər-sĭs′təns) *n.* the act of refusing to stop or be changed
For days, the girl practiced her flip turns, her persistence driving her to master them.

incredulous (ĭn-krĕj′ə-ləs) *adj.* doubtful; disbelieving
I was incredulous that I managed to win the race.

THROUGH THE
Tunnel

Short Story by
DORIS LESSING

BACKGROUND Born in Persia (now Iran), Doris
Lessing moved to Rhodesia (now Zimbabwe)
as a child with her British parents. Her self-
confidence, strength, and independence can be
traced to her youth in the unforgiving country of
the African bush. At an early age Lessing had to
deal with dangerous thunderstorms, droughts,
snakes, scorpions, and insects. Survival—
emotional and physical—is at the heart of
her life and work.

Going to the shore on the first morning of the vacation,
the young English boy stopped at a turning of the path
and looked down at a wild and rocky bay, and then over to the
crowded beach he knew so well from other years. His mother
walked on in front of him, carrying a bright striped bag in one
hand. Her other arm, swinging loose, was very white in the sun.
The boy watched that white, naked arm, and turned his eyes,
which had a frown behind them, toward the bay and back again
to his mother. When she felt he was not with her, she swung
10 around. "Oh, there you are, Jerry!" she said. She looked impatient,
then smiled. "Why, darling, would you rather not come with me?
Would you rather—" She frowned, conscientiously worrying over
what amusements he might secretly be longing for, which she had
been too busy or too careless to imagine. He was very familiar
with that anxious, apologetic smile. **Contrition** sent him running

contrition (kən-trĭsh'ən) *n.* a
feeling of regret for doing wrong

after her. And yet, as he ran, he looked back over his shoulder at the wild bay; and all morning, as he played on the safe beach, he was thinking of it. **A**

Next morning, when it was time for the routine of swimming
20 and sunbathing, his mother said, "Are you tired of the usual beach, Jerry? Would you like to go somewhere else?"

"Oh, no!" he said quickly, smiling at her out of that unfailing impulse of contrition—a sort of chivalry. Yet, walking down the path with her, he blurted out, "I'd like to go and have a look at those rocks down there."

She gave the idea her attention. It was a wild-looking place, and there was no one there; but she said, "Of course, Jerry. When you've had enough, come to the big beach. Or just go straight back to the villa, if you like." She walked away, that bare arm,
30 now slightly reddened from yesterday's sun, swinging. And he almost ran after her again, feeling it unbearable that she should go by herself, but he did not.

She was thinking, Of course he's old enough to be safe without me. Have I been keeping him too close? He mustn't feel he ought to be with me. I must be careful.

He was an only child, eleven years old. She was a widow. She was determined to be neither possessive nor lacking in devotion. She went worrying off to her beach. **B**

As for Jerry, once he saw that his mother had gained her
40 beach, he began the steep descent to the bay. From where he was, high up among red-brown rocks, it was a scoop of moving bluish green fringed with white. As he went lower, he saw that it spread among small **promontories** and inlets of rough, sharp rock, and the crisping, lapping surface showed stains of purple and darker blue. Finally, as he ran sliding and scraping down the last few yards, he saw an edge of white surf and the shallow, luminous movement of water over white sand, and, beyond that, a solid, heavy blue.

He ran straight into the water and began swimming. He was
50 a good swimmer. He went out fast over the gleaming sand, over a middle region where rocks lay like discolored monsters

A ANALYZE DETAILS
Reread lines 1–18. Circle the words that signal a contrast between the bay and the beach. Add these words to your chart.

B SETTING AS SYMBOL
What does Jerry's mother worry about? What do Jerry's mother's fears lead you to think about what the bay symbolizes?

_____

_____

_____

_____

_____

promontory (prŏm′ən-tôr′ē) *n.* a high ridge of land or rock jutting out into a body of water

C ANALYZE DETAILS
Circle the word in lines 49–54
that provide clues as to what the
rocks might symbolize. Why does
Jerry consider this "the real sea"?

_____

_____

_____

_____

_____

_____

_____

_____

supplication (sŭp'lĭ-kā'shən) *n.*
a humble request or prayer

D ANALYZE DETAILS
Why does Jerry feel proud of
himself?

_____

_____

_____

_____

_____

_____

under the surface, and then he was in the real sea—a warm
sea where irregular cold currents from the deep water shocked
his limbs. **C**

When he was so far out that he could look back not only on
the little bay but past the promontory that was between it and the
big beach, he floated on the buoyant surface and looked for his
mother. There she was, a speck of yellow under an umbrella that
looked like a slice of orange peel. He swam back to shore, relieved
60 at being sure she was there, but all at once very lonely.

On the edge of a small cape that marked the side of the bay
away from the promontory was a loose scatter of rocks. Above
them, some boys were stripping off their clothes. They came
running, naked, down to the rocks. The English boy swam
toward them, but kept his distance at a stone's throw. They were
of that coast; all of them were burned smooth dark brown and
speaking a language he did not understand. To be with them, of
them, was a craving that filled his whole body. He swam a little
closer; they turned and watched him with narrowed, alert dark
70 eyes. Then one smiled and waved. It was enough. In a minute, he
had swum in and was on the rocks beside them, smiling with a
desperate, nervous **supplication**. They shouted cheerful greetings
at him; and then, as he preserved his nervous, uncomprehending
smile, they understood that he was a foreigner strayed from his
own beach, and they proceeded to forget him. But he was happy.
He was with them.

They began diving again and again from a high point into
a well of blue sea between rough, pointed rocks. After they had
dived and come up, they swam around, hauled themselves up,
80 and waited their turn to dive again. They were big boys—men,
to Jerry. He dived, and they watched him; and when he swam
around to take his place, they made way for him. He felt he was
accepted and he dived again, carefully, proud of himself. **D**

Soon the biggest of the boys poised himself, shot down into the
water, and did not come up. The others stood about, watching.
Jerry, after waiting for the sleek brown head to appear, let out a
yell of warning; they looked at him idly and turned their eyes back

toward the water. After a long time, the boy came up on the other
side of a big dark rock, letting the air out of his lungs in a sputtering
90 gasp and a shout of triumph. Immediately the rest of them dived in.
One moment, the morning seemed full of chattering boys; the next,
the air and the surface of the water were empty. But through the
heavy blue, dark shapes could be seen moving and groping.

Jerry dived, shot past the school of underwater swimmers, saw
a black wall of rock looming at him, touched it, and bobbed up
at once to the surface, where the wall was a low barrier he could
see across. There was no one visible; under him, in the water, the
dim shapes of the swimmers had disappeared. Then one, and then
another of the boys came up on the far side of the barrier of rock,
100 and he understood that they had swum through some gap or hole
in it. He plunged down again. He could see nothing through the
stinging salt water but the blank rock. When he came up the boys
were all on the diving rock, preparing to attempt the feat again.
And now, in a panic of failure, he yelled up, in English, "Look at
me! Look!" and he began splashing and kicking in the water like
a foolish dog.

They looked down gravely, frowning. He knew the frown.
At moments of failure, when he clowned to claim his mother's
attention, it was with just this grave, embarrassed inspection that
110 she rewarded him. Through his hot shame, feeling the pleading
grin on his face like a scar that he could never remove, he looked
up at the group of big brown boys on the rock and shouted,
"Bonjour! Merci! Au revoir! Monsieur, monsieur!"[1] while he hooked
his fingers round his ears and waggled them. **E**

Water surged into his mouth; he choked, sank, came up.
The rock, lately weighted with boys, seemed to rear up out of
the water as their weight was removed. They were flying down
past him, now, into the water; the air was full of falling bodies.
Then the rock was empty in the hot sunlight. He counted one,
120 two, three. . . .

At fifty, he was terrified. They must all be drowning beneath
him, in the watery caves of the rock! At a hundred, he stared
around him at the empty hillside, wondering if he should yell for

E ANALYZE DETAILS
Underline details in lines 84–114
that explain what the bigger
boys are doing. What does Jerry
do in response?

_____

_____

_____

_____

_____

_____

_____

_____

_____

_____

_____

_____

_____

_____

_____

_____

_____

---

1. ***Bonjour! Merci! Au revoir! Monsieur, monsieur!*** (bôN-zhōōr′ mĕr-sē′ ō′rə-
vwär′ mə-syœ′ mə-syœ′) *French*: Good day! Thank you! Goodbye! Sir, sir!

F SETTING AS SYMBOL
How has the setting changed in
lines 121–135? What makes Jerry
upset?

_____

_____

_____

_____

G ANALYZE DETAILS
Underline details in lines 138–140
that describe the boulders. What
does this choice of words tell you
about what the boulders might
symbolize?

_____

_____

_____

_____

inquisitive (ĭn-kwĭz′ĭ-tĭv) adj.
curious; inquiring

Why does Jerry's mother give
him an **inquisitive** look? Why
does she find his request a bit
unusual?

_____

_____

_____

_____

_____

_____

help. He counted faster, faster, to hurry them up, to bring them
to the surface quickly, to drown them quickly—anything rather
than the terror of counting on and on into the blue emptiness
of the morning. And then, at a hundred and sixty, the water
beyond the rock was full of boys blowing like brown whales.
They swam back to the shore without a look at him.

130   He climbed back to the diving rock and sat down, feeling the
hot roughness of it under his thighs. The boys were gathering up
their bits of clothing and running off along the shore to another
promontory. They were leaving to get away from him. He cried
openly, fists in his eyes. There was no one to see him, and he cried
himself out. **F**

    It seemed to him that a long time had passed, and he swam out to
where he could see his mother. Yes, she was still there, a yellow spot
under an orange umbrella. He swam back to the big rock, climbed
up, and dived into the blue pool among the fanged and angry
140 boulders. Down he went, until he touched the wall of rock again.
But the salt was so painful in his eyes that he could not see. **G**

    He came to the surface, swam to shore, and went back to the
villa to wait for his mother. Soon she walked slowly up the path,
swinging her striped bag, the flushed, naked arm dangling beside
her. "I want some swimming goggles," he panted, defiant and
beseeching.

    She gave him a patient, **inquisitive** look as she said casually,
"Well, of course, darling."

    But now, now, now! He must have them this minute, and no
150 other time. He nagged and pestered until she went with him to
a shop. As soon as she had bought the goggles, he grabbed them
from her hand as if she were going to claim them for herself, and
was off, running down the steep path to the bay.

    Jerry swam out to the big barrier rock, adjusted the goggles,
and dived. The impact of the water broke the rubber-enclosed
vacuum, and the goggles came loose. He understood that he must
swim down to the base of the rock from the surface of the water.
He fixed the goggles tight and firm, filled his lungs, and floated,
face down, on the water. Now, he could see. It was as if he had

160 eyes of a different kind—fish eyes that showed everything clear and delicate and wavering in the bright water.

Under him, six or seven feet down, was a floor of perfectly clean, shining white sand, rippled firm and hard by the tides. Two grayish shapes steered there, like long, rounded pieces of wood or slate. They were fish. He saw them nose toward each other, poise motionless, make a dart forward, swerve off, and come around again. It was like a water dance. A few inches above them the water sparkled as if sequins were dropping through it. Fish again—myriads of minute fish, the length of his fingernail, were

170 drifting through the water, and in a moment he could feel the innumerable tiny touches of them against his limbs. It was like swimming in flaked silver. The great rock the big boys had swum through rose sheer out of the white sand—black, tufted lightly with greenish weed. He could see no gap in it. He swam down to its base.

Again and again he rose, took a big chestful of air, and went down. Again and again he groped over the surface of the rock, feeling it, almost hugging it in the desperate need to find the entrance. And then, once, while he was clinging to the black wall,

180 his knees came up and he shot his feet out forward and they met no obstacle. He had found the hole. **PAUSE & REFLECT**

He gained the surface, clambered about the stones that littered the barrier rock until he found a big one, and, with this in his arms, let himself down over the side of the rock. He dropped, with the weight, straight to the sandy floor. Clinging tight to the anchor of stone, he lay on his side and looked in under the dark shelf at the place where his feet had gone. He could see the hole. It was an irregular, dark gap; but he could not see deep into it. He let go of his anchor, clung with his hands to the edges of the hole,

190 and tried to push himself in.

He got his head in, found his shoulders jammed, moved them in sidewise, and was inside as far as his waist. He could see nothing ahead. Something soft and clammy touched his mouth; he saw a dark frond moving against the grayish rock, and panic

PAUSE & REFLECT
How do you think Jerry feels at this moment?

_____

_____

_____

_____

_____

_____

❶ ANALYZE DETAILS
Reread lines 191–201. How does Jerry's perception of the tunnel change? Why is he so determined to find his way through the hole?

_____

_____

_____

_____

_____

_____

_____

❶ SETTING AS SYMBOL
Underline the words in lines 217–224 that describe the big beach. What does this beach symbolize to Jerry now?

_____

_____

_____

_____

_____

_____

_____

filled him. He thought of octopuses, of clinging weed. He pushed himself out backward and caught a glimpse, as he retreated, of a harmless tentacle of seaweed drifting in the mouth of the tunnel. But it was enough. He reached the sunlight, swam to shore, and lay on the diving rock. He looked down into the blue well of

200 water. He knew he must find his way through that cave, or hole, or tunnel, and out the other side. ❶

First, he thought, he must learn to control his breathing. He let himself down into the water with another big stone in his arms, so that he could lie effortlessly on the bottom of the sea. He counted. One, two, three. He counted steadily. He could hear the movement of blood in his chest. Fifty-one, fifty-two. . . . His chest was hurting. He let go of the rock and went up into the air. He saw that the sun was low. He rushed to the villa and found his mother at her supper. She said only "Did you enjoy yourself?" and

210 he said "Yes."

All night the boy dreamed of the water-filled cave in the rock, and as soon as breakfast was over he went to the bay.

That night, his nose bled badly. For hours he had been underwater, learning to hold his breath, and now he felt weak and dizzy. His mother said, "I shouldn't overdo things, darling, if I were you."

That day and the next, Jerry exercised his lungs as if everything, the whole of his life, all that he would become, depended upon it. Again his nose bled at night, and his mother

220 insisted on his coming with her the next day. It was a torment to him to waste a day of his careful self-training, but he stayed with her on that other beach, which now seemed a place for small children, a place where his mother might lie safe in the sun. It was not his beach. ❶

He did not ask for permission, on the following day, to go to his beach. He went, before his mother could consider the complicated rights and wrongs of the matter. A day's rest, he discovered, had improved his count by ten. The big boys had made the passage while he counted a hundred and sixty. He

230 had been counting fast, in his fright. Probably now, if he tried, he could get through that long tunnel, but he was not going to try yet. A curious, most unchildlike **persistence**, a controlled impatience, made him wait. In the meantime, he lay underwater on the white sand, littered now by stones he had brought down from the upper air, and studied the entrance to the tunnel. He knew every jut and corner of it, as far as it was possible to see. It was as if he already felt its sharpness about his shoulders.

He sat by the clock in the villa, when his mother was not near, and checked his time. He was **incredulous** and then proud to
240 find he could hold his breath without strain for two minutes. The words "two minutes," authorized by the clock, brought close the adventure that was so necessary to him.

In another four days, his mother said casually one morning, they must go home. On the day before they left, he would do it. He would do it if it killed him, he said defiantly to himself. But two days before they were to leave—a day of triumph when he increased his count by fifteen—his nose bled so badly that he turned dizzy and had to lie limply over the big rock like a bit of seaweed, watching the thick red blood flow on to the rock and
250 trickle slowly down to the sea. He was frightened. Supposing he turned dizzy in the tunnel? Supposing he died there, trapped? Supposing—his head went around, in the hot sun, and he almost gave up. He thought he would return to the house and lie down, and next summer, perhaps, when he had another year's growth in him—*then* he would go through the hole. PAUSE & REFLECT

But even after he had made the decision, or thought he had, he found himself sitting up on the rock and looking down into the water; and he knew that now, this moment, when his nose had only just stopped bleeding, when his head was still sore and
260 throbbing—this was the moment when he would try. If he did not do it now, he never would. He was trembling with fear that he would not go; and he was trembling with horror at that long, long tunnel under the rock, under the sea. Even in the open sunlight,

persistence (pər-sĭs′təns) *n.* the act of refusing to stop or be changed

incredulous (ĭn-krĕj′ə-ləs) *adj.* doubtful; disbelieving

PAUSE & REFLECT
Do you think Jerry's fears are valid? Why or why not?

_____

_____

_____

_____

_____

ⓙ ANALYZE DETAILS
Underline the words and phrases in lines 243–267 that describe the danger of Jerry's quest. Why is Jerry so determined to try to swim through the tunnel now?

the barrier rock seemed very wide and very heavy; tons of rock pressed down on where he would go. If he died there, he would lie until one day—perhaps not before next year—those big boys would swim into it and find it blocked. ⓙ

He put on his goggles, fitted them tight, tested the vacuum. His hands were shaking. Then he chose the biggest stone he could carry and slipped over the edge of the rock until half of him was in the cool, enclosing water and half in the hot sun. He looked up once at the empty sky, filled his lungs once, twice, and then sank fast to the bottom with the stone. He let it go and began to count. He took the edges of the hole in his hands and drew himself into it, wriggling his shoulders in sidewise as he remembered he must, kicking himself along with his feet.

Soon he was clear inside. He was in a small rock-bound hole filled with yellowish-gray water. The water was pushing him up against the roof. The roof was sharp and pained his back. He pulled himself along with his hands—fast, fast—and used his legs as levers. His head knocked against something; a sharp pain dizzied him. Fifty, fifty-one, fifty-two. . . . He was without light, and the water seemed to press upon him with the weight of rock. Seventy-one, seventy-two. . . . There was no strain on his lungs. He felt like an inflated balloon, his lungs were so light and easy, but his head was pulsing.

He was being continually pressed against the sharp roof, which felt slimy as well as sharp. Again he thought of octopuses, and wondered if the tunnel might be filled with weed that could tangle him. He gave himself a panicky, convulsive kick forward, ducked his head, and swam. His feet and hands moved freely, as if in open water. The hole must have widened out. He thought he must be swimming fast, and he was frightened of banging his head if the tunnel narrowed.

A hundred, a hundred and one. . . . The water paled. Victory filled him. His lungs were beginning to hurt. A few more strokes and he would be out. He was counting wildly; he said a hundred

and fifteen, and then, a long time later, a hundred and fifteen
300 again. The water was a clear jewel-green all around him. Then
he saw, above his head, a crack running up through the rock.
Sunlight was falling through it, showing the clean, dark rock
of the tunnel, a single mussel shell, and darkness ahead.

He was at the end of what he could do. He looked up at the
crack as if it were filled with air and not water, as if he could
put his mouth to it to draw in air. A hundred and fifteen, he
heard himself say inside his head—but he had said that long
ago. He must go on into the blackness ahead, or he would
drown. His head was swelling, his lungs cracking. A hundred
310 and fifteen, a hundred and fifteen pounded through his head,
and he feebly clutched at rocks in the dark, pulling himself
forward, leaving the brief space of sunlit water behind. He felt
he was dying. He was no longer quite conscious. He struggled
on in the darkness between lapses into unconsciousness. An
immense, swelling pain filled his head, and then the darkness
cracked with an explosion of green light. His hands, groping
forward, met nothing; and his feet, kicking back, propelled
him out into the open sea. Ⓚ

He drifted to the surface, his face turned up to the air. He
320 was gasping like a fish. He felt he would sink now and drown;
he could not swim the few feet back to the rock. Then he was
clutching it and pulling himself up onto it. He lay face down,
gasping. He could see nothing but a red-veined, clotted dark.
His eyes must have burst, he thought; they were full of blood.
He tore off his goggles and a gout of blood went into the sea. His
nose was bleeding, and the blood had filled the goggles.

He scooped up handfuls of water from the cool, salty sea, to
splash on his face, and did not know whether it was blood or salt
water he tasted. After a time, his heart quieted, his eyes cleared,
330 and he sat up. He could see the local boys diving and playing half
a mile away. He did not want them. He wanted nothing but to get
back home and lie down.

Ⓚ ANALYZE DETAILS
Circle the words "a hundred and
fifteen" in line 298–299. How
many times do those words
appear in lines 296–318?

_____

Why does Jerry keep repeating
this number?

_____
_____
_____
_____
_____
_____
_____
_____
_____
_____
_____
_____
_____

Why does Jerry give in when his
mother advises him not to swim
for the rest of the day?

_____

_____

_____

_____

_____

_____

_____

_____

_____

_____

_____

In a short while, Jerry swam to shore and climbed slowly
up the path to the villa. He flung himself on his bed and slept,
waking at the sound of feet on the path outside. His mother was
coming back. He rushed to the bathroom, thinking she must not
see his face with bloodstains, or tearstains, on it. He came out of
the bathroom and met her as she walked into the villa, smiling,
her eyes lighting up.

340   "Have a nice morning?" she asked, laying her hand on his
warm brown shoulder a moment.

"Oh, yes, thank you," he said.

"You look a bit pale." And then, sharp and anxious, "How did
you bang your head?"

"Oh, just banged it," he told her.

She looked at him closely. He was strained; his eyes were
glazed-looking. She was worried. And then she said to herself, Oh,
don't fuss! Nothing can happen. He can swim like a fish.

They sat down to lunch together.

350   "Mummy," he said, "I can stay under water for two minutes—
three minutes, at least." It came bursting out of him.

"Can you, darling?" she said. "Well, I shouldn't overdo it.
I don't think you ought to swim any more today."

She was ready for a battle of wills, but he gave in at once.
It was no longer of the least importance to go to the bay. L

Text Analysis: Setting as Symbol

Consider each of the following aspects of the tunnel and write down your thoughts. Then decide what you think Jerry's swim through the tunnel symbolizes. The first example has been done for you.

Aspect of the Tunnel	My Thoughts
1. The danger it represents for Jerry	*Jerry risks his life to get through the tunnel and does it alone—without an adult present.*
2. Its connection to the older boys	
3. How it looks and feels	
4. How Jerry feels about it	
5. What Jerry's swim through the tunnel symbolizes	

Review the thoughts you noted in the chart above. Does Jerry accomplish his goal by swimming through the tunnel? How is Jerry different before and after his swim?

_____

_____

_____

_____

_____

Reading Skill: Analyze Details

Look back at the details you recorded about each setting as you read "Through the Tunnel." For each setting, find a passage in the text that best sums up that place's description and write it in the chart below.

Big Beach	Bay
As he played on the safe beach.	Wild and rocky bay

Write a sentence or two summing up the major differences between the big beach and the bay.

The beach was was more of a ~~forest~~ safe place, while the bay hent sharprocks jutting out, and the water was stronger

When is a **RISK** worth taking?

How would you decide if the potential rewards of a risk are worth taking the risk?

If one doesn't take any risks then there isn't much excitement in life.

Vocabulary Practice

Drawing on your understanding of the vocabulary words, circle **T** (true) or **F** (false) for each item below.

1. If you feel **contrition** for something you did, you feel proud of your actions. (T/**F**)

2. You should not live on a **promontory** if you are afraid of heights. (**T**/F)

3. You might hear a **supplication** at a prayer service. (**T**/F)

4. An **inquisitive** child will rarely ask why. (T/**F**)

5. A person shows **persistence** by repeating a job until she gets it right. (**T**/F)

6. If you are **incredulous** about a friend's advice, you likely will ignore it. (**T**/F)

Academic Vocabulary in Writing

aspect	circumstance	contribute	distinct	perceive

To *perceive* something means to notice something. What changes does Jerry's mother **perceive** in her son during their vacation? What changes does she fail to **perceive?** Answer these questions, using at least one Academic Vocabulary word in your response. Definitions for these terms are listed on page 111.

Jerry's mother perceives her son as a growing boy and not a baby anymore. She needs to change her aspect on her son, which is seen throughout the story.

Assessment Practice

DIRECTIONS Use "Through the Tunnel" to answer questions 1–6 below.

1 Which word *best* describes Jerry's journey through the tunnel?
- (A) interesting
- (B) relaxing
- (C) boring
- (D) frightening

2 What happens between Jerry and the older boys?
- (A) They show him how to swim through the tunnel.
- (B) They ignore him.
- (C) They are friendly at first, but then ignore him.
- (D) They make fun of him.

3 The tunnel is a bigger challenge than Jerry thought it would be because it is —
- (A) too narrow for him to fit through
- (B) deeper than he realized
- (C) lit in only one section
- (D) longer than he expected it to be

4 Which word *best* describes Jerry's character?
- (A) scared
- (B) shy
- (C) mature
- (D) determined

5 The sharp rocks and seaweed in the tunnel may symbolize —
- (A) the trials of life
- (B) slimy, disgusting plant life
- (C) his mother's hold on Jerry
- (D) the other boys

6 Which sentence *best* expresses the symbolic meaning of the story?
- (A) Children have to rebel against their parents to grow up.
- (B) Mothers and sons will never understand each other.
- (C) The journey to adulthood can be dangerous and frightening.
- (D) Life is nasty, brutish, and short.

The Cask of Amontillado
Short Story by **Edgar Allan Poe**

Is **REVENGE** ever justified?

Montresor, the narrator of "The Cask of Amontillado" wants revenge for a wrong done to him. Do acts of revenge ever resolve conflicts or do they just lead to more conflict?

PRESENT An act of revenge often causes a chain reaction. With a group, think of one act of revenge and chart out the possible chain of effects. Share your chain of events with the rest of the class.

Text Analysis: Mood

"The Cask of Amontillado" is a terrifying story about a man who plots a shocking act of revenge. From the beginning, the narrator's talk of injuries, insults, and revenge sets up a sinister feeling. As you read pay attention to the following:

- Notice the details of the **setting,** the time and place in which the story is set, that reveal information about the characters' lives and beliefs.

- Pay attention to Poe's use of **imagery**—descriptive words and phrases that create sensory experiences for the reader.

- Setting and imagery create the **mood,** or atmosphere of the story. A story's mood can affect the reader's emotional reaction.

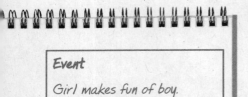

Event

Girl makes fun of boy.

↓

Act of Revenge

Boy spills ink on her uniform.

↓

Effects

_____

_____

_____

SIGHT: "Flashes of lightning illuminated the **ink-black sky.**"

TOUCH: "Another cobweb stuck to her **cold, clammy skin.**"

TASTE: "She could not get the **metallic taste of fear** out of her mouth."

SOUND: "Her heart thumped wildly when she heard an **ominous scratching on the door.**"

SMELL: "The **foul smell of dead mice** hung in the air."

Reading Skill: Paraphrase

Part of the challenge of reading Poe is getting through his long, complex sentences. To make sure you understand the events in this story, try **paraphrasing**—restating the information you've read in your own words. A paraphrase contains all the details of the original text but is written in simpler language. Here is an example:

Text	Paraphrase
"It must be understood, that neither by word nor deed had I given Fortunato cause to doubt my good-will." (lines 11–12)	*You must understand that I said and did nothing to make Fortunato mistrust me.*

As you read this story, you will be prompted to paraphrase some difficult passages.

Vocabulary in Context

Note: Words are listed in the order in which they appear in the story.

preclude (prĭ-klōōd′) *v.* to make impossible, especially by taking action in advance
*To preclude **pain,** she took an aspirin before her appointment.*

impunity (ĭm-pyōō′nĭ-tē) *n.* freedom from penalty or harm
*He thinks he can do what he wants because he has **impunity.***

immolation (ĭm′ə-lā′shən) *n.* death or destruction
*His thirst for revenge would only be satisfied by his enemy's complete **immolation.***

abscond (ăb-skŏnd′) *v.* to go away suddenly and secretly
*She **absconded** with the evidence so as not to implicate herself in the crime.*

repose (rĭ-pōz′) *v.* to lie dead or at rest
*Many buried bodies **repose** in the underground vaults.*

termination (tûr′mə-nā′shən) *n.* an end, limit, or edge
*We were coming to the **termination** of the tunnel.*

subside (səb-sīd′) *v.* to decrease in amount or intensity; settle down
*I waited for the temperature to **subside** before I stepped into the bath.*

aperture (ăp′ər-chər) *n.* an opening, such as a hole or a gap
*The **aperture** was so small he could not fit his entire hand inside.*

SET A PURPOSE
FOR READING
Read this story to find out
how a mysterious narrator
seeks revenge on his worst
enemy.

The Cask of Amontillado

Short Story by
EDGAR ALLAN POE

BACKGROUND Poe's story begins during carnival, which
is celebrated before the start of Lent, the season in which
Christians give up various pleasures. During carnival, people
often wore costumes and dance in the streets. The story's
setting soon shifts to the dark, cool burial vaults—called
catacombs—under the narrator's palace. Centuries ago,
Christians in Italy buried their dead in these underground
cemeteries where bodies were placed in carved recesses
along the walls of the burial chamber. The largest and most
famous catacombs are those of the early Christians in Rome.

The thousand injuries of Fortunato I had borne as I best
could; but when he ventured upon insult, I vowed revenge.
You, who so well know the nature of my soul, will not suppose,
however, that I gave utterance to a threat. *At length* I would
be avenged; this was a point definitively settled—but the very
definitiveness with which it was resolved, **precluded** the idea of
risk. I must not only punish, but punish with **impunity**. A wrong
is unredressed when retribution overtakes its redresser. It is equally
unredressed when the avenger fails to make himself felt as such to
10 him who has done the wrong.

preclude (prĭ-klōōd') *v.* to make
impossible, especially by taking
action in advance

impunity (ĭm-pyōō'nĭ-tē) *n.*
freedom from penalty or harm

It must be understood, that neither by word nor deed had I given Fortunato cause to doubt my good-will. I continued, as was my wont, to smile in his face, and he did not perceive that my smile *now* was at the thought of his **immolation**.

He had a weak point—this Fortunato—although in other regards he was a man to be respected and even feared. He prided himself on his connoisseurship[1] in wine. Few Italians have the true virtuoso spirit. For the most part their enthusiasm is adopted to suit the time and opportunity—to practice imposture upon the British and Austrian *millionaires*. In painting and gemmary[2] Fortunato, like his countrymen, was a quack—but in the matter of old wines he was sincere. In this respect I did not differ from him materially; I was skillful in the Italian vintages myself, and bought largely whenever I could.

It was about dusk, one evening during the supreme madness of the carnival[3] season, that I encountered my friend. He accosted me with excessive warmth, for he had been drinking much. The man wore motley.[4] He had on a tight-fitting parti-striped dress, and his head was surmounted by the conical cap and bells. I was so pleased to see him, that I thought I should never have done wringing his hand. **Ⓐ**

I said to him: "My dear Fortunato, you are luckily met. How remarkably well you are looking to-day! But I have received a pipe of what passes for Amontillado,[5] and I have my doubts."

"How?" said he. "Amontillado? A pipe? Impossible! And in the middle of the carnival!"

"I have my doubts," I replied; "and I was silly enough to pay the full Amontillado price without consulting you in the matter. You were not to be found, and I was fearful of losing a bargain."

"Amontillado!"

"I have my doubts."

immolation (ĭm′ə-lā′shən) *n.* death or destruction

Ⓐ MOOD
Circle the words in lines 25–31 that help set the mood, or atmosphere in the story.

1. **connoisseurship** (kŏn′ə-sûr′shĭp): expertise or authority, especially in the fine arts or in matters of taste.
2. **gemmary** (jĕm′ə-rē): knowledge of precious gems.
3. **carnival**: a festival before the fasting period of Lent, characterized by fanciful costumes, masquerades, and feasts.
4. **motley**: the costume of a court jester.
5. **a pipe . . . Amontillado** (ə-mŏn′tl-ä′dō): a barrel of a wine that is supposed to be a type of pale, dry sherry, named for a town in southern Spain.

B MOOD

Reread lines 32–58. How does Poe build a suspenseful mood in this conversation between the narrator and Fortunato? What does the narrator want Fortunato to do?

_____

_____

_____

_____

_____

_____

_____

_____

_____

abscond (ăb-skŏnd') v. to go away suddenly and secretly

Why is it convenient that the attendants have **abscond**ed to celebrate carnival?

_____

_____

_____

_____

_____

_____

_____

_____

_____

"Amontillado!"

"And I must satisfy them."

"Amontillado!"

"As you are engaged, I am on my way to Luchesi.[6] If anyone has a critical turn, it is he. He will tell me—"

"Luchesi cannot tell Amontillado from Sherry."

"And yet some fools will have it that his taste is a match for your own."

50   "Come, let us go."

"Whither?"

"To your vaults."

"My friend, no; I will not impose upon your good nature. I perceive you have an engagement. Luchesi—"

"I have no engagement;—come."

"My friend, no. It is not the engagement, but the severe cold with which I perceive you are afflicted. The vaults are insufferably damp. They are encrusted with niter."[7] **B**

"Let us go, nevertheless. The cold is merely nothing.

60 Amontillado! You have been imposed upon. And as for Luchesi, he cannot distinguish Sherry from Amontillado."

Thus speaking, Fortunato possessed himself of my arm. Putting on a mask of black silk, and drawing a *roquelaure*[8] closely about my person, I suffered him to hurry me to my palazzo.[9]

There were no attendants at home; they had **absconded** to make merry in honor of the time. I had told them that I should not return until the morning, and had given them explicit orders not to stir from the house. These orders were sufficient, I well knew, to insure their immediate disappearance, one and all, as

70 soon as my back was turned.

I took from their sconces two flambeaux,[10] and giving one to Fortunato, bowed him through several suites of rooms to the archway that led into the vaults. I passed down a long and

---

6. **Luchesi** (lōō-kā′sē).
7. **niter:** a white, gray, or colorless mineral, consisting of potassium nitrate.
8. *roquelaure* (rôk-lōr′) *French:* a man's knee-length cloak, popular during the 18th century.
9. **palazzo** (pə-lät′sō): a palace or mansion.
10. **from their sconces two flambeaux** (flăm′bōz′): from their wall brackets two lighted torches.

winding staircase, requesting him to be cautious as he followed. We came at length to the foot of the descent and stood together on the damp ground of the catacombs of the Montresors.

The gait of my friend was unsteady, and the bells upon his cap jingled as he strode.

"The pipe?" said he.

80 "It is farther on," said I; "but observe the white web-work which gleams from these cavern walls."

He turned toward me, and looked into my eyes with two filmy orbs that distilled the rheum of intoxication.[11]

"Niter?" he asked, at length.

"Niter," I replied. "How long have you had that cough?"

"Ugh! ugh! ugh!—ugh! ugh! ugh!—ugh! ugh! ugh!—ugh! ugh! ugh!—ugh! ugh! ugh!" **PAUSE & REFLECT**

My poor friend found it impossible to reply for many minutes.

"It is nothing," he said, at last.

90 "Come," I said, with decision, "we will go back; your health is precious. You are rich, respected, admired, beloved; you are happy, as once I was. You are a man to be missed. For me it is no matter. We will go back; you will be ill, and I cannot be responsible. Besides, there is Luchesi—"

"Enough," he said; "the cough is a mere nothing; it will not kill me. I shall not die of a cough."

"True—true," I replied; "and, indeed, I had no intention of alarming you unnecessarily; but you should use all proper caution. A draft of this Medoc[12] will defend us from the damps."

100 Here I knocked off the neck of a bottle that I drew from a long row of its fellows that lay upon the mold. **C**

"Drink," I said, presenting him the wine.

He raised it to his lips with a leer. He paused and nodded to me familiarly, while his bells jingled.

"I drink," he said, "to the buried that <u>repose</u> around us."

---

11. **filmy . . . intoxication:** eyes clouded and glazed over from drunkenness.

12. **Medoc** (mā-dôk'): a red wine from the Bordeaux region of France.

PAUSE & REFLECT

The narrator refers to Fortunato as "my poor friend." What clues suggest that the narrator means the opposite of what he says?

_____

_____

_____

_____

_____

_____

_____

C MOOD

Poe provides details in lines 82–101 to enhance the mood of the story. Where does the narrator lead Fortunato? Circle the words that show Fortunato's condition. Why is his "gait . . . unsteady"?

_____

_____

_____

_____

repose (rĭ-pōz') v. to lie dead or at rest

"And I to your long life."

He again took my arm, and we proceeded.

"These vaults," he said, "are extensive."

"The Montresors," I replied, "were a great and numerous
110 family."

"I forget your arms."

"A huge human foot d'or,[13] in a field azure; the foot crushes
a serpent rampant whose fangs are imbedded in the heel."

"And the motto?"

"Nemo me impune lacessit."[14]

"Good!" he said.

The wine sparkled in his eyes and the bells jingled. My own
fancy grew warm with the Medoc. We had passed through walls
of piled bones, with casks and puncheons[15] intermingling, into the
120 inmost recesses of the catacombs. I paused again, and this time
I made bold to seize Fortunato by an arm above the elbow.

"The niter!" I said; "see, it increases. It hangs like moss upon
the vaults. We are below the river's bed. The drops of moisture
trickle among the bones. Come, we will go back ere it is too late.
Your cough—" **D**

"It is nothing," he said; "let us go on. But first, another draft
of the Medoc."

I broke and reached him a flagon of De Grâve.[16] He
emptied it at a breath. His eyes flashed with a fierce light.
130 He laughed and threw the bottle upward with a gesticulation
I did not understand.

I looked at him in surprise. He repeated the movement—a
grotesque one.

"You do not comprehend?" he said.

"Not I," I replied.

"Then you are not of the brotherhood."

D MOOD
Underline the sensory details
and imagery in lines 117–125 that
help you visualize the setting.
What mood do they create?

_____

_____

_____

_____

_____

_____

_____

_____

_____

_____

---

13. **d'or** (dôr) *French:* colored gold. (Montresor is describing his coat of arms, the
    distinctive emblem of his family.)
14. *Nemo me impune lacessit* (nä′mō mā ĭm-pōō′nĕ lä-kĕs′ĭt) *Latin:* No one
    injures me with impunity.
15. **casks and puncheons:** large storage containers for wine.
16. **De Grâve** (də gräv′): a red wine from the Bordeaux region of France.

"How?"

"You are not of the masons."[17]

"Yes, yes," I said; "yes, yes."

"You? Impossible! A mason?"

"A mason," I replied.

"A sign," he said.

"It is this," I answered, producing a trowel[18] from beneath the folds of my *roquelaure*. PAUSE & REFLECT

"You jest," he exclaimed, recoiling a few paces. "But let us proceed to the Amontillado."

"Be it so," I said, replacing the tool beneath the cloak, and again offering him my arm. He leaned upon it heavily. We continued our route in search of the Amontillado. We passed through a range of low arches, descended, passed on, and descending again, arrived at a deep crypt, in which the foulness of the air caused our flambeaux rather to glow than flame.

At the most remote end of the crypt there appeared another less spacious. Its walls had been lined with human remains, piled to the vault overhead, in the fashion of the great catacombs of Paris. Three sides of this interior crypt were still ornamented in this manner. From the fourth the bones had been thrown down, and lay promiscuously upon the earth, forming at one point a mound of some size. Within the wall thus exposed by the displacing of the bones, we perceived a still interior recess, in depth about four feet, in width three, in height six or seven. It seemed to have been constructed for no especial use within itself, but formed merely the interval between two of the colossal supports of the roof of the catacombs, and was backed by one of their circumscribing walls of solid granite. E

---

17. **of the masons:** a Freemason, a member of a social organization with secret rituals and signs.

18. **producing a trowel:** Montresor is playing on another meaning of *mason*— "one who builds with stone or brick."

PAUSE & REFLECT

Why might Montresor be carrying a trowel, or shovel? What guess can you about his plans?

_____

_____

_____

_____

_____

_____

_____

_____

_____

_____

_____

E MOOD

Circle the sensory details in lines 147–165 that add to the mood of the story. To which senses do they appeal? How would you describe the mood here?

_____

_____

_____

_____

_____

termination (tûr′mə-nā′shən) *n.*
an end, limit, or edge

Ⓕ PARAPHRASE
What has happened in lines
171–181? Complete the
paraphrase started below.

"He is an idiot," my friend said

as he walked forward. I was

right behind him. Suddenly he

was at the end of the hall,

stopped by a wall of rock and

looking stupid and confused.

_____

_____

_____

_____

_____

_____

_____

_____

_____

_____

_____

_____

_____

It was in vain that Fortunato, uplifting his dull torch, endeavored to pry into the depth of the recess. Its **termination** the feeble light did not enable us to see.

"Proceed," I said; "herein is the Amontillado. As for
170 Luchesi—"

"He is an ignoramus," interrupted my friend, as he stepped unsteadily forward, while I followed immediately at his heels. In an instant he had reached the extremity of the niche, and finding his progress arrested by the rock, stood stupidly bewildered. A moment more and I had fettered him to the granite. In its surface were two iron staples, distant from each other about two feet, horizontally. From one of these depended a short chain, from the other a padlock. Throwing the links about his waist, it was but the work of a few seconds to secure it. He
180 was too much astounded to resist. Withdrawing the key I stepped back from the recess. Ⓕ

"Pass your hand," I said, "over the wall; you cannot help feeling the niter. Indeed it is *very* damp. Once more let me *implore* you to return. No? Then I must positively leave you. But I must first render you all the little attentions in my power."

"The Amontillado!" ejaculated my friend, not yet recovered from his astonishment.

"True," I replied; "the Amontillado."

As I said these words I busied myself among the pile of bones
190 of which I have before spoken. Throwing them aside, I soon uncovered a quantity of building stone and mortar. With these materials and with the aid of my trowel, I began vigorously to wall up the entrance of the niche.

I had scarcely laid the first tier of the masonry when I discovered that the intoxication of Fortunato had in a great measure worn off. The earliest indication I had of this was a low moaning cry from the depth of the recess. It was not the cry of a drunken man. There was then a long and obstinate silence. I laid the second tier, and the third, and the fourth; and then I heard
200 the furious vibrations of the chain. The noise lasted for several

minutes, during which, that I might hearken to it with the more satisfaction, I ceased my labors and sat down upon the bones. When at last the clanking **subsided**, I resumed the trowel, and finished without interruption the fifth, the sixth, and the seventh tier. The wall was now nearly upon a level with my breast. I again paused, and holding the flambeaux over the mason-work, threw a few feeble rays upon the figure within. **G**

A succession of loud and shrill screams, bursting suddenly from the throat of the chained form, seemed to thrust me violently

210 back. For a brief moment I hesitated—I trembled. Unsheathing my rapier,[19] I began to grope with it about the recess; but the thought of an instant reassured me. I placed my hand upon the solid fabric of the catacombs, and felt satisfied. I reapproached the wall. I replied to the yells of him who clamored. I re-echoed— I aided—I surpassed them in volume and in strength. I did this, and the clamorer grew still. **H**

It was now midnight, and my task was drawing to a close. I had completed the eighth, the ninth, and the tenth tier. I had finished a portion of the last and the eleventh; there remained

220 but a single stone to be fitted and plastered in. I struggled with its weight; I placed it partially in its destined position. But now there came from out the niche a low laugh that erected the hairs upon my head. It was succeeded by a sad voice, which I had difficulty in recognizing as that of the noble Fortunato. The voice said—

"Ha! ha! ha!—he! he!—a very good joke indeed—an excellent jest. We will have many a rich laugh about it at the palazzo—he! he! he! —over our wine—he! he! he!"

"The Amontillado!" I said.

"He! he! he!—he! he! he!—yes, the Amontillado. But is it not

230 getting late? Will not they be awaiting us at the palazzo, the Lady Fortunato and the rest? Let us be gone."

"Yes," I said, "let us be gone."

"For the love of God, Montresor!"

"Yes," I said, "for the love of God!" **I**

---

19. **rapier** (rā′pē-ər): a long, slender sword.

subside (səb-sīd′) *v.* to decrease in amount or intensity; settle down

G MOOD
Reread lines 194–207. Circle the details that make the description especially horrifying.

H PARAPHRASE
Restate what happens in lines 208–216. How does the narrator feel at this point in the story?

_____

_____

_____

_____

_____

_____

_____

_____

_____

I MOOD
Underline the **details** and **images** in lines 217–234 that create the mood of this scene. How would you describe the mood here?

_____

aperture (ăp′ər-chər) *n.* an opening, such as a hole or a gap

But to these words I hearkened in vain for a reply. I grew impatient. I called aloud,

"Fortunato!"

No answer. I called again,

"Fortunato!"

240   No answer still. I thrust a torch through the remaining **aperture** and let it fall within. There came forth in return only a jingling of the bells. My heart grew sick—on account of the dampness of the catacombs. I hastened to make an end of my labor. I forced the last stone into its position; I plastered it up. Against the new masonry I re-erected the old rampart of bones. For the half of a century no mortal has disturbed them. *In pace requiescat!*[20]

---

20. *In pace requiescat* (ĭn pä′kĕ rĕ-kwē-ĕs′kät) *Latin:* May he rest in peace.

Text Analysis: Mood

Descriptive words, the setting, sensory images, as well as the sound and rhythm of the language the writer uses contribute to the mood, or atmosphere, of a work. On the chart below, list examples of passages that help create the mood of the story. Identify the kind of mood that is created and explain how the mood is developed.

Passage	Mood that is Created	How Mood is Developed
"We are below the river's bed. The drops of moisture trickle among the bones." (lines 123–124)	gloomy, creepy, chilly, dark, and damp	descriptive words, setting

What is the overall mood, or atmosphere, of this story? What do you think contributes most to the mood—the setting, the sound and rhythm of the language, or the descriptions of Montresor's thoughts and feelings? Explain.

_____

_____

_____

_____

_____

_____

Reading Skills: Paraphrase

Reread the following passage from the beginning of "The Cask of Amontillado" and then paraphrase it in the space below.

TEXT	"*At length* I would be avenged; this was a point definitively settled—but the very definitiveness with which it was resolved, precluded the idea of risk. I must not only punish, but punish with impunity. A wrong is unredressed when retribution overtakes its redreseer. It is equally unredressed when the avenger fails to make himself felt as such to him who has done the wrong."

↓

MY PARAPHRASE	

Is **REVENGE** ever justified?

What do you think is the right way to address a wrong?

_____

Vocabulary Practice

Circle the letter of the situation that most closely relates to each vocabulary word.

1. aperture **(a)** a crack in a building's foundation **(b)** a large stack of lumber

2. subside **(a)** two cars racing **(b)** a heavy wind lessening in force

3. impunity **(a)** getting away with a crime **(b)** a tiny hole in a shirt

4. termination **(a)** someone starting a new job **(b)** someone getting fired

5. repose **(a)** lying on an empty beach **(b)** carrying a heavy load of books

6. abscond **(a)** making a public announcement **(b)** sneaking out of a meeting

7. immolation **(a)** deaths in a train accident **(b)** cartons of spoiled food

8. preclude **(a)** getting a flu shot **(b)** planting spring bulbs in autumn

Academic Vocabulary in Speaking

aspect	circumstance	contribute	distinct	perceive

An **aspect** is a part or feature of something. What **aspects** of Fortunato's character allow him to be fooled by Montresor? Identify two aspects and discuss how they affect the story's outcome. Use at least one Academic Vocabulary word in your discussion. Definitions for these terms are listed on page 111.

_____

_____

Assessment Practice

DIRECTIONS Use "The Cask of Amontillado" to answer questions 1–6 below.

1 Montresor, the narrator, wants revenge because —

  (A) Fortunato stole his amontillado

  (B) Fortunato insulted him

  (C) Fortunato insulted Luchesi

  (D) Luchesi misjudged Fortunato

2 Which of the following does Montresor *not* do to ensure the success of his plan?

  (A) He pretends to be Fortunato's friend.

  (B) He gives Fortunato wine to drink.

  (C) He carries out his plan when no attendants are at home.

  (D) He pushes Fortunato down to the catacombs.

3 Which of these lines from the story is an example of imagery?

  (A) "My poor friend found it impossible to reply for many minutes."

  (B) "We continued our route in search of the Amontillado."

  (C) "The foulness of the air caused our flambeaux rather to glow than flame."

  (D) "He was much too astounded to resist."

4 Which of the following is the *best* paraphrase of the following quotation:

  I was so pleased to see him, that I thought I should never have done wringing his hand.

  (A) I shook his hand for a very long time because I was so happy to see him.

  (B) I did not want to shake his hand even though I was happy to see him.

  (C) I was surprised to see that his hand would not stop shaking.

  (D) I kept shaking his hand because he seemed excited to see me.

5 Which of the following is *not* a result of the carnival setting?

  (A) Fortunato has a bad cold.

  (B) Fortunato has been drinking.

  (C) Montresor's servants are not at home.

  (D) Montresor and Fortunato wear costumes.

6 Which of the following words does *not* describe the story's mood?

  (A) sinister

  (B) ominous

  (C) upbeat

  (D) gloomy

from A Walk in the Woods
Travel Narrative by Bill Bryson

Where do you find ADVENTURE?

Do you find adventure in physically risky activities, such as rock climbing and skateboarding, or in the unexpected surprises you encounter every day? In this selection, you'll read about the adventures of Bill Bryson, a well-known travel writer whose hike along the Appalachian Trail takes some unexpected turns.

QUICKWRITE If you could create an adventure of your own, what would it be? Write a few sentences about your ideal adventure and why it's exciting to you.

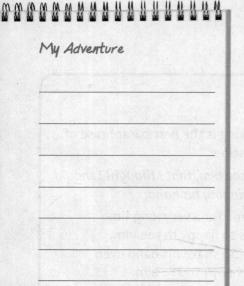

My Adventure

Text Analysis: Setting and Mood

Setting can play an important role in creating **mood**—the emotional effect or feeling the text creates. Often a writer's description of setting does more than just tell the location, weather, time of day, time of year, or historical period in which a work takes place. The writer's use of descriptive language in describing the setting helps to set the mood of the selection. Mood is often described by adjectives such as *upbeat*, *gloomy*, and *serious*.

In this selection, Bill Bryson describes the setting of the Appalachian trail by using **sensory language**—language that appeals to the senses. As you read, pay attention to the language Bryson uses to describe the setting and create a particular mood.

Description of Setting	Mood
"skies grew sullen and the air chillier" (lines 37–38)	tense and alarming

Reading Skill: Identify Author's Perspective

People often look at a subject from different perspectives, or viewpoints. For example, a person living in a warm climate may react negatively to a 40-degree day, while a person living in a cold climate may think 40 degrees is a comfortable temperature. An **author's perspective** is the combination of beliefs, values, and experiences that influence how a writer looks at situations and events. In order to figure out an author's perspective, pay attention to the following clues

- statements and opinions—personal ideas that cannot be proven true
- details and examples the writer chooses to include
- the writer's tone, or attitude (such as humorous or serious)

As you read Bill Bryson's account of hiking the Appalachian Trail, try to figure out his perspective using the prompts provided in the text.

Vocabulary in Context

Note: Words are listed in the order in which they appear in the narrative.

singularity (sĭng′gyə-lăr′ĭ-tē) *n.* something peculiar or unique
That vase has amazing singularity—I've never seen anything like it before.

veneer (və-nîr′) *v.* to cover with a thin layer of material
The cold weather veneered the trail with slippery ice.

unnerving (ŭn-nûr′vĭng) *adj.* causing loss of courage
Climbing down the steep hill was unnerving.

abysmal (ə-bĭz′məl) *adj.* very bad
The rain was too abysmal for us to safely continue our hike.

buffeted (bŭf′ĭ-tĭd) *adj.* knocked about or struck
During the long hike we were buffeted by heavy wind that made it difficult to reach the campground.

daunted (dôn′tĭd) *adj.* discouraged
The hikers, daunted by the storm, decided to head home.

reconnoiter (rē′kə-noi′tər) *v.* to make a preliminary inspection
The guide walked ahead to reconnoiter the trail and see if it was safe for us to continue.

superannuated (sōō′pər-ăn′yōō-ā′tĭd) *adj.* obsolete with age
The superannuated bridge was too worn for us to travel across it safely.

SET A PURPOSE FOR READING

Read this narrative to find out how a walk in the woods can also be an exciting adventure.

A Walk in the Woods

Travel Narrative by

BILL BRYSON

BACKGROUND The Appalachian Trail is a footpath that spans more than 2,100 miles from Maine to Georgia, passing through 14 states. The idea for the trail began in 1921 with a proposal by conservationist Benton MacKaye. The trail was completed on August 14, 1937.

Distance changes utterly when you take the world on foot. A mile becomes a long way, two miles literally considerable, ten miles whopping, fifty miles at the very limits of conception. The world, you realize, is enormous in a way that only you and a small community of fellow hikers know. Planetary scale is your little secret.

Life takes on a neat simplicity, too. Time ceases to have any meaning. When it is dark, you go to bed, and when it is light again you get up, and everything in between is just in between.

10 It's quite wonderful, really. Ⓐ

You have no engagements, commitments, obligations, or duties; no special ambitions and only the smallest, least complicated of wants; you exist in a tranquil tedium,[1] serenely beyond the reach of exasperation, "far removed from the seats of strife," as the early explorer and botanist William Bartram[2] put it. All that is required of you is a willingness to trudge.

Ⓐ AUTHOR'S PERSPECTIVE
Review lines 1–10. According to Bryson, what makes hiking "wonderful"?

_____

_____

_____

_____

---

1. **tranquil tedium:** calm and peaceful boredom.
2. **William Bartram** (bär′trəm): one of the first explorers of the Appalachian Mountains, who wrote about his experiences in a book published in 1791.

There is no point in hurrying because you are not actually going anywhere. However far or long you plod, you are always in the same place: in the woods. It's where you were yesterday, where
20 you will be tomorrow. The woods is one boundless **singularity**. Every bend in the path presents a prospect indistinguishable from every other, every glimpse into the trees the same tangled mass. For all you know, your route could describe a very large, pointless circle. In a way, it would hardly matter. **B**

At times, you become almost certain that you slabbed this hillside three days ago, crossed this stream yesterday, clambered over this fallen tree at least twice today already. But most of the time you don't think. No point. Instead, you exist in a kind of mobile Zen mode,[3] your brain like a balloon tethered with string,
30 accompanying but not actually part of the body below. Walking for hours and miles becomes as automatic, as unremarkable, as breathing. At the end of the day you don't think, "Hey, I did sixteen miles today," any more than you think, "Hey, I took eight-thousand breaths today." It's just what you do.

And so we walked, hour upon hour, over rollercoaster hills, along knife-edge ridges and over grassy balds, through depthless ranks of oak, ash, chinkapin, and pine. The skies grew sullen and the air chillier, but it wasn't until the third day that the snow came. It began in the morning as thinly scattered flecks, hardly
40 noticeable. But then the wind rose, then rose again, until it was blowing with an end-of-the-world fury that seemed to have even the trees in a panic, and with it came snow, great flying masses of it. By midday we found ourselves plodding into a stinging, cold, hard-blowing storm. Soon after, we came to a narrow ledge of path along a wall of rock. **PAUSE & REFLECT**

Even in ideal circumstances this path would have required delicacy and care. It was like a window ledge on a skyscraper, no more than fourteen or sixteen inches wide, and crumbling in places, with a sharp drop on one side of perhaps eighty feet, and
50 long, looming stretches of vertical granite on the other. Once or twice I nudged foot-sized rocks over the side and watched with

---

3. **mobile Zen mode:** walking, perfectly in tune with one's environment to the point of feeling at one with the surroundings.

singularity (sĭng′gyə-lăr′ĭ-tē) *n.* something peculiar or unique

B SETTING AND MOOD
Reread lines 17–24. Circle the descriptions in the passage that help create the mood. How would you describe this mood? Note this information in the following chart.

Description of Setting

↓

Mood

PAUSE & REFLECT
Reread lines 35–45. What changes in setting have occurred?

_____

_____

_____

_____

veneer (və-nîr′) *v.* to cover with a thin layer of material

C SETTING AND MOOD
Circle two examples of sensory language in lines 46–68. What mood does that language convey? Add this information to your chart.

_____

_____

unnerving (ŭn-nûr′vĭng) *adj.* causing loss of courage.

What specific conditions are **unnerving** for Bryson and Katz?

_____

_____

_____

_____

_____

_____

_____

_____

faint horror as they crashed and tumbled to improbably remote resting places. The trail was cobbled with rocks and threaded with wandering tree roots against which we constantly stubbed and stumbled, and **veneered** everywhere with polished ice under a thin layer of powdery snow. At exasperatingly frequent intervals, the path was broken by steep, thickly bouldered streams, frozen solid and ribbed with blue ice, which could only be negotiated in a crablike crouch. And all the time, as we crept along on this
60 absurdly narrow, dangerous perch, we were half-blinded by flying snow and jostled by gusts of wind, which roared through the dancing trees and shook us by our packs. This wasn't a blizzard; it was a tempest. We proceeded with painstaking deliberativeness, placing each foot solidly before lifting the one behind. Even so, twice Katz made horrified, heartfelt, comic-book noises ("AIEEEEE!" and "EEEARGH!") as his footing went, and I turned to find him hugging a tree, feet skating, his expression bug-eyed and fearful. **C**

It was deeply **unnerving**. It took us over two hours to cover
70 six-tenths of a mile of trail. By the time we reached solid ground at a place called Bearpen Gap, the snow was four or five inches deep and accumulating fast. The whole world was white, filled with dime-sized snowflakes that fell at a slant before being caught by the wind and hurled in a variety of directions. We couldn't see more than fifteen or twenty feet ahead, often not even that.

The trail crossed a logging road, then led straight up Albert Mountain,[4] a bouldered summit 5,250 feet above sea level, where the winds were so wild and angry that they hit the mountain with an actual wallop sound and forced us to shout to hear each other.
80 We started up and hastily retreated. Hiking packs leave you with no recognizable center of gravity at the best of times; here we were literally being blown over. Confounded, we stood at the bottom of the summit and looked at each other. This was really quite grave. We were caught between a mountain we couldn't climb and a ledge we had no intention of trying to renegotiate. Our only apparent option was to pitch our tents—if we could in this

---

4. **Albert Mountain:** a peak in western North Carolina.

wind—crawl in, and hope for the best. I don't wish to reach for melodrama, but people have died in less trying circumstances. **D**

90 I dumped my pack and searched through it for my trail map. Appalachian Trail maps are so monumentally useless that I had long since given up using them. They vary somewhat, but most are on an <u>abysmal</u> scale of 1:100,000, which ludicrously compresses every kilometer of real world into a mere centimeter of map. Imagine a square kilometer of physical landscape and all that it might contain—logging roads, streams, a mountaintop or two, perhaps a fire tower, a knob or grassy bald, the wandering AT,[5] and maybe a pair of important side trails—and imagine trying to convey all that information on an area the size of the nail on your little finger. That's an AT map.

100 Actually, it's far, far worse than that because AT maps—for reasons that bewilder me beyond speculation—provide less detail than even their meager scale allows. For any ten miles of trail, the maps will name and identify perhaps only three of the dozen or more peaks you cross. Valleys, lakes, gaps, creeks, and other important, possibly vital, topographical features are routinely left unnamed. Forest Service roads are often not included, and, if included, they're inconsistently identified. Even side trails are frequently left off. There are no coordinates, no way of directing rescuers to a particular place, no pointers to towns just off the

110 map's edge. These are, in short, seriously inadequate maps. **E**

In normal circumstances, this is merely irksome. Now, in a blizzard, it seemed closer to negligence. I dragged the map from the pack and fought the wind to look at it. It showed the trail as a red line. Nearby was a heavy, wandering black line, which I presumed to be the Forest Service road we stood beside, though there was no actual telling. According to the map, the road (if a road is what it was) started in the middle of nowhere and finished half a dozen miles later equally in the middle of nowhere, which clearly made no sense—indeed, wasn't even possible. (You can't

120 start a road in the middle of forest; earth-moving equipment can't spontaneously appear among the trees. Anyway, even if you could

---

5. **AT:** Appalachian Trail.

D AUTHOR'S PERSPECTIVE
What does Bryson's statement that "people have died in less trying circumstances" (line 88) tell you about his perspective on the situation?

_____

_____

_____

_____

abysmal (ə-bĭz′məl) *adj.*
very bad

E AUTHOR'S PERSPECTIVE
How would you describe Bryson's tone in lines 89–110? What is his opinion of AT maps?

_____

_____

_____

_____

_____

_____

build a road that didn't go anywhere, why would you?) There was, obviously, something deeply and infuriatingly wrong with this map.

"Cost me eleven bucks," I said to Katz a little wildly, shaking the map at him and then crumpling it into an approximately flat shape and jabbing it into my pocket.

"So what're we going to do?" he said.

I sighed, unsure, then yanked the map out and examined it
130 again. I looked from it to the logging road and back. "Well, it looks as if this logging road curves around the mountain and comes back near the trail on the other side. If it does and we can find it, then there's a shelter we can get to. If we can't get through, I don't know, I guess we take the road back downhill to lower ground and see if we can find a place out of the wind to camp." I shrugged a little helplessly. "I don't know. What do you think?"

He issued a single bitter guffaw and returned to the hysterical snow. I hoisted my pack and followed.

We plodded up the road, bent steeply, **buffeted** by winds.
140 Where it settled, the snow was wet and heavy and getting deep enough that soon it would be impassable and we would have to take shelter whether we wanted to or not. There was no place to pitch a tent here, I noted uneasily—only steep, wooded slope going up on one side and down on the other. For quite a distance—far longer than it seemed it ought to—the road stayed straight. Even if, farther on, it did curve back near the trail, there was no certainty (or even perhaps much likelihood) that we would spot it. In these trees and this snow you could be ten feet from the trail and not see it. It would be madness to leave the logging road and
150 try to find it. Then again, it was probably madness to be following a logging road to higher ground in a blizzard. **PAUSE & REFLECT**

Gradually, and then more decidedly, the trail began to hook around behind the mountain. After about an hour of dragging sluggishly through ever-deepening snow, we came to a high, windy, level spot where the trail—or at least *a* trail—emerged down the back of Albert Mountain and continued on into level

buffeted (bŭf′ĭ-tĭd) *adj.* knocked about or struck.

PAUSE & REFLECT
What would you do in this situation?

_____

_____

_____

_____

_____

_____

_____

_____

woods. I regarded my map with bewildered exasperation. It didn't give any indication of this whatever, but Katz spotted a white blaze twenty yards into the woods, and we whooped with joy. 160 We had refound the AT. A shelter was only a few hundred yards farther on. It looked as if we would live to hike another day.

The snow was nearly knee deep now, and we were tired, but we all but pranced through it, and Katz whooped again when we reached an arrowed sign on a low limb that pointed down a side trail and said "BIG SPRING SHELTER." The shelter, a simple wooden affair, open on one side, stood in a snowy glade—a little winter wonderland—150 yards or so off the main trail. Even from a distance we could see that the open side faced into the wind and that the drifting snow was nearly up to the lip 170 of the sleeping platform. Still, if nothing else, it offered at least a sense of refuge. **F**

We crossed the clearing, heaved our packs onto the platform, and in the same instant discovered that there were two people there already—a man and a boy of about fourteen. They were Jim and Heath, father and son, from Chattanooga,[6] and they were cheerful, friendly, and not remotely **daunted** by the weather. They had come hiking for the weekend, they told us (I hadn't even realized it was a weekend), and knew the weather was likely to be bad, though not perhaps quite this bad, and so were well prepared. 180 Jim had brought a big clear plastic sheet, of the sort decorators use to cover floors, and was trying to rig it across the open front of the shelter. Katz, uncharacteristically, leapt to his assistance. The plastic sheet didn't quite reach, but we found that with one of our groundcloths lashed alongside it we could cover the entire front. The wind walloped ferociously against the plastic and from time to time tore part of it loose, where it fluttered and snapped, with a retort like gunshot, until one of us leaped up and fought it back into place. The whole shelter was, in any case, incredibly leaky of air—the plank walls and floors were full of cracks through 190 which icy wind and occasional blasts of snow shot—but we were infinitely snugger than we would have been outside.

F SETTING AND MOOD
Bryson and Katz seem relieved to be nearing the shelter. Underline the descriptive words and phrases in lines 162–171 that convey this mood of relief. Add this information to your chart.

daunted (dôn′tĭd) *adj.* discouraged.

Compare Bryson and Katz to Jim and Heath. Would you say Bryson and Katz were more **daunted** by the weather than Jim and Heath? Explain.

_____

_____

_____

_____

_____

_____

_____

---

6. **Chattanooga** (chăt′ə-nōō′gə): a city in southeastern Tennessee.

So we made a little home of it for ourselves, spread out our sleeping pads and bags, put on all the extra clothes we could find, and fixed dinner from a reclining position. Darkness fell quickly and heavily, which made the wildness outside seem even more severe. Jim and Heath had some chocolate cake, which they shared with us (a treat beyond heaven), and then the four of us settled down to a long, cold night on hard wood, listening to a banshee[7] wind and the tossing of angry branches.

200   When I awoke, all was stillness—the sort of stillness that makes you sit up and take your bearings. The plastic sheet before me was peeled back a foot or so and weak light filled the space beyond. Snow was over the top of the platform and lying an inch deep over the foot of my sleeping bag. I shooed it off with a toss of my legs. Jim and Heath were already stirring to life. Katz slumbered heavily on, an arm flung over his forehead, his mouth a great open hole. It was not quite six.

     I decided to go out to **reconnoiter** and see how stranded we might be. I hesitated at the platform's edge, then jumped out into 210 the drift—it came up over my waist and made my eyes fly open where it slipped under my clothes and found bare skin—and pushed through it into the clearing, where it was slightly (but only slightly) shallower. Even in sheltered areas, under an umbrella of conifers, the snow was nearly knee deep and tedious to churn through. But everywhere it was stunning. Every tree wore a thick cloak of white, every stump and boulder a jaunty snowy cap, and there was that perfect, immense stillness that you get nowhere else but in a big woods after a heavy snowfall. Here and there clumps of snow fell from the branches, but otherwise there was no sound 220 or movement. I followed the side trail up and under heavily bowed limbs to where it rejoined the AT. The AT was a plumped blanket of snow, round and bluish, in a long, dim tunnel of overbent rhododendrons. It looked deep and hard going. I walked a few yards as a test. It was deep and hard going. **G**

     When I returned to the shelter, Katz was up, moving slowly and going through his morning groans, and Jim was studying his

---

reconnoiter (rē´kə-noi´tər) *v.* to make a preliminary inspection

G **SETTING AND MOOD**
Although Bryson knows he and the other hikers are in danger of being stranded, he is also appreciative of the beautiful setting. Underline the details in lines 208–224 that convey a mood of appreciation.

---

7. **banshee** (băn´shē): in Gaelic folklore, a female spirit who wails as a sign that death is coming.

maps, which were vastly better than mine. I crouched beside him and he made room to let me look with him. It was 6.1 miles to Wallace Gap and a paved road, old U.S. 64. A mile down the road

230 from there was Rainbow Springs Campground, a private campsite with showers and a store. I didn't know how hard it would be to walk seven miles through deep snow and had no confidence that the campground would be open this early in the year. Still, it was obvious this snow wasn't going to melt for days and we would have to make a move sometime; it might as well be now, when at least it was pretty and calm. Who knew when another storm might blow in and really strand us?

Jim had decided that he and Heath would accompany us for the first couple of hours, then turn off on a side trail called Long

240 Branch, which descended steeply through a ravine for 2.3 miles and emerged near a parking lot where they had left their car. He had hiked the Long Branch trail many times and knew what to expect. Even so, I didn't like the sound of it and asked him hesitantly if he thought it was a good idea to go off on a little-used side trail, into goodness knows what conditions, where no one would come across him and his son if they got in trouble. Katz, to my relief, agreed with me. "At least there's always other people on the AT," he said. "You don't know what might happen to you on a side trail." Jim considered the matter and said they would turn

250 back if it looked bad. ❽

Katz and I treated ourselves to two cups of coffee, for warmth, and Jim and Heath shared with us some of their oatmeal, which made Katz intensely happy. Then we all set off together. It was cold and hard going. The tunnels of boughed rhododendrons, which often ran on for great distances, were exceedingly pretty, but when our packs brushed against them they dumped volumes of snow onto our heads and down the backs of our necks. The three adults took it in turns to walk in front because the lead person always received the heaviest

260 dumping, as well as having all the hard work of dibbing holes in the snow.

❽ **AUTHOR'S PERSPECTIVE**
Circle the statements and details that convey Bryson's attitude toward Jim's plan. How would you describe Bryson's perspective of the situation?

_____

_____

_____

_____

_____

_____

_____

PAUSE & REFLECT

Irony occurs when a situation turns out to be the opposite of what you expect. What does Bryson mean by "the pathetic irony" of it being the first day of spring?

_____

_____

_____

_____

superannuated
(sōō′pər-ăn′yōō-ā′tĭd) *adj.*
obsolete with age

The Long Branch trail, when we reached it, descended steeply through bowed pines—too steeply, it seemed to me, to come back up if the trail proved impassable, and it looked as if it might. Katz and I urged Jim and Heath to reconsider, but Jim said it was all downhill and well-marked, and he was sure it would be all right. "Hey, you know what day it is?" said Jim suddenly and, seeing our blank faces, supplied the answer. "March twenty-first."

Our faces stayed blank.

270 "First day of spring," he said.

We smiled at the pathetic irony of it, shook hands all around, wished each other luck, and parted. **PAUSE & REFLECT**

Katz and I walked for three hours more, silently and slowly through the cold, white forest, taking it in turns to break snow. At about one o'clock we came at last to old 64, a lonesome, **superannuated** two-lane road through the mountains. It hadn't been cleared, and there were no tire tracks through it. It was starting to snow again, steadily, prettily. We set off down the road for the campground and had walked about a quarter of a mile

280 when from behind there was the crunching sound of a motorized vehicle proceeding cautiously through snow. We turned to see a big jeep-type car rolling up beside us. The driver's window hummed down. It was Jim and Heath. They had come to let us know they had made it, and to make sure we had likewise. "Thought you might like a lift to the campground," Jim said.

Text Analysis: Setting and Mood

As Bryson tells the story of his dangerous hike along the steep pathways near the Appalachian Trail, he uses sensory language to describe the quickly changing weather. How does the mood shift each time he writes about a change in the weather? Trace the shift in weather and mood from the beginning of the narrative to the end, noting examples of sensory language on the chart below.

Beginning	
Weather: The skies became "sullen and the air chillier" (lines 37–38)	Mood: Calm but becoming tense.

Middle	
Weather:	Mood:

End	
Weather:	Mood:

What elements of setting most strongly contribute to the mood of this selection? Consider the time of day, the season, the weather, and the natural setting.

_____

_____

_____

_____

_____

_____

Reading Skill: Identify Author's Perspective

At what points in the narrative was Bryson's perspective most clear? What clues helped you identify the writer's perspective in those sections? In the chart below, fill in an example for each type of clue and explain what each clue tells you about the author's perspective.

Clue	What It Reveals About Bryson
Statement/Opinion:	
Details/Examples:	
Writer's Tone/Attitude:	

In one or two sentences summarize Bryson's perspective about walking the Appalachian Trail. Explain how his perspective changes as the episode unfolds.

_____

_____

Where do you find ADVENTURE?

What types of activities or pursuits do you find adventurous?

_____

_____

Vocabulary Practice

Put an **S** next to the word pairs below that are synonyms (words with similar meanings). Put an **A** next to the word pairs that are antonyms (words with opposite meanings).

1. buffeted/battered _____

2. reconnoiter/inspect _____

3. daunted/inspired _____

4. abysmal/wonderful _____

5. veneer/uncover _____

6. superannuated/rejuvenated _____

7. unnerving/encouraging _____

8. singularity/commonality _____

Academic Vocabulary in Writing

aspect	circumstance	contribute	distinct	perceive

Jim and Heath, the father and son Bryson and Katz encounter on the trail, have a different attitude toward their **circumstances** than the writer does. Write a few sentences in which you identify Jim and Heath's attitude and explain what they **contributed** to the narrative. Use at least two Academic Vocabulary words in your response. Definitions for these terms are listed on page 111.

_____

_____

_____

_____

Assessment Practice

DIRECTIONS Use "A Walk in the Woods" to answer questions 1–6.

1 Bill Bryson and Stephen Katz have set out to —

- **A** see how long they can survive in the wilderness
- **B** vacation at Rainbow Springs Campground
- **C** rescue Jim and Heath from the storm
- **D** hike the Appalachian Trail

2 Bryson dislikes AT maps because —

- **A** they are difficult to fold
- **B** they don't offer detailed information
- **C** they never hold up in the rain or snow
- **D** they only show one route

3 Other than the storm, which of the following contributes to the suspense of the narrative?

- **A** Bryson's poor preparations
- **B** Meeting Jim and Heath
- **C** Finding the campground
- **D** Katz's poor attitude

4 In the end, the hikers survive the storm by —

- **A** calling for help
- **B** huddling together
- **C** following a logging route to shelter
- **D** sharing food and warm clothes

5 Which word best describes the mood when Bryson and Katz cross the narrow ledge in lines 46–68?

- **A** sorrowful
- **B** lighthearted
- **C** peaceful
- **D** tense

6 When Bryson and Katz reach the shelter the mood shifts from —

- **A** worrisome to relief
- **B** upbeat to gloomy
- **C** joyous to anxious
- **D** fearful to terror

Wilderness Letter

Background

In *A Walk in the Woods,* you read about some of the pleasures and pitfalls of hiking the Appalachian Trail. In the following letter from Wallace Stegner you will read one of many arguments that have been made in favor of preserving wilderness areas such as the Appalachian Trail.

Although not all of his stories are set in the West, Wallace Stegner is called the dean of Western writers. A passionate environmentalist, Stegner not only wrote about the importance of preserving the West, he fought for it. In 1960, Stegner wrote this letter, stating that wild places were in need of federal protection.

Standards Focus: Read Primary Sources

Primary sources are materials written by people who have witnessed the events portrayed first hand. Letters, speeches, interviews, and journal entries are all examples of primary sources. To get the most out of primary sources, consider

- the form and purpose of the text
- where and when it was written
- the intended audience
- the author's credibility (whether he or she is a reliable source of information)

To further analyze a primary source, summarize its main points. Then complete a chart like the one below to help you synthesize and connect the source with other information you have found. You will be prompted to answer some of these questions as you read the following letter.

Questions About Primary Source	My Answers
What is the form and purpose of this document?	
What, if anything, do I already know about the author and his times?	
What seems to be the relationship between the author and his audience?	
What does the document tell me about life at the time it was written?	

SET A PURPOSE FOR READING

Read this letter to learn about Wallace Stegner's argument for preserving wilderness.

Wilderness Letter

Wallace Stegner

Los Altos, Calif.
Dec. 3, 1960

David E. Pesonen
Wildland Research Center
Agricultural Experiment Station
243 Mulford Hall
University of California
Berkeley 4, Calif.

Dear Mr. Pesonen:

1   I believe that you are working on the wilderness portion of the Outdoor Recreation Resources Review Commission's report. If I may, I should like to urge some arguments for wilderness preservation that involve recreation, as it is ordinarily conceived, hardly at all. Hunting, fishing,

Ⓐ PRIMARY SOURCES
What does Stegner say is his purpose for writing? Add this information to your chart.

What is the form and purpose of this document?

↓

Ⓑ PRIMARY SOURCES
Reread lines 10–19. What does Stegner mean by the wilderness "idea"?

_____

_____

_____

_____

_____

_____

hiking, mountain-climbing, camping, photography, and the enjoyment of natural scenery will all, surely, figure in your report. So will the wilderness as a genetic reserve, a scientific yardstick by which we may measure the world in its natural
10 balance against the world in its man-made imbalance. What I want to speak for is not so much the wilderness uses, valuable as those are, but the wilderness <u>idea</u>, which is a resource in itself. Being an intangible and spiritual resource, it will seem mystical to the practical-minded—but then anything that cannot be moved by a bulldozer is likely to seem mystical to them. Ⓐ

I want to speak for the wilderness idea as something that has helped form our character and that has certainly shaped our history as a people. . . . Ⓑ
20 Something will have gone out of us as a people if we ever let the remaining wilderness be destroyed; if we permit the last virgin forests to be turned into comic books and plastic cigarette cases; if we drive the few remaining members of the wild species into zoos or to extinction; if we pollute the last clear air and dirty the last clean streams and push our paved roads through the last of the silence, so that never again will Americans be free in their own country from the noise, the exhausts, the stinks of human and automotive waste. And so that never again can we have the chance to see ourselves
30 single, separate, vertical and individual in the world, part of the environment of trees and rocks and soil, brother to the other animals, part of the natural world and competent to belong in it. Without any remaining wilderness we are committed wholly, without chance for even momentary reflection and rest, to a headlong drive into our technological

termite-life, the Brave New World[1] of a completely man-
controlled environment. We need wilderness preserved—as
much of it as is still left, and as many kinds—because it
was the challenge against which our character as a people
40 was formed. The reminder and the reassurance that it is still
there is good for our spiritual health even if we never once in
ten years set foot in it. It is good for us when we are young,
because of the incomparable sanity it can bring briefly, as
vacation and rest, into our insane lives. It is important to us
when we are old simply because it is there—important, that
is, simply as idea. **C**

    We are a wild species. . . . Nobody ever tamed or
domesticated or scientifically bred us. But for at least
three millennia we have been engaged in a cumulative
50 and ambitious race to modify and gain control of our
environment, and in the process we have come close to
domesticating ourselves. Not many people are likely, any
more, to look upon what we call "progress" as an unmixed
blessing. Just as surely as it has brought us increased comfort
and more material goods, it has brought us spiritual losses,
and it threatens now to become the Frankenstein that will
destroy us. One means of sanity is to retain a hold on the
natural world, to remain, insofar as we can, good animals.
Americans still have that chance, more than many peoples;
60 for while we were demonstrating ourselves the most efficient
and ruthless environment-busters in history, and slashing and
burning and cutting our way through a wilderness continent,
the wilderness was working on us. It remains in us as surely
as Indian names remain on the land. If the abstract dream
of human liberty and human dignity became, in America,

C PRIMARY SOURCES
In lines 20–46, what does
Stegner's description suggest
about life in the Unites States at
the time he wrote this letter?

_____

_____

_____

_____

_____

_____

_____

_____

_____

_____

_____

1. **Brave New World:** a reference to Aldous Huxley's 1932 science fiction
   novel, *Brave New World*, depicting a society in which happiness and the
   most basic natural life functions are controlled by technology.

something more than an abstract dream, mark it down at least partially to the fact that we were in subtle ways subdued by what we conquered. . . .

The American experience has been the confrontation 70 by old peoples and cultures of a world as new as if it had just risen from the sea. That gave us our hope and our excitement, and the hope and excitement can be passed on to newer Americans, Americans who never saw any phase of the frontier. But only so long as we keep the remainder of our wild as a reserve and a promise—a sort of wilderness bank. . . . **PAUSE & REFLECT**

We need to demonstrate our acceptance of the natural world, including ourselves; we need the spiritual refreshment that being natural can produce. And one of the best places 80 for us to get that is in the wilderness where the fun houses, the bulldozers, and the pavements of our civilization are shut out.

Sherwood Anderson, in a letter to Waldo Frank in the 1920's, said it better than I can. "Is it not likely that when the country was new and men were often alone in the fields and the forest they got a sense of bigness outside themselves that has now in some way been lost . . . Mystery whispered in the grass, played in the branches of trees overhead, was caught up and blown across the American line in clouds of dust at 90 evening on the prairies . . . I am old enough to remember tales that strengthen my belief in a deep semi-religious influence that was formerly at work among our people. The flavor of it

PAUSE & REFLECT
In lines 64–76, what does Stegner say has been the American experience? How can we pass on this experience to newer Americans?

_____

_____

_____

_____

_____

_____

_____

_____

_____

_____

hangs over the best work of Mark Twain . . . I can remember old fellows in my home town speaking feelingly of an evening spent on the big empty plains. It had taken the shrillness out of them. They had learned the trick of quiet . . ." **D**

We could learn it too, even yet; even our children and grand-children could learn it. But only if we save, for just such absolutely non-recreational, impractical, and mystical uses as this, all the wild that still remains to us. . . .

For myself, I grew up on the empty plains of Saskatchewan and Montana and in the mountains of Utah, and I put a very high valuation on what those places gave me. And if I had not been able periodically to renew myself in the mountains and deserts of western America I would be very near bughouse. Even when I can't get to the back country, the thought of the colored deserts of southern Utah, or the reassurance that there are still stretches of prairie where the world can be instantaneously perceived as disk and bowl, and where the little but intensely important human being is exposed to the five directions and the thirty-six winds, is a positive consolation. The idea alone can sustain me. But as the wilderness areas are progressively exploited or "improved," as the jeeps and bulldozers of uranium prospectors scar up the deserts and the roads are cut into the alpine timberlands, and as the remnants of the unspoiled and natural world are progressively eroded, every such loss is a little death in me. In us. . . . **E**

Let me say something on the subject of the kinds of wilderness worth preserving. Most of those areas contemplated are in the national forests and in high

D PRIMARY SOURCES
Circle the name of the writer that Stegner quotes in lines 83–96. How does this quotation add to Stegner's argument?

_____

_____

_____

_____

_____

_____

E PRIMARY SOURCES
Reread lines 101–118. Paraphrase, or state in your own words, what Stegner is saying about the benefits of wilderness in his own life.

_____

_____

_____

_____

_____

_____

_____

mountain country. For all the usual recreational purposes, the alpine and forest wildernesses are obviously the most important, both as genetic banks and as beauty spots. But for the spiritual renewal, the recognition of identity, the birth of awe, other kinds will serve every bit as well. Perhaps, because they are less friendly to life, more abstractly nonhuman, they will serve even better. On our Saskatchewan prairie, the nearest neighbor was four miles away, and at night we saw
130 only two lights on all the dark rounding earth. The earth was full of animals—field mice, ground squirrels, weasels, ferrets, badgers, coyotes, burrowing owls, snakes. I knew them as my little brothers, as fellow creatures, and I have never been able to look upon animals in any other way since. The sky in that country came clear down to the ground on every side, and it was full of great weathers, and clouds, and winds, and hawks. I hope I learned something from knowing intimately the creatures of the earth; I hope I learned something from looking a long way, from looking up, from being much alone.
140 A prairie like that, one big enough to carry the eye clear to the sinking, rounding horizon, can be as lonely and grand and simple in its forms as the sea. It is as good a place as any for the wilderness experience to happen; the vanishing prairie is as worth preserving for the wilderness idea as the alpine forests. **PAUSE & REFLECT**

So are great reaches of our western deserts, scarred somewhat by prospectors but otherwise open, beautiful, waiting. . . .

PAUSE & REFLECT
Underline the different kinds of wilderness Stegner identifies in lines 101–145. How has he benefited from wilderness?

_____

_____

_____

_____

_____

_____

These are some of the things wilderness can do for
150 us. That is the reason we need to put into effect, for its
preservation, some other principle than the principles of
exploitation or "usefulness" or even recreation. We simply
need that wild country available to us, even if we never do
more than drive to its edge and look in. For it can be a means
of reassuring ourselves of our sanity as creatures, a part of the
geography of hope. **F**

Very sincerely yours,

Wallace Stegner

Wallace Stegner

F **PRIMARY SOURCES**
Reread Stegner's closing
paragraph. Summarize his
conclusion.

_____

_____

_____

_____

_____

_____

Practicing Your Skills

Now that you have finished reading the letter, complete your primary sources chart. In the last row, write a brief summary of his main argument.

Questions About Primary Source	My Answers
What is the form and purpose of this document?	
What, if anything, do I already know about the author and the time in which he lived?	
What does the document tell me about life at the time it was written?	
SUMMARY	

Consider the information in your chart. Which selection did you find more convincing—Stegner's letter or Bryson's narrative? Support your response with specific quotations, ideas, and facts from the text.

_____

_____

_____

_____

Academic Vocabulary in Writing

aspect	circumstance	contribute	distinct	perceive

In the beginning of "A Walk in the Woods," Bill Bryson writes about the simplicity of being in the wilderness. Did reading Bryson's narrative **contribute** to your understanding of Stegner's argument in "A Wilderness Letter"? Explain, using at least one Academic Vocabulary word in your response. Definitions for these terms are listed on page 111.

_____

_____

_____

Assessment Practice

DIRECTIONS Use "Wilderness Letter" to answer questions 1–4.

1 Stenger's purpose for writing "Wilderness Letter" is —
- **A** to protect endangered species living in the wilderness
- **B** to ask that homes be torn down to create parks
- **C** to protect what's left of the wilderness
- **D** to ask that humans never enter protected areas

2 The intended audience for Stegner's audience is —
- **A** construction company owners
- **B** governmental decision makers
- **C** recreational park users
- **D** Utah residents

3 Which of the following aspects of Stenger's letter does *not* help establish credibility?
- **A** firsthand accounts of experiences with the wilderness
- **B** the author's background in environmental issues
- **C** quotations from others writing on the same subject
- **D** counterarguments about the importance of technology

4 Stegner believes that the existence of wilderness areas benefits us —
- **A** even if we only hear about them
- **B** only if we visit them frequently
- **C** only when we are in times of personal stress
- **D** even if very few of them are left

UNIT 4

Getting the Message
THEME AND SYMBOL

Be sure to read the Text Analysis Workshop on pp. 434–439 in *Holt McDougal Literature*.

Academic Vocabulary for Unit 4

Preview the following Academic Vocabulary words. You will encounter these words as you work through this book and will use them as you write and talk about the selections in this unit.

context (kŏn´tĕkst´) *n.* the words that surround a particular word or passage and make the meaning of that word or passage clear
*When thinking about symbols, it is important to consider them in the **context** of the story.*

---

interpret (in tər´prət) *v.* to explain the meaning of or translate
*To identify the theme of a story, readers must first **interpret** the writer's message.*

---

reveal (ri vēl´) *v.* to show, make known, or expose
*Themes **reveal** messages about life and human nature.*

---

significant (sig nif´ə kənt) *adj.* having meaning; important
*Evaluating the meaning of symbols is a **significant** part of understanding a story's message.*

---

tradition (trə-dĭsh´ən) *n.* a practice passed down from generation to generation
*Many cultures share a **tradition** of passing down stories.*

A symbol is an object, event, person, or animal that stands for something other than itself. Think of another widely used symbol and **interpret** its meaning. Use at least one Academic Vocabulary word in your response.

_____

_____

_____

The Scarlet Ibis

Short Story by James Hurst

Why do we **HURT** the ones we **LOVE?**

Even the most loving people can turn cruel when angry or disappointed. What do you do when you experience mixed emotions about those people who are closest to you? What harm can come from a thoughtless word or action?

QUICKWRITE Why are we sometimes harder on loved ones than on anyone else? Read the sentences in the notebook to the left and fill in your answers.

Why are we harder on those we love?

Sometimes I get mad at

_____ *because*

_____ *even though*

I like him/her.

I don't like it when

_____ *does*

_____ *because*

_____

Text Analysis: Symbol

A **symbol** is a literary device in which a person, animal, place, object, or activity stands for something beyond itself. For example, a heart often symbolizes love. Writers often use symbols to emphasize ideas which can act as clues to a story's **theme**—the underlying message about life or human nature that the author wants the reader to understand. The chart below shows how to analyze various clues to a story's theme.

CLUES TO THEME

TITLE

The title may reflect a story's subject or a significant idea. Ask what ideas the title highlights.

CHARACTERS

Characters can reflect theme by what they do or say. Ask what lessons the character learns.

PLOT AND CONFLICT

A story revolves around conflicts that are central to the theme. Consider what conflicts the characters face and how they are resolved.

SETTING

Setting can convey theme because of what it means to the characters and readers. Ask what the setting might represent.

IMPORTANT STATEMENTS

The narrator or the characters may make statements that hint at the theme. Ask what ideas these statements emphasize.

SYMBOLS

Characters, conflicts, and settings can serve as symbols that support the theme. Ask what ideas these symbols communicate.

As you read "The Scarlet Ibis," look for symbols that provide clues to the story's theme.

Reading Skill: Make Inferences About Characters

Writers often don't tell you directly what their characters are like. Instead, writers describe what characters say and do, allowing you to make your own **inferences**, or logical guesses about them. When you make an inference, you use your observations and prior experience to make an educated guess. As you read, you will be prompted to make and record inferences about the relationship between the narrator and his brother. See the example below.

Quotations	Inferences About Relationship
"Doodle ... was a nice crazy, like someone you meet in your dreams".	*Narrator basically liked his brother, but thought he was odd.*

Vocabulary in Context

NOTE: Words are listed in the order in which they appear in the story.

imminent (ĭm'ə-nənt) *adj.* about to occur
*He was an **imminent** danger of falling from the shaky ladder.*

infallibility (ĭn-făl'ə-bĭl'ĭ-tē) *n.* an inability to make errors
*The politician believed in the **infallibility** of his deeply-held beliefs.*

doggedness (dô'gĭd-nĭs) *n.* persistence; stubbornness
*The athlete trained hard and with **doggedness.***

reiterate (rē-ĭt'ə-rāt') *v.* to repeat
*When giving an oral presentation, you should **reiterate** your main idea for emphasis.*

precariously (prĭ-kâr'ē-əs-lē) *adv.* insecurely; in a dangerous or unstable way
*The car was balanced **precariously** on the edge of the cliff.*

exotic (ĭg-zŏt'ĭk) *adj.* excitingly strange
*She found some colorful **exotic** shells on the beach.*

evanesce (ĕv'ə-nĕs') *v.* to disappear; vanish
*As the sun rose, the morning mist **evanesced** slowly.*

heresy (hĕr'ĭ-sē) *n.* an action or opinion contrary to what is generally thought of as right
*The strangers dangerous beliefs bordered on **heresy**.*

SET A PURPOSE FOR READING

Read this story to find out what happens when a boy tries to change his younger brother.

The Scarlet Ibis

Short Story by
JAMES HURST

BACKGROUND "The Scarlet Ibis" takes its title from a tropical bird rarely found in coastal North Carolina, where the story takes place. The lush natural environment of this setting is prominent in the story. In addition to the ibis, Hurst uses the local names of plants for their symbolic associations. For example, in the story the ibis lands in a "bleeding tree," a type of pine that oozes a white sap when cut. "Graveyard flowers" are fragrant white gardenias often planted in cemeteries because they bloom year after year.

A SYMBOL
Symbols are often repeated throughout the story and can be a clue to the story's theme. Circle the words associated with death or dying in lines 1–9.

It was in the clove of seasons,[1] summer was dead but autumn had not yet been born, that the ibis lit in the bleeding tree. The flower garden was stained with rotting brown magnolia petals and ironweeds grew rank amid the purple phlox. The five o'clocks by the chimney still marked time, but the oriole nest in the elm was untenanted and rocked back and forth like an empty cradle. The last graveyard flowers were blooming, and their smell drifted across the cotton field and through every room of our house, speaking softly the names of our dead. **A**

---

1. **the clove of seasons:** a time between two seasons, in this case, summer and autumn.

10   It's strange that all this is still so clear to me, now that
that summer has long since fled and time has had its way.
A grindstone stands where the bleeding tree stood, just outside
the kitchen door, and now if an oriole sings in the elm, its song
seems to die up in the leaves, a silvery dust. The flower garden is
prim, the house a gleaming white, and the pale fence across the
yard stands straight and spruce. But sometimes (like right now),
as I sit in the cool, green-draped parlor, the grindstone begins
to turn, and time with all its changes is ground away—and
I remember Doodle.

20   Doodle was just about the craziest brother a boy ever had.
Of course, he wasn't a crazy crazy like old Miss Leedie, who
was in love with President Wilson and wrote him a letter
every day, but was a nice crazy, like someone you meet in your
dreams. He was born when I was six and was, from the outset,
a disappointment. He seemed all head, with a tiny body which
was red and shriveled like an old man's. Everybody thought
he was going to die—everybody except Aunt Nicey, who had
delivered him. She said he would live because he was born in
a caul,[2] and cauls were made from Jesus' nightgown. Daddy
30 had Mr. Heath, the carpenter, build a little mahogany coffin
for him. But he didn't die, and when he was three months
old, Mama and Daddy decided they might as well name him.
They named him William Armstrong, which was like tying
a big tail on a small kite. Such a name sounds good only on
a tombstone. **B**

I thought myself pretty smart at many things, like holding
my breath, running, jumping, or climbing the vines in Old
Woman Swamp, and I wanted more than anything else someone
to race to Horsehead Landing, someone to box with, and
40 someone to perch with in the top fork of the great pine behind
the barn, where across the fields and swamps you could see the
sea. I wanted a brother. But Mama, crying, told me that even
if William Armstrong lived, he would never do these things
with me. He might not, she sobbed, even be "all there." He

B MAKE INFERENCES
Underline the **details** about
Doodle presented in lines 20–35.
What inferences can you make
about him? Add them to the
chart below.

DETAILS

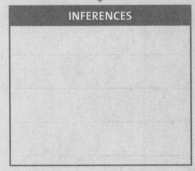

INFERENCES

---

2. **born in a caul:** born with a thin membrane covering the head.

might, as long as he lived, lie on the rubber sheet in the center of the bed in the front bedroom where the white marquisette curtains billowed out in the afternoon sea breeze, rustling like palmetto fronds.[3]

50　　It was bad enough having an invalid brother, but having one who possibly was not all there was unbearable, so I began to make plans to kill him by smothering him with a pillow. However, one afternoon as I watched him, my head poked between the iron posts of the foot of the bed, he looked straight at me and grinned. I skipped through the rooms, down the echoing halls, shouting, "Mama, he smiled. He's all there! He's all there!" and he was. **ⓒ**

When he was two, if you laid him on his stomach, he began to move himself, straining terribly. The doctor said that with his weak heart this strain would probably kill him, but it didn't.
60　Trembling, he'd push himself up, turning first red, then a soft purple, and finally collapse back onto the bed like an old worn-out doll. I can still see Mama watching him, her hand pressed tight across her mouth, her eyes wide and unblinking. But he learned to crawl (it was his third winter), and we brought him out of the front bedroom, putting him on the rug before the fireplace. For the first time he became one of us.

As long as he lay all the time in bed, we called him William Armstrong, even though it was formal and sounded as if we were referring to one of our ancestors, but with his creeping
70　around on the deerskin rug and beginning to talk, something had to be done about his name. It was I who renamed him. When he crawled, he crawled backward, as if he were in reverse and couldn't change gears. If you called him, he'd turn around as if he were going in the other direction, then he'd back right up to you to be picked up. Crawling backward made him look like a doodlebug, so I began to call him Doodle, and in time even Mama and Daddy thought it was a better name than William Armstrong. Only Aunt Nicey disagreed. She said caul babies should be treated with special respect since they might turn
80　out to be saints. Renaming my brother was perhaps the kindest

ⓒ MAKE INFERENCES
Lines 49–56 present the narrator's conflicted feelings about his brother. What inference can you make about the narrator from his reaction to Doodle's grin?

_____

_____

_____

_____

_____

_____

_____

_____

_____

_____

_____

_____

_____

_____

_____

---

3. **palmetto fronds:** the fanlike leaves of a kind of palm tree.

thing I ever did for him, because nobody expects much from someone called Doodle. **D**

Although Doodle learned to crawl, he showed no signs of walking, but he wasn't idle. He talked so much that we all quit listening to what he said. It was about this time that Daddy built him a go-cart and I had to pull him around.

At first I just paraded him up and down the piazza, but then he started crying to be taken out into the yard, and it ended up by my having to lug him wherever I went. If I so much as picked
90 up my cap, he'd start crying to go with me, and Mama would call from wherever she was, "Take Doodle with you."

He was a burden in many ways. The doctor had said that he mustn't get too excited, too hot, too cold, or too tired and that he must always be treated gently. A long list of don'ts went with him, all of which I ignored once we got out of the house. To discourage his coming with me, I'd run with him across the ends of the cotton rows and careen him around corners on two wheels. Sometimes I accidentally turned him over, but he never told Mama. His skin was very sensitive, and he had to wear a
100 big straw hat whenever he went out. When the going got rough and he had to cling to the sides of the go-cart, the hat slipped all the way down over his ears. He was a sight. Finally, I could see I was licked. Doodle was my brother and he was going to cling to me forever, no matter what I did, so I dragged him across the burning cotton field to share with him the only beauty I knew, Old Woman Swamp. I pulled the go-cart through the sawtooth fern, down into the green dimness where the palmetto fronds whispered by the stream. I lifted him out and set him down in the soft rubber grass beside a tall pine. His eyes were round with
110 wonder as he gazed about him, and his little hands began to stroke the rubber grass. Then he began to cry.

"For heaven's sake, what's the matter?" I asked, annoyed.

"It's so pretty," he said. "So pretty, pretty, pretty."

After that day Doodle and I often went down into Old Woman Swamp. I would gather wildflowers, wild violets, honeysuckle, yellow jasmine, snakeflowers, and water lilies, and

D SYMBOL
Reread lines 75–82. A nickname is often a kind of symbol. What is Doodle's real name?

What does Doodle's nickname tell you about the feelings the others have about him?

_____

_____

_____

_____

_____

_____

_____

_____

_____

_____

_____

_____

_____

_____

E MAKE INFERENCES
How would you describe the narrator's relationship with Doodle? Why does the narrator decide to take Doodle to Old Woman Swamp?

_____

_____

_____

_____

_____

_____

F SYMBOL
In lines 123–126, the narrator makes a direct statement that offers clues to the theme. Underline that statement and then paraphrase it in your own words.

_____

_____

_____

PAUSE & REFLECT
According to lines 138–145, what does Doodle fear most?

_____

_____

_____

_____

with wire grass we'd weave them into necklaces and crowns. We'd bedeck ourselves with our handiwork and loll about thus beautified, beyond the touch of the everyday world. Then when
120 the slanted rays of the sun burned orange in the tops of the pines, we'd drop our jewels into the stream and watch them float away toward the sea. **E**

There is within me (and with sadness I have watched it in others) a knot of cruelty borne by the stream of love, much as our blood sometimes bears the seed of our destruction, and at times I was mean to Doodle. One day I took him up to the barn loft and showed him his casket, telling him how we all had believed he would die. It was covered with a film of Paris green[4] sprinkled to kill the rats, and screech owls had built a nest
130 inside it. **F**

Doodle studied the mahogany box for a long time, then said, "It's not mine."

"It is," I said. "And before I'll help you down from the loft, you're going to have to touch it."

"I won't touch it," he said sullenly.

"Then I'll leave you here by yourself," I threatened, and made as if I were going down.

Doodle was frightened of being left. "Don't go leave me, Brother," he cried, and he leaned toward the coffin. His hand,
140 trembling, reached out, and when he touched the casket he screamed. A screech owl flapped out of the box into our faces, scaring us and covering us with Paris green. Doodle was paralyzed, so I put him on my shoulder and carried him down the ladder, and even when we were outside in the bright sunshine, he clung to me, crying, "Don't leave me. Don't leave me." **PAUSE & REFLECT**

When Doodle was five years old, I was embarrassed at having a brother of that age who couldn't walk, so I set out to teach him. We were down in Old Woman Swamp and it was spring and the sick-sweet smell of bay flowers hung everywhere
150 like a mournful song. "I'm going to teach you to walk, Doodle," I said.

_____

4. **Paris green:** a poisonous green powder used to kill pests.

He was sitting comfortably on the soft grass, leaning back against the pine. "Why?" he asked.

I hadn't expected such an answer. "So I won't have to haul you around all the time."

"I can't walk, Brother," he said.

"Who says so?" I demanded.

"Mama, the doctor—everybody."

"Oh, you can walk," I said, and I took him by the arms and
160 stood him up. He collapsed onto the grass like a half-empty flour sack. It was as if he had no bones in his little legs.

"Don't hurt me, Brother," he warned.

"Shut up. I'm not going to hurt you. I'm going to teach you to walk." I heaved him up again, and again he collapsed.

This time he did not lift his face up out of the rubber grass. "I just can't do it. Let's make honeysuckle wreaths."

"Oh yes you can, Doodle," I said. "All you got to do is try. Now come on," and I hauled him up once more.

It seemed so hopeless from the beginning that it's a miracle
170 I didn't give up. But all of us must have something or someone to be proud of, and Doodle had become mine. I did not know then that pride is a wonderful, terrible thing, a seed that bears two vines, life and death. Every day that summer we went to the pine beside the stream of Old Woman Swamp, and I put him on his feet at least a hundred times each afternoon. Occasionally I too became discouraged because it didn't seem as if he was trying, and I would say, "Doodle, don't you *want* to learn to walk?" **G**

He'd nod his head, and I'd say, "Well, if you don't keep trying,
180 you'll never learn." Then I'd paint for him a picture of us as old men, white-haired, him with a long white beard and me still pulling him around in the go-cart. This never failed to make him try again.

Finally one day, after many weeks of practicing, he stood alone for a few seconds. When he fell, I grabbed him in my arms and hugged him, our laughter pealing through the swamp like a ringing bell. Now we knew it could be done. Hope no longer hid

G MAKE INFERENCES
Why does the narrator try so hard to teach Doodle to walk?

_____

_____

_____

Underline the statements in lines 167–178 that support your answer.

in the dark palmetto thicket but perched like a cardinal in the lacy toothbrush tree, brilliantly visible.

190 "Yes, yes," I cried, and he cried it too, and the grass beneath us was soft and the smell of the swamp was sweet.

imminent (ĭm'ə-nənt) *adj.* about to occur

With success so **imminent**, we decided not to tell anyone until he could actually walk. Each day, barring rain, we sneaked into Old Woman Swamp, and by cotton-picking time Doodle was ready to show what he could do. He still wasn't able to walk far, but we could wait no longer. Keeping a nice secret is very hard to do, like holding your breath. We chose to reveal all on October eighth, Doodle's sixth birthday, and for weeks ahead we mooned around the house, promising everybody a most

200 spectacular surprise. Aunt Nicey said that, after so much talk, if we produced anything less tremendous than the Resurrection,[5] she was going to be disappointed.

At breakfast on our chosen day, when Mama, Daddy, and Aunt Nicey were in the dining room, I brought Doodle to the door in the go-cart just as usual and had them turn their backs, making them cross their hearts and hope to die if they peeked. I helped Doodle up, and when he was standing alone I let them look. There wasn't a sound as Doodle walked slowly across the room and sat down at his place at the table. Then Mama began

210 to cry and ran over to him, hugging him and kissing him. Daddy hugged him too, so I went to Aunt Nicey, who was thanks praying in the doorway, and began to waltz her around. We danced together quite well until she came down on my big toe with her brogans,[6] hurting me so badly I thought I was crippled for life.

Doodle told them it was I who had taught him to walk, so everyone wanted to hug me, and I began to cry.

"What are you crying for?" asked Daddy, but I couldn't answer. They did not know that I did it for myself; that pride, whose slave I was, spoke to me louder than all their voices, and

220 that Doodle walked only because I was ashamed of having a crippled brother. ⓗ

ⓗ MAKE INFERENCES
Why is the narrator ashamed of himself? Underline the words that explain his shame.

_____

_____

_____

_____

_____

---

5. **the Resurrection:** the rising of Jesus Christ from the dead after his burial.
6. **brogans** (brō'gənz): heavy, ankle-high work shoes.

Within a few months Doodle had learned to walk well and his go-cart was put up in the barn loft (it's still there) beside his little mahogany coffin. Now, when we roamed off together, resting often, we never turned back until our destination had been reached, and to help pass the time, we took up lying. From the beginning Doodle was a terrible liar and he got me in the habit. Had anyone stopped to listen to us, we would have been sent off to Dix Hill.[7]

230　　My lies were scary, involved, and usually pointless, but Doodle's were twice as crazy. People in his stories all had wings and flew wherever they wanted to go. His favorite lie was about a boy named Peter who had a pet peacock with a ten-foot tail. Peter wore a golden robe that glittered so brightly that when he walked through the sunflowers they turned away from the sun to face him. When Peter was ready to go to sleep, the peacock spread his magnificent tail, enfolding the boy gently like a closing go-to-sleep flower, burying him in the gloriously iridescent, rustling vortex.[8] Yes, I must admit it. Doodle could
240 beat me lying. **PAUSE & REFLECT**

Doodle and I spent lots of time thinking about our future. We decided that when we were grown we'd live in Old Woman Swamp and pick dog-tongue for a living. Beside the stream, he planned, we'd build us a house of whispering leaves and the swamp birds would be our chickens. All day long (when we weren't gathering dog-tongue) we'd swing through the cypresses on the rope vines, and if it rained we'd huddle beneath an umbrella tree and play stickfrog. Mama and Daddy could come and live with us if they wanted to. He even came up with the idea
250 that he could marry Mama and I could marry Daddy. Of course, I was old enough to know this wouldn't work out, but the picture he painted was so beautiful and serene that all I could do was whisper Yes, yes.

PAUSE & REFLECT
How would you describe Doodle's "lies"?

_____

_____

_____

_____

_____

_____

_____

_____

_____

_____

_____

---

7. **Dix Hill:** common name for a mental hospital in Raleigh, North Carolina.

8. **iridescent rustling vortex:** the shimmering, rainbow-colored peacock feathers are in a funnel shape, like a whirlpool or whirlwind (vortex).

infallibility (ĭn-făl′ə-bĭl′ĭ-tē) *n.*
an inability to make errors

**What does it mean that the
narrator believes in his own
infallibility?**

_____

_____

_____

_____

_____

_____

_____

● **MAKE INFERENCES**
Reread lines 261–276. Circle the
words that describe the spring
and the words that describe
summer. How do the descriptions
of the two seasons differ?

_____

_____

_____

_____

_____

_____

_____

_____

Once I had succeeded in teaching Doodle to walk, I began
to believe in my own **infallibility**, and I prepared a terrific
development program for him, unknown to Mama and Daddy,
of course. I would teach him to run, to swim, to climb trees, and
to fight. He, too, now believed in my infallibility, so we set the
deadline for these accomplishments less than a year away, when,
260 it had been decided, Doodle could start to school.

That winter we didn't make much progress, for I was in school
and Doodle suffered from one bad cold after another. But when
spring came, rich and warm, we raised our sights again. Success
lay at the end of summer like a pot of gold, and our campaign
got off to a good start. On hot days, Doodle and I went down to
Horsehead Landing, and I gave him swimming lessons or showed
him how to row a boat. Sometimes we descended into the cool
greenness of Old Woman Swamp and climbed the rope vines
or boxed scientifically beneath the pine where he had learned to
270 walk. Promise hung about us like the leaves, and wherever we
looked, ferns unfurled and birds broke into song.

That summer, the summer of 1918, was blighted. In May and
June there was no rain and the crops withered, curled up, then
died under the thirsty sun. One morning in July a hurricane came
out of the east, tipping over the oaks in the yard and splitting
the limbs of the elm trees. That afternoon it roared back out of
the west, blew the fallen oaks around, snapping their roots and
tearing them out of the earth like a hawk at the entrails of a
chicken. Cotton bolls were wrenched from the stalks and lay like
280 green walnuts in the valleys between the rows, while the cornfield
leaned over uniformly so that the tassels touched the ground.
Doodle and I followed Daddy out into the cotton field, where
he stood, shoulders sagging, surveying the ruin. When his chin
sank down onto his chest, we were frightened, and Doodle slipped
his hand into mine. Suddenly Daddy straightened his shoulders,
raised a giant knuckly fist, and with a voice that seemed to rumble
out of the earth itself began cursing heaven, hell, the weather, and
the Republican Party.[9] Doodle and I, prodding each other and
giggling, went back to the house, knowing that everything would
290 be all right. ●

---

9. **Republican Party:** In 1918, most Southerners were Democrats.

And during that summer, strange names were heard through the house: Château-Thierry, Amiens, Soissons, and in her blessing at the supper table, Mama once said, "And bless the Pearsons, whose boy Joe was lost at Belleau Wood."[10]

So we came to that clove of seasons. School was only a few weeks away, and Doodle was far behind schedule. He could barely clear the ground when climbing up the rope vines, and his swimming was certainly not passable. We decided to double our efforts, to make that last drive and reach our pot of gold. I made him swim until he turned blue and row until he couldn't lift an oar. Wherever we went, I purposely walked fast, and although he kept up, his face turned red and his eyes became glazed. Once, he could go no further, so he collapsed on the ground and began to cry.

"Aw, come on, Doodle," I urged. "You can do it. Do you want to be different from everybody else when you start school?"

"Does it make any difference?"

"It certainly does," I said. "Now, come on," and I helped him up.

As we slipped through dog days,[11] Doodle began to look feverish, and Mama felt his forehead, asking him if he felt ill. At night he didn't sleep well, and sometimes he had nightmares, crying out until I touched him and said, "Wake up, Doodle. Wake up." ❶

It was Saturday noon, just a few days before school was to start. I should have already admitted defeat, but my pride wouldn't let me. The excitement of our program had now been gone for weeks, but still we kept on with a tired **doggedness**. It was too late to turn back, for we had both wandered too far into a net of expectations and had left no crumbs behind.

Daddy, Mama, Doodle, and I were seated at the dining-room table having lunch. It was a hot day, with all the windows and doors open in case a breeze should come. In the kitchen Aunt Nicey was humming softly. After a long silence, Daddy spoke.

---

10. **Château-Thierry** (shä-tō-tyĕ-rē′), **Amiens** (ä-myăn′), **Soissons** (swä-sōn′), . . . **Belleau** (bel′ō) **Wood:** places in France where famous battles were fought near the end of World War I (1914–1918).

11. **dog days:** the hot, uncomfortable days between early July and early September (named after the Dog Star, Sirius, which rises and sets with the sun at this time).

❶ **MAKE INFERENCES**
Underline the words in lines 295–313 that describe a change in Doodle. What do you think is happening to him?

_____

_____

_____

_____

_____

doggedness (dô′gĭd-nĭs) *n.* persistence; stubbornness

Who shows more **doggedness**, the narrator or Doodle? Explain.

_____

_____

_____

_____

_____

_____

THE SCARLET IBIS **199**

"It's so calm, I wouldn't be surprised if we had a storm this afternoon."

"I haven't heard a rain frog," said Mama, who believed in signs, as she served the bread around the table.

"I did," declared Doodle. "Down in the swamp."

"He didn't," I said contrarily.

330   "You did, eh?" said Daddy, ignoring my denial.

"I certainly did," Doodle **reiterated**, scowling at me over the top of his iced-tea glass, and we were quiet again.

Suddenly, from out in the yard, came a strange croaking noise. Doodle stopped eating, with a piece of bread poised ready for his mouth, his eyes popped round like two blue buttons. "What's that?" he whispered.

I jumped up, knocking over my chair, and had reached the door when Mama called, "Pick up the chair, sit down again, and say excuse me."

340   By the time I had done this, Doodle had excused himself and had slipped out into the yard. He was looking up into the bleeding tree. "It's a great big red bird!" he called.

The bird croaked loudly again, and Mama and Daddy came out into the yard. We shaded our eyes with our hands against the hazy glare of the sun and peered up through the still leaves. On the topmost branch a bird the size of a chicken, with scarlet feathers and long legs, was perched **precariously**. Its wings hung down loosely, and as we watched, a feather dropped away and floated slowly down through the green leaves. **K**

350   "It's not even frightened of us," Mama said.

"It looks tired," Daddy added. "Or maybe sick."

Doodle's hands were clasped at his throat, and I had never seen him stand still so long. "What is it?" he asked.

Daddy shook his head. "I don't know, maybe it's—"

At that moment the bird began to flutter, but the wings were uncoordinated, and amid much flapping and a spray of flying feathers, it tumbled down, bumping through the limbs of the bleeding tree and landing at our feet with a thud. Its long,

reiterate (rē-ĭt′ə-rāt′) v. to repeat

precariously (prĭ-kâr′ē-əs-lē) adv. insecurely; in a dangerous or unstable way

K **SYMBOL**
The description of the bird seems to give it a special meaning. What character in the story does the bird remind you of, and why?

_____

_____

_____

_____

_____

_____

graceful neck jerked twice into an S, then straightened out, and
360   the bird was still. A white veil came over the eyes and the long
white beak unhinged. Its legs were crossed and its clawlike feet
were delicately curved at rest. Even death did not mar its grace, for
it lay on the earth like a broken vase of red flowers, and we stood
around it, awed by its **exotic** beauty.

"It's dead," Mama said.

"What is it?" Doodle repeated.

"Go bring me the bird book," said Daddy.

I ran into the house and brought back the bird book. As we
watched, Daddy thumbed through its pages. "It's a scarlet ibis," he
370   said, pointing to a picture. "It lives in the tropics—South America
to Florida. A storm must have brought it here."

Sadly, we all looked back at the bird. A scarlet ibis! How many
miles it had traveled to die like this, in *our* yard, beneath the
bleeding tree.

"Let's finish lunch," Mama said, nudging us back toward the
dining room.

"I'm not hungry," said Doodle, and he knelt down beside
the ibis.

"We've got peach cobbler
380   for dessert," Mama tempted
from the doorway.

Doodle remained
kneeling. "I'm going to bury
him."

"Don't you dare touch
him," Mama warned.
"There's no telling what
disease he might have had."

"All right," said Doodle.
390   "I won't."

Daddy, Mama, and I
went back to the dining-
room table, but we watched

exotic (ĭg-zŏt′ĭk) *adj.* excitingly
strange

Circle the details in lines 355–364
that describe the **exotic** beauty
of the bird.

Doodle through the open door. He took out a piece of string from his pocket and, without touching the ibis, looped one end around its neck. Slowly, while singing softly "Shall We Gather at the River," he carried the bird around to the front yard and dug a hole in the flower garden, next to the petunia bed. Now we were watching him through the front window, but he didn't know it. His awkwardness at digging the hole with a shovel whose handle was twice as long as he was made us laugh, and we covered our mouths with our hands so he wouldn't hear. **PAUSE & REFLECT**

When Doodle came into the dining room, he found us seriously eating our cobbler. He was pale and lingered just inside the screen door. "Did you get the scarlet ibis buried?" asked Daddy.

Doodle didn't speak but nodded his head.

"Go wash your hands, and then you can have some peach cobbler," said Mama.

"I'm not hungry," he said.

"Dead birds is bad luck," said Aunt Nicey, poking her head from the kitchen door. "Specially *red* dead birds!" **L**

As soon as I had finished eating, Doodle and I hurried off to Horsehead Landing. Time was short, and Doodle still had a long way to go if he was going to keep up with the other boys when he started school. The sun, gilded with the yellow cast of autumn, still burned fiercely, but the dark green woods through which we passed were shady and cool. When we reached the landing, Doodle said he was too tired to swim, so we got into a skiff and floated down the creek with the tide. Far off in the marsh a rail was scolding, and over on the beach locusts were singing in the myrtle trees. Doodle did not speak and kept his head turned away, letting one hand trail limply in the water.

After we had drifted a long way, I put the oars in place and made Doodle row back against the tide. Black clouds began to gather in the southwest, and he kept watching them, trying to pull the oars a little faster. When we reached Horsehead Landing, lightning was playing across half the sky and thunder roared

PAUSE & REFLECT

How does Doodle's reaction to the death of the ibis differ from the rest of the family's?

_____

_____

_____

_____

L SYMBOL

What similarities do you see between Doodle and the ibis?

_____

_____

_____

_____

_____

_____

_____

out, hiding even the sound of the sea. The sun disappeared
430 and darkness descended, almost like night. Flocks of marsh
crows flew by, heading inland to their roosting trees; and two
egrets, squawking, arose from the oyster-rock shallows and
careened away.

Doodle was both tired and frightened, and when he stepped
from the skiff he collapsed onto the mud, sending an armada
of fiddler crabs rustling off into the marsh grass. I helped him
up, and as he wiped the mud off his trousers, he smiled at me
ashamedly. He had failed and we both knew it, so we started back
home, racing the storm. We never spoke (What are the words
440 that can solder[12] cracked pride?), but I knew he was watching me,
watching for a sign of mercy. The lightning was near now, and
from fear he walked so close behind me he kept stepping on my
heels. The faster I walked, the faster he walked, so I began to run.
The rain was coming, roaring through the pines, and then, like
a bursting Roman candle, a gum tree ahead of us was shattered
by a bolt of lightning. When the deafening peal of thunder had
died, and in the moment before the rain arrived, I heard Doodle,
who had fallen behind, cry out, "Brother, Brother, don't leave me!
Don't leave me!"

450 The knowledge that Doodle's and my plans had come
to naught[13] was bitter, and that streak of cruelty within me
awakened. I ran as fast as I could, leaving him far behind with a
wall of rain dividing us. The drops stung my face like nettles, and
the wind flared the wet glistening leaves of the bordering trees.
Soon I could hear his voice no more. Ⓜ

I hadn't run too far before I became tired, and the flood of
childish spite **evanesced** as well. I stopped and waited for Doodle.
The sound of rain was everywhere, but the wind had died and
it fell straight down in parallel paths like ropes hanging from
460 the sky. As I waited, I peered through the downpour, but no one
came. Finally I went back and found him huddled beneath a red
nightshade bush beside the road. He was sitting on the ground,
his face buried in his arms, which were resting on his drawn-up
knees. "Let's go, Doodle," I said.

Ⓜ **MAKE INFERENCES**
Underline the details in
line 443 that show the
narrator's frustration.

Why does he continue to run
when he knows Doodle has
fallen behind him?

_____

_____

_____

_____

_____

_____

_____

_____

_____

_____

_____

evanesce (ĕv′ə-nĕs′) v. to
disappear; vanish

---

12. **solder** (sŏd′ər): to join or bond together.
13. **had come to naught:** had resulted in nothing.

N SYMBOL
The color red has come up several times in the story. What do you think the color might symbolize?

_____

_____

_____

_____

heresy (hĕr'ĭ-sē) *n.* an action or opinion contrary to what is generally thought of as right

He didn't answer, so I placed my hand on his forehead and lifted his head. Limply, he fell backward onto the earth. He had been bleeding from the mouth, and his neck and the front of his shirt were stained a brilliant red. **N**

"Doodle! Doodle!" I cried, shaking him, but there was no

470 answer but the ropy rain. He lay very awkwardly, with his head thrown far back, making his vermilion[14] neck appear unusually long and slim. His little legs, bent sharply at the knees, had never before seemed so fragile, so thin.

I began to weep, and the tear-blurred vision in red before me looked very familiar. "Doodle!" I screamed above the pounding storm and threw my body to the earth above his. For a long long time, it seemed forever, I lay there crying, sheltering my fallen scarlet ibis from the **heresy** of rain.

---

14. vermilion (vər-mĭl'yən): bright red to reddish orange.

Text Analysis: Symbol

In "The Scarlet Ibis," some of the people, places, things, and events stand for both themselves and for something beyond themselves. Fill out the chart below to see how symbols convey meaning in the story.

Story Passage	Symbol	Meaning
"When Peter was ready to go to sleep, the peacock spread his magnificent tail, enfolding the boy gently like a closing go-to-flower, burying him in the gloriously iridescent, rustling vortex." (lines 236–239)	*peacock*	*love and protection; a kinder, happier world*
"That winter we didn't make much progress, for I was in school and Doodle suffered from one bad cold after another. But when spring came, rich and warm, we raised our sights again." (lines 261–263)		
"Sadly, we all looked back at the bird. A scarlet ibis! How many miles it had traveled to die like this, in *our* yard, beneath the bleeding tree." (lines 372–374)		

What do the symbols in the story reveal about its theme? State the story's theme in a complete sentence.

_____

_____

_____

_____

_____

Reading Skill: Make Inferences About Characters

When you make inferences about characters, you make educated guesses about them based on their appearance, speech, actions, thoughts, and the reactions of other characters. Find details from the text that describe the narrator and make an inference for each one.

Detail from Text	My Inference

Why do we **HURT** the ones we **LOVE?**

What consequences can arise from being cruel to loved ones?

_____

_____

Vocabulary Practice

Circle the word that is not related in meaning to the other words in the set.

1. (a) exotic, (b) ordinary, (c) unusual, (d) foreign

2. (a) impending, (b) imminent, (c) approaching, (d) far away

3. (a) fidelity, (b) heresy, (c) conformity, (d) compliance

4. (a) echo, (b) repeat, (c) originate, (d) reiterate

5. (a) wrong, (b) infallible, (c) inaccurate, (d) imperfect

6. (a) insecurely, (b) cleverly, (c) precariously, (d) dangerously

7. (a) disappear, (b) float, (c) vanish, (d) evanesce

8. (a) doggedness, (b) perseverance, (c) willful, (d) laziness

Academic Vocabulary in Writing

context	interpret	reveal	significant	tradition

An author can **reveal,** or show, a character's personality in a number of ways: by describing the character's appearance, actions, and interactions with other people. How does the author of "The Scarlet Ibis" **reveal** Doodle's character? Explain, using at least one Academic Vocabulary word in your response.

_____

_____

_____

Assessment Practice

DIRECTIONS Use "The Scarlet Ibis" to answer questions 1–6 below.

1 Why does the narrator teach Doodle to walk?

- (A) He is a good teacher.
- (B) His parents asked him to.
- (C) He wants to prove that Doodle can walk.
- (D) He is embarrassed by Doodle's inability to walk.

2 Why does the narrator share with Doodle "the only beauty [he] knew, Old Woman Swamp"?

- (A) His mother makes the narrator take Doodle to the swamp.
- (B) Doodle asks the narrator to show him his favorite places.
- (C) The narrator realizes that Doodle is determined and is always going to be with him.
- (D) The narrator thinks it is the best place to run, swim, and climb trees.

3 The scarlet ibis symbolizes Doodle in that both the child and the bird are —

- (A) able to move very quickly
- (B) trying to learn to fly
- (C) rare, beautiful, and fragile
- (D) fond of being outside

4 Which of the following themes does the symbolism of the ibis best support?

- (A) Selfish pride causes more harm than good.
- (B) Delicate creatures need to be protected and cared for.
- (C) Cruelty toward a loved one often stems from wounded pride.
- (D) Some creatures are too fragile to live.

5 Which of the following does *not* describe the narrator's feelings toward Doodle?

- (A) generous
- (B) embarrassed
- (C) ashamed
- (D) jealous

6 What inference can you make about Doodle from his determination to bury the ibis?

- (A) Doodle killed the bird.
- (B) Doodle liked to bury things.
- (C) Doodle felt sorry for the bird.
- (D) Doodle did what his mother told him.

Poem on Returning to Dwell in the Country
Poem by T'ao Ch'ien

My Heart Leaps Up
Poem by William Wordsworth

The Sun
Poem by Mary Oliver

Where do you go to GET AWAY from it all?

What does nature do for you? Whether it's staring at a fishbowl or hiking in the mountains, many people look to nature for beauty, serenity, and relaxation. The poems that follow reflect on the natural world.

QUICKWRITE In the notebook to the left, list types of nature you enjoy and the reasons why. Then share your notes with a partner.

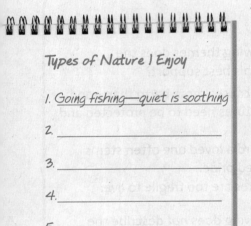

Types of Nature I Enjoy

1. *Going fishing—quiet is soothing*
2. _____
3. _____
4. _____
5. _____

Elements of Poetry: Influences

Modern-day poets often write with an awareness of the language and themes of poems from earlier historical periods. For example, a modern-day poet writing about nature would likely be influenced by England's Romantic poets who had a deep appreciation of nature. The poems that follow are from different time periods but each is about nature. As you read, pay attention to the background information for each poem and consider the influences each earlier poem may have had on the later one.

Text Analysis: Universal Theme

Some poems have a **universal theme;** they express ideas that people from many cultures and times have found to be true. Although the following poems were written by poets who lived in different cultures and times, all three poems touch upon the same universal theme. As you read each poem, use these questions to identify their shared universal theme:

• What idea about nature is each poet expressing?

• What theme does each poem convey?

• How are the poems similar or different?

Reading Strategy: Reading Poetry for Theme

The **theme** of a work is the central idea or insight about life it reveals. The words in a poem are carefully chosen and arranged to convey the poet's message. To understand theme in poetry, you need to look at details differently than you would when reading prose. Use the questions in the chart below to help you identify the theme in each poem.

Clue	Ask Yourself	Details from the Poem
Title	What is the title of the poem? Often the title of a work offers clues to its theme.	
Speaker	• Who is the speaker? • What is the speaker's attitude toward the subject of the poem?	
Key Words and Phrases	Are there any words or phrases that may hint at the writer's message?	
Images	• Are there any key images in the poem? • What is their meaning?	

SET A PURPOSE FOR READING

Read this poem to find out why the speaker returns to the mountains and hills that he loved as a child.

Poem on Returning to Dwell in the Country

Poem by

T'AO CH'IEN

BACKGROUND T'ao Ch'ien (365–427) worked for the government in China before he returned to his family farm to live as a farmer—a radical decision at the time. His poetry reflects Taoist philosophy, which emphasizes living simply and close to nature. Both his life and his natural, conversational writing style inspired many later Chinese writers.

Ⓐ READING POETRY

Think about the images in lines 9–12. The words *tame* and *house-pond* suggest captivity. Why would a tame bird long for his old forest?

_____

_____

_____

Why does the fish in the house-pond think of his ancient pool?

_____

_____

_____

In youth I had nothing
    that matched the vulgar tone,[1]
For my nature always
    loved the hills and mountains.
5 Inadvertently I fell
    into the Dusty Net,[2]
Once having gone
    it was more than thirteen years.
The tame bird
10   longs for his old forest—
The fish in the house-pond
    thinks of his ancient pool. Ⓐ
I too will break the soil
    at the edge of the southern moor,

---

1. **matched the vulgar tone:** The speaker is saying that he was never coarse or raucous in his youth.
2. **Dusty Net:** a term that refers to being caught up in professional ambition and materialism.

15 I will guard simplicity
      and return to my fields and garden.
   My land and house—
      a little more than ten acres,
   In the thatched cottage—
20   only eight or nine rooms.
   Elms and willows
      shade the back verandah,
   Peach and plum trees
      in rows before the hall.
25 Hazy and dimly seen
      a village in the distance,
   Close in the foreground
      the smoke of neighbors' houses.
   A dog barks
30   amidst the deep lanes,
   A cock is crowing
      atop a mulberry tree.
   No dust and confusion
      within my doors and courtyard;
35 In the empty rooms
      more than sufficient leisure. **PAUSE & REFLECT**
   Too long I was held
      within the barred cage.
   Now I am able
40   to return again to Nature. **B**

   Translated by William Acker

PAUSE & REFLECT
Reread lines 33–36. What statement is the speaker making about the difference between life in the country and life elsewhere?

_____

_____

_____

_____

_____

B UNIVERSAL THEME
Reread lines 37–40. What is the "barred cage"?

_____

_____

_____

**SET A PURPOSE
FOR READING**
Read this poem to find out what makes the speaker's heart leap.

My Heart Leaps Up

Poem by

WILLIAM WORDSWORTH

BACKGROUND William Wordsworth (1770–1850) grew up in northern England. As a boy, he loved being outdoors and appreciated the natural beauty of the region. This love of nature never left him. Wordsworth believed that nature was the best teacher and that the human mind was intimately related to the workings of the natural world.

C UNIVERSAL THEME
What does the speaker reveal in lines 1–6 about his feelings toward nature?

_____

_____

_____

_____

My heart leaps up when I behold
  A rainbow in the sky:
So was it when my life began;
So is it now I am a man;
5 So be it when I shall grow old,
  Or let me die! **C**
The Child is father of the Man;
And I could wish my days to be
Bound each to each by natural piety.[1]

---

1. **piety** (pī'ĭ-tē): the quality of showing devotion or being reverent.

The SUN

Poem by

MARY OLIVER

BACKGROUND Mary Oliver's poetry links the worlds of people, animals, and plants. Her work has won the Pulitzer Prize and the National Book Award.

> Have you ever seen
> anything
> in your life
> more wonderful
>
> 5 than the way the sun,
> every evening,
> relaxed and easy,
> floats toward the horizon
>
> and into the clouds or the hills,
> 10 or the rumpled sea,
> and is gone— **PAUSE & REFLECT**
> and how it slides again

SET A PURPOSE FOR READING
Read this poem to understand the speaker's appreciation for the sun.

PAUSE & REFLECT
How would you answer the question the speaker poses in lines 1–11? Explain your response.

_____

_____

_____

_____

_____

E READING POETRY
What can you infer, or guess, about the speaker's attitude toward nature from this description of the sun in lines 1–20?

_____

_____

_____

_____

_____

F UNIVERSAL THEME
Reread lines 31–36. What question does the speaker ask?

_____

_____

_____

_____

_____

_____

out of the blackness,
every morning,
15 on the other side of the world,
like a red flower **D**

        streaming upward on its heavenly oils,
say, on a morning in early summer,
at its perfect imperial distance—
20 and have you ever felt for anything **E**

such wild love—
do you think there is anywhere, in any language,
a word billowing enough
for the pleasure

25 that fills you,
as the sun
reaches out,
as it warms you

as you stand there,
30 empty-handed—
or have you too
turned from this world—

or have you too
gone crazy
35 for power,
for things? **F**

Text Analysis: Universal Theme

Consider the three poems you just read about nature. In the chart below write a theme statement for each poem. Then write down a single universal theme that all of the pieces share.

"Poem on Returning to Dwell in the Country"
Theme Statement:

"My Heart Leaps Up"
Theme Statement:

"The Sun"
Theme Statement:

Universal Theme:

_____

_____

_____

_____

Reading Skill: Reading Poetry for Theme

On the previous page you identified the themes of the three poems you just read. What clues led you to those themes? Identify those clues on the chart below.

	Theme	Clues: (Title, Speaker, Key Words/Phrases, Images)
"Poem on Returning to Dwell in the Country"		
"My Heart Leaps Up"		
"The Sun"		

England's Romantic poets had a deep appreciation for nature. Their works shows an emphasis on imagination, the expression of emotions, and wonder at the natural world. How does Wordsworth's poem reflect this tradition? To what extent do these traits appear in T'ao Ch'ien's and Mary Oliver's poem? Cite evidence to support your answer.

_____

_____

_____

_____

_____

Where do you go to GET AWAY from it all?

Do you have a special place that's all your own? Describe that place below.

_____

_____

_____

Academic Vocabulary in Writing

context	interpret	reveal	significant	tradition

What do the poems you just read **reveal** about the importance of nature to the human spirit? Use at least one Academic Vocabulary word in your response. Definitions for these terms are listed on page 187.

Assessment Practice

DIRECTIONS Use "Poem on Returning to Dwell in the Country," "My Heart Leaps Up," and "The Sun" to answer questions 1–4.

1 In "Poem on Returning to Dwell in the Country," what change does the speaker make in his life?

  (A) The speaker moves away from the country and to the city.

  (B) The speaker leaves his materialist lifestyle and moves to the country.

  (C) The speaker decides he no longer appreciates the country.

  (D) The speaker does not make any changes to his lifestyle.

2 In "My Heart Leaps Up," the speaker wishes to —

  (A) to never grow old

  (B) to see a rainbow everyday

  (C) always be devoted to nature

  (D) to fall in love

3 In "The Sun," what does the speaker regard as the most wonderful thing in life?

  (A) the sunrises and sunsets

  (B) the beauty of red flowers

  (C) the sky and sea

  (D) the summertime

4 Which of the following best expresses the universal theme found in all three poems?

  (A) One cannot live without nature.

  (B) Nature can be powerful and dangerous.

  (C) Connecting to nature provides a simple but powerful joy.

  (D) Some types of nature are more beautiful than others.

Two Kinds
Short Story by Amy Tan

Rice and Rose Bowl Blues
Poem by Diane Mei Lin Mark

How do EXPECTATIONS affect performance?

Think of a time when someone in a position of authority set a high goal for you. Perhaps a coach expected you to be the team's top scorer, or a parent expected you to get straight A's. How did you respond to these expectations? Were you motivated to work harder? Did you rebel?

DISCUSS With a small group of classmates, discuss why parents might have high expectations of their children. Record three reasons from your discussion to share with the class.

Reasons for High Expectations

1. _____

  _____

2. _____

  _____

3. _____

  _____

Text Analysis: Theme Across Genres

The short story and poem you are about to read are both about young people struggling to find their own identities—despite the expectations of their parents. The works have a similar **theme,** or message, about the topic, even though they are different genres, or types of literature. The short story writer and the poet use different techniques to express the theme of their work. The chart below shows the techniques used in each genre.

In the Short Story	In the Poem
• details about the main character's traits, motivations, and values • details about how the characters change the lessons they learn • the major internal and external conflicts • information about the setting • the story's title	• words and phrases describing the speaker's thoughts and feelings • key images • stanzas and lines that present an idea or compare images • sound devices, such as alliteration and repetition, that may emphasize an idea

As you read, try to infer the theme of each work by paying attention to the techniques listed above.

Reading Skill: Set a Purpose for Reading

When you **set a purpose for reading,** you establish specific reasons to read a work. For example, your purpose for reading "Two Kinds" and "Rice and Rose Bowl Blues" is to identify the theme of each so that you can compare and contrast them. As you read, think about the struggles each character faces and look for answers to the questions in the chart below.

Points of Comparison
What is the main conflict?
What lesson does the narrator or speaker learn?
What idea does the title emphasize?
Write is the theme of the work?
What techniques does the writer use to convey the theme?

Vocabulary in Context

Note: Words are listed in the order in which they appear in the story.

prodigy (prŏd'ə-jē) *n.* a person who is exceptionally talented or intelligent
The young composer was a **prodigy** *in his field, making him incredibly successful for his age.*

reproach (rĭ-prōch') *n.* blame; criticism
Despite poor reviews in the press, the famous movie director felt he was beyond **reproach.**

mesmerizing (mĕz'mə-rīz'ĭng) *adj.* holding one's attention in an almost hypnotic manner
I could not tear my eyes away from the ballerina's **mesmerizing** *performance.*

encore (ŏn'kôr') *n.* a repeated or additional performance
The audience enjoyed the performance so much that they cheered for an **encore.**

discordant (dĭ-skôr'dnt) *adj.* having a disagreeable or clashing sound
The **discordant** *notes coming from the poorly tuned piano made it unpleasant to listen to.*

lament (lə-mĕnt') *v.* to express grief or deep regret
The man **lamented** *over the loss of his wife.*

debut (dā-byōo') *n.* first public performance or showing
The singer nervously prepared for her **debut** *performance.*

fiasco (fē-ăs'kō) *n.* a complete failure
Due to the rain, the outdoor event was a **fiasco.**

Two Kinds

Short Story by
AMY TAN

BACKGROUND The main character in "Two Kinds," Jing-mei, is an American girl born to Chinese parents. Like many other children of immigrants, Chinese American children often have one foot in the world their parents left behind and one foot in the United States. The differences between the two cultures can cause conflict between second-generation American children and their parents.

prodigy (prŏd′ə-jē) *n.* a person who is exceptionally talented or intelligent

My mother believed you could be anything you wanted to be in America. You could open a restaurant. You could work for the government and get good retirement. You could buy a house with almost no money down. You could become rich. You could become instantly famous.

"Of course you can be **prodigy**, too," my mother told me when I was nine. "You can be best anything. What does Auntie Lindo know? Her daughter, she is only best tricky."

America was where all my mother's hopes lay. She had come here in 1949 after losing everything in China: her mother and father, her family home, her first husband, and two daughters, twin baby girls. But she never looked back with regret. There were so many ways for things to get better. **PAUSE & REFLECT**

We didn't immediately pick the right kind of prodigy. At first my mother thought I could be a Chinese Shirley Temple.[1] We'd

---

1. **Shirley Temple:** a popular child movie star of the 1930s.

watch Shirley's old movies on TV as though they were training films. My mother would poke my arm and say, *"Ni kan"*—You watch. And I would see Shirley tapping her feet, or singing a sailor song, or pursing her lips into a very round O while saying,
20 "Oh my goodness."

"Ni kan," said my mother as Shirley's eyes flooded with tears. "You already know how. Don't need talent for crying!"

Soon after my mother got this idea about Shirley Temple, she took me to a beauty training school in the Mission district[2] and put me in the hands of a student who could barely hold the scissors without shaking. Instead of getting big fat curls, I emerged with an uneven mass of crinkly black fuzz. My mother dragged me off to the bathroom and tried to wet down my hair.

"You look like Negro Chinese," she lamented, as if I had done
30 this on purpose.

The instructor of the beauty training school had to lop off these soggy clumps to make my hair even again. "Peter Pan is very popular these days," the instructor assured my mother. I now had hair the length of a boy's, with straight-across bangs that hung at a slant two inches above my eyebrows. I liked the haircut, and it made me actually look forward to my future fame. PAUSE & REFLECT

In fact, in the beginning, I was just as excited as my mother, maybe even more so. I pictured this prodigy part of me as many
40 different images, trying each one on for size. I was a dainty ballerina girl standing by the curtains, waiting to hear the right music that would send me floating on my tiptoes. I was like the Christ child lifted out of the straw manger, crying with holy indignity. I was Cinderella stepping from her pumpkin carriage with sparkly cartoon music filling the air.

In all of my imaginings, I was filled with a sense that I would soon become *perfect*. My mother and father would adore me. I would be beyond **reproach**. I would never feel the need to sulk for anything.

PAUSE & REFLECT
Why do you think Jing-mei wants to be a prodigy?

_____

_____

_____

_____

_____

_____

reproach (rĭ-prōch′) *n.* blame; criticism

---

2. **Mission district:** a residential neighborhood in San Francisco.

Ⓐ THEME

Reread lines 38–52. What are the narrator's conflicting feelings about becoming a prodigy?

_____

_____

_____

_____

_____

_____

_____

_____

_____

_____

PAUSE & REFLECT

Why do you think the narrator's mother sets up such impossible tests for the narrator? How do you think this makes the narrator feel?

_____

_____

_____

_____

_____

50   But sometimes the prodigy in me became impatient. "If you don't hurry up and get me out of here, I'm disappearing for good," it warned. "And then you'll always be nothing." Ⓐ

Every night after dinner, my mother and I would sit at the Formica[3] kitchen table. She would present new tests, taking her examples from stories of amazing children she had read in *Ripley's Believe It or Not,* or *Good Housekeeping, Reader's Digest,* and a dozen other magazines she kept in a pile in our bathroom. My mother got these magazines from people whose houses she cleaned. And since she cleaned many houses each week, we had a

60   great assortment. She would look through them all, searching for stories about remarkable children.

The first night she brought out a story about a three-year-old boy who knew the capitals of all the states and even most of the European countries. A teacher was quoted as saying the little boy could also pronounce the names of the foreign cities correctly.

"What's the capital of Finland?" my mother asked me, looking at the magazine story.

All I knew was the capital of California, because Sacramento was the name of the street we lived on in Chinatown. "Nairobi!"[4]

70   I guessed, saying the most foreign word I could think of. She checked to see if that was possibly one way to pronounce "Helsinki" before showing me the answer.

The tests got harder—multiplying numbers in my head, finding the queen of hearts in a deck of cards, trying to stand on my head without using my hands, predicting the daily temperatures in Los Angeles, New York, and London.

One night I had to look at a page from the Bible for three minutes and then report everything I could remember. "Now Jehoshaphat[5] had riches and honor in abundance and . . . that's all

80   I remember, Ma," I said. **PAUSE & REFLECT**

---

3. **Formica** (fôr-mī′kə): a heat-resistant material used on kitchen counters, table tops, and similar surfaces.

4. **Nairobi** (nī-rō′bē): the capital of the African nation of Kenya.

5. **Jehoshaphat** (jə-hŏsh′ə-făt′): a king of the ancient Biblical land of Judah in the ninth century B.C.

And after seeing my mother's disappointed face once again, something inside of me began to die. I hated the tests, the raised hopes and failed expectations. Before going to bed that night, I looked in the mirror above the bathroom sink and when I saw only my face staring back—and that it would always be this ordinary face—I began to cry. Such a sad, ugly girl! I made high-pitched noises like a crazed animal, trying to scratch out the face in the mirror.

90 And then I saw what seemed to be the prodigy side of me—because I had never seen that face before. I looked at my reflection, blinking so I could see more clearly. The girl staring back at me was angry, powerful. This girl and I were the same. I had new thoughts, willful thoughts, or rather thoughts filled with lots of won'ts. I won't let her change me, I promised myself. I won't be what I'm not. **B**

So now on nights when my mother presented her tests, I performed listlessly, my head propped on one arm. I pretended to be bored. And I was. I got so bored I started counting the bellows of the foghorns out on the bay while my mother drilled 100 me in other areas. The sound was comforting and reminded me of the cow jumping over the moon. And the next day, I played a game with myself, seeing if my mother would give up on me before eight bellows. After a while I usually counted only one, maybe two bellows at most. At last she was beginning to give up hope.

Two or three months had gone by without any mention of my being a prodigy again. And then one day my mother was watching *The Ed Sullivan Show*[6] on TV. The TV was old and the sound kept shorting out. Every time my mother got halfway 110 up from the sofa to adjust the set, the sound would go back on and Ed would be talking. As soon as she sat down, Ed would go silent again. She got up, the TV broke into loud piano music. She sat down. Silence. Up and down, back and forth, quiet and loud. It was like a stiff, embraceless dance between her and the TV set. Finally she stood by the set with her hand on the sound dial.

B THEME
Reread lines 89–95. Circle the statements that reveal the narrator's changing attitude toward her mother's tests. What conflict is developing?

_____

_____

_____

_____

_____

_____

_____

_____

_____

_____

_____

---

6. *The Ed Sullivan Show:* a popular television variety show in the 1950s and 1960s.

mesmerizing (mĕz′mə-rīz′ĭng) *adj.* holding one's attention in an almost hypnotic manner.

PAUSE & REFLECT
Reread lines 134–139. The narrator equates talent with effort. How does the mother's attitude toward talent and success differ from her daughter's?

_____

_____

_____

_____

_____

encore (ŏn′kôr′) *n.* a repeated or additional performance

She seemed entranced by the music, a little frenzied piano piece with this **mesmerizing** quality, sort of quick passages and then teasing lilting ones before it returned to the quick playful parts.

"*Ni kan,*" my mother said, calling me over with hurried hand
120 gestures, "Look here."

I could see why my mother was fascinated by the music. It was being pounded out by a little Chinese girl, about nine years old, with a Peter Pan haircut. The girl had the sauciness of a Shirley Temple. She was proudly modest like a proper Chinese child. And she also did this fancy sweep of a curtsy, so that the fluffy skirt of her white dress cascaded slowly to the floor like the petals of a large carnation.

In spite of these warning signs, I wasn't worried. Our family had no piano and we couldn't afford to buy one, let alone reams
130 of sheet music and piano lessons. So I could be generous in my comments when my mother bad-mouthed the little girl on TV.

"Play note right, but doesn't sound good! No singing sound," complained my mother.

"What are you picking on her for?" I said carelessly. "She's pretty good. Maybe she's not the best, but she's trying hard." I knew almost immediately I would be sorry I said that.

"Just like you," she said. "Not the best. Because you not trying." She gave a little huff as she let go of the sound dial and sat down on the sofa. **PAUSE & REFLECT**

140 The little Chinese girl sat down also to play an **encore** of "Anitra's Dance" by Grieg.[7] I remember the song, because later on I had to learn how to play it.

Three days after watching *The Ed Sullivan Show,* my mother told me what my schedule would be for piano lessons and piano practice. She had talked to Mr. Chong, who lived on the first floor of our apartment building. Mr. Chong was a retired piano teacher and my mother had traded housecleaning services for weekly lessons and a piano for me to practice on every day, two hours a day, from four until six.

---

7. **Grieg** (grēg): Norwegian composer Edvard Grieg (1843–1907).

150 When my mother told me this, I felt as though I had been sent to hell. I whined and then kicked my foot a little when I couldn't stand it anymore.

"Why don't you like me the way I am? I'm *not* a genius! I can't play the piano. And even if I could, I wouldn't go on TV if you paid me a million dollars!" I cried.

My mother slapped me. "Who ask you be genius?" she shouted. "Only ask you be your best. For you sake. You think I want you be genius? Hnnh! What for! Who ask you!"

"So ungrateful," I heard her mutter in Chinese. "If she had as
160 much talent as she has temper, she would be famous now." **C**

Mr. Chong, whom I secretly nicknamed Old Chong, was very strange, always tapping his fingers to the silent music of an invisible orchestra. He looked ancient in my eyes. He had lost most of the hair on top of his head and he wore thick glasses and had eyes that always looked tired and sleepy. But he must have been younger than I thought, since he lived with his mother and was not yet married.

I met Old Lady Chong once and that was enough. She had this peculiar smell like a baby that had done something in its pants.
170 And her fingers felt like a dead person's, like an old peach I once found in the back of the refrigerator; the skin just slid off the meat when I picked it up.

I soon found out why Old Chong had retired from teaching piano. He was deaf. "Like Beethoven!" he shouted to me. "We're both listening only in our head!"[8] And he would start to conduct his frantic silent sonatas.

Our lessons went like this. He would open the book and point to different things, explaining their purpose: "Key! Treble! Bass! No sharps or flats! So this is C major! Listen now and play after me!"
180 And then he would play the C scale a few times, a simple chord, and then, as if inspired by an old, unreachable itch, he gradually added more notes and running trills and a pounding bass until the music was really something quite grand.

C THEME
Reread lines 153–160 and consider what you know about the narrator's mother. Why does she continue to push her daughter?

---

8. **Beethoven . . . in our head!** (bā′tō′vən): Ludwig van Beethoven (1770–1827) continued to compose great music even after becoming totally deaf during the last years of his life.

I would play after him, the simple scale, the simple chord, and then I just played some nonsense that sounded like a cat running up and down on top of garbage cans. Old Chong smiled and applauded and then said, "Very good! But now you must learn to keep time!"

So that's how I discovered that Old Chong's eyes were too slow to keep up with the wrong notes I was playing. He went through the motions in half-time. To help me keep rhythm, he stood behind me, pushing down on my right shoulder for every beat. He balanced pennies on top of my wrists so I would keep them still as I slowly played scales and arpeggios.[9] He had me curve my hand around an apple and keep that shape when playing chords. He marched stiffly to show me how to make each finger dance up and down, staccato[10] like an obedient little soldier.

He taught me all these things, and that was how I also learned I could be lazy and get away with mistakes, lots of mistakes. If I hit the wrong notes because I hadn't practiced enough, I never corrected myself. I just kept playing in rhythm. And Old Chong kept conducting his own private reverie. **D**

So maybe I never really gave myself a fair chance. I did pick up the basics pretty quickly, and I might have become a good pianist at that young age. But I was so determined not to try, not to be anybody different, that I learned to play only the most ear-splitting preludes,[11] the most **discordant** hymns.

Over the next year, I practiced like this, dutifully in my own way. And then one day I heard my mother and her friend Lindo Jong both talking in a loud, bragging tone of voice so others could hear. It was after church, and I was leaning against the brick wall wearing a dress with stiff white petticoats. Auntie Lindo's daughter, Waverly, who was about my age, was standing farther down the wall about five feet away. We had grown up

D THEME
Review lines 199–203. What is the narrator's attitude toward her piano lessons? Do you think she'll be a successful student? Why or why not?

_____

_____

_____

_____

discordant (dĭ-skôr′dnt) *adj.* having a disagreeable or clashing sound

---

9. **arpeggios** (är-pĕj′ē-ōz′): chords in which the notes are played separately in quick sequence rather than at the same time.

10. **staccato** (stə-kä′tō): producing distinct, abrupt breaks between successive tones.

11. **preludes** (prĕl′yo̅o̅dz′): short piano compositions, each usually based on a single musical theme.

together and shared all the closeness of two sisters squabbling over crayons and dolls. In other words, for the most part, we hated each other. I thought she was snotty. Waverly Jong had gained a certain amount of fame as "Chinatown's Littlest Chinese
220 Chess Champion."

"She bring home too many trophy," <u>lamented</u> Auntie Lindo that Sunday. "All day she play chess. All day I have no time do nothing but dust off her winnings." She threw a scolding look at Waverly, who pretended not to see her.

"You lucky you don't have this problem," said Auntie Lindo with a sigh to my mother.

And my mother squared her shoulders and bragged: "Our problem worser than yours. If we ask Jing-mei[12] wash dish, she hear nothing but music. It's like you can't stop this natural talent."

230 And right then, I was determined to put a stop to her foolish pride. PAUSE & REFLECT

A few weeks later, Old Chong and my mother conspired to have me play in a talent show which would be held in the church hall. By then, my parents had saved up enough to buy me a secondhand piano, a black Wurlitzer spinet[13] with a scarred bench. It was the showpiece of our living room.

For the talent show, I was to play a piece called "Pleading Child" from Schumann's[14] *Scenes from Childhood*. It was a simple, moody piece that sounded more difficult than it was.
240 I was supposed to memorize the whole thing, playing the repeat parts twice to make the piece sound longer. But I dawdled over it, playing a few bars and then cheating, looking up to see what notes followed. I never really listened to what I was playing. I daydreamed about being somewhere else, about being someone else.

lament (lə-mĕnt') v. to express grief or deep regret

PAUSE & REFLECT
The narrator concludes that "foolish pride" motivates her mother. Based on what you know about her mother so far, do you agree? Explain.

_____

_____

_____

_____

_____

_____

_____

_____

_____

_____

_____

---

12. **Jing-mei** (jǐng'mā').

13. **Wurlitzer spinet:** Wurlitzer was a well-known manufacturer of organs and pianos, including the small upright piano known as a spinet.

14. **Schumann's** (shōō'mänz'): composed by Robert Schumann (1810–1856), a German composer famous for his piano works.

debut (dā-byōō') *n.* first public performance or showing

ⓔ THEME
Reread lines 258–267. Underline two statements that reveal the narrators expectations for her own performance.

The part I liked to practice best was the fancy curtsy: right foot out, touch the rose on the carpet with a pointed foot, sweep to the side, left leg bends, look up and smile.

My parents invited all the couples from the Joy Luck Club[15] to witness my **debut**. Auntie Lindo and Uncle Tin were there. Waverly and her two older brothers had also come. The first two rows were filled with children both younger and older than I was. The littlest ones got to go first. They recited simple nursery rhymes, squawked out tunes on miniature violins, twirled Hula-Hoops,[16] pranced in pink ballet tutus, and when they bowed or curtsied, the audience would sigh in unison, "Awww," and then clap enthusiastically.

When my turn came, I was very confident. I remember my childish excitement. It was as if I knew, without a doubt, that the prodigy side of me really did exist. I had no fear whatsoever, no nervousness. I remember thinking to myself, This is it! This is it! I looked out over the audience, at my mother's blank face, my father's yawn, Auntie Lindo's stiff-lipped smile, Waverly's sulky expression. I had on a white dress layered with sheets of lace, and a pink bow in my Peter Pan haircut. As I sat down I envisioned people jumping to their feet and Ed Sullivan rushing up to introduce me to everyone on TV. ⓔ

And I started to play. It was so beautiful. I was so caught up in how lovely I looked that at first I didn't worry how I would sound. So it was a surprise to me when I hit the first wrong note and I realized something didn't sound quite right. And then I hit another and another followed that. A chill started at the top of my head and began to trickle down. Yet I couldn't stop playing, as though my hands were bewitched. I kept thinking my fingers would adjust themselves back, like a train switching to the right track. I played this strange jumble through two repeats, the sour notes staying with me all the way to the end.

When I stood up, I discovered my legs were shaking. Maybe I had just been nervous and the audience, like Old Chong,

---

15. **Joy Luck Club:** the social group to which the family in this story belongs.
16. **Hula-Hoops:** plastic hoops that are whirled around the body by means of hip movements.

280 had seen me go through the right motions and had not heard anything wrong at all. I swept my right foot out, went down on my knee, looked up and smiled. The room was quiet, except for Old Chong, who was beaming and shouting, "Bravo! Bravo! Well done!" But then I saw my mother's face, her stricken face. The audience clapped weakly, and as I walked back to my chair, with my whole face quivering as I tried not to cry, I heard a little boy whisper loudly to his mother, "That was awful," and the mother whispered back, "Well, she certainly tried."

And now I realized how many people were in the audience,
290 the whole world it seemed. I was aware of eyes burning into my back. I felt the shame of my mother and father as they sat stiffly throughout the rest of the show. **PAUSE & REFLECT**

We could have escaped during intermission. Pride and some strange sense of honor must have anchored my parents to their chairs. And so we watched it all: the eighteen-year-old boy with a fake mustache who did a magic show and juggled flaming hoops while riding a unicycle. The breasted girl with white makeup who sang from *Madama Butterfly*[17] and got honorable mention. And the eleven-year-old boy who won first prize playing a tricky violin
300 song that sounded like a busy bee.

After the show, the Hsus,[18] the Jongs, and the St. Clairs from the Joy Luck Club came up to my mother and father.

"Lots of talented kids," Auntie Lindo said vaguely, smiling broadly.

"That was somethin' else," said my father, and I wondered if he was referring to me in a humorous way, or whether he even remembered what I had done.

Waverly looked at me and shrugged her shoulders. "You aren't a genius like me," she said matter-of-factly. And if I hadn't felt so
310 bad, I would have pulled her braids and punched her stomach.

---

17. **Madama Butterfly:** a famous opera by the Italian composer Giacomo Puccini.
18. **Hsus** (shüz).

PAUSE & REFLECT
Think about how the narrator feels now. How have her feelings toward her mother changed?

_____

_____

_____

_____

_____

_____

_____

_____

_____

_____

_____

_____

_____

_____

Monitor Your Comprehension

PAUSE & REFLECT

Why do you think the narrator's mother did not react as the narrator had expected in lines 311–322?

_____

_____

_____

_____

fiasco (fē-ăs'kō) n. a complete failure

What happened during the narrator's performance to turn it into a fiasco?

_____

_____

_____

_____

But my mother's expression was what devastated me: a quiet, blank look that said she had lost everything. I felt the same way, and it seemed as if everybody were now coming up, like gawkers at the scene of an accident, to see what parts were actually missing. When we got on the bus to go home, my father was humming the busy-bee tune and my mother was silent. I kept thinking she wanted to wait until we got home before shouting at me. But when my father unlocked the door to our apartment, my mother walked in and then went to the back, into the bedroom.

320 No accusations. No blame. And in a way, I felt disappointed. I had been waiting for her to start shouting, so I could shout back and cry and blame her for all my misery. **PAUSE & REFLECT**

I assumed my talent-show <u>fiasco</u> meant I never had to play the piano again. But two days later, after school, my mother came out of the kitchen and saw me watching TV. "Four clock," she reminded me as if it were any other day. I was stunned, as though she were asking me to go through the talent-show torture again. I wedged myself more tightly in front of the TV.

"Turn off TV," she called from the kitchen five minutes later.

330 I didn't budge. And then I decided. I didn't have to do what my mother said anymore. I wasn't her slave. This wasn't China. I had listened to her before and look what happened. She was the stupid one.

She came out from the kitchen and stood in the arched entryway of the living room. "Four clock," she said once again, louder.

"I'm not going to play anymore," I said nonchalantly. "Why should I? I'm not a genius."

She walked over and stood in front of the TV. I saw her chest
340 was heaving up and down in an angry way.

"No!" I said, and I now felt stronger, as if my true self had finally emerged. So this was what had been inside me all along.

"No! I won't!" I screamed.

230 INTERACTIVE READER / UNIT 4: THEME AND SYMBOL

She yanked me by the arm, pulled me off the floor, snapped off the TV. She was frighteningly strong, half pulling, half carrying me toward the piano as I kicked the throw rugs under my feet. She lifted me up and onto the hard bench. I was sobbing by now, looking at her bitterly. Her chest was heaving even more and her mouth was open, smiling crazily as if she were pleased
350 I was crying.

"You want me to be someone that I'm not!" I sobbed. "I'll never be the kind of daughter you want me to be!"

"Only two kinds of daughters," she shouted in Chinese. "Those who are obedient and those who follow their own mind! Only one kind of daughter can live in this house. Obedient daughter!" **F**

"Then I wish I wasn't your daughter. I wish you weren't my mother," I shouted. As I said these things I got scared. It felt like worms and toads and slimy things crawling out of my chest, but it also felt good, as if this awful side of me had surfaced, at last.
360 "Too late change this," said my mother shrilly.

And I could sense her anger rising to its breaking point. I wanted to see it spill over. And that's when I remembered the babies she had lost in China, the ones we never talked about. "Then I wish I'd never been born!" I shouted. "I wish I were dead! Like them."

It was as if I had said the magic words. Alakazam!—and her face went blank, her mouth closed, her arms went slack, and she backed out of the room, stunned, as if she were blowing away like a small brown leaf, thin, brittle, lifeless. **PAUSE & REFLECT**

F THEME
The title of a story is often a clue to its theme. The title of this story comes from the exchange between the narrator and her mother in lines 353–357. Circle the kind of daughter the narrator believes herself to be. Put a box around the kind of daughter her mother expects her daughter to be.

PAUSE & REFLECT
Why does the narrator mention the babies her mother lost? How does the mother react to her daughter's words in lines 361–365?

370 It was not the only disappointment my mother felt in me. In the years that followed, I failed her so many times, each time asserting my own will, my right to fall short of expectations. I didn't get straight A's. I didn't become class president. I didn't get into Stanford. I dropped out of college.

For unlike my mother, I did not believe I could be anything I wanted to be. I could only be me.

And for all those years, we never talked about the disaster at the recital or my terrible accusations afterward at the piano bench. All that remained unchecked, like a betrayal that was

380 now unspeakable. So I never found a way to ask her why she had hoped for something so large that failure was inevitable.

And even worse, I never asked her what frightened me the most: Why had she given up hope?

For after our struggle at the piano, she never mentioned my playing again. The lessons stopped. The lid to the piano was closed, shutting out the dust, my misery, and her dreams.

So she surprised me. A few years ago, she offered to give me the piano, for my thirtieth birthday. I had not played in all those years. I saw the offer as a sign of forgiveness, a tremendous

390 burden removed.

"Are you sure?" I asked shyly. "I mean, won't you and Dad miss it?"

"No, this your piano," she said firmly. "Always your piano. You only one can play."

"Well, I probably can't play anymore," I said. "It's been years."

"You pick up fast," said my mother, as if she knew this was certain. "You have natural talent. You could been genius if you want to."

"No I couldn't."

400 "You just not trying," said my mother. And she was neither angry nor sad. She said it as if to announce a fact that could never be disproved. "Take it," she said. PAUSE & REFLECT

PAUSE & REFLECT
Reread lines 387–404. How has the narrator's mother changed? Explain.

_____

_____

_____

_____

_____

_____

_____

_____

But I didn't at first. It was enough that she had offered it to me. And after that, every time I saw it in my parents' living room, standing in front of the bay windows, it made me feel proud, as if it were a shiny trophy I had won back.

Last week I sent a tuner over to my parents' apartment and had the piano reconditioned, for purely sentimental reasons. My mother had died a few months before and I had been getting

410 things in order for my father, a little bit at a time. I put the jewelry in special silk pouches. The sweaters she had knitted in yellow, pink, bright orange—all the colors I hated—I put those in mothproof boxes. I found some old Chinese silk dresses, the kind with little slits up the sides. I rubbed the old silk against my skin, then wrapped them in tissue and decided to take them home with me.

After I had the piano tuned, I opened the lid and touched the keys. It sounded even richer than I remembered. Really, it was a very good piano. Inside the bench were the same exercise notes

420 with handwritten scales, the same secondhand music books with their covers held together with yellow tape.

I opened up the Schumann book to the dark little piece I had played at the recital. It was on the left-hand side of the page, "Pleading Child." It looked more difficult than I remembered. I played a few bars, surprised at how easily the notes came back to me.

And for the first time, or so it seemed, I noticed the piece on the right-hand side. It was called "Perfectly Contented." I tried to play this one as well. It had a lighter melody but the same flowing

430 rhythm and turned out to be quite easy. "Pleading Child" was shorter but slower; "Perfectly Contented" was longer, but faster. And after I played them both a few times, I realized they were two halves of the same song.

SET A PURPOSE FOR READING

Read this poem to find out the expectations the speaker's mother has for her daughter.

RICE *and* ROSE BOWL BLUES

Poem by

DIANE MEI LIN MARK

BACKGROUND The Rose Bowl is a famous college football championship played in California each year on New Year's Day. The first Rose Bowl was held in 1902, but it did not become an annual game until 1916. The writer includes some football terminology in her poem, including the terms *pass interception* (line 10), which means "a throw that is caught by the other team" and *on our 20* (line 12), meaning "20 yards from our goal."

PAUSE & REFLECT

How do you think the speaker feels about being pulled away from the game to learn to wash rice?

_____

_____

_____

_____

I remember the day
Mama called me in from
the football game with brothers
and neighbor boys
5 in our front yard

said it was time
I learned to
wash rice for dinner **PAUSE & REFLECT**

glancing out the window
I watched a pass interception
10 setting the other team up
on our 20

    Pour some water
    into the pot,
    she said pleasantly,
15   turning on the tap
    Rub the rice
    between your hands,
    pour out the clouds,
    fill it again

20   (I secretly traced
    an end run through
    the grains in
    between pourings) **G**
with the rice
25 settled into a simmer
I started out the door
but was called back

the next day
Roland from across the street
30 sneeringly said he heard
I couldn't play football
anymore

I laughed loudly,
asking him
35 where
he'd heard
such a thing **H**

G THEME
Reread the text in parentheses.
What do you learn about the
speaker's feelings and interests?

_____

_____

_____

_____

_____

_____

_____

H THEME
What can you tell about the
speaker's feelings from her
reaction to Roland?

_____

_____

_____

_____

_____

Comparing Themes Across Genres

Now that you have read both selections about parental expectations, you are ready to identify each writer's **theme**, or message. The following chart will help you get started.

Points of Comparison	In the Short Story	In the Poem
What is the main conflict?	Mother wants Jing-Mei to be a prodigy and daughter just wants to be herself.	
What lesson does the narrator or speaker learn?		
What idea does the title emphasize?		
Write a sentence stating your interpretation of the theme.		
What techniques does the writer use to convey the theme?		

Looking at your answers in the chart above, make a statement about how the themes in each selection differ.

_____

_____

_____

_____

How do **EXPECTATIONS** affect performance?

What best motivates you to succeed? Why?

_____

_____

_____

Academic Vocabulary in Speaking

context	interpret	reveal	significant	tradition

"Two Kinds" and "Rice Bowl Blues" both feature **traditions,** or customs of Chinese culture. With a partner, discuss those **traditions** and their place in the selection. Use at least one Academic Vocabulary word in your response. Definitions for these terms can be found on page 187.

Assessment Practice

DIRECTIONS Use "Two Kinds" and "Rice and Rose Bowl Blues" to answer questions 1–4.

1 In "Two Kinds" the narrator's mother want her to become a —
   - (A) straight A student
   - (B) prodigy
   - (C) chess player
   - (D) pianist

2 What does the following statement by Jing-Mei's mother reveal about the narrator of "Two Kinds"?

   "You already know how. Don't need talent for crying."
   - (A) Her mother cries a lot.
   - (B) Jing-Mei likes to cry.
   - (C) Jing-Mei cries a lot.
   - (D) Jing-Mei never cries.

3 At the end of the story, the narrator realizes that the Schumann pieces —
   - (A) reminded her of the conflict with her mother
   - (B) possesses the same qualities she sees in herself
   - (C) brought back the memories of her recital
   - (D) meant very little to her

4 In "Rice and Rose Bowl Blues," what is the speaker's main conflict with her mother?
   - (A) Her mother won't let her play with Roland.
   - (B) Her brothers won't let her play football.
   - (C) She does not know how to wash rice.
   - (D) Her mother makes her stop playing football so she can learn how to wash rice.

5

Ideas Made Visible

AUTHOR'S PURPOSE

Be sure to read the Text Analysis Workshop on pp. 552–557 in *Holt McDougal Literature*.

Academic Vocabulary for Unit 5

Preview the following Academic Vocabulary words. You will encounter these words as you work through this book and will use them as you write and talk about the selections in this unit.

conclude (kən klōōd') *v.* to decide or infer by reasoning

*After reading the article, one will likely **conclude** that the facts prove the scientist's theory to be correct.*

●

construct (kən strukt') *v.* to systematically create or build

*The writer **constructed** a convincing argument.*

●

implicit (im plis'it) *adj.* not plainly obvious or exhibited; suggested or implied

*I was confused by the article because the author's purpose was **implicit**.*

●

primary (prī'mĕr-ē) *adj.* highest in rank, or first in importance

*The writer's **primary** objective is to inform the reader of the war in Sudan.*

●

specific (spĭ-sĭf'k) *adj.* definite; of a special sort

*The directions were very **specific** and I was able to follow them easily.*

Have you ever read a poorly **constructed** article or document? What **specific** things made the text difficult to follow? Use at least one Academic Vocabulary word in your response.

_____

_____

_____

_____

Who Killed the Iceman?
Magazine Article

Skeletal Sculptures
Process Description by **Donna M. Jackson**

How do scientists **UNLOCK** the past?

As you may know from true-crime shows or sci-fi thrillers, human remains often have their own stories to tell. As police detectives unravel difficult cases and scientists investigate unexplained phenomena, the bones of humans often tell stories that help piece the past together.

DISCUSS What types of criminal or scientific investigations do you know about? With a small group, discuss the types of investigations you've read about or seen featured on a television program. Then, list each method you think of and its purpose in the notebook at the left.

Criminal Investigation

Method	Purpose
1. Finger-printing	Identify suspect
2.	
3.	

Text Analysis: Text Features

Many magazine articles and expository texts contain **text features**—design elements that help organize and highlight key information in a document. These features can also help you preview what you are reading.

- **Subheadings** signal the beginning of a new topic of section and identify the subject of the text to follow. They are usually set off from the selection text by a different color or font.

- **Graphic aids,** such as maps and photographs, present information visually. Photographs usually include **captions,** textual descriptions explaining the images.

- **Numbered lists** often show steps in a process. The numbers show the order in which the steps should be followed.

As you read the magazine article and the process description, look for text features that provide you with additional information.

Reading Strategy: Take Notes

When you **take notes,** you record a text's main ideas in a way that is easy for you to understand and remember. Since text features highlight main ideas and key information, including them in your notes is helpful.

As you read each section of "Who Killed the Iceman?" jot down its subheadings in a chart like the one below. The underlined head "Background" is the first subhead in the article, and the bulleted items are the main points under that subhead.

As you read, "Skeletal Sculptures," you will be prompted to note the key information in each step.

Who Killed the Iceman?	Skeletal Sculptures
<u>Background</u>	<u>Facial Reconstruction</u>
• He was frozen for 5,000 years.	1. _____
	_____
• Hikers found him in 1991 on the border between Austria and Italy.	2. _____
	_____
• _____	3. _____
_____	_____

Vocabulary in Context

Note: Words are listed in the order in which they appear in the selections.

artifact (är′tə-făkt′) *n.* something created by humans, usually for a practical purpose
   *The explorers found other **artifacts** alongside the mummy.*

refute (rĭ-fyōōt′) *v.* to prove false by argument or evidence
   *The new discovery may **refute** the scientist's previous theory.*

compile (kəm-pīl′) *v.* to put together by gathering from many sources
   *In order to come up with the best theories, scientists **compile** results from many studies.*

anthropology (ăn′thrə-pŏl′ə-jē) *n.* the science or study of human beings, including their physical characteristics and cultures
   *Because he loved studying other cultures, he decided to major in **anthropology**.*

presumed (prĭ-zōōmd′) *adj.* thought to be true
   *When the hikers failed to return on time, we **presumed** they were lost.*

SET A PURPOSE FOR READING

Read this article to discover the mystery of a 5,000-year-old mummy found frozen in an Italian glacier.

A TEXT FEATURES

Examine the **photograph** on this page and the accompanying **caption**. What information does the caption provide that the photograph does not?

_____

_____

_____

_____

_____

FROM NATIONAL GEOGRAPHIC MAGAZINE

WHO KILLED THE ICEMAN?

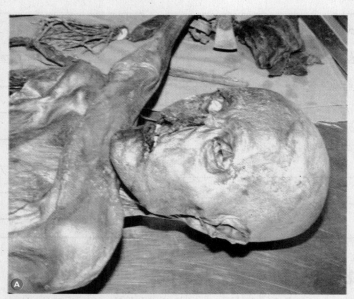

A

The world's oldest mummy, Ötzi, who roamed the Alps over five thousand years ago. Scientists took samples from him in order to help them learn more about him and his death.

BACKGROUND "Who Killed the Iceman?" chronicles some of the theories surrounding the death of a man who died nearly 3,000 B.C. The "Iceman" was discovered by German hikers vacationing in the Alps. When they spied a body embedded in the ice, the hikers assumed they found the remains of a fellow hiker. They had no idea they had stumbled onto the oldest mummy ever found.

He spent some 5,000 years frozen in a mountain glacier on the Austro-Italian border before passing hikers discovered him, sprawled in the melting snow, in 1991. He now resides in a refrigerated room at a museum in Italy. Over the 11 years since his discovery the Iceman mummy has been examined from every possible angle. But not until this past summer did those studying his still frozen body notice a crucial piece of evidence that dramatically rewrites his story: "Ötzi," nicknamed for the Ötztal Alps where he was found, 10 didn't freeze to death in a sudden snow storm while tending sheep as some had suggested. Instead he was killed, a victim of warfare, murder, or human sacrifice. **B**

Clues Discovered

X-rays reveal an arrowhead buried deep in the Iceman's left shoulder—an injury that could not possibly have been self-inflicted. This discovery consequently led archaeologists to believe that the Iceman had been killed. The wound, visible as a small dark smudge beneath the mummy's leathery skin, had been overlooked in all previous examinations.

B TAKE NOTES
What is the most important information provided in lines 1–12?

_____

_____

_____

_____

_____

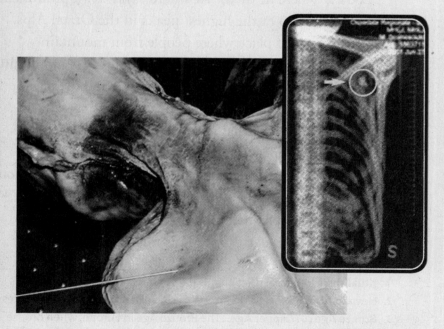

X-Ray Vision It was not until scientists performed a CT scan—a type of 3-D X-ray—that they saw the arrowhead buried in the Iceman's shoulder blade.

C TEXT FEATURES
What is the second subhead in this article?

_____

What is the main idea in this section?

_____

_____

_____

_____

D TAKE NOTES
The subheading "Different Theories" alerts you that there are different ideas about how the Iceman died. Underline the clues in lines 22–39 that explain what Reinhard believes happened.

artifact (är′tə-făkt′) *n.* something created by humans, usually for a practical purpose

20 Though no arrow shaft protrudes from the wound and no blood marks the arrow's entrance, it's now clear that the Iceman was shot in the back. But who did it? And why? **C**

Differing Theories

"There's no way anyone can ever really know," says archaeologist Johan Reinhard, a National Geographic Society explorer-in-residence. "It might have been murder. Or it might have been ritual sacrifice."[1]

Reinhard knows mummies. Among the many he has discovered is the Inca "ice maiden," a victim of sacrifice, on the frozen slopes of Peru's Nevado Ampato[2] in 1995. His experience studying mountain cultures in the Andes,
30 the Himalayas, and elsewhere has convinced him that the Iceman's death was not a random killing.

"Look at where he died," Reinhard says. "It's a prominent pass, between two of the highest peaks in the Ötztal Alps. This is the kind of place where people from mountain cultures have traditionally made offerings to their mountain gods. We know that mountain worship was important in prehistoric Europe during the Bronze Age," he says. "And there is good evidence that it may also have played a role earlier, in the Copper Age."[3] **D**
40 Reinhard's interpretation seems to answer questions about **artifacts** found with the mummy that have long puzzled experts. For example, breaking objects was a ceremonial practice in Neolithic[4] Europe. This might explain the

---

1. **ritual sacrifice:** a sacrifice that is part of a religious ceremony.
2. **Nevado Ampato** (nə-vä′dō äm-pä′tō): a volcano in the Central Andes.
3. **Bronze Age . . . Copper Age:** The Bronze Age in Europe, when bronze tools began to be used, lasted roughly from 3500 B.C. to 1000 B.C. The Copper Age overlaps with the earliest part of the Bronze Age.
4. **Neolithic** (nē′ə-lĭth′ĭk): having to do with the prehistoric period when food growing began, but before metal tools were used— about 4000 B.C. in Europe.

broken arrows lying near the mummy. The Iceman's copper ax—the oldest prehistoric ax in Europe with its bindings and handle intact—is also significant. Its copper had to have been mined, and mountains, as the source of valuable metals used to make tools, "were worshiped by miners throughout the world," says Reinhard. "This helps explain why the ax
50 was left with the body after the killing." Murderers would likely have taken something so useful with them. But people performing a ritual might have left it for the Iceman's use in the afterlife or as a tribute to the gods.

Where Ötzi Died

JUTLAND PENINSULA

SWITZERLAND
AUSTRIA
Innsbruck
Similaun
Venice
ITALY

E GRAPHICAL SOURCES
Examine the map on this page. What information does this map convey that the article does not? List two details.

_____

_____

_____

_____

_____

_____

_____

_____

_____

_____

_____

_____

Ötzi was found at approximately 10,500 feet in the Ötztal Alps on the border between Austria and Italy. After closely examining Ötzi's clothing and possessions—including a sheath and dagger (shown at left)—archaeologists realized they had uncovered a 5,300-year-old find.

PAUSE & REFLECT
What do you think about
Reinhard's theory? Do you find it
convincing? Why or why not?

_____

_____

_____

_____

_____

_____

refute (rĭ-fyōōt′) *v.* to prove false
by argument or evidence

**Why do other experts refute
Reinhard's theory?**

_____

_____

_____

_____

_____

compile (kəm-pīl′) *v.* to put
together by gathering from
many sources

Another clue: The Iceman's body was found in a naturally
formed trench along the pass. Prior explanations had him
taking shelter there from sudden bad weather. "But the
trench is not deep and is at a high point of the pass. It would
have been a poor place to sit out a storm," explains Reinhard.
Perhaps, instead, the Iceman was buried there by whoever
60 killed him, which would account for the body's being so well
preserved. **PAUSE & REFLECT**

Reinhard's ideas have not been met with enthusiasm by
European experts. In contrast with his beliefs, the mummy's
caretaker, pathologist Eduard Egarter Vigl of South Tyrol
Museum of Archaeology, believes that Ötzi may have been
fleeing from an attacker, saying, "The Iceman was hit by
an arrow from behind." Others maintain that arrows aren't
efficient means of ritual killing and that no clear evidence of
any other Copper Age sacrifice exists.

So Who Killed the Iceman?

70 "They view the idea of human sacrifice as too sensational,"
says Reinhard. "But they can't <u>refute</u> what I've pointed out,
and I believe my theory better explains the known facts.

"I know it's controversial," he admits. "But it's time to
<u>compile</u> all the evidence and reexamine it from a different
perspective. Let's look at these artifacts not only relative to
each other but also within social, sacred, and geographical
contexts."

Skeletal SCULPTURES

Process Description by

DONNA M. JACKSON

SET A PURPOSE
FOR READING

Read the process
description to learn how
forensic anthropologists
help detectives identify
human remains.

BACKGROUND "Skeletal Sculptures" explains how
forensic anthropologists help police track down the
truth. Forensics is the use of science to solve crimes.
Forensic anthropologists use their knowledge of
human characteristics to assist police in cracking
tough cases.

Dr. Michael Charney is an expert in forensic[1] **anthropology**.
His expertise has enabled him to take a few pieces of a
skeleton found in Missouri and compile a portrait of a five-foot,
120-pound Asian woman in her mid-twenties. Still, that isn't
enough to identify her.

The dead woman's "face" needs to be brought back to life.

Reconstructing the likeness of a person in clay, using the
skull as a guide, is a last resort at identification, Dr. Charney
says. It gives police a new lead to follow, a visual clue that can
10 be photographed and displayed in the media.

Facial reconstruction is not an identifying tool, he warns.
The goal is to trigger someone to recognize the model and to
identify the person through scientific means. **F**

"All that's needed is a general recognition that it looks like
so-and-so," he says.

anthropology (ăn′thrə-pŏl′ə-jē)
n. the science or study of human
beings, including their physical
characteristics and cultures

F TAKE NOTES
Reread lines 11–13. Underline the
goal of facial reconstruction.

---

1. **forensic:** having to do with applying scientific methods to crime
investigation.

Before re-creating a face, Dr. Charney and forensic sculptor Nita Bitner search the skull for signs of disease, injury, and structural defects.

"We look for things that shouldn't be there," Bitner says. 20 "Sometimes we find broken noses, cuts, or dentures." These affect the face's appearance and aid in the identification process. If the nose bone is curved to one side, for example, it's important to show it in the face because it's a distinguishing feature.

"We have to be careful, how-ever, not to include anything that happened at the time of death," Bitner notes, "because it wouldn't be recognizable to others."

Age also influences how a face is built. Wrinkled skin, which might help illustrate an older person, is often incorporated into a sculpture for accuracy.

30 After studying the Missouri woman's skull, Bitner makes a latex mold and pours a plaster cast. Now she's ready to sculpt the face. **G**

G TAKE NOTES
According to this article, what does Nita Bitner do after examining the skull?

_____

_____

_____

_____

H TEXT FEATURES
Reread the caption for photo 1. What items in the caption can you identify in the photograph?

_____

_____

_____

_____

1. Forensic sculptor Nita Bitner begins a facial restoration by cutting round rubber pegs into different lengths. The pegs, called landmarks, represent the thickness of the soft tissue (muscle, fat, and skin) at different points on the face. These tissue depths, which vary for men and women of varying ages, were first calculated from corpses by nineteenth-century scientists and later updated. **H**

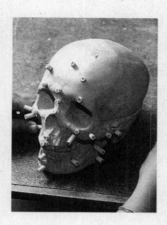

2. She then glues the rubber pegs to the skull cast.

3. Bitner "connects the dots" with strips of modeling clay. When attaching the strips of clay, she begins at the forehead and works her way down to the cheekbones, nasal area, chin, and mouth.

4. Once the dots are connected, Bitner fills in the spaces with clay and fleshes out the face. Now the prominent cheekbones of the Missouri woman become strikingly clear. Suddenly her broad face and delicate nose emerge. ❶

❶ **TAKE NOTES**
What is the main idea in step 4?

_____

_____

_____

_____

_____

5. As Bitner smooths the clay with her thumb and fingers, the face develops like a photograph.

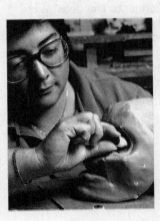

6. Bitner sets the plastic brown eyes in their sockets.

7. Next come the eyelids.

8. Bitner then sculpts the sides of the nose.

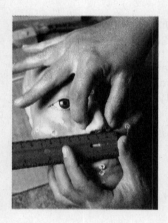

9. She measures the nose with a ruler to ensure it is the correct width. **PAUSE & REFLECT**

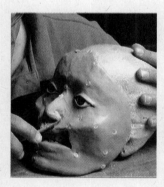

10. Now it's time to mold the upper lip.

PAUSE & REFLECT

How do the pictures on this page help you understand the process of facial reconstruction?

_____

_____

_____

_____

_____

_____

_____

_____

_____

_____

_____

_____

_____

presumed (prĭ-zoōmd') *adj.*
thought to be true.

11. The face is nearly complete.
Because the Missouri woman
is **presumed** to be Asian,
Bitner will add a black wig.
She will then add a scarf for a
finishing touch.

12. The model is now ready to be
photographed and publicized
in the media so that millions
of amateur detectives can
help solve the riddle of her
identity. **J**

J TEXT FEATURES
Review the **photographs**
illustrating the process. Circle the
photograph that you think is the
most important for transforming
a skull into a recognizable face.
Explain your choice.

_____

_____

_____

_____

_____

_____

_____

_____

_____

_____

_____

Text Analysis: Text Features

Text features, including graphic aids, help you gain more information from an article than just a simple paragraph of text might. Go back to the articles you just read and fill in the chart below, identifying the type of text features you found and the purpose of each.

Text Feature	Purpose of Text Feature

If you had simply scanned the text features of "Who Killed the Iceman?" would you have had an accurate idea of what the article was about? Explain your answer.

_____

_____

_____

Reading Strategy: Take Notes

Look back at the notes that you took as you read. Review each article and make sure that the main ideas are accurately represented in your set of notes. Did you miss any important ideas or details? If so, add them to this chart under an appropriate subhead.

"Who Killed the Iceman?"	"Skeletal Sculptures"

How do scientists UNLOCK the past?

How does learning about the past give us insight into our own time?

_____

_____

Vocabulary Practice

For each statement below, circle **T** for true or **F** for false.

1. A wildflower originally identified centuries ago is an ancient **artifact.**

   T   F

2. If I **refute** an argument, I make a convincing case against it.

   T   F

3. To write a good report, you should **compile** information from several sources.

   T   F

4. A person interested in animal behavior might want to study **anthropology.**

   T   F

5. Someone **presumed** to be at fault has already been proved wrong.

   T   F

Academic Vocabulary in Writing

conclude	construct	implicit	primary	specific

Something **specific** is definite or clearly defined. Which **specific** details in the description of Otzi in "Who Killed the Iceman?" stuck out to you? Use at least one Academic Vocabulary word in your response. Definitions of these words are provided on page 239.

_____

_____

_____

Assessment Practice

DIRECTIONS Use "Who Killed the Iceman?" and "Skeletal Sculptures" to answer questions 1–6.

1 What is Johan Reinhard's theory about how the Iceman died?

  (A) The Iceman was killed by other hunters.
  (B) The Iceman was killed by ritual sacrifice.
  (C) The Iceman was killed by animals.
  (D) The Iceman bled to death.

2 What piece of evidence did scientists find that led them to conclude the Iceman had been killed?

  (A) a sheath and dagger
  (B) hair on his clothes
  (C) a copper ax
  (D) an arrowhead in his shoulder

3 According to "Skeletal Sculptures," facial reconstruction is used for —

  (A) showing how a person might age
  (B) determining a skeleton's age
  (C) triggering recognition of skeletal remains
  (D) as an identifying tool

4 Subheads are used for all of the following reasons *except* —

  (A) to preview the following text
  (B) to signal a new topic or idea
  (C) to visually break up the text
  (D) to explain the main idea of the article

5 "Who Killed the Iceman?" contains all of the following text features *except* —

  (A) captions
  (B) subheads
  (C) numbered lists
  (D) graphics

6 According to "Skeletal Sculptures," what do forensic sculptors use as a guide to facial reconstruction?

  (A) crime scene photographs
  (B) the person's skull
  (C) descriptions from the victim's friends and family
  (D) x-ray images

The Lost Boys
Magazine Article by Sara Corbett

How far would you go to find FREEDOM?

It's impossible for most of us to imagine life as a refugee—someone who faces such terrible danger in his or her home country that leaving becomes the only way to find freedom. What would it take to make you leave your home and seek refuge in a strange, new place?

CHART IT Think about how you might respond if you were forced to leave everything you knew—your home, your family, your friends, and your belongings. In the chart at left, list what you would miss most about each part of your life if you suddenly became a refugee.

What I Would Miss Most

Home: _____

_____

Family: _____

_____

Friends: _____

_____

Belongings: _____

_____

Text Analysis: Author's Purpose

An author's purpose is what the writer hopes to achieve by writing a particular work. Although a writer may have more than one purpose, usually one stands out. An author's purpose can be:

- to inform or explain
- to persuade
- to entertain
- to express thoughts and feelings

AUTHOR'S PURPOSE	CLUES IN THE WRITING
TO INFORM OR EXPLAIN Examples: encyclopedia or magazine articles, documentaries, instruction manuals, Web sites	Facts and statistics, directions, steps in a process, diagrams or illustrated explanations
TO PERSUADE Examples: editorials, TV ads, political speeches	A statement of opinion, supporting evidence, appeals to emotion, a call to action
TO ENTERTAIN Examples: short stories, novels, plays, humorous essays, movies	Suspenseful or exciting situations, humorous or fascinating details, intriguing characters
TO EXPRESS THOUGHTS OR FEELINGS Examples: personal essays, poems, diaries, journals	Thoughtful descriptions, insightful observations, the writer's personal feelings

As you read "The Lost Boys," look for clues in the writing such as those listed in the chart above.

Reading Skill: Interpret Graphic Aids

Magazine articles often include **graphic aids**—such as charts, maps, and photographs—to present key information. When you read an article with graphic aids:

1. Examine the **photographs** that accompany this article. What information do they provide that is not in the article itself?

2. Study any **maps or charts** in the article and note the information they provide. How does a map or chart enhance your understanding of an article?

As you read, you will be prompted to answer questions about the graphic aids in this article.

Vocabulary in Context

Note: Words are listed in the order in which they appear in the article.

fractious (frăk′shəs) *adj.* hard to manage or hold together; unruly
   *The refugees were a **fractious** group of children from all over the country.*

posse (pŏs′ē) *n.* a band
   *The students had formed a **posse** and traveled in a group.*

exodus (ĕk′sə-dəs) *n.* a mass departure
   *Because of the threats of the bandits, the villagers made an **exodus** to leave their homeland.*

marauding (mə-rô′dĭng) *adj.* roaming about in search of plunder
   *The **marauding** men set fire to the villages once they were done robbing them.*

subsist (səb-sĭst′) *v.* to support oneself at a minimal level
   *We had barely enough food to **subsist** on.*

boon (bo͞on) *n.* a benefit; blessing
   *Help from aid workers was a **boon** for the refugees.*

Vocabulary Practice

Review the meanings of the vocabulary words above. Think about what you already know about refugees from Sudan or other areas. Write a few sentences using as many of the vocabulary words as you can.

_____

_____

_____

THE LOST BOYS

Magazine Article by

SARA CORBETT

BACKGROUND The young refugees profiled in
this article are from Sudan, the largest country
in Africa. Sudan has been torn apart by Africa's
longest-running civil war. Since 1972, over
4 million Sudanese people have been driven from
their homes and more than 2 million people
have died. At the heart of the war is a conflict
between the Islamic Sudanese government and
the southern Sudanese groups that demand
religious freedom and economic power.

**THESE YOUNG AFRICAN REFUGEES SURVIVED LIONS,
CROCODILES, AND STARVATION. NOW THEY'RE STARTING
LIFE OVER IN AMERICA.**

One evening in late January, Peter Dut, 21, leads his two
teenage brothers through the brightly lit corridors of the
Minneapolis airport, trying to mask his confusion. Two days
earlier, the brothers, refugees from Africa, had encountered their
first light switch and their first set of stairs. An aid worker in
Nairobi[1] had demonstrated the flush toilet to them—also the
seat belt, the shoelace, the fork. And now they find themselves
alone in Minneapolis, three bone-thin African boys confronted
by a swirling river of white faces and rolling suitcases.

---

1. **Nairobi** (nī-rō′bē): the capital city of Kenya, a country in Africa.

10   Finally, a traveling businessman recognizes their uncertainty. "Where are you flying to?" he asks kindly, and the eldest brother tells him in halting, bookish English. A few days earlier, they left a small mud hut in a blistering-hot Kenyan refugee camp, where they had lived as orphans for nine years after walking for hundreds of miles across Sudan.[2] They are now headed to a new home in the U.S.A. "Where?" the man asks in disbelief when Peter Dut says the city's name. "Fargo? North Dakota? You gotta be kidding me. It's too cold there. You'll never survive it!" **B**

And then he laughs. Peter Dut has no idea why.

20   In the meantime, the temperature in Fargo has dropped to 15 below. The boys tell me that, until now, all they have ever known about cold is what they felt grasping a bottle of frozen water. An aid worker handed it to them one day during a "cultural orientation" session at the Kakuma[3] Refugee Camp, a place where the temperature hovers around 100 degrees.

Peter Dut and his two brothers belong to an unusual group of refugees referred to by aid organizations as the Lost Boys of Sudan, a group of roughly 10,000 boys who arrived in Kenya in 1992 seeking refuge from their country's **fractious** civil war. The 30 fighting pits a northern Islamic government against rebels in the south who practice Christianity and tribal religions.

The Lost Boys were named after Peter Pan's **posse** of orphans. According to U.S. State Department estimates, some 17,000 boys were separated from their families and fled southern Sudan in an **exodus** of biblical proportions after fighting intensified in 1987. They arrived in throngs, homeless and parentless, having trekked about 1,000 miles from Sudan to Ethiopia, back to Sudan, and finally to Kenya. The majority of the boys belonged to the Dinka or Nuer tribes, and most were between the ages of 40 8 and 18. (Most of the boys don't know for sure how old they are; aid workers assigned them approximate ages after they arrived in 1992.) **C**

Along the way, the boys endured attacks from the northern army and **marauding** bandits, as well as lions who preyed on the slowest and weakest among them. Many died from starvation or

---

2. **Sudan:** a country in eastern Africa northwest of Kenya.
3. **Kakuma** (kə-kōo′mä).

B AUTHOR'S PURPOSE
The writer begins this article with an anecdote, or short story, instead of immediately presenting statistics about Sudan. How does this choice affect your view of the subject matter?

_____

_____

_____

_____

_____

fractious (frăk′shəs) adj. hard to manage or hold together; unruly

posse (pŏs′ē) n. a band

exodus (ĕk′sə-dəs) n. a mass departure

C AUTHOR'S PURPOSE
What is the author's purpose for including these statistics?

_____

_____

_____

_____

marauding (mə-rô′dĭng) adj. roaming about in search of plunder.

thirst. Others drowned or were eaten by crocodiles as they tried to cross a swollen Ethiopian river. By the time the Lost Boys reached the Kakuma Refugee Camp, their numbers had been cut nearly in half.

Ⓓ GRAPHIC AIDS
List two details included on this map that are not provided in the article. What do you think is the most important piece of information communicated by this map?

_____

_____

_____

_____

_____

subsist (səb-sĭst′) *v.* to support oneself at a minimal level

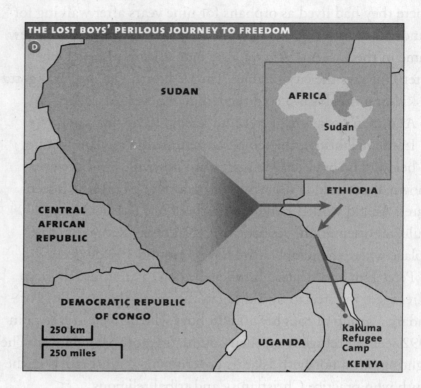

THE LOST BOYS' PERILOUS JOURNEY TO FREEDOM

Ⓓ

SUDAN

AFRICA

Sudan

ETHIOPIA

CENTRAL AFRICAN REPUBLIC

DEMOCRATIC REPUBLIC OF CONGO

250 km

250 miles

UGANDA

Kakuma Refugee Camp

KENYA

50   Now, after nine years of <u>subsisting</u> on rationed corn mush and lentils and living largely ungoverned by adults, the Lost Boys of Sudan are coming to America. In 1999, the United Nations High Commissioner for Refugees, which handles refugee cases around the world, and the U.S. government agreed to send 3,600 of the boys to the U.S.—since going back to Sudan was out of the question. About 500 of the Lost Boys still under the age of 18 will be living in apartments or foster homes across the U.S. by the end of this year. The boys will start school at a grade level normal for their age, thanks to a tough English-language program at their
60 refugee camp. The remaining 3,100 Lost Boys will be resettled as adults. After five years, each boy will be eligible for citizenship, provided he has turned 21.

NIGHTTIME IN AMERICA?

On the night that I stand waiting for Peter Dut and his brothers to land in Fargo, tendrils of snow are snaking across the tarmac. The three boys file through the gate without money or coats or luggage beyond their small backpacks. The younger brothers, Maduk, 17, and Riak, 15, appear petrified. As a social worker passes out coats, Peter Dut studies the black night through the airport window. "Excuse me," he says worriedly. "Can you tell me,
70 please, is it now night or day?" **PAUSE & REFLECT**

This is a stove burner. This is a can opener. This is a brush for your teeth. The new things come in a tumble. The brothers' home is a sparsely furnished, two-bedroom apartment in a complex on Fargo's south side. Rent is $445 a month. It has been stocked with donations from area churches and businesses: toothpaste, bread, beans, bananas.

A caseworker empties a garbage bag full of donated clothing, which looks to have come straight from the closet of an elderly man. I know how lucky the boys are: The State Department
80 estimates that war, famine, and disease in southern Sudan have killed more than 2 million people and displaced another 4 million. Still I cringe to think of the boys showing up for school in these clothes.

The next day, when I return to the apartment at noon, the boys have been up since 5 and are terribly hungry. "What about your food?" I ask, gesturing to the bread and bananas and the box of cereal sitting on the counter.

Peter grins sheepishly. I suddenly realize that the boys, in a lifetime of cooking maize and beans over a fire pit, have never
90 opened a box. I am placed in the role of teacher. And so begins an opening spree. We open potato chips. We open a can of beans. We untwist the tie on the bagged loaf of bread. Soon, the boys are seated and eating a hot meal. **E**

PAUSE & REFLECT
Notice in lines 64–65 that the author is now part of the article. Underline the word that shows you this shift in perspective. How does Peter's question help you understand the confusion of the boys?

E AUTHOR'S PURPOSE
What is the author's purpose in lines 85–93? Circle the words or phrases in these lines that provide clues to her purpose for writing.

boon (bo͞on) *n.* a benefit; blessing

Why would finding a warthog carcass be a **boon** for the Lost Boys?

_____

_____

_____

Given the experiences of the three brothers in Africa, how do you think they might react to life in America?

_____

_____

_____

_____

Ｆ AUTHOR'S PURPOSE

Why might the author have included these anecdotes about the boys's transition to life in Fargo?

_____

_____

_____

_____

_____

_____

_____

LIVING ON LEAVES AND BERRIES

The three brothers have come a long way since they fled their village in Sudan with their parents and three sisters—all of whom were later killed by Sudanese army soldiers. The Lost Boys first survived a 6- to 10-week walk to Ethiopia, often subsisting on leaves and berries and the occasional **boon** of a warthog carcass. Some boys staved off dehydration by drinking their own urine.
100 Many fell behind; some were devoured by lions or trampled by buffalo.

The Lost Boys lived for three years in Ethiopia, in UN-supported camps, before they were forced back into Sudan by a new Ethiopian government no longer sympathetic to their plight. Somehow, more than 10,000 of the boys miraculously trailed into Kenya's UN camps in the summer of 1992—as Sudanese government planes bombed the rear of their procession.

For the Lost Boys, then, a new life in America might easily
110 seem to be the answer to every dream. But the real world has been more complicated than that. Within weeks of arriving, Riak is placed in a local junior high; Maduk starts high school classes; and Peter begins adult-education classes. PAUSE & REFLECT

REFUGEE BLUES

Five weeks later, Riak listens quietly through a lesson on Elizabethan history at school, all but ignored by white students around him.

Nearby at Fargo South High School, Maduk is frequently alone as well, copying passages from his geography textbook, trying not to look at the short skirts worn by many of the girls.
120 Peter Dut worries about money. The three brothers say they receive just $107 in food stamps each month and spend most of their $510 monthly cash assistance on rent and utilities. Ｆ

Resettlement workers say the brothers are just undergoing the normal transition. Scott Burtsfield, who coordinates resettlement efforts in Fargo through Lutheran Social Services, says: "The first three months are always the toughest. It really does get better."

The Lost Boys can only hope so; they have few other options. A return to southern Sudan could be fatal. "There is nothing 130 left for the Lost Boys to go home to—it's a war zone," says Mary Anne Fitzgerald, a Nairobi-based relief consultant.

Some Sudanese elders have criticized sending boys to the U.S. They worry their children will lose their African identity. One afternoon, an 18-year-old Lost Boy translated a part of a tape an elder had sent along with many boys: "He is saying: 'Don't drink. Don't smoke. Don't kill. Go to school every day, and remember, America is not your home.'"

But if adjustment is hard, the boys also experience consoling moments.

140 One of these comes on a quiet Friday night last winter. As the boys make a dinner of rice and lentils, Peter changes into an African outfit, a finely woven green tunic, with a skullcap to match, bought with precious food rations at Kakuma.

Just then, the doorbell rings unexpectedly. And out of the cold tumble four Sudanese boys—all of whom have resettled as refugees over the last several years. I watch one, an 18-year-old named Sunday, wrap his arms encouragingly around Peter Dut. "It's a hard life here," Sunday whispers to the older boy, "but it's a free life, too." **PAUSE & REFLECT**

PAUSE & REFLECT
How do you think the boys feel about their new visitors?

_____

_____

_____

_____

_____

Text Analysis: Author's Purpose

Use the following chart to help you determine the author's main purpose for writing "The Lost Boys." Look back at the article for evidence that supports each purpose below and jot down line numbers in the chart. Whichever column has the most supporting evidence is the author's main purpose.

Author's Purpose in "The Lost Boys"
To Persuade:
To Entertain:
To Inform or Explain:
To Express Thoughts and Feelings:

Reading Skill: Graphic Aids

What other graphic aids—maps, photographs, charts—could be added to this article to make it more informative? What do you think would be the most helpful? Explain.

_____

_____

_____

How far would you go to find FREEDOM?

When is freedom worth other sacrifices?

_____

_____

_____

Vocabulary Practice

Circle the word that is not related in meaning to the other words.

1. migration, exodus, compassion, flight

2. boon, building, structure, edifice

3. inspiring, ravaging, plundering, marauding

4. amusement, posse, recreation, entertainment

5. subsist, survive, manage, reconsider

6. irritable, divisive, fractious, connected

Academic Vocabulary in Speaking

conclude	construct	implicit	primary	specific

To **conclude** means to come to a decision about something. What can you **conclude** about life as a refugee after reading this article? Discuss with a partner or small group and use at least one Academic Vocabulary word in your discussion. Definitions for these terms are listed on page 239.

Assessment Practice

DIRECTIONS Use "The Lost Boys" to answer questions 1–4.

1 The author most likely begins the article with the brothers' arrival at the airport to —

  A introduce a funny story about them
  B show that the boys are unhappy
  C emphasize the climate change the boys experience
  D highlight the difference between where the boys left and their new home

2 What is the main reason the Lost Boys are unable to return to Sudan?

  A They don't want to return.
  B The Sudanese government will not let them return.
  C Their villages have been destroyed.
  D The United States will not let them go back.

3 The author most likely included the anecdote in lines 63–70 to —

  A gain readers' sympathy for the boys
  B share her own feelings about how the boys were treated by the Americans
  C argue that the boys should have had escorts traveling with them
  D make the article more interesting

4 Why did the Lost Boys leave Ethiopia?

  A They wanted to return home.
  B The new Ethiopian government forced them out.
  C They were chased by lions.
  D Boys from Kakuma Refugee Camp told them it was safe.

Consumer Documents: From the Manufacturer to You

Product Information, Safety Information, Warranty

Why are **PROCEDURAL** texts necessary?

Have you ever tried to read a product warranty or an instruction manual and found yourself totally confused? Sometimes **procedural texts**—texts that provide instructions or other detailed, step-by-step information—can be difficult to understand. Good readers know not to panic. They slow down the pace of their reading and pay attention to details in the text.

QUICKWRITE What was the last product you bought that came with instructions? Did you find the instructions helpful? Why or why not? Record your thoughts in the notebook page to the left.

Product Instructions

Text Analysis: Consumer Documents

A consumer is someone who uses a product or service. You, your parents, and your classmates are all consumers. Many of the things you buy—even a product as simple as a backpack—come with **consumer documents.**

The purpose of most consumer documents is to give you information so that you can use the product effectively, safely, and—the company hopes—happily. Designers of consumer documents try to organize information well and explain the product clearly so that their documents meet this objective. As you read the consumer documents that follow, consider how they are organized and whether they are clear and easy to understand. Here are some questions that will help you evaluate consumer documents.

- Does the structure and format of the document make it easy to follow? For example, are key words boldface?

- If there are steps to follow, are they in the proper order?

- Does the document include graphics, charts, diagrams, or illustrations to help you find the information you need?

- Are the graphics and charts easy to understand?

Reading Skill: Adjust Reading Rate

When reading consumer documents, it is important to **adjust your reading rate** so that you don't miss important information. You may read quickly through information you think you already know, but you should slow down when you come across technical information that is more difficult to understand. Often, you'll find this kind of data in graphs, charts, tables, and pictures.

As you read the documents that follow, you will be asked to take notes about your reading rate in a chart like the one below. An example has been filled in for you.

Product Information	Safety Information	Warranty
I quickly scanned the row headings in the table, but then I slowed down to compare the numbers to what I learned from the product.		

**SET A PURPOSE
FOR READING**
Test your knowledge of
consumer documents by
reading the following texts.

CONSUMER DOCUMENTS:

From the Manufacturer to You

BACKGROUND So many of the things that you'll want to
do in life—such as making purchases, finding a job, and
becoming involved in your community—require you to
read and understand functional documents, procedural
and work-related texts that serve a practical purpose. As a
consumer, or user of a product or service, you will also need
to read consumer documents such as instruction manuals,
warranties, and product information to get the most out of
your purchase.

Picture before you an unopened box. In it is the latest
and greatest computer game console. In your hurry to
get it out of the box, you let a sheaf of papers slide to the
floor. There they lie in danger of being thrown out with all
the packing materials. Be sure you retrieve and read them
carefully. These **consumer documents** can make a big
difference in how much you enjoy your new game.

Elements and Features of Consumer Documents

Here are some types of consumer documents and the elements, or types of information, that each document provides:

- **product information**—descriptions of what the product will do
- **instruction manual**—information on how to use the product, often including safety information and any directions required for installation
- **warranty**—details of company and owner responsibilities if the product does not work **Ⓐ**

Consumer documents itemize, or detail, the unique features of each product. Here are some samples.

Product Information **Ⓑ**

WYSIWYGAME ARTS		
	CPU	800MHz
	Video card	250 MHz GPU
	Resolution	1920 × 1080 maximum
	Memory	128 MB
	Storage	Memory Card—Hard Drive
	Sound card	64 Channels
	DVD	Yes
	Media	12 × DVD-ROM 6.2 GB Capacity
	Hard drive	8 GB
	Modem	Yes
	Ethernet port	Yes
	Controllers	4

Ⓐ CONSUMER DOCUMENTS
What type of document should you consult if you need to find product safety information for an item you have purchased?

_____

_____

_____

_____

Ⓑ ADJUST READING RATE
The product information will help you decide if you want to purchase the WYSI WYGame Arts game console. What reading rate would you use to read this information? Add this info to the chart below.

Production Information
My Reading Rate:

C CONSUMER DOCUMENTS

How is the safety information on the page organized for easy use by readers?

_____

_____

_____

_____

_____

_____

_____

_____

_____

PAUSE & REFLECT

Why is it important to have a qualified professional service this product?

_____

_____

_____

_____

_____

_____

Safety Information

C Please follow these safeguards regarding the installation and use of your game console:

1. When installing your game console, be certain that the unit receives proper ventilation. Vents in the console covering are provided for this purpose. Never block or cover these vents with any objects, such as fabric, books, or magazines.
2. Do not install your game console in a bookcase or entertainment rack where it cannot receive proper ventilation.
3. Do not place the game console in direct sunlight or near a heat source, such as a radiator or hot-air duct.
4. Do not set the game console on a soft surface, such as a bed, sofa, or rug, since doing so may result in damage to the appliance.
5. Unplug this appliance from the wall outlet and contact a qualified service person under the following conditions:
    a. The power-supply cord or plug is damaged.
    b. Liquid has been spilled on, or objects have fallen into, the game console.
    c. The game console has been exposed to rain or water.
    d. The game console does not operate normally after you follow the operating instructions.
    e. The game console has been dropped, or the cabinet has been damaged.
    f. The game console exhibits a distinct change in performance.

Do not attempt to service this product yourself. Opening or removing the outside covers may expose you to dangerous voltage or other hazards. All service must be done by qualified service personnel.

PAUSE & REFLECT

Limited Warranty

WYSIWYGame Arts makes the following limited warranties. These limited warranties extend to the original consumer purchaser or any person receiving this product as a gift from the original consumer purchaser and to no other purchaser or transferee.

Limited Ninety [90] Day Warranty

WYSIWYGame Arts warrants this product and its parts against defect in materials and workmanship for a period of ninety [90] days after the dated or original retail purchase. During this period, WYSIWYGame Arts will
10   replace any defective product or part without charge to you. For replacement you must deliver the entire product to the place of purchase.

Limited One [1] Year Warranty of Parts

WYSIWYGame Arts further warrants the parts of this product against defects in materials or workmanship for a period of one [1] year after the date of original retail purchase. During this period, WYSIWYGame Arts will replace a defective part without charge to you, except that if a defective part is replaced after ninety [90] days from the date of original purchase, you pay labor charges
20   involved in the replacement. You must also deliver the entire product to an authorized WYSIWYGame Arts service station. You pay all transportation and insurance charges for the product to and from the service station.

D CONSUMER DOCUMENTS

Review the information under "Limited Ninety [90] Day Warranty." Underline the items that the manufacturer is willing to replace if the product breaks within 90 days of purchase. What must you include in order to get a replacement?

_____

_____

_____

_____

_____

_____

_____

_____

E ADJUST READING RATE

The warranty provides information about what the game company is willing and not willing to do if the product does not work correctly. How would you read this document in order to find out how to get a warranty?

_____

_____

_____

What do you need to do to ensure the warranty will be effective?

_____

_____

_____

_____

E Owner's Manual and Warranty Registration

Read the owner's manual thoroughly before operating this product. WYSIWYGame Arts does not warrant any defect caused by improper installation or operation. Complete and mail the attached registration card within fourteen [14] days; the warranty is effective only if your name, address, and date of purchase are on file as the

30   new owner of a WYSIWYGame Arts product.

Text Analysis: Consumer Documents

Evaluate the organization of the information in the consumer documents
you just read. Was the document easy to understand? What features of the
documents are intended to help you accomplish the document's objective?
Record your answers in the chart below.

Document	Type of Information	How Well the Information is Organized
Product Information		
Safety Information		
Warranty		

Reading Skill: Adjust Reading Rate

Now that you have read the three types of consumer documents, how would you recommend another person read them? Write notes about how you adjusted your reading rate in the spaces in the chart below.

Product Information	Safety Information	Warranty

Now that you have carefully read the product information, safety information, and warranty for the WYSIWYGame Arts console, consider whether you would purchase this product. Does the product information seem reliable? Is the product safe to use? Are the terms of the warranty satisfactory? Explain.

_____

_____

_____

_____

_____

_____

Why are **PROCEDURAL** texts necessary?

How are they different from other things you read?

_____

_____

_____

Academic Vocabulary in Speaking

conclude	construct	implicit	primary	specific

From reading these consumer documents, what can you **conclude,** or decide about the best reading rate to use? What **specific** information would you look for? Discuss with a partner, using at least one Academic Vocabulary word in your response. Definitions for these terms appear on page 239.

_____

_____

_____

Assessment Practice

DIRECTIONS Use the consumer documents to answer questions 1–6.

1 The purpose of the product information is to inform consumers about the product's —

- **A** safety hazards
- **B** cost
- **C** specifications
- **D** warranty

2 The purpose of a warranty is to provide —

- **A** some protection if a product is defective
- **B** a list of product hazards
- **C** directions for operating a product
- **D** a lifetime guarantee of a product

3 According to the Safety Information, what should you do if the product does not operate normally after following the operating instructions?

- **A** Return the product to the nearest store.
- **B** Try to repair the product yourself.
- **C** Call the product manufacturer.
- **D** Unplug it and contact a service person.

4 The format of the Warranty includes —

- **A** boldface headers
- **B** key words in boldface
- **C** graphic illustrations
- **D** a chronological order

5 What time limits on the parts and workmanship does the Warranty impose?

- **A** One month
- **B** Ninety days
- **C** One year
- **D** None

6 According to the Product Information, you would not want to purchase this product if you were looking for a product with —

- **A** more than 4 controllers
- **B** more than 6 GB of hard drive space
- **C** a modem and ethernet port
- **D** a memory card

UNIT 6

Argument and Persuasion

TAKING SIDES

Be sure to read the Text Analysis Workshop on pp. 654–659 in *Holt McDougal Literature*.

Academic Vocabulary for Unit 6

Preview the following Academic Vocabulary words. You will encounter these words as you work through this book and will use them as you write and talk about the selections in the unit.

coherent (kō-hîr′ənt) *adj.* logical, consistent, or connected

*The paragraph is **coherent** because each example relates to the main idea.*

differentiate (dĭf′ə-rĕn′shē-āt′): *v.* to perceive or create a difference between

*Read closely to **differentiate** the various types of appeals used in the argument.*

evident (ĕv′ĭ-dənt): *adj.* obvious, easy to see or understand

*The main idea is **evident** because it is restated several times.*

relevant (rĕl′ə-vənt): *adj.* related or pertinent to the matter at hand

*Any support used in an argument must be **relevant** to the claim.*

technique (tĕk-nēk′): *n.* a method of procedure or a manner of doing something

*His argument uses a variety of persuasive **techniques**.*

Think about an article or speech you read or heard that had a convincing argument. What **techniques** were used to make it effective? Write a few sentences about it, using at least one Academic Vocabulary word in your response.

_____

_____

_____

I Have a Dream
Speech by **Dr. Martin Luther King Jr.**

Can a **DREAM** change the world?

Time and again someone has a dream, or vision, of how to make the world a better place. Powerful words can help turn a person's dream into reality. In the speech you are about to read, Dr. Martin Luther King Jr., sets forth his vision for the future.

QUICKWRITE What is your vision for a better world? Does it involve better schools? safer communities? cleaner air? Complete the sentence in the notebook at the left for your idea for a better world.

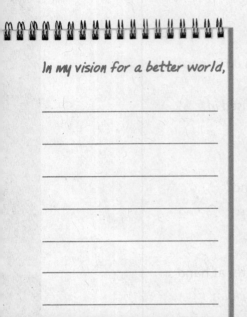

In my vision for a better world,

Text Analysis: Argument

You may think of an argument as an angry discussion. In formal speaking and writing, however, an **argument** expresses a position on an issue and supports the position with reasons and evidence. A sound argument includes these elements:

• a **claim**—the writer or speaker's position on an issue

• the **support**—the reasons and evidence that support the claim

In "I Have a Dream," King makes this claim about the status of African Americans:

But one hundred years later [after the Emancipation Proclamation], *the Negro is still not free.*

As you read the speech, look for this claim and the reasons and evidence King provides to support it.

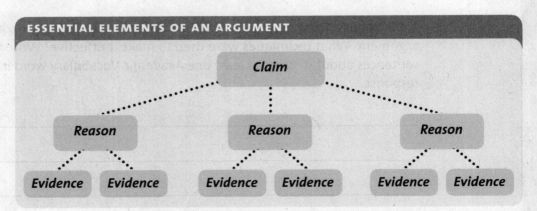

ESSENTIAL ELEMENTS OF AN ARGUMENT

Claim

Reason   *Reason*   *Reason*

Evidence *Evidence*   *Evidence* *Evidence*   *Evidence* *Evidence*

Reading Skill: Understand Rhetorical Devices

Writers and speakers typically use more than just arguments to persuade. They also use rhetorical devices, techniques to enhance their arguments and communicate more effectively. In the following examples, notice how the wording makes the message more memorable.

RHETORICAL DEVICE	EXAMPLE
REPETITION Uses the same word or words more than once for emphasis	Let there be justice for all. Let there be peace for all. Let there be work, bread, water and salt for all. —from "Glory and Hope" by Nelson Mandela
PARALLELISM Uses similar grammatical constructions to express ideas that are related or equal in importance. Often creates a rhythm.	We cannot, we must not, refuse to protect the right of every American to vote in every election. . . . And we ought not, and we cannot, and we must not wait another eight months before we get a bill. —from "We Shall Overcome" by Lyndon Baines Johnson
ANALOGY Makes a comparison between two subjects that are alike in some ways	Have you heard the canned, frozen and processed product being dished up to the world as American popular music today? —from a commencement address by Billy Joel

As you read "I Have a Dream," you will be prompted to find examples of these devices.

Vocabulary in Context

Note: Words are listed in the order in which they appear in the speech.

momentous (mō-měn′təs) *adj.* of great importance
*The inauguration of the president was a **momentous** occasion.*

default (dĭ-fôlt′) *v.* to fail to keep a promise, especially a promise to repay a loan
*Banks charge penalties if you miss payments and **default** on a loan.*

legitimate (lə-jĭt′ə-mĭt) *adj.* justifiable, reasonable
*The student had a **legitimate** excuse for being late to class.*

militancy (mĭl′ĭ-tənt-sē) *n.* the act of aggressively supporting a political or social cause
*The group's outrage at injustice fueled its **militancy**.*

inextricably (ĭn-ĕk′strĭ-kə-blē) *adv.* in a way impossible to untangle
*Employee efforts were **inextricably** linked to the company's success.*

SET A PURPOSE FOR READING

Read "I Have a Dream" to find out what kind of future Dr. Martin Luther King Jr. dreams about.

I Have a Dream

Speech by

DR. MARTIN LUTHER KING JR.

BACKGROUND On August 28, 1963, more than 250,000 Americans of all races and from all over the country took part in a march on Washington, D.C. to urge Congress to pass a civil rights bill. Late in the day, Dr. Martin Luther King Jr. delivered this speech, encouraging people to use nonviolent protest to bring about social change.

I am happy to join with you today in what will go down in history as the greatest demonstration for freedom in the history of our nation.

Five score[1] years ago, a great American, in whose symbolic shadow we stand today, signed the Emancipation Proclamation.[2] This **momentous** decree came as a great beacon light of hope to millions of Negro slaves who had been seared in the flames of withering injustice. It came as a joyous daybreak to end the long night of their captivity.

10 But one hundred years later, the Negro still is not free; one hundred years later, the life of the Negro is still sadly crippled by the manacles of segregation and the chains of discrimination; one hundred years later, the Negro lives on a lonely island of poverty in the midst of a vast ocean of material prosperity; one

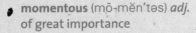

momentous (mō-mĕn′təs) *adj.* of great importance

Why was the Emancipation Proclamation a **momentous** event?

This documnat is important because it abolished Slavery in America.

---

1. **five score:** 100; *score* means "twenty." (This phrasing recalls the beginning of Abraham Lincoln's Gettysburg Address: "Four score and seven years ago . . .")
2. **Emancipation Proclamation:** a document signed by President Lincoln in 1863, during the Civil War, declaring that all slaves in states still at war with the Union were free.

hundred years later, the Negro is still languishing in the corners of American society and finds himself in exile in his own land. **Ⓐ**

So we've come here today to dramatize a shameful condition. In a sense we've come to our nation's capital to cash a check. When the architects of our republic wrote the magnificent words of the Constitution and the Declaration of Independence, they were signing a promissory note[3] to which every American was to fall heir. This note was the promise that all men, yes, black men as well as white men, would be guaranteed the unalienable rights of life, liberty, and the pursuit of happiness.

It is obvious today that America has **defaulted** on this promissory note insofar as her citizens of color are concerned. Instead of honoring this sacred obligation, America has given the Negro people a bad check, a check which has come back *still* marked "insufficient funds." But we refuse to believe that the bank of justice is bankrupt. We refuse to believe that there are insufficient funds in the great vaults of opportunity of this nation. And so we've come to cash this check, a check that will give us upon demand the riches of freedom and the security of justice. **Ⓑ**

We have also come to this hallowed spot to remind America of the fierce urgency of now. This is no time to engage in the luxury of cooling off or to take the tranquilizing drug of gradualism.[4] Now is the time to make real the promises of democracy; now is the time to rise from the dark and desolate valley of segregation to the sunlit path of racial justice; now is the time to lift our nation from the quicksands of racial injustice to the solid rock of brotherhood; now is the time to make justice a reality for all of God's children. It would be fatal for the nation to overlook the urgency of the moment. This sweltering summer of the Negro's **legitimate** discontent will not pass until there is an invigorating autumn of freedom and equality.

Nineteen sixty-three is not an end, but a beginning. And those who hope that the Negro needed to blow off steam and will

Ⓐ ARGUMENT
Reread lines 8–16. Underline the evidence King uses to **support** his **claim** that "the Negro is still not free." What problems does "the Negro" still face?

he states the fact that 100 yrs. after slavery discrimination and segregation evist

default (dĭ-fôlt') v. to fail to keep a promise, especially a promise to repay a loan

Ⓑ RHETORICAL DEVICE
Circle the **analogy**, or comparison, King uses in lines 25–34. To what situation does King compare the plight of "citizens of color"?

He compares the situation AA's face with a Bad check.

legitimate (lə-jĭt′ə-mĭt) *adj.* justifiable; reasonable

---

3. **promissory** (prŏm′ĭ-sôr′ē) **note:** a written promise to repay a loan.
4. **gradualism:** a policy of seeking to reach a goal slowly, in gradual stages.

now be content will have a rude awakening if the nation returns
50 to business as usual. There will be neither rest nor tranquility
in America until the Negro is granted his citizenship rights.
The whirlwinds of revolt will continue to shake the foundations of
our nation until the bright day of justice emerges.

But there is something that I must say to my people, who
stand on the worn threshold which leads into the palace of
justice. In the process of gaining our rightful place we must not
be guilty of wrongful deeds. Let us not seek to satisfy our thirst
for freedom by drinking from the cup of bitterness and hatred.
We must forever conduct our struggle on the high plain of
60 dignity and discipline. We must not allow our creative protests to
degenerate into physical violence. Again and again we must rise
to the majestic heights of meeting physical force with soul force.
The marvelous new **militancy**, which has engulfed the Negro
community, must not lead us to a distrust of all white people.
For many of our white brothers, as evidenced by their presence
here today, have come to realize that their destiny is tied up with
our destiny. And they have come to realize that their freedom is
inextricably bound to our freedom. We cannot walk alone. And
as we walk, we must make the pledge that we shall always march
70 ahead. We cannot turn back.   **PAUSE & REFLECT**

There are those who are asking the devotees of civil rights,
"When will you be satisfied?" We can never be satisfied as long
as the Negro is the victim of the unspeakable horrors of police
brutality; we can never be satisfied as long as our bodies, heavy
with the fatigue of travel, cannot gain lodging in the motels of
the highways and the hotels of the cities; we cannot be satisfied
as long as the Negro's basic mobility is from a smaller ghetto to
a larger one; we can never be satisfied as long as our children
are stripped of their selfhood and robbed of their dignity by
80 signs stating For Whites Only; we cannot be satisfied as long as
the Negro in Mississippi cannot vote and a Negro in New York
believes he has nothing for which to vote. No! No, we are not

militancy (mĭl'ĭ-tənt-sē) *n.* the act of aggressively supporting a political or social cause

inextricably (ĭn-ĕk'strĭ-kə-blē) *adv.* in a way impossible to untangle

PAUSE & REFLECT
Reread lines 54–70. How does King's message address his followers and also encourage support from a wider audience?

He ~~uses~~ ~~coffe makes~~ ~~the audin~~ addresses the white community/ audience and he asks them to stand w/ us

satisfied, and we will not be satisfied until "justice rolls down like waters and righteousness like a mighty stream." **C**

I am not unmindful that some of you have come here out of great trials and tribulations. Some of you have come fresh from narrow jail cells. Some of you have come from areas where your quest for freedom left you battered by the storms of persecution and staggered by the winds of police brutality.
90 You have been the veterans of creative suffering. Continue to work with the faith that unearned suffering is redemptive.[5] Go back to Mississippi. Go back to Alabama. Go back to South Carolina. Go back to Georgia. Go back to Louisiana. Go back to the slums and ghettos of our Northern cities, knowing that somehow this situation can and will be changed. Let us not wallow in the valley of despair.

I say to you today, my friends, even though we face the difficulties of today and tomorrow, I still have a dream. It is a dream deeply rooted in the American dream. I have a dream that
100 one day this nation will rise up and live out the true meaning of its creed, "We hold these truths to be self-evident; that all men are created equal." I have a dream that one day on the red hills of Georgia, sons of former slaves and the sons of former slave owners will be able to sit down together at the table of brotherhood. I have a dream that one day even the state of Mississippi, a state sweltering with the heat of injustice, sweltering with the heat of oppression, will be transformed into an oasis of freedom and justice. I have a dream that my four little children will one day live in a nation where they will not be judged by the color of their
110 skin, but by the content of their character. **D**

I have a dream today!

I have a dream that one day down in Alabama—with its vicious racists, with its Governor having his lips dripping with the words of interposition and nullification[6]—one day right there in Alabama, little black boys and black girls will be able

---

5. **unearned suffering is redemptive:** undeserved suffering is a way of earning freedom or salvation.

6. **Governor . . . nullification:** Rejecting a federal order to desegregate the University of Alabama, Governor George Wallace claimed that the principle of nullification (a state's alleged right to refuse a federal law) allowed him to resist federal "interposition," or interference, in state affairs.

C ARGUMENT
Underline examples of racial injustice that King provides in lines 71–84. How does King suggest his supporters should respond to this injustice?

to fight back for the rights they deserve and to never be satisfied by compromise

D RHETORICAL DEVICES
What rhetorical device does King use in lines 97–110? Fill out your answers in the chart below.

Word, Phrase, or Sentence
I Have a dream

↓

Type of Device
Repetition

↓

Effect
makes an effect of emphasis

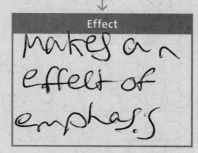

to join hands with little white boys and white girls as sisters and brothers.

<u>I have a dream today!</u>

I have a dream that one day every valley shall be exalted, and
120 every hill and mountain shall be made low. The rough places
will be plain and the crooked places will be made straight, "and
the glory of the Lord shall be revealed, and all flesh shall see
it together."

This is our hope. <u>This is the faith that</u> I go back to the South
with. With this faith we will be able to hew out of the mountain
of despair a stone of hope. <u>With this</u> faith we will be able to
transform the jangling discords of our nation into a beautiful
symphony of brotherhood. <u>With this</u> faith we will be able to
<u>work together</u>, to <u>pray together</u>, to <u>struggle together</u>, to <u>go to jail
130 together</u>, to stand up for freedom together, knowing that we will
be free one day. And this will be the day. This will be the day
when all of God's children will be able to sing with new meaning,
"My country 'tis of thee, sweet land of liberty, of thee I sing. Land
where my fathers died, land of the pilgrims' pride, from every
mountainside, let freedom ring." And if America is to be a great
nation, this must become true. **E**

So let freedom ring from the prodigious hilltops of
New Hampshire; let <u>freedom ring</u> from the mighty mountains
of New York; let freedom ring from the heightening Alleghenies
140 of Pennsylvania; <u>let freedom ring</u> from the snowcapped
Rockies of Colorado; <u>let freedom ring</u> from the curvaceous
slopes of California. But not only that. Let freedom ring from
Stone Mountain of Georgia; let freedom ring from Lookout
Mountain of Tennessee; let freedom ring from every hill
and molehill of Mississippi. "From every mountainside, let
freedom ring."

And when this happens, and when we allow freedom to ring,
when we let it ring from every village and every hamlet, from every
state and every city, we will be able to speed up that day when all
150 of God's children—<u>black men and white men</u>, Jews and Gentiles,
<u>Protestants and Catholics</u>—will be able to join hands and sing
<u>in the words of the old Negro spiritual</u>, "Free at last. Free at last.
Thank God Almighty, we are free at last." **PAUSE & REFLECT**

E **RHETORICAL DEVICES**
Reread lines 124–136. Underline
the words that King repeats.
What effect does this have?

The effect of emphasis using the words "I Have a Dream"

PAUSE & REFLECT
How does King appeal to a wide
audience in this last portion of
his speech?

He verbally mentions a lot of different etnics/religions saying all will be free

---

Text Analysis: Argument

Dr. Martin Luther King Jr. dreams of an America where all people live in freedom and harmony. Complete the graphic organizer with reasons and evidence King provides to support his argument that this freedom and harmony does not exist for African Americans.

Reasons/Evidence: Police brutality, even now, is evident in our society.

Reasons/Evidence: Basic Mobility

Claim:
Racial injustice still exists.

Reasons/Evidence: Hotells and Highways were not open to Negroes

Review your notes for "I Have a Dream" and the completed graphic organizer. Then, write a brief summary of King's argument.

_____

_____

_____

_____

Reading Skill: Understand Rhetorical Devices

Think about the rhetorical devices you noticed as you read King's speech. Which device had the strongest effects? List your ideas in the chart below.

Device	

↓

Example	

↓

Why it was effective	

Can a DREAM change the world?

How can you turn a dream for change into a reality?

_____

_____

_____

Vocabulary Practice

Circle the answer to each question below.

1. Which would be more **momentous**?
   the birth of a baby/the first snow of the season

2. What does it mean to **default** on a loan?
   sign up to borrow money/fail to make a payment

3. What would occur if your doctor's note was deemed **legitimate**?
   sent to the principal's office/allowed to miss gym

4. Who would be more likely to support a course of **militancy**?
   someone starting a new job/someone unfairly denied employment

5. Which items are more likely to be **inextricably** linked?
   products on a grocery store shelf/necklaces kept in a dresser drawer

Academic Vocabulary in Writing

coherent	differentiate	evident	relevant	technique

Dr. King gave this speech almost fifty years ago. What, if anything, has changed about racial relations in this country? Are King's arguments still **relevant** today? Explain, using at least one Academic Vocabulary word in your response. Definitions for these terms appear on page 277.

_____

_____

_____

_____

Assessment Practice

DIRECTIONS Use "I Have a Dream" to answer questions 1–4.

1 Which answer best explains why King refers to the Emancipation Proclamation at the start of his speech?
  - **A** He is at the march to celebrate the end of slavery.
  - **B** He wants people to remember how shameful slavery was.
  - **C** He plans to explain that African Americans are still not free.
  - **D** He is honoring President Lincoln for signing the document.

2 In lines 27–29, what does King mean when he says that America has given African Americans a "bad check"?
  - **A** It failed to support racial equality.
  - **B** It prevented banks from insuring funds.
  - **C** It continued to allow slavery in the South.
  - **D** It broke its promise to provide economic support.

3 Which of the following facts does King use to support his argument that African Americans are not free?
  - **A** African Americans live in poverty.
  - **B** Slavery was outlawed but still continues.
  - **C** Unalienable rights restrict African Americans.
  - **D** The Constitution only gives citizenship rights to whites.

4 In lines 72–84, how does King's repetition of the phrase "we can never be satisfied" support his argument?
  - **A** He appeals to feelings of guilt among the audience.
  - **B** He helps people understand his ideas by restating them.
  - **C** He provides examples of injustice each time he uses the phrase.
  - **D** He makes the speech memorable by adding rhythm and rhyme.

Testimony Before the Senate

Speech by **Michael J. Fox**

How do you SELL AN IDEA?

As a teenager, you've seen hundreds of ads that try to sell you everything from snacks to clothes to electronic devices. But did you know that many organizations work hard to sell you on people and ideas, too?

DISCUSS Brainstorm a list of images or advertisements you've seen that have tried to sell you an idea, an image, or a person's expertise. One example is provided in the notebook at left. Think of another example and list the pitch, or technique, used.

Idea: Say "no" to drugs.

Pitch Used: Commercial about saving a friend who's drowning; slogan is "Friends, the anti-drug."

Idea: _____

_____

Pitch Used: _____

_____

_____

_____

Text Analysis: Persuasive Techniques

To sway their audiences, writers and speakers use **persuasive techniques**—messages and language that appeal to people's emotions, values, and desires. The chart below shows some examples.

TECHNIQUE	EXAMPLE
Appeals by Association	
"Plain Folks" Appeal Implies that ordinary people would agree with the proposition	Any mother knows that milk is part of a nutritious diet.
Testimonial Relies on endorsements from well-known people or satisfied customers	As an Olympic athlete, I need all the energy I can get. That's why I start my day with Grain Puffs.
Transfer Connects a product or a cause with a positive image or idea	Freedom is in your hands the minute you hit the road in a Mountainback XRV.
Emotional Appeals	
Appeal to Pity, Fear, or Vanity Uses words that evoke strong feelings, rather than facts and evidence, to persuade	**Appeal to Pity** For just one dollar a day, you can give a stray pet a second chance.
Appeal to Values	
Ethical Appeal Taps into people's values or moral standards	Volunteer today—because it's the right thing to do.

Reading Strategy: Summarize

A **summary** is a brief retelling of the main ideas of a written or spoken text. When you summarize, use your own words to restate the main ideas. As you read Fox's speech, you will be prompted to summarize it by jotting down main ideas and important details in a chart like the one shown.

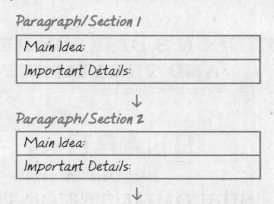

Paragraph/Section 1

| Main Idea: |
| Important Details: |

↓

Paragraph/Section 2

| Main Idea: |
| Important Details: |

↓

Vocabulary in Context

Note: Words are listed in the order in which they appear in the selection.

status quo (stăt′əs kwō) *n.* the existing state of affairs
*We don't want to change this policy because we like the **status quo.***

meager (mē′gər) *adj.* lacking in quantity or quality
*How can the cafeteria serve healthy meals on such a **meager** budget?*

neurological (nŏŏr′ə-lŏj′ĭ-kəl) *adj.* having to do with the nervous system
*Alzheimer's disease is a **neurological** disorder that affects memory and other brain functions.*

eradicate (ĭ-răd′ĭ-kāt′) *v.* to do away with completely
*If elected, the candidate promises to **eradicate** poverty in the city.*

Vocabulary Practice

Review the vocabulary words and their meanings. Then try to write a sentence for each word in the lines below.

_____

_____

_____

_____

SET A PURPOSE
FOR READING
Read this speech to find out
why Michael J. Fox decided to
become a spokesperson for
Parkinson's disease.

PARKINSON'S DISEASE RESEARCH AND TREATMENT

HEARING

BEFORE A
SUBCOMMITTEE OF THE
COMMITTEE ON APPROPRIATIONS
UNITED STATES SENATE
ONE HUNDRED SIXTH CONGRESS

FIRST SESSION

SPECIAL HEARING

Printed for the use of the Committee on Appropriations

BACKGROUND A successful actor, Michael J. Fox was
diagnosed with Parkinson's disease at the age of 30.
Parkinson's disease results from a loss of brain cells that
produce dopamine, a chemical that sends signals to
the brain. The disease can cause tremors, slowness of
movement, and problems with balance that make walking
and other ordinary activities difficult. Fox is devoted to
promoting Parkinson's research.

Senator SPECTER. We have with us today Mr. Michael J.
Fox, a successful actor for many years. First, as Alex P. Keaton,
on the television series "Family Ties." You always work with
a middle initial, do you not, Mr. Fox? Later in many movies,
including "Back to the Future," and, most recently, on
television again in the highly acclaimed "Spin City." Michael
was diagnosed with Parkinson's in 1991, at the age of 30.

He has become very, very active in Parkinson's advocacy. One of the facts of life is that when someone like
10 Michael J. Fox steps forward, it very heavily personalizes the problem, focuses a lot of public attention on it, and has the public understanding of the need for doing whatever we can as a country to conquer this disease and many, many others. So we thank you for being here, Michael J. Fox, and look forward to your testimony.

Again, we will put the lights on, for 5 minutes, on testimony.

Mr. FOX. Mr. Chairman, Senator Harkin, and members of the Subcommittee—thank you for inviting me to testify
20 today about the need for a greater federal investment in Parkinson's research. I would like to thank you, in particular, for your tremendous leadership in the fight to double funding for the National Institutes of Health.[1] Ⓐ

Some, or perhaps most of you are familiar with me from 20 years of work in film and television. What I wish to speak to you about today has little or nothing to do
30 with celebrity—save for this brief reference.

When I first spoke publicly about my 8 years of experience as a person with Parkinson's, many were surprised, in part because

Ⓐ **PERSUASIVE TECHNIQUES**
In lines 18–23, underline the sentence in which Fox uses an appeal to vanity. On the lines below, explain how Fox uses it.

_____

_____

_____

_____

_____

_____

_____

---

1. **National Institutes of Health:** a government organization that conducts and supports research designed to improve the health of the nation.

B Reread lines 32–49. Record this paragraph's main idea and details in the chart below.

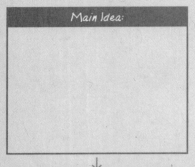

Main Idea:

↓

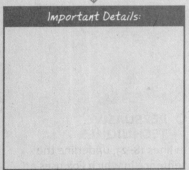

Important Details:

of my age (although 30 percent of all Parkinson's patients are under 50, and 20 percent are under 40,

40 and that number is growing). I had hidden my symptoms and struggles very well, through increasing amounts of medication, through surgery, and by employing the hundreds of little tricks and techniques a person with Parkinson's learns to mask his or her condition for as long as possible. B

50 While the changes in my life were profound and progressive, I kept them to myself for a number of reasons: fear, denial for sure, but I also felt that it was important for me to just quietly "soldier on."

When I did share my story, the response was overwhelming, humbling, and deeply inspiring. I heard from thousands of Americans affected by Parkinson's, writing and calling to offer encouragement and to tell me of their experience. They spoke of pain, frustration, fear and hope. Always hope.

60 What I understood very clearly is that the time for quietly "soldiering on" is through. The war against Parkinson's is a winnable war, and I am resolved to play a role in that victory.

What celebrity has given me is the opportunity to raise the visibility of Parkinson's disease and focus more attention on the desperate need for more research dollars. While I am able, for the time being, to continue to do what I love best, others are not so fortunate. There are doctors, teachers, policemen, nurses, and parents who are no longer able to work, to provide for their families, and live out their dreams. **C**

70   The one million Americans living with Parkinson's want to beat this disease. So do millions more Americans who have family members suffering from Parkinson's. But it won't happen until Congress adequately funds Parkinson's research.

    For many people with Parkinson's, managing their disease is a full-time job. It is a constant balancing act. Too little medicine causes tremors and stiffness. Too much medicine produces uncontrollable movement and slurring. And far too often, Parkinson's patients wait and wait for the medicines to "kick-in." New investigational therapies have helped some

80 people like me control my symptoms, but in the end, we all face the same reality: the medicines stop working. **D**

    For people living with Parkinson's, the <u>status quo</u> isn't good enough.

    As I began to understand what research might promise for the future, I became hopeful I would not face the terrible suffering so many with Parkinson's endure. But I was shocked and frustrated to learn that the amount of funding for Parkinson's research is so <u>meager</u>. Compared with the amount of federal funding going to other diseases, research

90 funding for Parkinson's lags far behind.

    In a country with a $15 billion investment in medical research we can and we must do better.

    At present, Parkinson's is inadequately funded, no matter how one cares to spin it. Meager funding means a continued lack of effective treatments, slow progress in understanding the cause of the disease, and little chance that a cure will

---

C PERSUASIVE TECHNIQUES

What kind of appeal does Fox make by referring to "doctors, teachers, policemen, nurses, and parents"? Explain your answer.

_____

_____

_____

D PERSUASIVE TECHNIQUES

Underline the words that Fox repeats in lines 74–81. What affect does this repetition have on you?

_____

_____

_____

_____

status quo (stăt′əs kwō) *n.* the existing state of affairs

meager (mē′gər) *adj.* lacking in quantity or quality

come in time. I applaud the steps we are taking to fulfill the promise of the Udall Parkinson's Research Act, but we must be clear—we aren't there yet.

100   If, however, an adequate investment is made, there is much to be hopeful for. We have a tremendous opportunity to close the gap for Parkinson's. We are learning more and more about this disease. The scientific community believes that with a significant investment in Parkinson's research, new discoveries and improved treatments strategies are close-at-hand. Many have called Parkinson's the most curable **neurological** disorder and the one expected to produce a breakthrough first. Scientists tell me that a cure is possible, some say even by the end of the

110 next decade—if the research dollars match the research opportunity. **E**

Mr. Chairman, you and the members of the Subcommittee have done so much to increase the investment in medical research in this country. I thank you for your vision. Most people don't know just how important this research is until they or someone in their family faces a serious illness. I know I didn't.

The Parkinson's community strongly supports your efforts to double medical research funding. At the same

120 time, I implore you to do more for people with Parkinson's. Take up Parkinson's as if your life depended on it. Increase funding for Parkinson's research by $75 million over current levels for the coming fiscal year.[2] Make this a down

neurological (no͝or´ə-lŏj´ĭ-kəl) *adj.* having to do with the nervous system

E SUMMARIZE
In lines 100–111, circle the details Fox provides to support the idea that there is reason to be hopeful about Parkinson's disease. Then summarize the paragraph in your own words.

_____

_____

_____

_____

---

2. **fiscal year:** a 12-month period—which may or may not coincide with the calendar year—during which a company or organization keeps accounting records.

payment for a fully funded Parkinson's research agenda that will make Parkinson's nothing more than a footnote in medical textbooks. **PAUSE & REFLECT**

I would like to close on a personal note. Today you will hear from, or have already heard from, more than a few experts, in the fields of science, book-keeping and other areas. 130 I am an expert in only one—what it is like to be a young man, husband, and father with Parkinson's disease. With the help of daily medication and selective exertion, I can still perform my job, in my case in a very public arena. I can still help out with the daily tasks and rituals involved in home

PAUSE & REFLECT
What does Fox want the senators to do? Underline the sentence in this paragraph that states his proposition most directly and specifically.

eradicate (ĭ-rădʹĭ-kāt') *v.* to do away with completely

Use a dictionary or a thesaurus to find a synonym for eradicate.

_____

_____

Ⓕ PERSUASIVE TECHNIQUES

In lines 127–142, circle the positive image that Fox connects with increased funding for Parkinson's disease. What persuasive technique is he using here?

_____

_____

_____

_____

life. But I don't kid myself . . . that will change. Physical and mental exhaustion will become more and more of a factor, as will increased rigidity, tremor and dyskinesia.[3] I can expect in my 40s to face challenges most wouldn't expect until their 70s and 80s—if ever. But with your help, if we all do
140 everything we can to **eradicate** this disease, in my 50s I'll be dancing at my children's weddings. And mine will be just one of millions of happy stories. Ⓕ

Thank you again for your time and attention.

Senator SPECTER. Thank you very much, Mr. Fox, for those very profound and moving words.

---

3. **dyskinesia** (dĭsʹkə-nēʹzhə): inability to control bodily movements.

Text Analysis: Persuasive Techniques

Michael J. Fox uses a variety of persuasive techniques in his speech to the Senate. Find an example of each type of technique listed on the chart below. The first one has been done for you.

PERSUASIVE TECHNIQUE	EXAMPLE FROM SPEECH
Testimonial (an appeal or endorsement by well-known people or satisfied customers)	"When I first spoke publicly about my 8 years of experience as a person with Parkinsons, many were surprised . . . When I did share my story, the response was overwhelming . . ."
Ethical Appeal (an appeal that taps into people's values or moral standards)	
"Plain Folks" Appeal (implies that ordinary people would agree with this position)	
Emotional Appeal (an appeal to a reader or listener's emotions, using words and images to evoke strong feelings)	

Of the persuasive techniques you noticed in Fox's speech, which did you find the most persuasive? Explain your answer.

_____

_____

_____

Reading Strategy: Summarize

In a persuasive speech, the speaker's proposition, or claim, is the main idea of his or her argument. Use the notes you made while reading Michael J. Fox's speech to write three important ideas that support his claim.

Claim: Congress must adequately fund Parkinson's Research

Supporting idea:

Supporting idea:

Supporting idea:

How do you SELL AN IDEA?

What makes some ideas easier—or harder—to sell than others?

_____

_____

_____

Vocabulary Practice

Write the word from the Word Bank that best completes each sentence.

1. _____ diseases can damage the brain.

2. The goal of medical research is to _____ these diseases.

3. A _____ increase in funding won't speed the progress toward finding a cure.

4. Clearly, it is important to move forward instead of maintaining the _____.

> **WORD BANK**
> eradicate
> meager
> neurological
> status quo

Academic Vocabulary in Speaking

coherent	differentiate	evident	relevant	technique

TURN AND TALK Imagine you are a senator who has just heard Fox's testimony. With a partner, role-play a conversation with a fellow senator in which you describe your responses to the testimony. For example, you might want to discuss which supporting details you thought were the most **relevant** to Fox's argument. Use at least one Academic Vocabulary word in your conversation. Definitions for these terms are listed on page 277.

Assessment Practice

DIRECTIONS Use "Testimony Before the Senate" to answer questions 1–6.

1 What does Michael J. Fox want to persuade the senators to do?

- **A** increase funding for Parkinson's research
- **B** forget that he is a celebrity
- **C** feel sorry for people with neurological disorders
- **D** double the funding for the National Institutes of Health

2 Which of these is the best summary of lines 74–81?

- **A** Tremors and stiffness are side effects of taking too little Parkinson's medicine.
- **B** It can take a long time for Parkinson's medicines to start working.
- **C** Medicating Parkinson's patients is difficult, and eventually the medicines stop working.
- **D** Parkinson's symptoms can be controlled with the right medications.

3 Fox makes an appeal to pity when he —

- **A** asks the Senate to increase funding by $75 million
- **B** describes the suffering of Parkinson's patients
- **C** mentions his career as a famous movie actor
- **D** praises the senators for supporting medical research

4 For eight years, Fox kept his illness a secret by —

- **A** refusing to take any Parkinson's medications
- **B** pretending to be younger than he was
- **C** using tricks to hide his symptoms
- **D** giving up his acting career

5 According to Fox, there is hope for Parkinson's patients because —

- **A** they can use many techniques to mask their symptoms
- **B** many celebrities are supporting the cause
- **C** the disease gets more funding than other neurological disorders
- **D** scientists believe a cure is possible if enough funding is available

6 When Fox mentions "dancing at my children's weddings," he is looking forward to a time when —

- **A** he learns to control his tremors and stiffness
- **B** his children no longer have to take care of him
- **C** people have more sympathy for Parkinson's patients
- **D** Parkinson's disease has been cured

How Private Is Your Private Life?
Magazine Article by Andrea Rock

The Privacy Debate: One Size Doesn't Fit All
Newspaper Editorial by Arthur M. Ahalt

Is **PRIVACY** an illusion?

Your phone number appears in a hundred databases. Your favorite Web site keeps track of your every click. Are these elements of technology a threat to your privacy?

DEBATE Do you think your privacy is at risk in today's society? Write notes in the notebook at the left to use in a debate about personal privacy in today's society.

Text Analysis: Fact and Opinion

Most persuasive writers use facts and opinions to support their **claims**—or positions on a topic. In order to properly evaluate a work of nonfiction, you need to be able to determine what is fact and what is an opinion.

- A **fact** is a statement that can be proved, or verified.

- An **opinion** is a statement that cannot be proved because it expresses a person's beliefs, feelings, or thoughts.

Unless opinions come from experts and are well **substantiated**, or established by evidence, they are not considered as reliable support for an argument.

When you read more than one article on a topic, you can identify facts and opinions in a chart like the one below.

Location	Example	Fact / Opinion
lines 2–3	A 1999 poll found that loss of privacy is the number-one concern of Americans.	[Fact]

Privacy at Risk?

Privacy is something that people _____

_____

_____

Privacy needs to be _____

_____

_____

_____

_____

Reading Skill: Recognize Bias

Bias is an unfair preference for or against an issue. To detect bias, look for the following:

- an argument in which the evidence gives one side stronger support than the other
- the presence of **loaded language**—words that create intensely positive or negative impressions
- opinions stated as if they were facts with no supporting evidence
- the use of **stereotyping** and other faulty reasoning

Vocabulary in Context

Note: Words are listed in the order in which they appear in the selections.

pervasive (pər-vā′sĭv) *adj.* spreading widely through an area or group of people
*The **pervasive** practice of gathering information may invade privacy.*

advocacy (ăd′və-kə-sē) *adj.* involving public support for an idea or policy
*The **advocacy** group worked to convince people to support their cause.*

surveillance (sər-vā′ləns) *adj.* having to do with close observation
*Many stores and streets are now protected by **surveillance** devices.*

disconcerting (dĭs′kən-sûr′tĭng) *adj.* causing one to feel confused or embarrassed
*Knowing you are being filmed can be a **disconcerting** experience.*

affiliate (ə-fĭl′ē-ĭt) *n.* a person or an organization officially connected to a larger body
*A business may use an **affiliate** to help meet the specific needs of its customers.*

browser (brou′zər) *n.* a program used to navigate the Internet
*A **browser** makes it possible to quickly find information on the Internet.*

anonymity (ăn′ə-nĭm′ĭ-tē) *n.* the condition of being unknown
*It is difficult to achieve **anonymity** in a small community.*

articulate (är-tĭk′yə-lĭt) *adj.* able to speak clearly and coherently; well-spoken
*The speaker at the conference was well prepared and **articulate**.*

nonpartisan (nŏn-pär′tĭ-zən) *adj.* not controlled by any political group
*Some **nonpartisan** groups help people learn about political issues.*

awry (ə-rī′) *adj.* off course; wrong
*It is easy for things to go **awry** when you are not paying attention.*

**SET A PURPOSE
FOR READING**

Read the following selection
to find out how your privacy
might be threatened.

How Private Is Your Private Life?

ANDREA ROCK

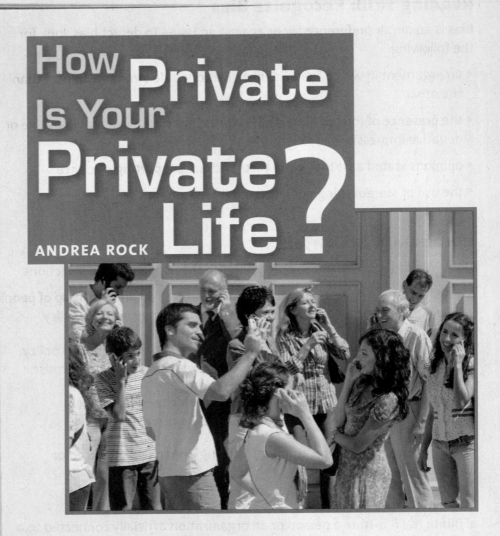

BACKGROUND Many Americans are becoming increasingly
concerned that the miracles of technology have come at the
cost of personal privacy. Some Americans want Congress to
pass stronger privacy laws.

*When you go online, file an insurance claim or even eat out, you
reveal personal information to strangers. Here's what you need to
know about who's watching you—and how to protect yourself.*

Rapid advances in technology have fostered an ever-
growing assault on our private lives. A 1999 *Wall Street
Journal* poll found that loss of privacy ranked as Americans'

number-one concern for the new century—ahead of depression, war and terrorism. **Ⓐ**

Regulators and lawmakers alike have proposed measures to safeguard privacy, but they face strong opposition from businesses whose aim is to collect as much information as possible about consumers' financial and medical histories, 10 their shopping habits and other personal details. Companies profit by selling this information to advertisers and other businesses, or simply by using it to tailor their own advertising.

To find out how <u>pervasive</u> the system really is, the editors of LHJ[1] asked me to see how often in a single day my activities resulted in a legal invasion of privacy. I was surprised by what I learned:

9:00 A.M.

After sending my two sons off to school, I go to the grocery store. At the register, I hand the cashier my 20 supermarket discount card. Later, I discover that this card allows retailers to track exactly what I've purchased, how much I spend and how often I shop. These details can then be shared with product manufacturers so that coupons and other offers can be targeted to me. "People should be aware that when they use these cards, they are literally selling their privacy," says Ari Schwartz, senior policy analyst at the Center for Democracy and Technology, an advocacy organization in Washington, D.C. Schwartz adds that his group has already seen cases where these records have been 30 used in lawsuits. **Ⓑ**

9:25 A.M.

After returning a video, I stop at the post office to mail an insurance claim form. Amazingly, the privacy

---

1. **editors of LHJ:** The author was given this assignment by the editors of *Ladies' Home Journal*.

Ⓐ RECOGNIZE BIAS
Reread lines 1–5 and circle any words or phrases that seem like **loaded language**. Does this language support a positive or negative view of technology? Explain.

_____

_____

_____

_____

pervasive (pər-vā′sĭv) *adj.* spreading widely through an area or group of people

advocacy (ăd′və-kə-sē) *adj.* involving public support for an idea or policy

Ⓑ FACT AND OPINION
Reread lines 18–30. Underline any facts that you find. What support is provided for these facts?

_____

_____

_____

_____

_____

PAUSE & REFLECT
Based on lines 31–43, who has
the right to see the author's
medical records? Does the
author think this is a good or bad
thing? Explain.

_____

_____

_____

_____

_____

_____

_____

_____

C FACT AND OPINION
Underline the fact in lines 50–53.
How might you confirm this
information?

_____

_____

_____

_____

_____

_____

of my video-rental records is protected by federal law,
but not the data in my medical records. By signing
the claim form, I authorize doctors to release sensitive
information about myself to insurers and other third
parties,[2] such as the Medical Information Bureau, which
keeps records of health problems reported on some
insurance applications and informs insurers (on request)
40 about pre-existing conditions.

Although my medical records can be shared with people
I don't know, in about half the states in the U.S., I don't have
the legal right to see them myself. **PAUSE & REFLECT**

10:00 A.M.

I call the car dealer about the 1997 Subaru I just
purchased. When I register a car or apply for a driver's license
in New York, my name, address, date of birth and the model
of my car may be sold to marketers, private investigators and
others who access the state's database. Policies may vary by
state, with some selling Social Security numbers, too.

50 The federal Driver's Privacy Protection Act of 1994
requires application forms to inform consumers that personal
information may be disclosed to third parties and that they
must be given an opportunity to prohibit such disclosures. **C**

10:20 A.M.

On my way into New York City to meet a friend for
lunch, I save time by paying the toll with my E-Z Pass, a
radio tag that deducts the toll from my account. But using
the pass means that a record of my travels is being kept.
While it can help track criminals, the data could also be used

2. **release sensitive information . . . other third parties:** Congress
attempted to address this problem by passing the Health Insurance
Portability and Accountability Act, which makes the unauthorized
release of medical information a crime.

to legally obtain personal information about law-abiding
60 citizens.

11:30 A.M.

As I'm waiting to cross the corner of 45th Street and
Fifth Avenue, I'm being filmed by a hidden video camera.
At twenty-second intervals, the device transmits the images
onto an Internet site. The camera is operated by a private
company simply for the use of promotional purposes and
entertainment on its Web site, but <u>surveillance</u> cameras are
increasingly being used by police and merchants to fight
crime, as well.

"By the end of the decade, I imagine most public places
70 will have surveillance cameras connected to a computer that
spontaneously compares faces shown on a monitor with
mug shots of people wanted by the police," says John Pike,
a security analyst at the Federation of American Scientists, a
private policy group in Washington D.C.

NOON

My friend Diane joins me at Daniel, a lovely French
restaurant. In my research, I found out that tiny cameras
strategically positioned in the ceiling allow the chefs to watch
diners eating so that they can time their delivery of the
courses. The food is delicious, but it's <u>disconcerting</u> to know
80 that every bite I take is being filmed. **◐**

Diane tells me that a friend of hers just received a ticket
by mail for running a red light six months earlier in Los
Angeles. A police surveillance camera caught the license plate
of the rental car, which the authorities used to track down his
name and address.

surveillance (sər-vā′ləns)
adj. having to do with close
observation

**How do police use surveillance
cameras?**

_____

_____

_____

_____

disconcerting
(dĭs′kən-sûr′tĭng) *adj.* causing
one to feel confused or
embarrassed.

◐ FACT AND OPINION
Fill in the chart with one fact and
one opinion from lines 75–80.

FACT:

↓

OPINION:

E FACT AND OPINION
Who is John Pike?

_____

_____

Is his statement a fact or an
opinion? Explain your answer.

_____

_____

_____

_____

_____

_____

_____

affiliate (ə-fĭl'ē-ĭt) *n.* a person
or an organization officially
connected to a larger body

1:30 A.M.

I use Diane's cell phone to leave a message for a friend,
aware that my conversation could be intercepted by someone
with a radio receiver. Says Pike: "If you are discussing
something highly sensitive that you wouldn't want your
90 prying neighbor or worst enemy to know, don't have that
conversation on a cell or portable phone." **E**

4:00 P.M.

After I check my e-mail on my home-office computer, my
older son, Adam, visits a site that provides all the research
he needs for his fifth-grade science project. I feel much more
comfortable about his use of the Internet now that a new
federal law prohibits commercial Web sites from collecting
personal information from children under thirteen without
parental consent.

6:11 P.M.

I use online banking services to see if a recent deposit has
100 been credited to my account. When I first signed up for this
service, I was instructed to use my Social Security number
as my customer access code. I avoid giving out that number
when possible, but in this case, I had no choice. The bank
protects my account information from hackers and other
unauthorized third parties, but it does share that data with
inside **affiliates**, such as brokerage partners.[3]

Consumer advocates say financial privacy has been
further endangered by a federal law that made it easier
for banks to merge with other financial firms, such as
110 brokerages and insurance companies. Though the law
includes provisions to protect consumer privacy, critics say
there are loopholes that could lead, for example, to a bank

---

3. **brokerage partners:** individuals or companies that buy and sell stocks
   or other assets for others.

denying a loan to a customer because its health-insurance affiliate's data reveals that he or she is being treated for a life-threatening illness. **PAUSE & REFLECT**

9:35 P.M.

When I visit *Amazon.com* to check out a book, a message on my computer screen says that the Web site is trying to place a "cookie," a tag that identifies me to an Internet company whenever I visit its site, on my hard drive. Normally,
120 consumers don't receive this alert, but I've learned how to activate a feature on my computer's **browser** that will warn me every time a cookie is about to be placed, giving me the option of accepting it or not. Adam and I have visited eleven Web sites today, accumulating forty-nine cookies in all.

Cookies can give you more than you bargained for. A Web site may share its data with an ad network, such as DoubleClick, which places banner ads on more than 1,800 Web sites. An online profile of you is created, which associates your computer with any sites you visit on that
130 ad network, noting what you look at or buy. Your profile continues to expand and can be sold to anyone without your knowledge or consent. Visiting a gardening Web site just to learn about varieties of roses might trigger a deluge of seed catalogs in your mailbox later. **G**

10:45 P.M.

To wrap up, I return to my Excite home page to read my horoscope. "Your home is your castle," it says, "and you are the supreme ruler within its walls." After today, I'm not so sure.

PAUSE & REFLECT
Is it fair for a bank to deny a loan to a customer with a life-threatening illness? Explain why or why not.

_____

_____

_____

_____

_____

browser (brou'zər) *n.* a program used to navigate the Internet

G RECOGNIZE BIAS
Reread lines 125–134. Loaded language can sometimes take the form of **hyperbole,** or exaggeration. Underline an example of hyperbole in these lines. How might this influence a reader?

_____

_____

_____

_____

_____

**SET A PURPOSE
FOR READING**
Read this selection for another
side to the privacy debate.

The Privacy Debate

Arthur M. Ahalt

One Size Doesn't Fit All

BACKGROUND The U.S. Constitution does not specify privacy as a right. Although many Supreme Court cases have addressed a range of privacy issues, privacy remains difficult to define and protect. This article explores the current debate over privacy issues.

"One man's justice is another man's injustice," said Ralph Waldo Emerson, neatly summarizing the complexity of most debates.

Unfortunately, the current debate over privacy issues rarely illuminates both sides of this complex issue. Instead, we are told there should be no debate over the need for privacy.

This article will explore the other side of the privacy debate and demonstrate the benefit of access and openness, particularly in the area of public records.

10   As a retired state circuit court judge with 17 years on the bench, I've observed firsthand the benefits to our judicial, government and economic systems of open access to public records. Unfortunately, too many Americans seem willing to reduce such access in the name of privacy.

Why is the siren call[1] of privacy so strong?

Maybe it stems from the impersonal nature of modern society, lack of community and the rise of the global economy, all of which makes us wish for more **anonymity**. There now are 280 million Americans, and we're long past

20   doing business at the corner store where everybody knew your name.

Maybe technology is to blame, with credit cards and consumer information automated to move consumers from the practical obscurity of paper records to huge computer databases. **G**

Maybe it's some politicians, the media and any number of self-styled advocates and experts who traffic in scare headlines, breathless press releases and emotional soapbox speeches. It's no mystery—privacy concerns affect **articulate**

30   middle class citizens who buy papers and vote—creating a "squeaky" wheel that gets the grease.

Privacy is also a **nonpartisan** concern which neither political party owns, and represents an issue where conservatives and liberals often meet in unison. Media stories about privacy issues often are human-interest heart-tuggers that sell and gather an audience. Think tanks,

---

1. **siren call:** alluring but possibly dangerous appeal (after the Sirens, mythological creatures whose irresistible songs lured sailors into danger).

G FACT AND OPINION
Underline a fact and circle an opinion in lines 16–25. Is the opinion you identified substantiated with evidence? Explain.

_____

_____

_____

_____

_____

anonymity (ăn′ə-nĭm′ĭ-tē) *n.* the condition of being unknown

articulate (är-tĭk′yə-lĭt) *adj.* able to speak clearly and coherently; well-spoken

nonpartisan (nŏn-pär′tĭ-zən) *adj.* not supporting or controlled by any political group

Underline the context clues in lines 32–34 that help you determine the meaning of **nonpartisan**.

H **RECOGNIZE BIAS**
Circle the loaded words in lines
32–39. How do these words help
or hinder Ahalt's argument?
Explain.

_____

_____

_____

_____

_____

PAUSE & REFLECT
Why does Ahalt believe instant
credit is the "very basis of the
underlying strength and power
of our economic system"? Do
you think he's right? Explain.

_____

_____

_____

_____

_____

clearinghouses[2] and "experts" flock to issue press releases,
hold seminars, appear on television and generally stoke the
fires of paranoia[3] and emotionalism. **H**

40 In this atmosphere, confusion, fear and concern replace a
balanced view of the privacy issue.

Politicians and the media quote polls—"93 percent
of people are concerned about privacy." Well, no doubt.
(I would like to know about the 7 percent who are not
concerned about privacy, but that is another matter.)
Those polls, however, don't appear to probe the trade-offs,
such as "would you prefer a bank loan in three days or
three months?" Most Americans not only prefer to obtain
immediate credit and debt, they demand it.

50 But instant credit and debt is more than a convenience;
it's also the very basis of the underlying strength and power
of our economic system, which moves at the speed of light
as a direct result of the transparency of information available
to economic decision makers. Car, home and bank loans and
the issuance of credit and debit cards can be made quickly
because information about most of us is available. It's the
source of our retail sector's[4] strength. It's the reason we can
buy and sell property in weeks; not months or years. Federal
Trade Commission Chairman Tim Muris calls this system,
60 which we all take for granted, "the miracle of instant credit."

Economist Walter Kitchenman says that our consumer
credit system is the "secret ingredient of the U.S. economy's
resilience." **PAUSE & REFLECT**

---

2. **think tanks, clearinghouses:** A think tank is a research institute
   organized to investigate social problems; a clearinghouse is an
   organization that collects and distributes information.
3. **stoke the fires of paranoia:** increase fear and suspicion.
4. **retail sector's:** of the branch of the nation's economy that deals with
   products people buy and use.

Aside from economic benefits, transparency also provides other specific benefits. It makes it possible to find absent spouses and enforce child support payments; to screen day care workers and school bus drivers to keep our kids safe from substance abusers and child molesters; to check the background of bank tellers to avoid embezzlement; to
70 connect heirs with fortunes; and to help prevent identity theft, and make it easier to fix if it occurs.

There are real problems that affect real people in the privacy arena, but it's the classic case of bad news always selling, and good news remaining invisible.

Each day, billions of financial transactions occur in our economy. Do some go <u>**awry?**</u> Of course, but it is a small percentage. Unfortunately, no one wants to read a headline "Today 299,999,033 Americans Did Not Suffer Privacy-Related Problems."

awry (ə-rī′) *adj.* off course; wrong

List two words that are antonyms for awry.

_____

_____

PAUSE & REFLECT
Do you agree with this adage in lines 95–96? Why or why not?
_____
_____
_____
_____
_____

80   There is also a need to segment privacy from one huge ball of confusion into separate, more manage-able and different issues, which require different approaches.

Tracking Internet surfing and purchases is different from identity theft, which is different from telemarketing calls, which is different from access to public records, which is also different from the use of Social Security numbers as a unique identifier.

Privacy supporters would have us believe that "one size fits all" when it comes to addressing matters of privacy.

90   I hold no portfolio on some of these issues, but as one who now is working directly in the area of public records accessibility, I am vitally concerned about access to these records and their contents. Remember the old adage when you hear self-styled privacy experts expound on the need to keep information hidden: "for every problem, there is a simple solution, which is usually wrong." **PAUSE & REFLECT**

Text Analysis: Fact and Opinion

Complete the chart below with two facts and two opinions from each article.

FACT vs OPINION
"How Private is Your Private Life?"
Fact #1:
Fact #2:
Opinion #1:
Opinion #12:
"The Privacy Debate"
Fact #1:
Fact #2:
Opinion #1:
Opinion #2:

Which article do you think provides better support for its main proposition, or claim? Explain your choice.

_____

_____

Reading Skill: Recognize Bias

Complete the chart below with examples of bias from both articles. Explain how each example shows loaded language, stereotyping, unbalanced evidence for an argument, or an opinion stated as a fact.

Example from Article	Explanation of Bias

Is **PRIVACY** an illusion?

What steps do you regularly take to ensure your privacy?

_____

_____

_____

Vocabulary Practice

Circle the word that is not related in meaning to the other words.

1. awry, amiss, assemble, astray

2. namelessness, disguise, anonymity, fretfulness

3. distressing, embarrassing, disconcerting, inspiring

4. electrician, browser, plumber, carpenter

5. pervasive, widespread, arrogant, extensive

6. enemy, associate, affiliate, partner

7. broadcasting, spying, observing, surveillance

8. impartial, uneasy, nonpartisan, unbiased

9. articulate, illogical, eloquent, expressive

10. rejection, advocacy, rebuff, disdain

Academic Vocabulary in Writing

coherent	differentiate	evident	relevant	technique

How are the arguments these two writers make about privacy **relevant,** or important, to your life? In a few sentences, state your opinion and support it with evidence and a **coherent** argument. Use at least one Academic Vocabulary word in your response. Definitions for these terms are listed on page 277.

_____

_____

_____

Assessment Practice

DIRECTIONS Use "How Private is Your Private Life?" and "The Privacy Debate" to answer questions 1–4.

1 In "How Private Is Your Private Life?" the author says that supermarket discount cards —

  (A) help customers share common interests
  (B) let businesses track shopping choices
  (C) keep track of shopper's spending
  (D) give away people's social security numbers

2 Writers use loaded language in order to persuade readers with —

  (A) phrases using faulty reasoning
  (B) arguments that give stronger evidence for one side than the other
  (C) opinions stated as if they were facts
  (D) language containing positive and negative connotations

3 Which fact from the selections supports the idea that privacy is threatened?

  (A) "Confusion, fear and concern replace a balanced view of the privacy issue."
  (B) "Your profile continues to expand and can be sold to anyone without your knowledge or consent."
  (C) Access to records "makes it possible to find absent spouses and enforce child support payments."
  (D) "We're long past doing business at the corner store where everybody knew your name."

4 Ahalt's article is persuasive because —

  (A) he presents only one side of the issue
  (B) his argument focuses only on opinions, not on facts
  (C) as a former judge, he has direct experience with the topic
  (D) he emphasizes the use of loaded language

UNIT 7

Special Effects

THE LANGUAGE OF POETRY

Be sure to read the Text Analysis Workshop on pp. 740–747 in *Holt McDougal Literature*.

Academic Vocabulary for Unit 7

Preview the following Academic Vocabulary words. You will encounter these words as you work through this book and will use them as you write and talk about the selections in the unit.

conventional (kən-věn′shə-nəl) *adj.* conforming to traditional standards

*This poet does not adhere to **conventional** rules of punctuation.*

•

effect (ǐ-fěkt′) *n.* something brought about by a cause; result

*Find an example of a literary technique and explain its **effect** on the work's meaning.*

•

evoke (ǐ-vōk′) *v.* to call to mind

*The poem uses an image of rippling waters to **evoke** feelings of peacefulness.*

•

form (fôrm) *n.* the structure of something

*The sonnet is a traditional **form** of poetry.*

•

refer (rǐ-fûr′) *v.* to pertain or concern

*When you **refer** to a quotation, be sure to include the line number.*

Think about a movie or television show you saw that **evoked** a particular reaction. Write a few sentences describing this reaction. Use at least two Academic Vocabulary words in your response.

_____

_____

_____

_____

Spring is like a perhaps hand
Poem by E. E. Cummings

Elegy for the Giant Tortoises
Poem by Margaret Atwood

Today
Poem by Billy Collins

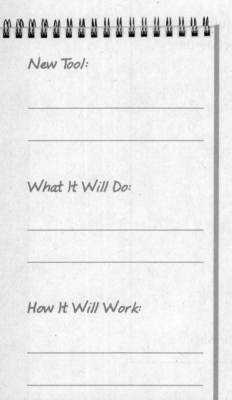

New Tool:

_____

_____

What It Will Do:

_____

_____

How It Will Work:

_____

_____

Can you think OUT OF THE BOX?

Some of the best things in life are those unlike anything ever thought of before. Whether it's a brilliant invention (light bulb) or an entertaining story (dog bites man), a new idea makes life more interesting and worthwhile. Creativity is a poet's bread and butter; a good poet always looks at things in a new way.

PRESENT With a small group, plan a design for a new tool. You might want to create a tool to help with a dreaded chore, such as cleaning your room or mowing the yard. Record your ideas in the notebook at left. Then share your plans with other groups.

Poetic Form: Elegy

Poetry is as much about form as it is about language and sound. Form refers to the poem's structure—the way the words are arranged on the page. All poems are made up of a series of lines. The length of the lines, where they break, and how they are punctuated contribute to the poem's rhythm and meaning.

An **elegy** is a specific type of lyric poem—a poem in which a speaker shares personal thoughts and feelings about a subject. In an elegy, the speaker writes about death, usually as a tribute to one who has recently died. The second poem in this lesson is an elegy. It expresses sadness not about the death of a person but about the possible loss of a species of animals.

Text Analysis: Diction

Poets are known for their concise and exact use of language. When reading poetry, pay special attention to the poet's **diction** (choice of words) and its effects. For example, Billy Collins chooses his words carefully in these lines from "Today":

Diction	Effects
"it made you want to throw / open all the windows in the house"	*creates a sense of joy, freedom, and movement*

This particular use of words adds more emphasis than if Collins had simply said he felt like opening a window. Like any good poet, Collins has chosen his words carefully to create a specific effect. As you read the poems in this lesson, you will be prompted to notice striking or unusual examples of diction.

Reading Skill: Paraphrase

Sometimes poems can be difficult to understand because of their unusual structure. When you **paraphrase** a line or stanza in a poem, you rephrase the poet's words with your own words. To paraphrase, you should:

• find the main ideas and important details

• think of simpler or more familiar ways of saying what the writer has written

• rewrite sentences in standard, subject-verb order

As you read each of the poems that follow, you will be prompted to paraphrase difficult passages like the one in the chart below.

"Elegy for the Giant Tortoises"		
Original Wording		Paraphrase
"on the road where I stand they will materialize, / plodding past me in a straggling line / awkward without water"	⟷	*They [the tortoises] will appear on the road where I stand, walking slowly by in a scattered line, looking clumsy because they are not in the water.*

**SET A PURPOSE
FOR READING**

Read "Spring is like a
perhaps hand" to discover
the speaker's ideas about
the change in seasons.

Spring is like a perhaps hand

Poem by
E. E. CUMMINGS

BACKGROUND Critics have ranked
E. E. Cummings among the most innovative of
20th century poets. In his writing, Cummings
often used lowercase letters, unusual word
spacing, and his own brand of punctuation.
Even though Cummings's style is unique, his
themes are familiar. He celebrated the wonder
of life and the glory of the individual.

Ⓐ PARAPHRASE
Reread lines 1–9. Underline
words and phrases that describe
spring. Then **paraphrase** the
comparison.

_____

_____

_____

_____

_____

Spring is like a perhaps hand
(which comes carefully
out of Nowhere) arranging
a window, into which people look (while
5 people stare
arranging and changing placing
carefully there a strange
thing and a known thing here) and

changing everything carefully Ⓐ

10 spring is like a perhaps
Hand in a window
(carefully to
and fro moving New and
Old things, while
15 people stare carefully
moving a perhaps
fraction of flower here placing
an inch of air there) and

without breaking anything.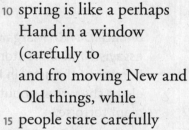

B DICTION
Notice the **diction** in lines
16–18. Circle the words used
as measurements. What do
these words suggest about the
speaker's idea of spring?

_____

_____

_____

_____

_____

_____

SET A PURPOSE FOR READING

Read this poem to discover how the speaker feels about the extinction of the giant tortoise.

ⓒ PARAPHRASE

Use the chart to **paraphrase** lines 7–12. In the first box, list synonyms for the most important words on these lines. Then use the synonyms to help you restate the passage in your own words.

Words From The Poem

↓

Paraphrase

Elegy for the GIANT TORTOISES

Poem by
MARGARET ATWOOD

BACKGROUND Margaret Atwood, a poet, novelist, essayist, and short story writer, has been called "a heroine of the arts" in her native Canada. In this elegy, she writes about the likely extinction of the giant tortoise.

Let others pray for the passenger pigeon
the dodo, the whooping crane,[1] the eskimo:
everyone must specialize

I will confine myself to a meditation
5 upon the giant tortoises
withering finally on a remote island.

I concentrate in subway stations,
in parks, I can't quite see them,
they move to the peripheries of my eyes

10 but on the last day they will be there;
already the event
like a wave travelling shapes vision: ⓒ

---

1. **the passenger pigeon/the dodo, the whooping crane:** extinct or extremely endangered birds.

on the road where I stand they will materialize,
plodding past me in a straggling line
15 awkward without water

their small heads pondering
from side to side, their useless armour
sadder than tanks and history,

in their closed gaze ocean and sunlight paralysed,
20 lumbering up the steps, under the archways
toward the square glass altars

where the brittle gods are kept,
the relics of what we have destroyed,
our holy and obsolete symbols. **D**

D ELEGY
Circle the religious words in lines 21–24. What effect does this choice of words have on the overall tone of the poem?

_____

_____

_____

Why is such language appropriate in an elegy?

_____

_____

_____

SET A PURPOSE FOR READING

Read "Today" to find out how the speaker describes a spring day.

Today

Poem by
BILLY COLLINS

BACKGROUND A teacher and poet, Billy Collins is known for his use of surprising and playful images. His poetry has brought him many awards as well as wide popularity. Some have called him the most popular poet in America.

E DICTION
Reread lines 3–8. Underline phrases that suggest quick actions. What is the effect of these words on the poem's meaning?

_____

_____

_____

If ever there were a spring day so perfect,
so uplifted by a warm intermittent breeze

that it made you want to throw
open all the windows in the house

5 and unlatch the door to the canary's cage,
indeed, rip the little door from its jamb,

a day when the cool brick paths
and the garden bursting with peonies **E**

seemed so etched in sunlight
10 that you felt like taking

a hammer to the glass paperweight
on the living room end table,

releasing the inhabitants
from their snow-covered cottage

15 so they could walk out,
holding hands and squinting

into this larger dome of blue and white, **F**
well, today is just that kind of day.

PAUSE & REFLECT

F DICTION
Circle the words the speaker uses to describe what happens to the inhabitants of the glass paperweight. What sense or feeling is evoked by this language?

_____

_____

_____

_____

_____

PAUSE & REFLECT
What is unusual about how Collins describes the perfect day?

_____

_____

_____

_____

_____

Text Analysis: Diction

The poets in this lesson have chosen their words carefully to convey certain ideas. Use the chart below to list unusual or striking examples of diction from each poem. Then describe the effects of each poet's choice of words.

"Spring is like a perhaps hand"
Words and Phrases:
Effects on Tone:

"Elegy for the Giant Tortoises"
Words and Phrases:
Effects on Tone:

"Today"
Words and Phrases:
Effects on Tone:

Reading Skill: Paraphrase

Review some of the paraphrases you made as you read each poem. Then read aloud one of your paraphrases and the original passage. Which one has the stronger impact? Explain.

_____

_____

_____

_____

Can you think OUT OF THE BOX?

Why is innovative thinking so important?

_____

_____

_____

Academic Vocabulary in Speaking

conventional	effect	evoke	form	refer

TURN AND TALK A poem's **form** refers to its structure, or the way the words are arranged on the page. Think about the different forms of the poems you just read. With a partner, discuss how each poem's form contributes to its meaning. Use at least one Academic Vocabulary word in your discussion. Definitions for these terms are listed on page 317.

Assessment Practice

DIRECTIONS Use "Spring is like a perhaps hand," "Elegy for the Giant Tortoises," and "Today" to answer questions 1–4.

1 What qualities of spring does "Spring is like a perhaps hand" emphasize?

- (A) joy, fun, and excitement
- (B) novelty, subtlety, and delicacy
- (C) weakness, hesitancy, and failure
- (D) intensity, durability, and vitality

2 "Their useless armour" in line 17 of "Elegy for the Giant Tortoises" describes defenseless —

- (A) army tanks
- (B) tortoise shells
- (C) immune systems
- (D) animal protection laws

3 What does "this larger dome" refer to in line 17 of "Today"?

- (A) the roof of the canary cage
- (B) the sky above the real world
- (C) the top of the glass paperweight
- (D) the blooming flowers in the garden

4 An elegy is best described as a —

- (A) rhyming poem
- (B) lyric poem
- (C) poem written to someone has died
- (D) figure of speech

UNIT

8

A Way with Words

AUTHOR'S STYLE AND VOICE

Be sure to read the Text Analysis Workshop on pp. 820–825 in *Holt McDougal Literature*.

Academic Vocabulary for Unit 8

Preview the following Academic Vocabulary words. You will encounter these words as you work through this book and will use them as you write and talk about the selections in the unit.

---

appreciate (ə-prē′shē-āt′) *v.* to think highly of; to recognize favorably the quality or value of

*What quality of the author's writing do you **appreciate** the most?*

•

attribute (ăt′rə-byōōt′) *n.* a quality thought of as a natural part of someone or something

*Vivid imagery is one **attribute** of this writer's work.*

•

indicate (ĭn′dĭ-kāt) *v.* to point out or show

*Which lines of dialogue **indicate** that the character is feeling nervous?*

•

unique (yōō-nēk′) *adj.* the only one; having no equal

*The writer's **unique** style makes her stories different from any others.*

•

vary (vâr′ē) *v.* to modify or alter; to change the characteristics of something

*If you **vary** the length of your sentences, your essay will be more interesting to read.*

Think about one of your favorite books, movies, or television shows. What do you especially like about it? Describe the reasons you **appreciate** it. Use at least two Academic Vocabulary words in your response.

_____

_____

_____

Where Have You Gone, Charming Billy?
Short Story by Tim O'Brien

Tim O'Brien: The Naked Soldier
Interview from *Verbicide* Magazine

Is FEAR our worst enemy?

Your heart pounds. Your hands shake. You are gripped by fear—how do you respond? In "Where Have You Gone, Charming Billy?" a young soldier struggles against his growing terror during his first night in Vietnam.

LIST IT In the notebook to the left, list situations that cause people to feel fear. Then share your list with a small group of classmates. Discuss this question: Are there times when is fear useful?

Situations that Cause Fear

1. Meeting a large, growling dog

2. _____

3. _____

4. _____

5. _____

Text Analysis: Realism

A writer's style is reflected in the dialogue, word choice, and sentence structure he or she uses. In "Where Have You Gone, Charming Billy?" Tim O'Brien uses the style of **realism** to depict the horrors of combat as seen through the eyes of a young soldier. The chart below describes three elements of O'Brien's style.

Element of O'Brien's Style	Example
Dialogue that sounds natural, like actual speech	"'Rats. . . . Don't matter, really. Goes faster if you don't know the time, anyhow.'"
Vivid, realistic descriptions of what the soldier sees	"Stretching ahead of him like dark beads on an invisible chain, the string of shadow-soldiers whose names he did not yet know moved with the silence and slow grace of smoke."
A mix of long and short sentences to communicate the soldier's thoughts and feelings	"Now as he stepped out of the paddy onto a narrow dirt path, now the fear was mostly the fear of being so terribly afraid again. He tried not to think."

Reading Skill: Analyze Sequence

The **sequence** of a story is the order in which events occur. Sometimes a writer interrupts this linear order with a **flashback,** an account of events that happened before the beginning of the story's action. A flashback provides more background information about the current situation and helps the reader understand the story's events. To identify flashbacks, look for sudden changes in scene. As you read "Where Have You Gone, Charming Billy?" keep track of its sequence of events by filling in a sequence chain like the one below.

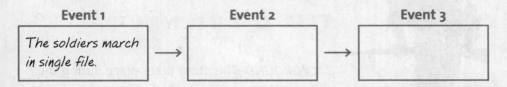

Event 1

The soldiers march in single file.

Event 2

Event 3

Vocabulary in Context

Note: Words are listed in the order in which they appear in the story.

stealth (stĕlth) *n.* cautious or secret action or movement
*The cat moved with **stealth** through the tall grass so that her prey would not notice her.*

fecund (fē′kənd) *adj.* producing much growth; fertile
*The settlers looked for a region of **fecund** earth where they could grow their crops.*

diffuse (dĭ-fyōōs′) *adj.* unfocused
*The professor's rambling lecture was so **diffuse** that we could not identify his main idea.*

inertia (ĭ-nûr′shə) *n.* tendency to continue to do what one has been doing
*I did not mow the lawn because I couldn't break the **inertia** of relaxing in the shade.*

Vocabulary Practice

Review the meanings of the vocabulary words. How might each word relate to a story about a soldier's experience in combat? Use each word in a sentence that describes what a soldier might do, see, think, or feel.

_____

_____

_____

_____

Where Have You Gone, Charming Billy?

Short Story by

TIM O'BRIEN

BACKGROUND This story takes place during the
Vietnam War—a war in which 58,000 Americans
died. Rebels backed by Communist-ruled North
Vietnam tried to take over South Vietnam in 1957.
The U.S. entered the war as a South Vietnamese
ally in 1964. Between 1965 and 1973, over 2 million
Americans were sent to Vietnam, including author
Tim O'Brien. In 1973, O'Brien published his first
book, an account of his time in Vietnam. The war
has been the main subject of his writing ever since.

stealth (stĕlth) *n.* cautious or
secret action or movement

Think about O'Brien's phrase "the
primitive stealth of warfare" in
lines 7–8. Why would **stealth** be
a part of all wars, from ancient
times to the present?

_____

_____

_____

_____

_____

The platoon of twenty-six soldiers moved slowly in the dark,
single file, not talking.

One by one, like sheep in a dream, they passed through the
hedgerow, crossed quietly over a meadow and came down to
the rice paddy.[1] There they stopped. Their leader knelt down,
motioning with his hand, and one by one the other soldiers
squatted in the shadows, vanishing in the primitive **stealth** of
warfare. For a long time they did not move. Except for the sounds
of their breathing, . . . the twenty-six men were very quiet: some

10 of them excited by the adventure, some of them afraid, some of
them exhausted from the long night march, some of them looking
forward to reaching the sea where they would be safe. At the rear
of the column, Private First Class Paul Berlin lay quietly with his
forehead resting on the black plastic stock of his rifle, his eyes
closed. He was pretending he was not in the war, pretending he

_____

1. **hedgerow . . . rice paddy:** A hedgerow is a thick hedge separating fields or
farms; a rice paddy is a flooded field in which rice is grown.

had not watched Billy Boy Watkins die of a heart attack that afternoon. He was pretending he was a boy again, camping with his father in the midnight summer along the Des Moines River. In the dark, with his eyes pinched shut, he pretended.

20 He pretended that when he opened his eyes, his father would be there by the campfire and they would talk softly about whatever came to mind and then roll into their sleeping bags, and that later they'd wake up and it would be morning and there would not be a war, and that Billy Boy Watkins had not died of a heart attack that afternoon. He pretended he was not a soldier. **Ⓐ**

In the morning, when they reached the sea, it would be better. The hot afternoon would be over, he would bathe in the sea and he would forget how frightened he had been on his first day at the war. The second day would not be so bad. He would learn.

30 There was a sound beside him, a movement and then a breathed: "Hey!"

He opened his eyes, shivering as if emerging from a deep nightmare.

"Hey!" a shadow whispered. "We're *moving*. . . . Get up."

"Okay."

"You sleepin', or something?"

"No." He could not make out the soldier's face. With clumsy, concrete hands he clawed for his rifle, found it, found his helmet.

The soldier-shadow grunted. "You got a lot to learn, buddy. I'd 40 shoot you if I thought you was sleepin'. Let's go." **Ⓑ**

Private First Class Paul Berlin blinked.

Ahead of him, silhouetted against the sky, he saw the string of soldiers wading into the flat paddy, the black outline of their shoulders and packs and weapons. He was comfortable. He did not want to move. But he was afraid, for it was his first night at the war, so he hurried to catch up, stumbling once, scraping his knee, groping as though blind; his boots sank into the thick paddy water and he smelled it all around him. He would tell his mother how it smelled: mud and algae and cattle manure 50 and chlorophyll, decay, breeding mosquitoes and leeches as

Ⓐ REALISM
Reread lines 12–25, circling repeating words and phrases and underlining short sentences. Is O'Brien's use of both long and short sentences a realistic way to convey this soldier's thoughts? Explain your answer.

_____

_____

_____

_____

_____

_____

_____

_____

_____

Ⓑ REALISM
Reread lines 30–40. Underline specific words and phrases in the characters' speech that make this **dialogue** sound realistic.

fecund (fē'kənd) *adj.* producing much growth; fertile

PAUSE & REFLECT
Reread lines 48–53. Why would Paul plan to tell his mother about how things looked and smelled but not about how frightened he was?

_____

_____

_____

_____

diffuse (dĭ-fyo͞os') *adj.* unfocused

big as mice, the **fecund** warmth of the paddy waters rising up to his cut knee. But he would not tell how frightened he had been. **PAUSE & REFLECT**

Once they reached the sea, things would be better. They would have their rear guarded by three thousand miles of ocean, and they would swim and dive into the breakers and hunt crayfish and smell the salt, and they would be safe.

He followed the shadow of the man in front of him. It was a clear night. Already the Southern Cross[2] was out. And other stars he could not yet name—soon, he thought, he would learn their names. And puffy night clouds. There was not yet a moon. Wading through the paddy, his boots made sleepy, sloshing sounds, like a lullaby, and he tried not to think. Though he was afraid, he now knew that fear came in many degrees and types and peculiar categories, and he knew that his fear now was not so bad as it had been in the hot afternoon, when poor Billy Boy Watkins got killed by a heart attack. His fear now was **diffuse** and unformed: ghosts in the tree line, nighttime fears of a child, a boogieman in the closet that his father would open to show empty, saying "See? Nothing there, champ. Now you can sleep." In the afternoon it had been worse: the fear had been bundled and tight and he'd been on his hands and knees, crawling like an insect, an ant escaping a giant's footsteps and thinking nothing, brain flopping like wet cement in a mixer, not thinking at all, watching while Billy Boy Watkins died.

Now as he stepped out of the paddy onto a narrow dirt path, now the fear was mostly the fear of being so terribly afraid again.

He tried not to think.

There were tricks he'd learned to keep from thinking. Counting: He counted his steps, concentrating on the numbers, pretending that the steps were dollar bills and that each step through the night made him richer and richer, so that soon

---

2. **Southern Cross:** a cross-shaped group of stars visible in the Southern Hemisphere.

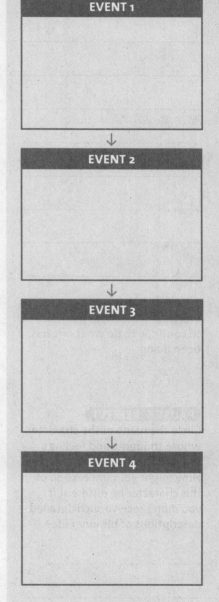

he would become a wealthy man, and he kept counting and considered the ways he might spend the money after the war and what he would do. He would look his father in the eye and shrug and say, "It was pretty bad at first, but I learned a lot and I got used to it." Then he would tell his father the story of Billy Boy Watkins. But he would never let on how frightened he had been. "Not so bad," he would say instead, making his father feel proud.

90   Songs, another trick to stop from thinking: *Where have you gone, Billy Boy, Billy Boy, Oh, where have you gone, charming Billy? I have gone to seek a wife, she's the joy of my life, but she's a young thing and cannot leave her mother,* and other songs that he sang in his thoughts as he walked toward the sea. And when he reached the sea he would dig a deep hole in the sand and he would sleep like the high clouds, and he would not be afraid any more. **C**

The moon came out. Pale and shrunken to the size of a dime.

The helmet was heavy on his head. In the morning he would adjust the leather binding. He would clean his rifle, too.
100 Even though he had been frightened to shoot it during the hot afternoon, he would carefully clean the breech and the muzzle and the ammunition so that next time he would be ready and not so afraid. In the morning, when they reached the sea, he would begin to make friends with some of the other soldiers. He would learn their names and laugh at their jokes. Then when the war was over he would have war buddies, and he would write to them once in a while and exchange memories.

Walking, sleeping in his walking, he felt better. He watched the moon come higher.

110   Once they skirted a sleeping village. The smells again—straw, cattle, mildew. The men were quiet. On the far side of the village, buried in the dark smells, a dog barked. The column stopped until the barking died away; then they marched fast away from the village, through a graveyard filled with conical-shaped burial mounds and tiny altars made of clay and stone. The graveyard had a perfumy smell. A nice place to spend the night, he thought. The mounds would make fine battlements,

C **ANALYZE SEQUENCE**
Use the sequence chain below to summarize the story's main events up to this point. Do not include scenes the narrator imagines in the future or remembers from his past. Record only events from the story's present time.

EVENT 1

↓

EVENT 2

↓

EVENT 3

↓

EVENT 4

D **REALISM**
Reread lines 110–120. Underline the **sensory details** that O'Brien includes. How do these details add to the vivid, realistic style of the story?

_____

_____

_____

_____

_____

_____

_____

_____

inertia (ĭ-nûr′shə) *n.* tendency to continue to do what one has been doing

PAUSE & REFLECT
Circle the name of the character whose thoughts and feelings the narrator shares with readers. How might your impression of this character be different if you didn't receive such detailed descriptions of his inner life?

_____

_____

_____

_____

_____

and the smell was nice and the place was quiet. But they went on, passing through a hedgerow and across another paddy and east
120 toward the sea. **D**

He walked carefully. He remembered what he'd been taught: Stay off the center of the path, for that was where the land mines and booby traps were planted, where stupid and lazy soldiers like to walk. Stay alert, he'd been taught. Better alert than inert. Agile, mo-bile, hos-tile.[3] He wished he'd paid better attention to the training. He could not remember what they'd said about how to stop being afraid; they hadn't given any lessons in courage—not that he could remember—and they hadn't mentioned how Billy Boy Watkins would die of a heart attack, his face turning pale and
130 the veins popping out.

Private First Class Paul Berlin walked carefully.

Stretching ahead of him like dark beads on an invisible chain, the string of shadow-soldiers whose names he did not yet know moved with the silence and slow grace of smoke. Now and again moonlight was reflected off a machine gun or a wrist watch. But mostly the soldiers were quiet and hidden and far-away-seeming in a peaceful night, strangers on a long street, and he felt quite separate from them, as if trailing behind like the caboose on a night train, pulled along by **inertia**, sleepwalking, an afterthought
140 to the war.

So he walked carefully, counting his steps. When he had counted to three thousand, four hundred and eighty-five, the column stopped.

One by one the soldiers knelt or squatted down.

The grass along the path was wet. Private First Class Paul Berlin lay back and turned his head so that he could lick at the dew with his eyes closed, another trick to forget the war. He might have slept. "I *wasn't* afraid," he was screaming or dreaming, facing his father's stern eyes. "I wasn't afraid," he was saying.
150 When he opened his eyes, a soldier was sitting beside him, quietly chewing a stick of Doublemint gum. **PAUSE & REFLECT**

---

3. **Better alert . . . hos-tile:** sayings and chants reminding soldiers to pay attention rather than be lifeless (inert), and to be light on their feet (agile), ready to move (mobile), and aggressive (hostile).

"You sleepin' again?" the soldier whispered.

"No," said Private First Class Paul Berlin. . . .

The soldier grunted, chewing his gum. Then he twisted the cap off his canteen, took a swallow and handed it through the dark.

"Take some," he whispered.

"Thanks."

"You're the new guy?"

"Yes." He did not want to admit it, being new to the war.

160   The soldier grunted and handed him a stick of gum. "Chew it quiet—okay? Don't blow no bubbles or nothing."

"Thanks. I won't." He could not make out the man's face in the shadows.

They sat still and Private First Class Paul Berlin chewed the gum until all the sugars were gone; then the soldier said, "Bad day today, buddy."

Private First Class Paul Berlin nodded wisely, but he did not speak.

"Don't think it's always so bad," the soldier whispered. "I don't
170 wanna scare you. You'll get used to it soon enough. . . . They been fighting wars a long time, and you get used to it."

"Yeah."

"You will."

They were quiet awhile. And the night was quiet, no crickets or birds, and it was hard to imagine it was truly a war. He searched for the soldier's face but could not find it. It did not matter much. Even if he saw the fellow's face, he would not know the name; and even if he knew the name, it would not matter much. **PAUSE & REFLECT**

180   "Haven't got the time?" the soldier whispered.

"No."

"Rats. . . . Don't matter, really. Goes faster if you don't know the time, anyhow."

"Sure."

"What's your name, buddy?"

"Paul."

PAUSE & REFLECT

In lines 174–186, underline two examples in which the soldiers prefer not to know all the facts about something. Why do you think they have this attitude?

_____

_____

_____

_____

_____

_____

_____

"Nice to meet ya," he said, and in the dark beside the path they shook hands. "Mine's Toby. Everybody calls me Buffalo, though." The soldier's hand was strangely warm and soft. But it was a very big hand. "Sometimes they just call me Buff," he said.

And again they were quiet. They lay in the grass and waited. The moon was very high now and very bright, and they were waiting for cloud cover.

The soldier suddenly snorted.

"What is it?"

"Nothin'," he said, but then he snorted again. "A bloody *heart attack!*" the soldier said. "Can't get over it—old Billy Boy croaking from a lousy heart attack. . . . A heart attack—can you believe it?"

The idea of it made Private First Class Paul Berlin smile. He couldn't help it.

"Ever hear of such a thing?"

"Not till now," said Private First Class Paul Berlin, still smiling.

"Me neither," said the soldier in the dark.

". . . Dying of a heart attack. Didn't know him, did you."

"No."

"Tough as nails."

"Yeah."

"And what happens? A heart attack. Can you imagine it?" **E**

"Yes," said Private First Class Paul Berlin. He wanted to laugh. "I can imagine it." And he imagined it clearly. He giggled—he couldn't help it. He imagined Billy's father opening the telegram: SORRY TO INFORM YOU THAT YOUR SON BILLY BOY WAS YESTERDAY SCARED TO DEATH IN ACTION IN THE REPUBLIC OF VIETNAM, VALIANTLY SUCCUMBING TO[4] A HEART ATTACK SUFFERED WHILE UNDER ENORMOUS STRESS, AND IT IS WITH

E **REALISM**
Reread lines 194–208 and circle examples of slang, or informal expressions, in the characters' speech. Does this language make the **dialogue** seem more realistic? Explain.

_____

_____

_____

_____

_____

_____

_____

_____

_____

_____

_____

---

4. **valiantly succumbing** (sə-kŭm′ĭng) **to:** bravely dying from.

GREATEST SYMPATHY THAT . . . He giggled again. He rolled onto his belly and pressed his face into his arms. His body was shaking with giggles. PAUSE & REFLECT

220   The big soldier hissed at him to shut up, but he could not stop giggling and remembering the hot afternoon, and poor Billy Boy, and how they'd been drinking Coca-Cola from bright-red aluminum cans, and how they'd started on the day's march, and how a little while later poor Billy Boy stepped on the mine, and how it made a tiny little sound—*poof*—and how Billy Boy stood there with his mouth wide-open, looking down at where his foot had been blown off, and how finally Billy Boy sat down very casually, not saying a word, with his foot lying behind him, most of it still in the boot.

230   He giggled louder—he could not stop. He bit his arm, trying to stifle it, but remembering: "War's over, Billy," the men had said in consolation, but Billy Boy got scared and started crying and said he was about to die. "Nonsense," the medic said, Doc Peret, but Billy Boy kept bawling, tightening up, his face going pale and transparent and his veins popping out. Scared stiff. Even when Doc Peret stuck him with morphine,[5] Billy Boy kept crying. **F**

    "Shut up!" the big soldier hissed, but Private First Class Paul Berlin could not stop. Giggling and remembering, he covered his mouth. His eyes stung, remembering how it was when Billy Boy
240 died of fright.

    "Shut up!"

    But he could not stop giggling, the same way Billy Boy could not stop bawling that afternoon.

    Afterward Doc Peret had explained: "You see, Billy Boy really died of a heart attack. He was scared he was gonna die—so scared, he had himself a heart attack—and that's what really killed him. I seen it before."

---

5. **morphine** (môr′fēn′): a powerful drug used as a painkiller.

Monitor Your Comprehension

PAUSE & REFLECT
Why is Paul laughing as he imagines Billy's father reading the telegram?

_____

_____

_____

_____

_____

_____

_____

_____

F ANALYZE SEQUENCE
Reread lines 220–236. Circle the clue word(s) that signal a change in time. What happens to the story's sequence in these lines?

_____

_____

_____

_____

_____

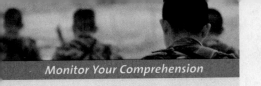
So they wrapped Billy in a plastic poncho, his eyes still wide-open and scared stiff, and they carried him over the meadow to a
250 rice paddy, and then when the Medevac helicopter[6] arrived they carried him through the paddy and put him aboard, and the mortar rounds[7] were falling everywhere, and the helicopter pulled up and Billy Boy came tumbling out, falling slowly and then faster, and the paddy water sprayed up as if Billy Boy had just executed a long and dangerous dive, as if trying to escape Graves Registration, where he would be tagged and sent home under a flag, dead of a heart attack.

"Shut up, . . . !" the soldier hissed, but Paul Berlin could not stop giggling, remembering: scared to death.

260 Later they waded in after him, probing for Billy Boy with their rifle butts, elegantly and delicately probing for Billy Boy in the stinking paddy, singing—some of them—*Where have you gone, Billy Boy, Billy Boy, Oh, where have you gone, charming Billy?* Then they found him. Green and covered with algae, his eyes still wide-open and scared stiff, dead of a heart attack suffered while—

"Shut up, . . . !" the soldier said loudly, shaking him.

But Private First Class Paul Berlin could not stop. The giggles were caught in his throat, drowning him in his own laughter:
270 scared to death like Billy Boy.

Giggling, lying on his back, he saw the moon move, or the clouds moving across the moon. Wounded in action, dead of fright. A fine war story. He would tell it to his father, how Billy Boy had been scared to death, never letting on . . . He could not stop.

The soldier smothered him. He tried to fight back, but he was weak from the giggles.

The moon was under the clouds and the column was moving. The soldier helped him up. "You okay now, buddy?"
280 "Sure."

G ANALYZE SEQUENCE
What information has been communicated to the reader in the **flashback** found on lines 237–266? Explain, giving details from the text.

_____

_____

_____

_____

_____

_____

_____

_____

_____

_____

_____

---

6. **Medevac** (mĕd′ĭ-văk′) **helicopter:** a helicopter used for transporting injured people to places where they can receive medical care. "Medevac" is a contraction of "medical evacuation."

7. **mortar rounds:** shells fired from small, portable cannons.

"What was so bloody funny?"

"Nothing."

"You can get killed, laughing that way."

"I know. I know that."

"You got to stay calm, buddy." The soldier handed him his rifle. "Half the battle, just staying calm. You'll get better at it," he said. "Come on, now."

He turned away and Private First Class Paul Berlin hurried after him. He was still shivering.

290   He would do better once he reached the sea, he thought, still smiling a little. A funny war story that he would tell to his father, how Billy Boy Watkins was scared to death. A good joke. But even when he smelled salt and heard the sea, he could not stop being afraid. **PAUSE & REFLECT**

PAUSE & REFLECT

Underline the sentence that tells how Paul feels when he finally reaches the sea. What is O'Brien saying about war?

_____

_____

_____

_____

_____

SET A PURPOSE
FOR READING
Read this interview to learn
more about Tim O'Brien's
experiences as a writer.

Tim O'Brien: **The Naked Soldier**

Douglas Novielli, Christopher Connal, and Jackson Ellis,
Verbicide *Magazine*

BACKGROUND In this revealing interview, Tim O'Brien talks
about two kinds of bravery and discusses the courage it took
to make one frightening choice.

Verbicide Do you think you would have pursued writing
if you hadn't gone to Vietnam?

O'Brien Probably. It probably would've been something
different. If I'd gone to Canada I'd be writing about that.
Life provides you plenty of material, with girlfriends or
whatever.

V Do you think you romanticize Vietnam at all?

O No. I think a lot of veterans think I haven't done that
enough, but I refuse to do it.

10 **V** **Is there a reason they think it should be romanticized?**

O Yeah, they look back on it as more heroic, and with nostalgia, and they talk about the fellowship or fraternity among men, and there's some truth to that. But it's an artificial one; it's borne of necessity. Even if you don't like someone, you've got to trust them at night when they're on guard and you're sleeping. And you learn who to trust and who not to trust, and you bond that way. But I never found it very heroic, I just found it stone-man, gotta stay alive stuff. And that's all there was to it. **PAUSE & REFLECT**

20 **V** **Are soldiers heroes?**

O In some ways. It's heroic just not to stop. Physically, there are always alternatives, I mean, just stop walking. What can they do? Court martial you, but they're not gonna kill you. It looks pretty attractive, especially in bad days when guys have been dropping like flies. . . .

You just keep humping. There's a weird heroism in that. Unglamorous kind of valor to just keep going, knowing you might die with every step, and just keep walking.

V **Is the heroism there in your books to be interpreted if**
30 **the reader wants it, or is it directly implied?**

O I remember one part in *The Things They Carried* when I was talking about humping and just taking one step after the next, and at one point I called it a kind of courage, which it is, just to keep your legs moving. I'm kind of explicit about that kind of courage, but there are other kinds of courage just like there are kinds of truth. It took a lot of guts, for example, to go to Canada. Your whole hometown is going to think of you as a sissy or a coward, even though it's totally conscientious.

PAUSE & REFLECT
O'Brien notes that some veterans wish he had presented a more nostalgic or romantic view of the war, although he refuses to do it. Why? Explain.

So I admire the heroism and courage it took. I didn't have the guts to do it, to cross over the border.

V **Do you still regret that?**

O Yeah, you can't live your life over, but it would have been the right thing to do. I mean, think how hard it would be, even now it would be hard and I'm grown up. It was the thing that was worse than anything about the war, just going to it. Once you're in the war, it's pretty much what you'd expect. But, boy, making that decision, because you're in control of things. You can go in the army, or you can go to Canada. I never actually made that drive and went to the Rainy River.[1] That's invented. But it did happen in my head all summer long. I thought about driving to Canada. **PAUSE & REFLECT**

PAUSE & REFLECT

When O'Brien talks about going to Canada, he's talking about avoiding the war. According to him, why is avoiding the war require courage?

_____

_____

_____

_____

_____

_____

_____

---

1. **Rainy River:** a river on the U.S.– Canadian border. In O'Brien's short story "On the Rainy River," the main character drives to the river and considers whether he should cross the border into Canada and dodge the draft.

Text Analysis: Realism

In "Where Have You Gone, Charming Billy?" Tim O'Brien uses realism to bring his main character's experiences to life for the reader. Complete the chart by finding an example in the text that illustrates each element of O'Brien's style.

Element of O'Brien's Style	Example
Dialogue that sounds natural, like actual speech	
Vivid, realistic descriptions of what Paul sees	
A mix of long and short sentences to communicate Paul's thoughts and feelings	

Use your completed chart to explain how O'Brien's use of realism adds to the reader's perceptions of Paul and his situation.

_____

_____

_____

_____

Reading Skill: Analyze Sequence

Review your notes about the **flashback** in lines 220–247. Why might O'Brien have included the flashback at this point in the story? Complete the chart to show what O'Brien reveals about Paul through the flashback.

What Reader Knows from Main Story Events	What Happens in Flashback	What Reader Learns from Flashback
His situation:		
His actions: →	→	

Is FEAR our worst enemy?

Does Paul think that fear is his enemy or his friend? Do you agree with him? Explain.

_____

_____

_____

Vocabulary Practice

diffuse	fecund	inertia	stealth

Write the vocabulary word from the list above that best completes each sentence.

1. The soldiers moved with _____ across the countryside so that they would not be spotted by the enemy.

2. In spite of all the bombing it had suffered, the land they traveled through was still _____.

3. In their nervousness, it was hard to bring their _____ thoughts back into clear focus.

4. They relied on _____ and force of habit to keep them on the path.

Academic Vocabulary in Speaking

appreciate	attribute	indicate	unique	vary

TURN AND TALK An **attribute** is an essential quality of someone or something. What **attributes** does a hero have? Discuss this question with a partner, using at least two Academic Vocabulary words in your discussion. Definitions for these terms are listed on page 329.

Assessment Practice

DIRECTIONS Use "Where Have You Gone, Charming Billy?" and the interview with Tim O'Brien to answer questions 1–6.

1 The death of Billy Boy Watkins takes place —
   A in Paul's fevered imagination
   B after the platoon reaches the sea
   C shortly before the main action of the story
   D about a year before Paul arrives in Vietnam

2 Why does Paul imagine telling his father that he was not scared in Vietnam?
   A His father was a brave soldier.
   B He thinks his father will enjoy the joke.
   C He knows that none of the other soldiers are scared.
   D He is trying to convince himself that he is not scared.

3 One element that gives this story a realistic style is —
   A dialogue that reflects the way people actually talk
   B a flashback to an event that happened at a different time
   C a narrator who is outside the story
   D its setting in a country far from the United States

4 The author uses a flashback to show —
   A why Billy Boy and Paul were such close friends
   B why Paul is afraid of being overwhelmed by his own fear
   C that Paul has a sense of humor about death
   D that soldiers have nothing to fear as long as they remain calm

5 Paul cannot stop giggling because —
   A he remembers a joke his father once told him
   B he thinks Billy Boy's death was funny
   C his fear of dying causes him to lose control
   D Toby is shaking him in a way that tickles

6 What does the interview with Tim O'Brien reveal about the story?
   A The story draws upon O'Brien's actual experiences in Vietnam.
   B O'Brien does not think Paul is a courageous character.
   C O'Brien wanted his story to romanticize the Vietnam War.
   D The story shows how O'Brien wishes he had acted in the war.

A Few Words

Essay by Mary Oliver

Is "CUTE" a compliment?

Before you answer, think about it. What does *cute* really mean? Can you be cute and still be taken seriously? In this essay, Mary Oliver has a few words to say about what happens when we label something cute.

DEBATE With a group of classmates, use the notebook at left to jot down what comes to mind when you think of something cute. Would you want to be described this way? Form two teams and square off to settle the question of whether or not *cute* is a compliment.

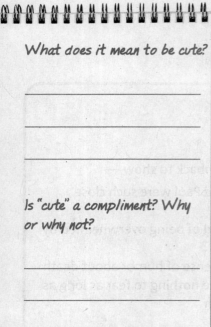

What does it mean to be cute?

_____

_____

_____

Is "cute" a compliment? Why or why not?

_____

_____

_____

Text Analysis: Tone

A writer's **tone** is his or her attitude about a subject as expressed through word choice and details. Some writers imply their tone carefully while others like to surprise readers by boldly hitting you over the head in the first paragraph. To detect a writer's tone, look carefully at his or her choice of words and details. For example, notice the tone Mary Oliver sets forth in the opening sentence of her essay:

Nothing in the forest is charming.

> **What is Oliver's tone in this opening statement?**
>
> blunt

> **How do you know?**
>
> She begins with a declaration that immediately challenges a common perception of the forest.

As you read "A Few Words," note striking words, details, and images that Oliver uses, and consider the tone they convey.

Reading Skill: Paraphrase

To understand difficult passages or sentences, it is sometimes helpful to **paraphrase,** or restate the writer's ideas in your own words. When you paraphrase, be sure to

- restate both the main idea and any important details

- use simpler words than those in the original text (you may want to use a thesaurus to help you find synonyms of more difficult terms)

As you read, you will be prompted to paraphrase this essay's difficult passages. See the chart below for an example.

Passage	My Paraphrase
"Gardens are charming, and man-made grottos, and there is a tranquility about some scenes of husbandry and agriculture that is charming—orderly rows of vegetation, or lazy herds, or the stalks of harvest lashed and leaning together."	Man-made elements of nature, like gardens and grottos, are pleasant. Some farm scenes, like orderly rows of crops, tame animals, and harvested produce, look peaceful and calm.

Vocabulary in Context

Note: Words are listed in the order in which they appear in the selection.

stalk (stôk) *n.* a stem or main axis of a plant
*The tall **stalks** of corn formed a maze.*

diminutive (dǐ-mǐn'yə-tǐv) *adj.* very small
*The study resulted in only a **diminutive** difference between the two groups.*

deftness (dĕft'nǐs) *n.* the quality of quickness and skillfulness
*The **deftness** with which the technician assembled the parts was remarkable.*

valorous (văl'ər-əs) *adj.* brave
*The medal honored the captain for his **valorous** achievements.*

Vocabulary Practice

Use the vocabulary words to write a few sentences about a walk in the forest.

_____

_____

_____

SET A PURPOSE
FOR READING
Read this essay to find out Oliver's view on the problems of "cuteness" in the natural world.

A Few Words

Essay by
MARY OLIVER

BACKGROUND Mary Oliver has been mesmerized by the natural world ever since she was a child growing up in Ohio. A keen observer, she writes about the mysteries and wisdom that it reveals to us. For inspiration, she takes solitary walks in the fields and woods, which she calls part of her writing process.

stalk (stôk) *n.* a stem or main axis of a plant

Ⓐ TONE
Reread lines 1–10. How would you describe Oliver's **tone?** Underline words and phrases the author uses to create this tone.

_____

_____

_____

_____

_____

_____

Nothing in the forest is charming. Gardens are charming, and man-made grottos,[1] and there is a tranquility about some scenes of husbandry[2] and agriculture that is charming—orderly rows of vegetation, or lazy herds, or the **stalks** of harvest lashed and leaning together.

And nothing in the forest is cute. The dog fox is not cute, nor the little foxes. I watch them as they run up and down the dune. One is carrying the soiled wing of a gull; the others grab onto it and pull. They fly in and out of the blond grasses, their small
10 teeth snapping. They are not adorable, or charming, or cute.

The owl is not cute. The milk snake is not cute, nor the spider in its web, nor the striped bass. Neither is the skunk cute, and its name is not "Flower." Nor is there a rabbit in the forest whose name is "Thumper," who is cute. Ⓐ

---

1. **man-made grottos** (grŏt′ōz): artificial caves created for coolness and pleasure.
2. **husbandry** (hŭz′bən-drē): farming.

Toys are cute. But animals are not toys. Neither are trees, rivers, oceans, swamps, the Alps, the mockingbird singing all night in the bowers of thorn, the snapping turtle, or the purple-fleshed mushroom.

Such words—"cute," "charming," "adorable"—miss the
20 mark, for what is perceived of in this way is stripped of dignity, and authority. What is cute is entertainment, and replaceable. The words lead us and we follow: what is cute is **diminutive**, it is powerless, it is capturable, it is trainable, it is ours. It is all a mistake. At our feet are the ferns—savage and resolute they rose, when the race of man was *nowhere* and altogether unlikely ever to be at all, in the terrifying shallows of the first unnamed and unnameable oceans. We find them pretty, delicate, and charming, and carry them home to our gardens.

Thus we manage to put ourselves in the masterly way—if
30 nature is full of a hundred thousand things adorable and charming, diminutive and powerless, then who is in the position of power? We are! We are the parents, and the governors. The notion facilitates a view of the world as playground and laboratory, which is a meager view surely. And it is disingenuous, for it seems so harmless, so responsible. But it is neither.

For it makes impossible the other view of nature, which is of a realm both sacred and intricate, as well as powerful, of which we are no more than a single part. Nature, the total of all of us, is the wheel that drives our world; those who ride it willingly might yet
40 catch a glimpse of a dazzling, even a spiritual restfulness, while those who are unwilling simply to hang on, who insist that the world must be piloted by man for his own benefit, will be dragged around and around all the same, gathering dust but no joy. **B**

diminutive (dĭ-mĭn′yə-tĭv) *adj.* very small

B PARAPHRASE
What is Oliver saying about human attitudes toward nature in lines 38–40? Use the chart to help you restate her ideas in your own words.

Original: "Nature, the total of all of us, is the wheel that drives our world"
My Paraphrase:

Original: "those who ride it willingly might yet catch a glimpse of a dazzling, even a spiritual restfulness"
My Paraphrase:

deftness (dĕft′nĭs) *n.* the quality of quickness and skillfulness

valorous (văl′ər-əs) *adj.* brave

PAUSE & REFLECT
According to Oliver, why shouldn't anything in nature be labeled "cute"?

_____

_____

_____

_____

_____

_____

Humans or tigers, tigers or tiger lilies—note their differences and still how alike they are! Don't we all, a few summers, stand here, and face the sea and, with whatever physical and intellectual **deftness** we can muster, improve our state—and then, silently, fall back into the grass, death's green cloud? What is cute or charming as it rises, as it swoons? Life is Niagara, or nothing. I would not
50 be the overlord of a single blade of grass, that I might be its sister. I put my face close to the lily, where it stands just above the grass, and give it a good greeting from the stem of my heart. We live, I am sure of this, in the same country, in the same household, and our burning comes from the same lamp. We are all wild, **valorous**, amazing. We are, none of us, cute. **PAUSE & REFLECT**

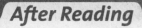

Text Analysis: Tone

"A Few Words" expresses a distinct tone. Fill in the chart below to understand
how Oliver establishes her tone. In the Example column, list words, details,
and images that contribute to the tone. Then, in the Tone column, describe
the tone that each example conveys.

Example	Tone

Review your notes for "A Few Words" and your completed chart. What is the
overall tone of this essay?

_____

_____

_____

Reading Skill: Paraphrase

Using the paraphrase you made as you read, summarize the main idea of this essay. Then list details that support the main idea.

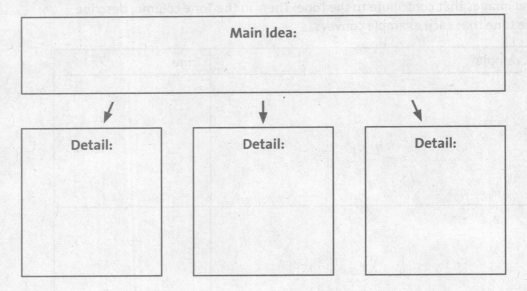

Main Idea:

Detail:

Detail:

Detail:

Is **"CUTE"** a compliment?

Did reading "A Few Words" change how you think of the word *cute?* Explain.

_____

_____

_____

Vocabulary Practice

In which situation might you use each vocabulary word? Circle the correct answers.

1. **diminutive: (a)** describing a miniature poodle, **(b)** listing the pros and cons of a school committee's proposal, **(c)** explaining how to draw trees

2. **stalk: (a)** explaining how to apply paint, **(b)** describing a field of wheat, **(c)** listing the reasons you like bungee jumping

3. **valorous: (a)** telling about a peaceful day in the country, **(b)** describing how the hero of a movie saved the day, **(c)** detailing how to lay a brick sidewalk

4. **deftness: (a)** watching leaves fall in a windstorm, **(b)** describing how a runner broke away from the pack to win, **(c)** choosing a birthday card for your brother

Academic Vocabulary in Writing

| appreciate | attribute | indicate | unique | vary |

Mary Oliver describes two views of the natural world that **vary** considerably. In a few sentences, explain which view you agree with most and why. Use at least one Academic Vocabulary in your response. Definitions for these terms are listed on page 329.

_____

_____

_____

_____

_____

_____

Assessment Practice

DIRECTIONS Use "A Few Words" to answer questions 1–4.

1 The image of the foxes in lines 6–10 is used in contrast with the idea that —
- **A** nature has an intricate order
- **B** animals are cute and adorable
- **C** animals should kill other animals
- **D** animals are easier to tame than plants

2 The tone of lines 11–14 is —
- **A** forceful
- **B** playful
- **C** melancholy
- **D** contemplative

3 Oliver says that viewing humans in a position of power is disingenuous because it —
- **A** strips people of their dignity
- **B** suggests that people are replaceable
- **C** prevents expressions of individuality
- **D** fails to acknowledge the power of nature

4 Which of these best describes who Oliver means by the pronoun "we" in lines 52–55?
- **A** all humans
- **B** all animals
- **C** everything in nature
- **D** everyone in this country

The Sneeze

Drama by **Neil Simon**

Based on a Story by **Anton Chekhov**

Who makes you LAUGH?

Can your best friend or a favorite comedian make you laugh every time? What's so funny about this person? If you get a kick out of ridiculous characters and their out-of-control bodily functions, you'll love "The Sneeze."

QUICKWRITE Think about the last time you had a laughing fit. In the notebook at left, create your own top-five list of the things and people you find funniest. Then, compare your list with a small group. Do your lists have items in common?

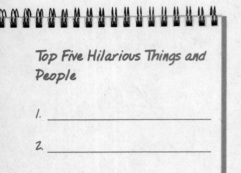

Top Five Hilarious Things and People

1. _____
2. _____
3. _____
4. _____
5. _____

Text Analysis: Farce

A **farce** is a humorous play that presents ridiculous situations, comic dialogue, and physical humor. Sometimes the purpose of a farce is simply to keep the audience laughing. In other cases, the writer might want to poke fun at someone or something in particular. As you read "The Sneeze" look out for the following elements.

Elements of a Farce	Examples
An absurd plot driven by a humorous conflict	The main character, Cherdyakov, keeps sneezing at inconvenient times.
Exaggerated behavior and language	After sneezing, Cherdyakov says, "It's unpardonable. It was monstrous of me —"
Characters who often exhibit just one comic trait or quality	Cherdyakov is so nervous about offending his boss that he apologizes over and over for his sneeze.
Clever wordplay, including puns and double meanings	"You shouldn't let people sneeze on you, dear. You're not to be sneezed at."
Physical comedy	Cherdyakov sneezes in an exaggerated way, leaning his head back and then snapping it forward.

Reading Strategy: Visualize

When you **visualize,** you use details, description, and dialogue to create mental images of what you read. Visualizing this play can help you monitor your understanding of it and enjoy its humor. Try the following:

- Read the stage directions to get a mental picture of the setting and of the actions taking place.

- Pay attention to the narrator's description of the other characters. Do you get an image of how they might look and behave?

- To help you picture each character, try mentally casting one of your favorite actors in the role.

- Use your own imagination and sense of humor.

As you read, track the details that help you visualize different aspects of the play in the following chart.

Details from the Text	My Visualization
"He is in his mid-thirties, mild-mannered and unassuming." (lines 3–4)	I picture a timid-looking, boring man with a pale, slightly anxious face.

**SET A PURPOSE
FOR READING**

Read this play to
determine which character,
Cherdyakov or the General,
deserves more sympathy.

THE sNEEZE

Drama by
NEIL SIMON

from The Good Doctor
Based on a Story by Anton Chekhov

BACKGROUND Anton Chekhov is one of Russia's greatest
authors. He is known for his short stories, one-act farces,
and full-length plays. Neil Simon's *The Good Doctor* is a
series of dramatic sketches based on one of Chekhov's
stories. The sketches are tied together through the
character of the Writer, who reveals his ideas for stories
to the audience. "The Sneeze" is one of these sketches.

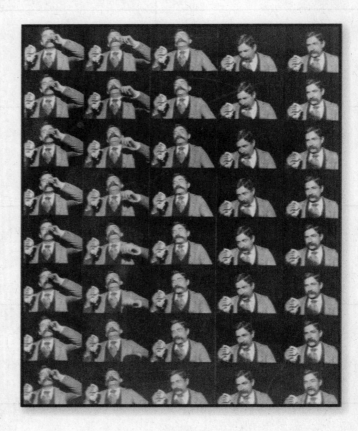

Writer. If Ivan Ilyitch Cherdyakov,[1] a civil servant, a clerk in the Ministry of Public Parks, had any passion in life at all, it was the theater. (*Enter* Ivan Cherdyakov *and his* Wife. *He is in his mid-thirties, mild-mannered and unassuming. He and his* Wife *are dressed in their best, but are certainly no match for the grandeur around them. They are clearly out of their element here. They move into their seats. As his* Wife *peruses her program,* Cherdyakov *is beaming with happiness as he looks around and in back at the theater and its esteemed audience. He is a happy man tonight.*) He certainly
10 had hopes and ambitions for higher office and had dedicated his life to hard work, zeal and patience. Still, he would not deny himself his one great pleasure. So he purchased two tickets in the very best section of the theater for the opening night performance of Rostov's *The Bearded Countess.*[2] (*A splendidly uniformed* General *and his* Wife *enter, looking for their seats.*) As fortune would have it, into the theater that night came His Respected Superior, General Mikhail Brassilhov,[3] the Minister of Public Parks himself. **Ⓐ**

(*The* General *and his* Wife *take their seats in the first row, the* General *directly in front of* Cherdyakov.)

20 **Cherdyakov** (*leans over to the* General). Good evening, General.

General (*turns, looks at* Cherdyakov *coldly*). Hmm? . . . What? Oh, yes. Yes. Good evening.

(*The* General *turns front again, looks at his program.*)

Cherdyakov. Permit me, sir. I am Cherdyakov . . . Ivan Ilyitch. This is a great honor for me, sir.

General (*turns; coldly*). Yes.

Cherdyakov. Like yourself, dear General, I too serve the Ministry of Public Parks . . . That is to say, I serve *you*, who is indeed *himself* the Minister of Public Parks. I am the Assistant Chief
30 Clerk in the Department of Trees and Bushes.

General. Ahh, yes. Keep up the good work . . . Lovely trees and bushes this year. Very nice.

Ⓐ VISUALIZE
Reread lines 1–17. What details help you visualize the play's setting and characters? Underline these details, and then choose the two best examples to add to the chart on page 357.

---

1. **Ivan Ilyitch Cherdyakov** (ē-vän′ ĭl-yēch′ chĕrd′yə-kəv).
2. **Rostov's** *The Bearded Countess*: a made-up author and play.
3. **Mikhail Brassilhov** (mē′kä-ēl′ bräs′ĭl-əv).

PAUSE & REFLECT
Reread lines 20–36. What kind
of humorous conflict might
develop between Cherdyakov
and the General?

_____

_____

_____

_____

_____

_____

_____

(*The* General *turns back.* Cherdyakov *sits back, happy, grinning
like a cat. The* General's Wife *whispers to him and he shrugs back.
Suddenly the unseen curtain rises on the play and they all applaud.*
Cherdyakov *leans forward again.*) **PAUSE & REFLECT**

Cherdyakov. My wife would like very much to say hello, General.
This is she. My wife, Madame Cherdyakov.

Wife (*smiles*). How do you do?

40 **General.** My pleasure.

Wife. *My* pleasure, General.

General. How do you do?

(*He turns front, flustered.* Cherdyakov *beams at his* Wife; *then*)

Cherdyakov (*to the* General's Wife). Madame Brassilhov—my
wife, Madame Cherdyakov.

Wife. How do you do, Madame Brassilhov?

Madame Brassilhov (*coldly*). How do you do?

Wife. I just had the pleasure of meeting your husband.

Cherdyakov (*to* Madame Brassilhov). And I am my wife's
50 husband. How do you do, Madame Brassilhov?

(*The* Writer *"shushes" them.*)

General (*to the* Writer). Sorry. Terribly sorry.

(*The* General *tries to control his anger as they all go back to
watching the play.*)

Cherdyakov. I hope you enjoy the play, sir.

General. I will if I can watch it.

(*He is getting hot under the collar. They all go back to watching
the performance.*)

Writer. Feeling quite pleased with himself for having made the
60 most of this golden opportunity, Ivan Ilyitch Cherdyakov sat

back to enjoy *The Bearded Countess*. He was no longer a stranger
to the Minister of Public Parks. They had become, if one wanted
to be generous about the matter, familiar with each other . . .
And then, quite suddenly, without any warning, like a bolt from
a gray thundering sky, Ivan Ilyitch Cherdyakov reared his head
back, and—

Cherdyakov. AHHHHHHHH—CHOOOOOOOO!!!
(Cherdyakov *unleashes a monstrous sneeze, his head snapping
forward. The main blow of the sneeze discharges on the back of the*
70 General's *completely bald head. The* General *winces and his hand
immediately goes to his now-dampened head.*) Ohhh, my goodness,
I'm *sorry,* your Excellency! I'm so terribly sorry! **B**

(*The* General *takes out his handkerchief and wipes his head.*)

General. Never mind. It's all right.

Cherdyakov. *All right?* . . . It certainly is *not* all right!
It's unpardonable. It was monstrous of me—

General. You make too much of the matter. Let it rest.

(*He puts away his handkerchief.*)

Cherdyakov (*quickly takes out his own handkerchief*). How can I let
80 it rest? It was inexcusable. Permit me to wipe your neck, General.
It's the least I can do.

(*He starts to wipe the* General's *head. The* General *pushes his
hand away.*)

General. Leave it be! It's all right, I say.

Cherdyakov. But I splattered you, sir. Your complete head is
splattered. It was an accident, I assure you—but it's *disgusting!*

Writer. Shhhh!

General. I'm sorry. My apologies.

Cherdyakov. The thing is, your Excellency, it came completely
90 without warning. It was out of my nose before I could stifle it.

Madame Brassilhov. Shhh! PAUSE & REFLECT

Monitor Your Comprehension

B FARCE
Reread lines 64–72 and underline
language that exaggerates
Cherdyakov's sneeze. What
elements of **farce** does the
sneeze represent? List at least
two.

_____

_____

_____

_____

_____

_____

_____

_____

_____

PAUSE & REFLECT
Do you think Cherdyakov's
apologies after the sneeze make
the situation better or worse?
Explain.

_____

_____

_____

_____

_____

_____

_____

Cherdyakov. Shhh, yes, certainly. I'm sorry . . . (*He sits back, nervously. He blows his nose with his handkerchief. Then* Cherdyakov *leans forward.*) It's not a cold, if that's what you were worrying about, sir. Probably a particle of dust in the nostril—

General. Shhh!

(*They watch the play in silence, and* Cherdyakov *sits back, unhappy with himself.*)

Writer. But try as he might, Cherdyakov could not put the
100 incident out of his mind. The sneeze, no more than an innocent anatomical accident,[4] grew out of all proportion in his mind, until it resembled the angry roar of a cannon aimed squarely at the enemy camp. He played the incident back in his mind, slowing the procedure down so he could view again in horror the infamous deed.

(Cherdyakov, *in slow motion, repeats the sneeze again, but slowed down so that it appears to us as one frame at a time. It also seems to be three times as great in intensity as the original sneeze. The* General, *also in slow motion, reacts as though he has just taken a fifty-pound*
110 *hammer blow at the base of his skull. They all go with the slow motion of the "sneeze" until it is completed, when the unseen curtain falls and they applaud. They all rise and begin to file out of the theater, chattering about the lovely evening they have just spent.*) **C**

General. Charming . . . Charming.

Madame Brassilhov. Yes, charming.

General. Charming . . . Simply charming. Wasn't it charming, my dear?

Madame Brassilhov. I found it utterly charming.

(Cherdyakov *stands behind them tapping the* General.)

120 **Writer.** I was completely charmed by it.

Cherdyakov (*still tapping away at the* General). Excuse me, Excellency—

C VISUALIZE

In lines 99–113, underline details that help you visualize the way Cherdyakov remembers his sneeze. (Review lines 64–72 if necessary.) Then add one more row to your chart on page 357.

---

4. **innocent anatomical accident:** A biological act over which Cherdyakov had no control.

General. Who's tapping? Somebody's tapping me. Who's that tapping?

Cherdyakov. I'm tapping, sir. I'm the tapper . . . Cherdyakov.

Madame Brassilhov (*quickly pulls the* General *back*). Stand back, dear, it's the sneezer.

Cherdyakov. No, no, it's all right. I'm all sneezed out . . . I was just concerned about your going out into the night air with a
130 damp head.

General. Oh, that. It was a trifle. A mere faux pas. Forget it, young man. Amusing play, don't you think? Did you find it amusing?

Cherdyakov. Amusing? Oh, my goodness, yes. Ha, ha. So true. Ha, ha. I haven't laughed as much in years. Ha, ha, ha . . .

General. Which part interested you the most?

Cherdyakov. The sneeze. When I sneezed on you. It was unforgivable, sir. **D**

General. Forget it, young man. Come, my dear. It looks like rain.
140 I don't want to get my head wet again.

Madame Brassilhov. You shouldn't let people sneeze on you, dear. You're not to be sneezed at.

(*They are gone.*)

Cherdyakov. I'm ruined! Ruined! He'll have me fired from Trees and Bushes. They'll send me down to Branches and Twigs. **E**

Wife. Come, Ivan.

Cherdyakov. What?

Wife. You mustn't let it concern you. It was just a harmless little sneeze. The General's probably forgotten it already.

150 **Cherdyakov.** Do you really think so?

Wife. No! I'm scared, Ivan.

Writer. And so they walked home in despair.

Monitor Your Comprehension

D FARCE
Reread the dialogue in lines 121–138. What comic trait does Cherdyakov reveal in this passage?

_____

_____

_____

E FARCE
Reread lines 114–145 and circle any examples of wordplay that you find. You may want to read the lines aloud. Restate in your own words what you find funny about the author's language.

_____

_____

_____

_____

_____

_____

_____

_____

_____

_____

_____

_____

Ⓕ FARCE
When the Writer says in lines 155–156 that Cherdyakov's "career had literally been blown away," he is using a **pun**. In this form of wordplay, a word or phrase has a double meaning. *Blown away* means "destroyed," but it also refers to Cherdyakov's sneeze. Circle another pun in lines 179–180 and explain it below.

_____

_____

_____

_____

_____

_____

_____

_____

_____

_____

_____

_____

_____

_____

_____

_____

_____

_____

Cherdyakov. Perhaps I should send him a nice gift. Maybe some Turkish towels.

Writer. Cherdyakov's once-promising career had literally been blown away.

Cherdyakov (*as they arrive home*). Why did this happen to me? Why did I go to the theater at all? Why didn't I sit in the balcony with people of our own class? They love sneezing on each other.

160 **Wife.** Come to bed, Ivan.

Cherdyakov. Perhaps if I were to call on the General and explain matters again, but in such a charming, honest and self-effacing manner, he would have no choice but to forgive me . . .

Wife. Maybe it's best not to remind him, Ivan.

Cherdyakov. No, no. If I ever expect to become a gentleman, I must behave like one.

Writer. And so the morning came. It so happened this was the day the General listened to petitions, and since there were fifty or sixty petitions ahead of Cherdyakov, he waited from morning till 170 late, late afternoon . . .

(Cherdyakov *moves into the office set.*)

General. Next! . . . NEXT!

Cherdyakov. I'm not next, your Excellency . . . I'm last.

General. Very well, then . . . Last!

Cherdyakov. That's me, sir.

General. Well, what is your petition?

Cherdyakov. I have no petition, sir. I'm not a petitioner.

General. Then you waste my time.

Cherdyakov. Do you not recognize me, sir? We met last night 180 under rather "explosive" circumstances . . . I am the splatterer. Ⓕ

General. The what?

Cherdyakov. The sneezer. The one who sneezed. The sneezing splatterer.

General. Indeed? And what is it you want now? A *Gesundheit?*[5]

Cherdyakov. No, Excellency . . . Your forgiveness. I just wanted to point out there was no political or antisocial motivation behind my sneeze. It was a nonpartisan, nonviolent act of God. I curse the day the protuberance formed itself on my face. It's a hateful nose, sir, and I am not responsible for its indiscretions . . . (*grabbing his own nose*) Punish that which committed the crime, but absolve the innocent body behind it. Exile my nose, but forgive me, your kindship. Forgive me.

General. My dear young man, I'm not angry with your nose. I'm too busy to have time for your nasal problems. I suggest you go home and take a hot bath—or a cold one—take *something,* but don't bother me with this silly business again . . . Gibber, gibber gibber, that's all I've heard all day. (*going offstage*) Gibber, gibber, gibber, gibber . . .

(Cherdyakov *stands alone in the office sobbing.*) **G**

Cherdyakov. Thank you, sir. God bless you and your wife and your household. May your days be sweet and may your nights be better than your days.

Writer. The feeling of relief that came over Cherdyakov was enormous . . .

Cherdyakov. May the birds sing in the morning at your window and may the coffee in your cup be strong and hot . . .

Writer. The weight of the burden that was lifted was inestimable . . .

Cherdyakov. I worship the chair you sit on and the uniform you wear that sits on the chair that I worship . . . **H**

Writer. He walked home, singing and whistling like a lark. Life was surely a marvel, a joy, a heavenly paradise . . .

Cherdyakov. Oh, God, I am happy! PAUSE & REFLECT

---

5. **Gesundheit** (gə-zŏŏnt′hīt′): German for "good health," this term is often used after someone sneezes.

G VISUALIZE
Reread lines 185–199. Circle the stage directions that describe his actions, and consider how an actor would portray his emotions. Then, in the chart on page 357, describe how you visualize this scene.

H FARCE
Underline examples of exaggeration in the apology and the blessings Cherdyakov gives to the General (lines 185–209).

PAUSE & REFLECT
Do you expect Cherdyakov to stay happy? Why or why not?

① FARCE
Reread lines 212–227. What is amusing about this section of dialogue?

_____

_____

_____

_____

_____

_____

PAUSE & REFLECT
In lines 216–242, underline examples of exaggeration. Do you think there is any truth to Cherdyakov's conclusion that the General meant to humiliate him? Explain your answer.

_____

_____

_____

_____

_____

_____

_____

_____

_____

Writer. And yet—

Cherdyakov. And yet—

Writer. When he arrived home, he began to think . . .

Cherdyakov. Have I been the butt of a cruel and thoughtless joke?

Writer. Had the Minister toyed with him?

Cherdyakov. If he had no intention of punishing me, why did he torment me so unmercifully?

220 **Writer.** If the sneeze meant so little to the Minister, why did he deliberately cause Cherdyakov to writhe in his bed?

Cherdyakov. . . . to twist in agony the entire night?

Writer. Cherdyakov was furious!

Cherdyakov. I AM FURIOUS!

Writer. He foamed and fumed and paced the night through, and in the morning he called out to his wife, "SONYA!"

Cherdyakov. SONYA! (_She rushes in._) I have been humiliated. **①**

Wife. _You,_ Ivan? Who would humiliate _you?_ You're such a kind and generous person.

230 **Cherdyakov.** Who? I'll tell you who! General Brassilhov, the Minister of Public Parks.

Wife. What did he do?

Cherdyakov. The swine! I was humiliated in such subtle fashion, it was almost indiscernible. The man's cunning is equal only to his cruelty. He practically forced me to come to his office to grovel and beg on my knees. I was reduced to a gibbering idiot.

Wife. You were that reduced?

Cherdyakov. I must go back and tell him what I think of him. The lower classes must speak up . . . (_He is at the door._) The

240 world must be made safe so that men of all nations and creeds, regardless of color or religion, will be free to sneeze on their superiors! It is _he_ who will be humiliated by _I!_ **PAUSE & REFLECT**

Writer. And so, the next morning, Cherdyakov came to humiliate *he*.[6]

(*Lights up on the* General *at his desk.*)

General. Last! (Cherdyakov *goes to the* General's *desk. He stands there glaring down at the* General *with a faint trace of a smile on his lips. The* General *looks up.*) Well?

Cherdyakov (*smiles*). Well? Well, you say? . . . Do you not recognize me, your Excellency? Look at my face . . . Yes. You're quite correct. It is I once again.

General (*looks at him, puzzled*). It is you once again who?

Cherdyakov (*confidentially*). Cherdyakov, Excellency. I have returned, having taken neither a hot bath nor a cold one.

General. Who let this filthy man in? What is it? ❿

Cherdyakov (*on top of the situation now*). What is it? . . . What is it, you ask? You sit there behind your desk and ask, What is it? You sit there in your lofty position as General and Minister of Public Parks, a member in high standing among the upper class and ask me, a lowly civil servant, What is it? You sit there with full knowledge that there is no equality in this life, that there are those of us who serve and those that are served, those of us that obey and those that are obeyed, those of us who bow and those that are bowed to, that in this life certain events take place that cause some of us to be humiliated and those that are the cause of that humiliation . . . and still you ask, "WHAT IS IT?"!

General (*angrily*). *What is it?* Don't stand there gibbering like an idiot! What is it you want?

Cherdyakov. *I'll tell you what I want!* . . . I wanted to apologize again for sneezing on you . . . I wasn't sure I made it clear. It was an accident, an accident, I assure you . . .

General (*stands and screams out*). *Out! Out, you idiot!* Fool! Imbecile! Get out of my sight! I never want to see you again. If you ever cross my line of vision I'll have you exiled forever . . . WHAT'S YOUR NAME?

❿ **FARCE**
The use of the word *filthy* in line 255 is a pun. Explain the two meanings the word has in this context.

1. _____

2. _____

_____

_____

---

6. **humiliated by *I* . . . humiliate *he*:** Cherdyakov uses an incorrect pronoun, and the Writer mimics him.

K FARCE
How does the ending of the play
in lines 276–293 illustrate the
qualities of a farce?

_____

_____

_____

_____

_____

_____

_____

_____

_____

_____

Cherdyakov. Ch—Cherdyakov!

(*It comes out as a sneeze in the* General's *face.*)

General (*wiping himself*). You germ spreader! You maggot! You
insect! You are lower than an insect. You are the second cousin
280 to a cockroach! The son-in-law of a bed bug! You are the nephew
of a *ringworm!* You are nothing, nothing, do you hear me? . . .
NOTHING!

(Cherdyakov *backs away, and returns home.*)

Writer. At that moment, something broke loose inside of
Cherdyakov . . . Something so deep and vital, so organic, that
the damage that was done seemed irreparable . . . Something
drained from him that can only be described as the very life force
itself . . . (Cherdyakov *takes off his coat. He sits on the sofa, head
in hands.*) The matter was over, for once, for all, forever. What
290 happened next was quite simple . . . (Cherdyakov *lies back on the
sofa.*) Ivan Ilyitch Cherdyakov arrived at home . . . removed his
coat . . . lay down on the sofa—and died! (Cherdyakov's *head
drops and his hand falls to the floor.*) **K**

Blackout

Text Analysis: Farce

Use the chart below to record examples of ridiculous situations, exaggerated behavior or language, and physical comedy that appear in "The Sneeze." Refer to the notes you took while reading to help you identify examples for each column of the chart.

Ridiculous Situations	Exaggerated Behavior or Language	Physical Comedy

The playwright, Neil Simon, uses these conventions of farce to make fun of something. What in particular does he seem to be mocking? Explain.

_____

_____

_____

_____

_____

Reading Strategy: Visualize

Which scenes in the play were you able to visualize most clearly? Review the chart you completed on page 357 for ideas. Then, think about how you might update this play for a more modern audience. Use your visualization skills to help you fill out the chart below.

Elements of the Play	Visualizing an Update
Main characters: Who would you have play the General, Cherdyakov, the Writer, and the wives?	
Setting: Where could the opening of the play be set, other than in the theater?	
Conflict: "The Sneeze" focuses on class issues in Russian society. How would you update the play to show two different sides of today's society?	

Who makes you LAUGH?

What did you find funniest about "The Sneeze"?

_____

_____

_____

_____

_____

_____

Academic Vocabulary in Writing

appreciate	attribute	indicate	unique	vary

What **attributes,** or characteristics, do Cherdyakov and the General have in common? What traits make each character **unique?** Write a few sentences about these two characters. Use at least one Academic Vocabulary word in your response. Definitions for these terms are listed on page 329.

_____

_____

_____

_____

Assessment Practice

DIRECTIONS Use "The Sneeze" to answer questions 1–5.

1 Cherdyakov's great passion in life is —
- (A) caring for trees and bushes
- (B) going to the theater
- (C) advancing his social position
- (D) sneezing on other people

2 Cherdyakov's sneeze creates a conflict because —
- (A) he is thrown out of the theater
- (B) the General refuses to forgive him
- (C) his wife fears he will lose his job
- (D) he cannot stop apologizing for it

3 Which element of farce is conveyed mostly through the stage directions that describe Cherdyakov's actions?
- (A) physical comedy
- (B) clever wordplay
- (C) exaggerated language
- (D) humorous conflict

4 Which of the following is an example of humorous exaggeration?
- (A) "This is a great honor for me, sir." (line 25)
- (B) "I'm *sorry*, your Excellency! I'm so terribly sorry!" (line 72)
- (C) "The sneezer. The one who sneezed. The sneezing splatterer." (lines 182–183)
- (D) "The [General's] cunning is equal only to his cruelty." (lines 234–235)

5 Why does Cherdyakov return to the General's office a second time?
- (A) to invite the General and his wife to a play
- (B) to express his anger at being humiliated by the General
- (C) to ask for a promotion in the Ministry of Public Parks
- (D) to apologize for sneezing on the General

9

Putting It in Context

HISTORY, CULTURE, AND THE AUTHOR

Be sure to read the Text Analysis Workshop on pp. 918–923 in *Holt McDougal Literature*.

Academic Vocabulary for Unit 9

Preview the following Academic Vocabulary words. You will encounter these words as you work through this book and will use them as you write and talk about the selections in the unit.

contrast (kən-trăst') *v.* to show differences
*Authors often **contrast** a character's life with the life of another character.*

environment (ĕn-vī'rən-mənt) *n.* surroundings; the land, water, climate, plants, and animals of an area
*A person grows up in an **environment** created by family and society.*

factor (făk'tər) *n.* elements or conditions
*It is difficult to find just one **factor** that is responsible for an event.*

incorporate (ĭn-kôr'pə-rāt') *v.* to join or combine into a single whole
*Children often **incorporate** friends' ideas to develop new games.*

predominant (prĭ-dăm'ə-nənt) *adj.* the most frequent or the most important
*The **predominant** feature of the house was the large windows.*

Think about the place where you live. Describe the **environment** in your area. For example, do you live in rural or urban surroundings? Use at least two Academic Vocabulary words in your description.

_____

_____

_____

_____

from *Angela's Ashes*
Memoir by Frank McCourt

How does FRIENDSHIP begin?

What makes two people connect? Something special happens to turn a mere acquaintance into a friend. In his memoir *Angela's Ashes*, writer Frank McCourt describes a friendship that develops under unusual circumstances.

QUICKWRITE Have you ever formed an unlikely friendship? Perhaps it was with someone much older than you—or simply with someone very different from you. In the notebook at the left write notes about how your friendship formed.

My Unlikely Friendship

Text Analysis: Memoir

A **memoir** is a form of autobiographical writing in which a writer shares his or her personal experiences and observations of significant events and people in his or her own life. Memoirs usually give readers insights into the influence of history on people's lives. The chart below gives examples of the historical and cultural factors that can affect a writer's work.

Historical Influences	
Political U.S. internment of Japanese citizens	**Social** the women's movement
Economic the Great Depression	**Environmental** the effects of pollution
Cultural Influences	
Ethnicity struggles to fit in while maintaining identity	**Values/Beliefs** the writer's religion
Technology world-altering inventions, such as the railroad or computer	**Arts/Entertainment** popular culture such as rock 'n' roll and baseball

In this selection, Frank McCourt is hospitalized with typhoid, a highly infectious, life-threatening illness that was common during his childhood in Ireland. As you read, note what you learn about Irish history and culture, especially the influence of the Roman Catholic Church.

Reading Skill: Use Allusions to Make Inferences

An **allusion** is a reference to a well-known person, place, event, or literary work. For example, a writer might refer to a strong character as having the strength of Hercules (a Greek hero famous for his strength). Writers use allusions

- to help characterize people or situations
- to evoke ideas or feelings in the reader's mind
- to clarify or highlight important ideas, including the theme

As you read, you will be prompted to notice allusions and make inferences about what they mean. See the chart below for an example.

Allusion	Significance	Inference
"…I don't care because it's Shakespeare and it's like having jewels in my mouth when I say the words" (lines 181–183)	Refers to William Shakespeare, revered English poet and playwright of the Elizabethan era.	Frank loves language and poetry.

Vocabulary in Context

Note: Words are listed in the order in which they appear in the story.

relapse (rē′lăps) *n.* a worsening of an illness after a partial recovery
The **relapse** *of his illness put him back in the hospital.*

induced (ĭn-dōōst′) *adj.* led on; persuaded
Her persuasive speech **induced** *me to support her cause.*

torrent (tôr′ənt) *n.* a heavy, uncontrolled outpouring
The **torrent** *of rain caused the road to flood.*

perfidy (pûr′fĭ-dē) *n.* treachery; betrayal of trust
The officer's **perfidy** *led him to be charged with treason.*

Vocabulary Practice

Work with a partner to substitute a different word for each vocabulary word in two of the sentences above. Write your new sentences below.

_____

_____

_____

SET A PURPOSE
FOR READING

Read this excerpt from "Angela's Ashes" to find out how a special friendship makes Frank McCourt's hospital stay more bearable.

Angela's Ashes

Memoir by **Frank McCourt**

BACKGROUND "Angela's Ashes" is Frank McCourt's memoir of growing up in Ireland in the late 1930s and 1940s. McCourt's family lived in a filthy, overcrowded slum, at a time when diseases such as typhoid and diphtheria were common. Because such diseases spread easily, people with these illnesses were isolated in "fever hospitals." Most of these hospitals were run by the Catholic Church and staffed by nuns.

Ⓐ MEMOIR
Reread lines 1–14. What **inferences** can you make about life in Ireland at this time? Underline clues in the text and then write your answer on the lines below.

_____

_____

_____

_____

_____

_____

Mam comes with Dr. Troy. He feels my forehead, rolls up my eyelids, turns me over to see my back, picks me up and runs to his motor car. Mam runs after him and he tells her I have typhoid fever. Mam cries, . . . am I to lose the whole family? Will it ever end? She gets into the car, holds me in her lap and moans all the way to the Fever Hospital at the City Home.[1]

The bed has cool white sheets. The nurses have clean white uniforms and the nun, Sister Rita, is all in white. Dr. Humphrey and Dr. Campbell have white coats and things hanging from their
10 necks which they stick against my chest and all over. I sleep and sleep but I'm awake when they bring in jars of bright red stuff that hang from tall poles above my bed and they stick tubes into my ankles and the back of my right hand. Sister Rita says, You're getting blood, Francis. Soldier's blood from the Sarsfield Barracks. Ⓐ

---

1. **Mam cries, . . . City Home:** The Fever Hospital was a special section of the Limerick City Home Hospital where patients who had fever-related illnesses like typhoid were treated. The McCourt family had already lost a baby daughter and twin boys to childhood disease.

Mam is sitting by the bed and the nurse is saying, You know, missus, this is very unusual. No one is ever allowed into the Fever Hospital for fear they'd catch something but they made an exception for you with his crisis coming. If he gets over this he'll surely recover.

20   I fall asleep. Mam is gone when I wake but there's movement in the room and it's the priest, Father Gorey, from the Confraternity[2] saying Mass at a table in the corner. I drift off again and now they're waking me and pulling down the bedclothes. Father Gorey is touching me with oil and praying in Latin. I know it's Extreme Unction[3] and that means I'm going to die and I don't care. They wake me again to receive Communion. I don't want it, I'm afraid I might get sick. I keep the wafer on my tongue and fall asleep and when I wake up again it's gone. **B**

It's dark and Dr. Campbell is sitting by my bed. He's holding
30   my wrist and looking at his watch. He has red hair and glasses and he always smiles when he talks to me. He sits now and hums and looks out the window. His eyes close and he snores a little. . . .

Sister Rita's white habit is bright in the sun that comes in the window. She's holding my wrist, looking at her watch, smiling. Oh, she says, we're awake, are we? Well, Francis, I think we've come through the worst. Our prayers are answered and all the prayers of those hundreds of little boys at the Confraternity. Can you imagine that? Hundreds of boys saying the rosary[4] for you and offering up their communion. **C**

40   My ankles and the back of my hand are throbbing from the tubes bringing in the blood and I don't care about boys praying for me. I can hear the swish of Sister Rita's habit and the click of her rosary beads when she leaves the room. I fall asleep and when I wake it's dark and Dad is sitting by the bed with his hand on mine.

Son, are you awake?

---

2. **Confraternity** (kŏn'frə-tûr'nĭ-tē): a religious society or association.
3. **Extreme Unction** (ŭngk'shən): a Roman Catholic sacrament given to a person thought to be near death.
4. **rosary** (rō'zə-rē): a series of prayers repeated by Roman Catholics as a form of devotion to the Virgin Mary—usually counted off on a string of beads as they are said.

B **MEMOIR**
In line 25, Frank says that he doesn't care if he dies. Why does he think he's going to die? Why do you think he doesn't care if he does?

_____

_____

_____

_____

_____

C **MEMOIR**
Reread lines 33–39. Underline details about the Catholic Church. How were Irish children influenced by the Church?

_____

_____

_____

_____

_____

PAUSE & REFLECT

Reread lines 51–62. How would you describe Frank's relationship with his father? Underline details in the text that support your answer.

I try to talk but I'm dry, nothing will come out and I point to my mouth. He holds a glass of water to my lips and it's sweet and cool. He presses my hand and says I'm a great old soldier and why wouldn't I? Don't I have the soldier's blood in me?

50　　The tubes are not in me anymore and the glass jars are gone.

Sister Rita comes in and tells Dad he has to go. I don't want him to go because he looks sad. When he looks sad it's the worst thing in the world and I start crying. Now what's this? says Sister Rita. Crying with all that soldier blood in you? There's a big surprise for you tomorrow, Francis. You'll never guess. Well, I'll tell you, we're bringing you a nice biscuit[5] with your tea in the morning. Isn't that a treat? And your father will be back in a day or two, won't you, Mr. McCourt?

Dad nods and puts his hand on mine again. He looks at me,
60 steps away, stops, comes back, kisses me on the forehead for the first time in my life and I'm so happy I feel like floating out of the bed. **PAUSE & REFLECT**

The other two beds in my room are empty. The nurse says I'm the only typhoid patient and I'm a miracle for getting over the crisis.

The room next to me is empty till one morning a girl's voice says, Yoo hoo, who's there?

I'm not sure if she's talking to me or someone in the room beyond.

70　Yoo hoo, boy with the typhoid, are you awake?

I am.

Are you better?

I am.

Well, why are you here?

I don't know. I'm still in the bed. They stick needles in me and give me medicine.

What do you look like?

---

5. **biscuit:** cookie.

I wonder, What kind of a question is that? I don't know what to tell her. **D**

80   Yoo hoo, are you there, typhoid boy?

I am.

What's your name?

Frank.

That's a good name. My name is Patricia Madigan. How old are you?

Ten.

Oh. She sounds disappointed.

But I'll be eleven in August, next month.

Well, that's better than ten. I'll be fourteen in September. Do 90 you want to know why I'm in the Fever Hospital?

I do.

I have diphtheria[6] and something else.

What's something else?

They don't know. They think I have a disease from foreign parts because my father used to be in Africa. I nearly died. Are you going to tell me what you look like?

I have black hair.

You and millions.

I have brown eyes with bits of green that's called hazel.

100   You and thousands.

I have stitches on the back of my right hand and my two feet where they put in the soldier's blood.

Oh, . . . did they?

They did.

You won't be able to stop marching and saluting.

There's a swish of habit and click of beads and then Sister Rita's voice. Now, now, what's this? There's to be no talking between

---

6. **diphtheria** (dĭf-thîr′ē-ə): a highly infectious disease caused by the bacterium *Corynebacterium diphtheriae*. It is spread by infected secretions from the nose and throat and can create toxins that destroy the heart and nervous system.

D MEMOIR

Go back to the end of page 378 and circle the question the girl asks Frank. Why does Frank think this is an odd question?

two rooms especially when it's a boy and a girl. Do you hear me, Patricia?

110   I do, Sister.

Do you hear me, Francis?

I do, Sister.

You could be giving thanks for your two remarkable recoveries. You could be saying the rosary. You could be reading *The Little Messenger of the Sacred Heart*[7] that's beside your beds. Don't let me come back and find you talking. She comes into my room and wags her finger at me. Especially you, Francis, after thousands of boys prayed for you at the Confraternity. Give thanks, Francis, give thanks. She leaves and there's silence for awhile. Then Patricia
120 whispers, Give thanks, Francis, give thanks, and say your rosary, Francis, and I laugh so hard a nurse runs in to see if I'm all right. She's a very stern nurse from the County Kerry[8] and she frightens me. What's this, Francis? Laughing? What is there to laugh about? Are you and that Madigan girl talking? I'll report you to Sister Rita. There's to be no laughing for you could be doing serious damage to your internal apparatus.[9] **E**

She plods out and Patricia whispers again in a heavy Kerry accent, No laughing, Francis, you could be doin' serious damage to your internal apparatus. Say your rosary, Francis, and pray for
130 your internal apparatus.

Mam visits me on Thursdays, I'd like to see my father, too, but I'm out of danger, crisis time is over, and I'm allowed only one visitor. Besides, she says, he's back at work at Rank's Flour Mills and please God this job will last a while with the war on and the English desperate for flour. She brings me a chocolate bar and that proves Dad is working. She could never afford it on the dole.[10] He sends me notes. He tells me my brothers are all praying for me, that I should be a good boy, obey the doctors, the nuns, the nurses, and don't forget to say my prayers. He's sure St. Jude
140 pulled me through the crisis because he's the patron saint of desperate cases and I was indeed a desperate case. **F**

E ALLUSIONS
Reread lines 114–126. Circle the name of the magazine Sister Rita mentions. Why do you think she wants Frank to read this?

_____

_____

_____

_____

_____

_____

F MEMOIR
Reread lines 131–141. Underline the details that describe Frank's family and the role of religion in their lives.

---

7. *The Little . . . Heart:* a Roman Catholic magazine.

8. **Country Kerry:** a largely rural county to the west of Limerick.

9. **internal apparatus:** the internal organs of the body.

10. **on the dole:** living on government unemployment payments.

Patricia says she has two books by her bed. One is a poetry book and that's the one she loves. The other is a short history of England and do I want it? She gives it to Seamus,[11] the man who mops the floors every day, and he brings it to me. He says, I'm not supposed to be bringing anything from a diphtheria room to a typhoid room with all the germs flying around and hiding between the pages and if you ever catch diphtheria on top of the typhoid they'll know and I'll lose my good job and be out on the
150 street singing patriotic songs with a tin cup in my hand, which I could easily do because there isn't a song ever written about Ireland's sufferings I don't know. . . .

Oh, yes, he knows Roddy McCorley.[12] He'll sing it for me right enough but he's barely into the first verse when the Kerry nurse rushes in. What's this, Seamus? Singing? Of all the people in this hospital you should know the rules against singing. I have a good mind to report you to Sister Rita.

Ah, . . . don't do that, nurse.

Very well, Seamus. I'll let it go this one time. You know the
160 singing could lead to a **relapse** in these patients.

When she leaves he whispers he'll teach me a few songs because singing is good for passing the time when you're by yourself in a typhoid room. He says Patricia is a lovely girl the way she often gives him sweets from the parcel her mother sends every fortnight.[13] He stops mopping the floor and calls to Patricia in the next room, I was telling Frankie you're a lovely girl, Patricia, and she says, You're a lovely man, Seamus. He smiles because he's an old man of forty and he never had children but the ones he can talk to here in the Fever Hospital. He says, Here's the
170 book, Frankie. Isn't it a great pity you have to be reading all about England after all they did to us, that there isn't a history of Ireland to be had in this hospital. **G**

The book tells me all about King Alfred and William the Conqueror and all the kings and queens down to Edward, who

relapse (rē'lăps) *n.* a worsening of an illness after a partial recovery

G ALLUSIONS
Reread lines 161–172. Underline the **allusion** that Seamus makes to the troubled relationship between England and Ireland. What does this reveal about him? about Irish culture?

_____

_____

_____

_____

_____

_____

_____

_____

---

11. **Seamus** (shā'məs).

12. **Roddy McCorley:** a song about Roddy McCorley, a local leader during an Irish uprising. McCorley was hanged by the English in 1798.

13. **fortnight:** two weeks.

induced (ĭn-dōōst′) *adj.* led on; persuaded

ⓗ MEMOIR
Reread lines 173–184. Circle the comparison that Frank makes about reading Shakespeare. What does this first encounter with Shakespeare reveal about Frank?

_____

_____

_____

_____

_____

_____

_____

torrent (tôr′ənt) *n.* a heavy, uncontrolled outpouring

What other word is a synonym of **torrent**? Replace **torrent** with a word with a similar meaning. What effect does this have on the line from the poem?

_____

_____

_____

_____

had to wait forever for his mother, Victoria, to die before he could be king. The book has the first bit of Shakespeare I ever read.

> *I do believe, __induced__ by potent circumstances*
> *That thou art mine enemy.*

The history writer says this is what Catherine, who is a wife
180 of Henry the Eighth, says to Cardinal Wolsey, who is trying to have her head cut off. I don't know what it means and I don't care because it's Shakespeare and it's like having jewels in my mouth when I say the words. If I had a whole book of Shakespeare they could keep me in the hospital for a year. ⓗ

Patricia says she doesn't know what induced means or potent circumstances and she doesn't care about Shakespeare, she has her poetry book and she reads to me from beyond the wall a poem about an owl and a pussycat that went to sea in a green boat with honey and money[14] and it makes no sense and when I say that
190 Patricia gets huffy and says that's the last poem she'll ever read to me. She says I'm always reciting the lines from Shakespeare and they make no sense either. Seamus stops mopping again and tells us we shouldn't be fighting over poetry because we'll have enough to fight about when we grow up and get married. Patricia says she's sorry and I'm sorry too so she reads me part of another poem which I have to remember so I can say it back to her early in the morning or late at night when there are no nuns or nurses about,

> *The wind was a __torrent__ of darkness among the gusty trees,*
> *The moon was a ghostly galleon tossed upon cloudy seas,*
> 200 *The road was a ribbon of moonlight over the purple moor,*
> *And the highwayman came riding*
> *Riding riding*
> *The highwayman came riding, up to the old inn-door.*
> *He'd a French cocked-hat on his forehead,*
> *a bunch of lace at his chin,*

---

14. **a poem . . . money:** "The Owl and the Pussycat," a humorous poem by the 19th-century British poet and artist Edward Lear.

A coat of the claret velvet, and breeches of brown doe-skin,
They fitted with never a wrinkle, his boots were up to the thigh.
And he rode with a jeweled twinkle,
His pistol butts a-twinkle,
210 *His rapier hilt a-twinkle, under the jeweled sky.*[15]

Every day I can't wait for the doctors and nurses to leave me
alone so I can learn a new verse from Patricia and find out what's
happening to the highwayman and the landlord's red-lipped
daughter. I love the poem because it's exciting and almost as
good as my two lines of Shakespeare. The redcoats are after the
highwayman because they know he told her, I'll come to thee
by moonlight. . . . ❶

I'd love to do that myself, come by moonlight for Patricia in
the next room. . . . She's ready to read the last few verses when
220 in comes the nurse from Kerry shouting at her, shouting at me,
I told ye there was to be no talking between rooms. Diphtheria
is never allowed to talk to typhoid and visa versa. I warned ye.
And she calls out, Seamus, take this one. Take the by.[16] Sister Rita
said one more word out of him and upstairs with him. We gave
ye a warning to stop the blathering but ye wouldn't. Take the by,
Seamus, take him.

Ah, now, nurse, sure isn't he harmless. 'Tis only a bit o' poetry.
Take that by, Seamus, take him at once. ❷

He bends over me and whispers, Ah, . . . I'm sorry, Frankie.
230 Here's your English history book. He slips the book under my
shirt and lifts me from the bed. He whispers that I'm a feather.
I try to see Patricia when we pass through her room but all I can
make out is a blur of dark head on a pillow.

Sister Rita stops us in the hall to tell me I'm a great
disappointment to her, that she expected me to be a good boy
after what God had done for me, after all the prayers said by

---

15. **The wind . . . jeweled sky:** the opening lines of "The Highwayman," a
romantic, action-packed narrative poem by the 20th-century British
writer Alfred Noyes.
16. **by:** boy (spelled to indicate the nurse's dialectal pronunciation).

❶ **MEMOIR**
Reread lines 211–217. How is
Frank and Patricia's situation like
that of the characters in "The
Highwayman"?

_____

_____

_____

_____

_____

_____

_____

❷ **MEMOIR**
In lines 221–228, McCourt uses
dialect—a form of language
spoken in a particular place or by
a particular group of people—to
provide a realistic portrayal
of the nurse. How does this
influence your reaction to her?

_____

_____

_____

_____

_____

_____

_____

_____

_____

PAUSE & REFLECT

What does Sister Rita tell Frank to say in confession? Why?

_____

_____

_____

_____

_____

hundreds of boys at the Confraternity, after all the care from the nuns and nurses of the Fever Hospital, after the way they let my mother and father in to see me, a thing rarely allowed, and this is
240 how I repaid them lying in the bed reciting silly poetry back and forth with Patricia Madigan knowing very well there was a ban on all talk between typhoid and diphtheria. She says I'll have plenty of time to reflect on my sins in the big ward upstairs and I should beg forgiveness for my disobedience reciting a pagan English poem about a thief on a horse and a maiden with red lips who commits a terrible sin when I could have been praying or reading the life of a saint. She made it her business to read that poem so she did and I'd be well advised to tell the priest in confession.

PAUSE & REFLECT

The Kerry nurse follows us upstairs gasping and holding on
250 to the banister. She tells me I better not get the notion she'll be running up to this part of the world every time I have a little pain or a twinge.

There are twenty beds in the ward, all white, all empty. The nurse tells Seamus put me at the far end of the ward against the wall to make sure I don't talk to anyone who might be passing the door, which is very unlikely since there isn't another soul on this whole floor. She tells Seamus this was the fever ward during the Great Famine[17] long ago and only God knows how many died here brought in too late for anything but a wash before they were
260 buried and there are stories of cries and moans in the far reaches of the night. She says 'twould break your heart to think of what the English did to us, that if they didn't put the blight[18] on the potato they didn't do much to take it off. No pity. No feeling at all for the people that died in this very ward, children suffering and dying here while the English feasted on roast beef and guzzled the best of wine in their big houses, little children with their

---

17. **Great Famine** (făm′ĭn): a devastating food shortage in Ireland in the late 1840s, caused by a failure of the potato crop. Over a million Irish people died of starvation during the famine, and about 1.5 million emigrated, mainly to the United States.

18. **blight:** a plant disease—in this case, the one that destroyed the Irish potato crop.

mouths all green from trying to eat the grass in the fields beyond, God bless us and save us and guard us from future famines. **K**

270 Seamus says 'twas a terrible thing indeed and he wouldn't want to be walking these halls in the dark with all the little green mouths gaping at him. The nurse takes my temperature, 'Tis up a bit, have a good sleep for yourself now that you're away from the chatter with Patricia Madigan below who will never know a gray hair.[19]

She shakes her head at Seamus and he gives her a sad shake back.

Nurses and nuns never think you know what they're talking about. If you're ten going on eleven you're supposed to be simple like my uncle Pat Sheehan who was dropped on his head. You can't ask questions. You can't show you understand what the nurse 280 said about Patricia Madigan, that she's going to die, and you can't show you want to cry over this girl who taught you a lovely poem which the nun says is bad. **PAUSE & REFLECT**

The nurse tells Seamus she has to go and he's to sweep the lint from under my bed and mop up a bit around the ward. Seamus tells me . . . that you can't catch a disease from a poem. . . . He never heard the likes of it, a little fella shifted upstairs for saying a poem and he has a good mind to go to the *Limerick Leader*[20] and tell them print the whole thing except he has this job and he'd lose it if ever Sister Rita found out. Anyway, Frankie, you'll be 290 outa here one of these fine days and you can read all the poetry you want though I don't know about Patricia below, I don't know about Patricia. . . .

He knows about Patricia in two days because she got out of the bed to go to the lavatory when she was supposed to use a bedpan and collapsed and died in the lavatory. Seamus is mopping the floor and there are tears on his cheeks and he's saying, 'Tis a dirty rotten thing to die in a lavatory when you're lovely in yourself. She told me she was sorry she had you reciting that poem and getting you shifted from the room, Frankie. She 300 said 'twas all her fault. **L**

---

19. **never know a gray hair:** won't live to be old.
20. *Limerick Leader:* a newspaper published in Limerick.

K MEMOIR

In lines 257–268, underline the lines where the Kerry nurse talks about the sufferings the Irish endured during the famine. What effect did the famine have on the Irish culture?

_____

_____

_____

_____

_____

PAUSE & REFLECT

Reread lines 271–282 and underline what the nurse tells Seamus about Patricia Madigan. How does Frank respond to this news?

_____

_____

_____

_____

_____

_____

L MEMOIR

In line 286 Seamus uses the expression *the likes of* to mean "anything like" and *fella* to mean "fellow." Underline other examples of informal language in these two paragraphs.

It wasn't, Seamus.

I know and didn't I tell her that.

Patricia is gone and I'll never know what happened to the highwayman and Bess, the landlord's daughter. I ask Seamus but he doesn't know any poetry at all especially English poetry. He knew an Irish poem once but it was about fairies and had no sign of a highwayman in it. Still he'll ask the men in his local pub where there's always someone reciting something and he'll bring it back to me. Won't I be busy meanwhile reading my short history

310 of England and finding out all about their **perfidy**. That's what Seamus says, perfidy, and I don't know what it means and he doesn't know what it means but if it's something the English do it must be terrible.

He comes three times a week to mop the floor and the nurse is there every morning to take my temperature and pulse. The doctor listens to my chest with the thing hanging from his neck. They all say, And how's our little soldier today? A girl with a blue dress brings meals three times a day and never talks to me. Seamus says she's not right in the head so don't say a word to her.

320 The July days are long and I fear the dark. There are only two ceiling lights in the ward and they're switched off when the tea tray is taken away and the nurse gives me pills. The nurse tells me go to sleep but I can't because I see people in the nineteen beds in the ward all dying and green around their mouths where they tried to eat grass and moaning for soup Protestant soup[21] any soup and I cover my face with the pillow hoping they won't come and stand around the bed clawing at me and howling for bits of the chocolate bar my mother brought last week.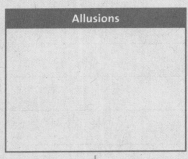

No, she didn't bring it. She had to send it in because I can't

330 have any more visitors. Sister Rita tells me a visit to the Fever Hospital is a privilege and after my bad behavior with Patricia Madigan and that poem I can't have the privilege anymore. She says I'll be going home in a few weeks and my job is to

perfidy (pûr´fĭ-dē) *n.* treachery; betrayal of trust

Reread lines 310–313 and underline the context clue that can help you determine the meaning of **perfidy**.

Ⓜ **ALLUSIONS**
Reread lines 320–328. In the chart below, record allusions to the Great Famine. What inference can you make about this allusion?

Allusions

↓

Inference

---

21. **Protestant soup:** soup provided by the English to the starving Irish during the famine, often in return for renouncing Catholicism and joining the Protestant faith.

concentrate on getting better and learn to walk again after being in bed for six weeks and I can get out of bed tomorrow after breakfast. I don't know why she says I have to learn how to walk when I've been walking since I was a baby but when the nurse stands me by the side of the bed I fall to the floor and the nurse laughs, See, you're a baby again.

340   I practice walking from bed to bed back and forth back and forth. I don't want to be a baby. I don't want to be in this empty ward with no Patricia and no highwayman and no red-lipped landlord's daughter. I don't want the ghosts of children with green mouths pointing bony fingers at me and clamoring for bits of my chocolate bar.

Seamus says a man in his pub knew all the verses of the highwayman poem and it has a very sad end. Would I like him to say it because he never learned how to read and he had to carry the poem in his head? He stands in the middle of the ward
350 leaning on his mop and recites,

> *Tlot-tlot, in the frosty silence! Tlot-tlot in the echoing night!*
> *Nearer he came and nearer! Her face was like a light!*
> *Her eyes grew wide for a moment, she drew one last deep breath,*
> *Then her finger moved in the moonlight,*
> *Her musket shattered the moonlight,*
> *Shattered her breast in the moonlight and warned him—with*
>   *her death.*

N MEMOIR
What does Seamus's recitation tell you about the relationship between him and Frank?

_____
_____
_____
_____
_____
_____
_____

Why do you think this phase of McCourt's life became an important part of his memoir?

_____

_____

_____

_____

_____

_____

_____

_____

_____

He hears the shot and escapes but when he learns at dawn how Bess died he goes into a rage and returns for revenge only to be shot down by the redcoats.

360　　　*Blood-red were his spurs in the golden noon; wine-red was his*
　　　　　　velvet coat,
　　　　When they shot him down on the highway,
　　　　Down like a dog on the highway,
　　　　And he lay in his blood on the highway, with a bunch of lace
　　　　　　at his throat.

Seamus wipes his sleeve across his face and sniffles. He says, There was no call at all to shift you up here away from Patricia when you didn't even know what happened to the highwayman and Bess. 'Tis a very sad story and when I said it to my wife she wouldn't stop crying the whole night till we went to bed. She said

370 there was no call for them redcoats to shoot that highwayman, they are responsible for half the troubles of the world and they never had any pity on the Irish, either. Now if you want to know any more poems, Frankie, tell me and I'll get them from the pub and bring 'em back in my head. **PAUSE & REFLECT**

Text Analysis: Memoir

In "Angela's Ashes," Frank McCourt shares his personal experiences and observations of significant events in his youth. Fill in the chart below with information from the selection that shows ideas and events that influenced McCourt. Refer back to the chart on page 374 for examples. Note: If you think there is no information from the selection to add to a category, explain your reasoning.

Historical Influences	
Political	Social
Economic	Environmental

Cultural Influences	
Ethnicity	Values/Beliefs
Technology	Arts/Entertainment

Review your notes for "Angela's Ashes" and your completed chart. Then write a few sentences about what you learned about Irish history and culture while reading this selection.

_____

_____

_____

_____

Reading Skill: Use Allusions to Make Inferences

In the chart below, list four allusions to Catholic clergy, rituals, practices, or beliefs that appear in this selection. In the second box, explain what these allusions tell you about McCourt's view of the Catholic Church and its influence on Irish culture and society in the 1940s.

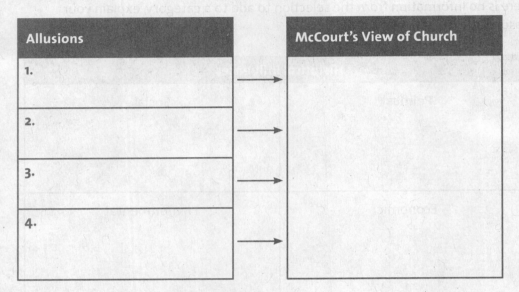

Allusions	McCourt's View of Church
1.	
2.	
3.	
4.	

How does **FRIENDSHIP** begin?

How does friendship end?

_____

_____

_____

Vocabulary Practice

Circle the phrase that best clarifies the meaning of each vocabulary word.

1. Experiencing a **relapse** of the flu usually means that **(a)** one will be sick for little longer, **(b)** it is time for a flu shot, **(c)** it is time to go back to school or work.

2. A **torrent** of water could most likely be produced by **(a)** a leaky hose, **(b)** a large rain cloud, **(c)** a spray bottle.

3. Experiencing an act of **perfidy** might make you **(a)** get interested in mountain climbing, **(b)** feel angry and betrayed, **(c)** decide to read historical fiction.

4. If you have **induced** a friend to join you on a boring errand, you are probably good at **(a)** persuading others, **(b)** staying on schedule, **(c)** working alone.

Academic Vocabulary in Writing

contrast	environment	factor	incorporate	predominant

In a few sentences, discuss the **environment** in the hospital where Frank is taken. **Contrast** this environment to a hospital today. What are the **predominant,** or most important, differences? Use at least one Academic Vocabulary word in your response. Definitions for these terms are listed on page 373.

_____

_____

_____

Assessment Practice

DIRECTIONS Use "Angela's Ashes" to answer questions 1–4.

1 How does Sister Rita expect Frank to act after she mentions the prayers of the Confraternity boys?

- **A** She knows that Frank will not appreciate the prayers.
- **B** She expects that Frank will want all the boys to visit him.
- **C** She thinks that Frank will be grateful and obey her rules.
- **D** She worries that Frank will act ungrateful.

2 What can the reader infer about McCourt's father?

- **A** His father is a soldier stationed at Sarsfield Barracks.
- **B** It is uncommon for Frank's father to show that he cares.
- **C** His father doesn't care about Frank or his brothers.
- **D** It is common for Frank's father to be working steadily.

3 The reference to "Protestant soup" in line 325 is an allusion because it —

- **A** helps the reader understand the people's hunger
- **B** allows McCourt to think about interesting history
- **C** supports the inference that McCourt is dreaming
- **D** refers to a well-known event in Irish history

4 What effect did the friendship with Patricia have on Frank's life?

- **A** It brought romance and beauty into Frank's lonely and isolated world.
- **B** It taught him how important it was to listen to the nuns and obey the rules.
- **C** It meant that he wasn't afraid of dying.
- **D** It kept him from being bored even though he wasn't interested in poetry.

American History

Short Story by **Judith Ortiz Cofer**

When do **WORLD EVENTS** hit home?

Once in a while, something tragic happens that makes people stop everything. The following story takes place on November 22, 1963, when the assassination of President John F. Kennedy stunned an entire nation.

SURVEY What news story really shocked you when you first heard it? Survey three classmates to find out what news event stands out most clearly in their memories. Record your results at left. Then draw a conclusion about the kind of event that affects people most deeply.

Survey: What news event do you remember most vividly?

My answer:

_____

Classmates' answers:

1. _____

_____

2. _____

_____

3. _____

_____

Text Analysis: Influence of Author's Background

An **author's background**—that is, the writer's life experiences and cultural heritage—shapes his or her perspective on the world and influences what he or she writes. This chart gives some tips for analyzing the influence of an author's background.

CONSIDERING AN AUTHOR'S BACKGROUND	
First, analyze the clues within the text. Ask yourself • What values are conveyed? (*Look for direct comments as well as characters' actions.*) • What is the tone, or the writer's attitude toward his or her subject? (*Notice characters and ideas that are respected or criticized.*)	**Then consider how the text may reflect certain aspects of the author's background. Ask** • What do I know about the writer's personal history? • How does this information shed light on my reading?

To prepare for reading "American History," read the background that appears on page 394.

As you read the story, look for the following:

• references to places Cofer has lived or visited

• characters whose heritage, beliefs, or values are similar to Cofer's

• events and circumstances that reflect Cofer's own life

Reading Strategy: Connect

Good readers **connect** what they know about a person, a place, or a situation to what they are reading in order to better understand the text. As you read "American History," connect your own life experiences to what you find in the story. See an example below.

Detail from Story	Connection	Better Understanding
tenement called El Building (lines 3–4)	I read about tenements in social studies. They are large, rundown apartment buildings with poor tenants.	El Building must be big and rundown.

Vocabulary in Context

Note: Words are listed in the order in which they appear in the story.

muted (myo͞o′tĭd) *adj.* softened or muffled
*While the baby is sleeping, please speak with a **muted** voice.*

hierarchy (hī′ə-rär′kē) *n.* a body of persons having authority
*King Henry VIII was at the top of England's political **hierarchy.***

maneuvering (mə-no͞o′vər-ĭng) *n.* an action designed to achieve a goal
*Her quick **maneuvering** on the soccer field allowed her to score.*

infatuated (ĭn-făch′o͞o-ā′tĭd) *adj.* possessed by an unreasoning attraction
*The new boy was so handsome that Emma soon became **infatuated** with him.*

vigilant (vĭj′ə-lənt) *adj.* on the alert; watchful
*The watch dog was **vigilant,** making sure no one entered the yard.*

enthralled (ĕn-thrôld′) *adj.* charmed greatly
*Bryan was **enthralled** by the movie, but I found it boring.*

distraught (dĭ-strôt′) *adj.* deeply upset
*The whole family was **distraught** after their cat died.*

resigned (rĭ-zīnd′) *adj.* marked by acceptance of a condition as unavoidable
*I was **resigned** to failing math until I met my excellent tutor.*

dilapidated (dĭ-lăp′ĭ-dā′tĭd) *adj.* broken down and shabby
*The **dilapidated** house needed a lot of work before we could move in.*

solace (sŏl′ĭs) *n.* comfort from sorrow or misfortune
*After a difficult day, she found **solace** in playing the piano.*

**SET A PURPOSE
FOR READING**

Read to find out how this
short story is connected
with real events in
American history.

American History

Short Story by

JUDITH ORTIZ COFER

BACKGROUND Judith Ortiz Cofer was born
in Puerto Rico in 1952 but moved at a young
age to Paterson, New Jersey. There she lived
in a large apartment building known by its
residents as *El Building*. Whenever her father,
a navy man, was on active duty, her mother
would take the family back to Puerto Rico
to live with their grandmother. Her father
pushed her to adopt American ways, while
her mother counseled her to hold on to
Puerto Rican customs.

I once read in a "Ripley's Believe It or Not" column that
Paterson, New Jersey, is the place where the Straight and
Narrow (streets) intersect. The Puerto Rican tenement known as
El Building was one block up from Straight. It was, in fact, the
corner of Straight and Market; not "at" the corner, but *the* corner.
At almost any hour of the day, El Building was like a monstrous
jukebox, blasting out *salsas*[1] from open windows as the residents,
mostly new immigrants just up from the island,[2] tried to drown
out whatever they were currently enduring with loud music. But
10 the day President Kennedy was shot there was a profound silence
in El Building; even the abusive tongues of viragoes,[3] the cursing
of the unemployed, and the screeching of small children had been
somehow **muted**. President Kennedy was a saint to these people.

muted (myo͞o′tĭd) *adj.* softened
or muffled

---

1. *salsas* (säl′säs): Latin-American dance tunes.
2. **the island:** Puerto Rico.
3. **abusive tongues of viragoes** (və-rä′gōz): hurtful comments of noisy, scolding
   women.

In fact, soon his photograph would be hung alongside the Sacred Heart and over the spiritist altars[4] that many women kept in their apartments. He would become part of the **hierarchy** of martyrs they prayed to for favors that only one who had died for a cause would understand. **Ⓐ**

On the day that President Kennedy was shot, my ninth grade
20 class had been out in the fenced playground of Public School Number 13. We had been given "free" exercise time and had been ordered by our P.E. teacher, Mr. DePalma, to "keep moving." That meant that the girls should jump rope and the boys toss basketballs through a hoop at the far end of the yard. He in the meantime would "keep an eye" on us from just inside the building.

It was a cold gray day in Paterson. The kind that warns of early snow. I was miserable, since I had forgotten my gloves, and my knuckles were turning red and raw from the jump rope. I was also
30 taking a lot of abuse from the black girls for not turning the rope hard and fast enough for them.

"Hey, Skinny Bones, pump it, girl. Ain't you got no energy today?" Gail, the biggest of the black girls had the other end of the rope, yelled, "Didn't you eat your rice and beans and pork chops for breakfast today?"

The other girls picked up the "pork chop" and made it into a refrain: "pork chop, pork chop, did you eat your pork chop?" They entered the double ropes in pairs and exited without tripping or missing a beat. I felt a burning on my cheeks and then
40 my glasses fogged up so that I could not manage to coordinate the jump rope with Gail. The chill was doing to me what it always did; entering my bones, making me cry, humiliating me. I hated the city, especially in winter. I hated Public School Number 13. I hated my skinny flat-chested body, and I envied the black girls who could jump rope so fast that their legs became a blur. They always seemed to be warm while I froze. **Ⓑ**

---

4. **alongside the Sacred Heart . . . spiritist altars:** The Sacred Heart, an image showing the physical heart of Jesus Christ, symbolizes Christ's love to some Roman Catholics. Spiritist altars are places of worship set up to observe spiritism, a set of religious beliefs based on the idea that spirits of the dead communicate with the living.

hierarchy (hī′ə-rär′kē) *n.* a body of persons having authority

Ⓐ AUTHOR'S BACKGROUND
Reread lines 1–18. Underline details that appear to come from the author's background.

Ⓑ CONNECT
Why does the narrator continue to turn the jump rope, even though she is miserable doing it? Fill in the chart to make a connection between the character's actions and something that might have happened in your own life.

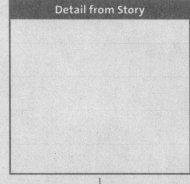

Detail from Story

↓

Connection

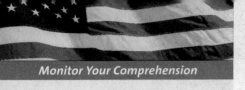

What can you conclude about the narrator from the way she observes the people in the house below her fire escape?

_____

_____

_____

_____

_____

_____

_____

_____

_____

_____

_____

_____

_____

There was only one source of beauty and light for me that school year. The only thing I had anticipated at the start of the semester. That was seeing Eugene. In August, Eugene and his
50 family had moved into the only house on the block that had a yard and trees. I could see his place from my window in El Building. In fact, if I sat on the fire escape I was literally suspended above Eugene's backyard. It was my favorite spot to read my library books in the summer. Until that August the house had been occupied by an old Jewish couple. Over the years I had become part of their family, without their knowing it, of course. I had a view of their kitchen and their backyard, and though I could not hear what they said, I knew when they were arguing, when one of them was sick, and many other things. I knew all this by watching
60 them at mealtimes. I could see their kitchen table, the sink, and the stove. During good times, he sat at the table and read his newspapers while she fixed the meals. If they argued, he would leave and the old woman would sit and stare at nothing for a long time. When one of them was sick, the other would come and get things from the kitchen and carry them out on a tray. The old man had died in June. The last week of school I had not seen him at the table at all. Then one day I saw that there was a crowd in the kitchen. The old woman had finally emerged from the house on the arm of a stocky, middle-aged woman, whom I had seen there a
70 few times before, maybe her daughter. Then a man had carried out suitcases. The house had stood empty for weeks. I had had to resist the temptation to climb down into the yard and water the flowers the old lady had taken such good care of. **PAUSE & REFLECT**

By the time Eugene's family moved in, the yard was a tangled mass of weeds. The father had spent several days mowing, and when he finished, from where I sat, I didn't see the red, yellow, and purple clusters that meant flowers to me. I didn't see this family sit down at the kitchen table together. It was just the mother, a red-headed tall woman who wore a white uniform—a

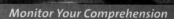
80 nurse's, I guessed it was; the father was gone before I got up in the
morning and was never there at dinner time. I only saw him on
weekends when they sometimes sat on lawn chairs under the oak
tree, each hidden behind a section of the newspaper; and there
was Eugene. He was tall and blond, and he wore glasses. I liked
him right away because he sat at the kitchen table and read books
for hours. That summer, before we had even spoken one word to
each other, I kept him company on my fire escape.

Once school started I looked for him in all my classes, but P.S.
13 was a huge, overpopulated place and it took me days and many
90 discreet questions to discover that Eugene was in honors classes
for all his subjects; classes that were not open to me because
English was not my first language, though I was a straight A
student. After much **maneuvering**, I managed "to run into him"
in the hallway where his locker was—on the other side of the
building from mine—and in study hall at the library where he
first seemed to notice me, but did not speak; and finally, on the
way home after school one day when I decided to approach him
directly, though my stomach was doing somersaults.

I was ready for rejection, snobbery, the worst. But when I came
100 up to him, practically panting in my nervousness, and blurted out:
"You're Eugene. Right?" he smiled, pushed his glasses up on his
nose, and nodded. I saw then that he was blushing deeply. Eugene
liked me, but he was shy. I did most of the talking that day. He
nodded and smiled a lot. In the weeks that followed, we walked
home together. He would linger at the corner of El Building for
a few minutes then walk down to his two-story house. It was
not until Eugene moved into that house that I noticed that El
Building blocked most of the sun, and that the only spot that got
a little sunlight during the day was the tiny square of earth the old
110 woman had planted with flowers.

I did not tell Eugene that I could see inside his kitchen from
my bedroom. I felt dishonest, but I liked my secret sharing of his
evenings, especially now that I knew what he was reading since we
chose our books together at the school library. **PAUSE & REFLECT**

maneuvering (mə-nōō′vər-ĭng)
n. an action designed to achieve
a goal.

**What kind of maneuvering
might the narrator have done in
order to "run into" Eugene?**

_____

_____

_____

_____

PAUSE & REFLECT
Is the narrator being dishonest
by not telling Eugene she can see
inside his house? Explain.

_____

_____

_____

_____

_____

_____

_____

_____

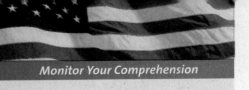
infatuated (ĭn-făch′ōō-ā′tĭd) *adj.* possessed by an unreasoning love or attraction

vigilant (vĭj′ə-lənt) *adj.* on the alert; watchful

Underline details in the text that prove Elena's mother behaves in a **vigilant** way.

C AUTHOR'S BACKGROUND

Recall what you read about Judith Ortiz Cofer on page 394. Then reread lines 123–142 and circle details that show how the author's experiences are reflected in Elena's life. On the lines below, summarize the facts from Cofer's life that influenced this story.

_____

_____

_____

_____

_____

_____

_____

_____

_____

_____

_____

_____

One day my mother came into my room as I was sitting on the window-sill staring out. In her abrupt way she said: "Elena, you are acting 'moony.'" *Enamorada*[5] was what she really said, that is—like a girl stupidly **infatuated**. Since I had turned fourteen . . . , my mother had been more **vigilant** than ever. She acted as if I was

120 going to go crazy or explode or something if she didn't watch me and nag me all the time about being a *señorita*[6] now. She kept talking about virtue, morality, and other subjects that did not interest me in the least. My mother was unhappy in Paterson, but my father had a good job at the bluejeans factory in Passaic[7] and soon, he kept assuring us, we would be moving to our own house there. Every Sunday we drove out to the suburbs of Paterson, Clifton, and Passaic, out to where people mowed grass on Sundays in the summer, and where children made snowmen in the winter from pure white snow, not like the gray slush of Paterson which

130 seemed to fall from the sky in that hue. I had learned to listen to my parents' dreams, which were spoken in Spanish, as fairy tales, like the stories about life in the island paradise of Puerto Rico before I was born. I had been to the island once as a little girl, to grandmother's funeral, and all I remembered was wailing women in black, my mother becoming hysterical and being given a pill that made her sleep two days, and me feeling lost in a crowd of strangers all claiming to be my aunts, uncles, and cousins. I had actually been glad to return to the city. We had not been back there since then, though my parents talked constantly about

140 buying a house on the beach someday, retiring on the island— that was a common topic among the residents of El Building. As for me, I was going to go to college and become a teacher. **C**

But after meeting Eugene I began to think of the present more than of the future. What I wanted now was to enter that house I had watched for so many years. I wanted to see the other rooms where the old people had lived, and where the boy spent his time. Most of all, I wanted to sit at the kitchen table with Eugene like two adults, like the old man and his wife had done, maybe drink

---

5. **enamorada** (ĕ-nä′mô-rä′dä) *Spanish:* in love.

6. **señorita** (sĕ′nyō-rē′tä) *Spanish:* young lady.

7. **Passaic** (pə-sā′ĭk).

some coffee and talk about books. I had started reading *Gone with*
150 *the Wind*.[8] I was **enthralled** by it, with the daring and the passion
of the beautiful girl living in a mansion, and with her devoted
parents and the slaves who did everything for them. I didn't
believe such a world had ever really existed, and I wanted to ask
Eugene some questions since he and his parents, he had told me,
had come up from Georgia, the same place where the novel was
set. His father worked for a company that had transferred him
to Paterson. His mother was very unhappy, Eugene said, in his
beautiful voice that rose and fell over words in a strange, lilting
way. The kids at school called him "the hick" and made fun of
160 the way he talked. I knew I was his only friend so far, and I liked
that, though I felt sad for him sometimes. "Skinny Bones" and
the "Hick" was what they called us at school when we were seen
together. **PAUSE & REFLECT**

The day Mr. DePalma came out into the cold and asked us to
line up in front of him was the day that President Kennedy was
shot. Mr. DePalma, a short, muscular man with slicked-down
black hair, was the science teacher, P.E. coach, and disciplinarian
at P.S. 13. He was the teacher to whose homeroom you got
assigned if you were a troublemaker, and the man called out to
170 break up playground fights, and to escort violently angry teenagers to the office. And Mr. DePalma was the man who called
your parents in for "a conference."

That day, he stood in front of two rows of mostly black and
Puerto Rican kids, brittle from their efforts to "keep moving" on
a November day that was turning bitter cold. Mr. DePalma, to
our complete shock, was crying. Not just silent adult tears, but
really sobbing. There were a few titters from the back of the line
where I stood shivering.

"Listen," Mr. DePalma raised his arms over his head as if
180 he were about to conduct an orchestra. His voice broke, and he

---

8. ***Gone with the Wind:*** a 1936 novel, written by Margaret Mitchell and set in
the South during and immediately after the Civil War.

enthralled (ĕn-thrôld') *adj.*
charmed greatly.

PAUSE & REFLECT
Why do you think Elena likes the
fact that she is Eugene's only
friend so far?

_____

_____

_____

_____

_____

_____

_____

_____

_____

_____

_____

_____

_____

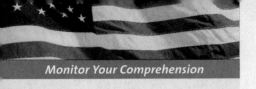
D CONNECT

Reread lines 173–186 and think about how different people receive bad news. Why do you think the students are reacting this way to Mr. DePalma?

_____

_____

_____

_____

_____

_____

_____

_____

_____

E CONNECT

Have you ever seen something, on TV or in real life, that you couldn't stop watching even though it was terrible? Make a connection to your own experience to explain why Elena's mother can't take her eyes off the television set.

_____

_____

_____

_____

covered his face with his hands. His barrel chest was heaving. Someone giggled behind me.

"Listen," he repeated, "something awful has happened." A strange gurgling came from his throat, and he turned around and spat on the cement behind him.

"Gross," someone said, and there was a lot of laughter. **D**

"The President is dead, you idiots. I should have known that wouldn't mean anything to a bunch of losers like you kids. Go home." He was shrieking now. No one moved for a minute or

190 two, but then a big girl let out a "Yeah!" and ran to get her books piled up with the others against the brick wall of the school building. The others followed in a mad scramble to get to their things before somebody caught on. It was still an hour to the dismissal bell.

A little scared, I headed for El Building. There was an eerie feeling on the streets. I looked into Mario's drugstore, a favorite hangout for the high school crowd, but there were only a couple of old Jewish men at the soda-bar talking with the short order cook in tones that sounded almost angry, but they were keeping their

200 voices low. Even the traffic on one of the busiest intersections in Paterson—Straight Street and Park Avenue—seemed to be moving slower. There were no horns blasting that day. At El Building, the usual little group of unemployed men were not hanging out on the front stoop making it difficult for women to enter the front door. No music spilled out from open doors in the hallway. When I walked into our apartment, I found my mother sitting in front of the grainy picture of the television set.

She looked up at me with a tear-streaked face and just said: "*Dios mio,*"[9] turning back to the set as if it were pulling at her

210 eyes. I went into my room. **E**

Though I wanted to feel the right thing about President Kennedy's death, I could not fight the feeling of elation that stirred in my chest. Today was the day I was to visit Eugene in his house. He had asked me to come over after school to study for an American history test with him. We had also planned to

---

9. *Dios mio* (dyôs mē'ô) *Spanish:* my God.

walk to the public library together. I looked down into his yard. The oak tree was bare of leaves and the ground looked gray with ice. The light through the large kitchen window of his house told me that El Building blocked the sun to such an extent that they had to turn lights on in the middle of the day. I felt ashamed about it. But the white kitchen table with the lamp hanging just above it looked cozy and inviting. I would soon sit there, across from Eugene, and I would tell him about my perch just above his house. Maybe I should.

In the next thirty minutes I changed clothes, put on a little pink lipstick, and got my books together. Then I went in to tell my mother that I was going to a friend's house to study. I did not expect her reaction.

"You are going out *today?*" The way she said "today" sounded as if a storm warning had been issued. It was said in utter disbelief. Before I could answer, she came toward me and held my elbows as I clutched my books.

"*Hija,*[10] the President has been killed. We must show respect. He was a great man. Come to church with me tonight."

PAUSE & REFLECT

PAUSE & REFLECT
Why is Elena's mother so surprised that she wants to go to her friend's house?

_____

_____

_____

_____

_____

_____

_____

_____

_____

_____

_____

_____

10. **hija** (ē'hä) *Spanish:* daughter.

distraught (dĭ-strôt′) *adj.* deeply upset

resigned (rĭ-zīnd′) *adj.* marked by acceptance of a condition or action as unavoidable

Why do you think Elena's mother's tone is resigned?

_____

_____

_____

dilapidated (dĭ-lăp′ĭ-dā′tĭd) *adj.* broken down and shabby

She tried to embrace me, but my books were in the way. My first impulse was to comfort her, she seemed so **distraught**, but I had to meet Eugene in fifteen minutes.

"I have a test to study for, Mama. I will be home by eight."

"You are forgetting who you are, *Niña*.[11] I have seen you staring
240 down at that boy's house. You are heading for humiliation and pain." My mother said this in Spanish and in a **resigned** tone that surprised me, as if she had no intention of stopping me from "heading for humiliation and pain." I started for the door. She sat in front of the TV holding a white handkerchief to her face.

I walked out to the street and around the chainlink fence that separated El Building from Eugene's house. The yard was neatly edged around the little walk that led to the door. It always amazed me how Paterson, the inner core of the city, had no apparent logic to its architecture. Small, neat, single residences like this
250 one could be found right next to huge, **dilapidated** apartment buildings like El Building. My guess was that the little houses had been there first, then the immigrants had come in droves, and the monstrosities had been raised for them—the Italians, the Irish, the Jews, and now us, the Puerto Ricans and the blacks. The door was painted a deep green: *verde*, the color of hope, I had heard my mother say it: *Verde-Esperanza*. I knocked softly. A few suspenseful moments later the door opened just a crack. The red, swollen face of a woman appeared. She had a halo of red hair floating over a delicate ivory face—the face of a doll—with
260 freckles on the nose. Her smudged eye make-up made her look unreal to me, like a mannequin seen through a warped store window.

"What do you want?" Her voice was tiny and sweet-sounding, like a little girl's, but her tone was not friendly.

"I'm Eugene's friend. He asked me over. To study." I thrust out my books, a silly gesture that embarrassed me almost immediately.

---

11. **Niña** (nē′nyä) *Spanish:* little girl.

"You live there?" She pointed up to El Building, which looked particularly ugly, like a gray prison with its many dirty windows and rusty fire escapes. The woman had stepped halfway out and

270 I could see that she wore a white nurse's uniform with St. Joseph's Hospital on the name tag.

"Yes. I do."

She looked intently at me for a couple of heartbeats, then said as if to herself, "I don't know how you people do it." Then directly to me: "Listen. Honey. Eugene doesn't want to study with you. He is a smart boy. Doesn't need help. You understand me. I am truly sorry if he told you you could come over. He cannot study with you. It's nothing personal. You understand? We won't be in this place much longer, no need for him to get close to people—it'll just make it

280 harder for him later. Run back home now." **PAUSE & REFLECT**

I couldn't move. I just stood there in shock at hearing these things said to me in such a honey-drenched voice. I had never heard an accent like hers, except for Eugene's softer version. It was as if she were singing me a little song.

"What's wrong? Didn't you hear what I said?" She seemed very angry, and I finally snapped out of my trance. I turned away from the green door, and heard her close it gently. **F**

Our apartment was empty when I got home. My mother was in someone else's kitchen, seeking the **solace** she needed. Father

290 would come in from his late shift at midnight. I would hear them talking softly in the kitchen for hours that night. They would not discuss their dreams for the future, or life in Puerto Rico, as they often did; that night they would talk sadly about the young widow and her two children, as if they were family. For the next few days, we would observe *luto* in our apartment;

that is, we would practice restraint and silence—no loud music
or laughter. Some of the women of El Building would wear black
for weeks. **G**

That night, I lay in my bed trying to feel the right thing for
300 our dead President. But the tears that came up from a deep source
inside me were strictly for me. When my mother came to the
door, I pretended to be sleeping. Sometime during the night, I saw
from my bed the streetlight come on. It had a pink halo around
it. I went to my window and pressed my face to the cool glass.
Looking up at the light I could see the white snow falling like a
lace veil over its face. I did not look down to see it turning gray as
it touched the ground below.

Text Analysis: Influence of Author's Background

Review the background information about Judith Ortiz Cofer on page 394 and the notes you took while reading "American History." In the chart, list three facts from Cofer's background and specific details from the story that reflect those facts.

Fact from the Author's Background	Story Detail(s)

Cofer likely remembers very clearly the day President Kennedy was assassinated. When he died, many Americans felt that the dreams and hopes he had championed, such as racial equality, died with him. Why might Cofer have chosen to set Elena's story on this day in history?

_____

_____

_____

_____

Reading Strategy: Connect

Recall the connections you made while reading the story. What were some of your strongest connections, and how did they help you understand the story better? Use the chart to record your responses.

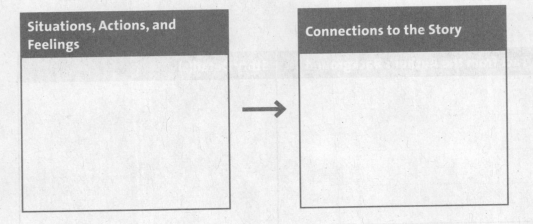

Situations, Actions, and Feelings	Connections to the Story

When do **WORLD EVENTS** hit home?

What world events, either tragic or inspiring, do you remember best?

_____

_____

_____

Vocabulary Practice

Circle the word that is most different in meaning from the others.

1. **(a)** spellbound, **(b)** enthralled, **(c)** considerate, **(d)** thrilled

2. **(a)** cowardly, **(b)** watchful, **(c)** observant, **(d)** vigilant

3. **(a)** muted, **(b)** noisy, **(c)** deafening, **(d)** boisterous

4. **(a)** consolation, **(b)** solace, **(c)** depression, **(d)** sympathy

5. **(a)** rejecting, **(b)** jockeying, **(c)** maneuvering, **(d)** strategizing

6. **(a)** hierarchy, **(b)** order, **(c)** religion, (d) classification

7. **(a)** perplexed, **(b)** infatuated, **(c)** surprised, **(d)** confounded

8. **(a)** fired, **(b)** accepting, **(c)** resigned, **(d)** submissive

9. **(a)** enlivened, **(b)** entertained, **(c)** amused, **(d)** distraught

10. **(a)** dilapidated, **(b)** antique, **(c)** decaying, **(d)** neglected

Academic Vocabulary in Writing

contrast	environment	factor	incorporate	predominant

TURN AND TALK Think about Elena's life in El Building. Write down some of the positive and negative aspects of growing up in that **environment**. Use at least one Academic Vocabulary word in your response. Definitions for these terms are listed on page 373.

_____

_____

_____

Assessment Practice

DIRECTIONS Use "American History" to answer questions 1–6.

1 The story take place on the day when —
- (A) Elena and her family move to Paterson
- (B) a funeral is held for President Kennedy
- (C) Eugene moves into a house near El Building
- (D) President Kennedy is assassinated

2 One of Elena's favorite activities is —
- (A) jumping rope in the school playground
- (B) studying with Eugene at his kitchen table
- (C) watching television with her mother
- (D) reading books on the tenement fire escape

3 Which of the following reflects the author's background?
- (A) Eugene speaks with a Southern accent.
- (B) Elena's family is from Puerto Rico.
- (C) Elena puts on pink lipstick.
- (D) Eugene's mother is a nurse.

4 When Elena first talks to Eugene, she finds out that —
- (A) they have both read the book *Gone with the Wind*
- (B) he likes her but has been too shy to speak
- (C) they both take the same honors classes
- (D) he has been watching her window from his house

5 Eugene's mother won't let Elena study with her son because —
- (A) Eugene is a better student
- (B) she doesn't want Elena to get hurt
- (C) Elena is Puerto Rican
- (D) Eugene no longer likes Elena

6 Which aspect of Puerto Rican culture is expressed in the story?
- (A) deep respect for the dead
- (B) belief in an afterlife
- (C) love of flowers and gardens
- (D) children's obedience to elders

Special Report
Magazine Article

Background

On the 40th anniversary of President John F. Kennedy's assassination, *U.S. News & World Report* featured this special report. The article discusses how Kennedy's assassination on November 22, 1963, affected the nation. It also analyzes how and why Kennedy's presidency of just over 1,000 days remains significant today.

Standards Focus: Identify Controlling Idea

In a sense, the controlling idea of an expository text "controls" the writer's development of the text—it suggests which details the writer should include to achieve his or her purpose and how he or she should organize those details. From the reader's perspective, the **controlling idea** is the most important point that an expository text conveys.

Here are some tips to help you determine the controlling idea of a magazine article:

1. Preview the first paragraph or two of the article. Sometimes the controlling idea will be stated outright at the beginning. More often, however, you'll have to infer the controlling idea.

2. Distinguish between the details in each paragraph. Identify which ones are more important and which are less important.

3. Try to state the key idea of each paragraph in your own words. Taken together, these key ideas should suggest the controlling idea of the article.

You can keep track of details and key ideas in a chart like the one below.

Paragraph	Important Details	Key Idea
1	After 9/11, many Americans visited the JFK Library and Museum. . . .	Kennedy was a strong and skillful leader during trying times.
2		
Article's Controlling Idea:		

BY KENNETH T. WALSH
NOVEMBER 24, 2003

SET A PURPOSE
FOR READING
Read the article to learn more about how President Kennedy's death affected the nation.

In the days immediately after 9/11, Americans in large numbers showed up at the John F. Kennedy Library and Museum in Boston, apparently looking for strength and hope at a time of national peril and sorrow. They were drawn in particular to a film recounting the Cuban missile crisis, when Kennedy guided the nation through a confrontation with the Soviet Union that could easily have led to nuclear war. Many visitors seemed comforted by the idea that prudent leadership and common sense could make all the difference, even in the
10 worst of times.

The fact that Kennedy still has such a hold on America's imagination comes as no surprise to historians and other observers of popular culture. This connection will become even more apparent in the coming weeks as the nation marks the 40th anniversary of his assassination, on Nov. 22, 1963.

Yet the reasons for his mystique are less clear. The fact that he was assassinated in the prime of life goes only so far in explaining it. President William McKinley, another popular leader, was murdered in 1901, but his death generated no
20 vast outpouring of emotion and no enduring sense of a lost

Ⓐ CONTROLLING IDEA
Reread lines 1–15. Underline words and phrases that give clues to the **controlling idea** of the article. Then write the controlling idea that you can infer from these clues.

_____

_____

_____

_____

_____

_____

_____

_____

B CONTROLLING IDEA
Reread lines 16–28. Underline the topic sentence in this paragraph. Then rewrite the sentence as a question. As you continue reading, look for the answer.

_____

_____

_____

_____

_____

_____

_____

C CONTROLLING IDEA
What is the author suggesting in lines 37–47 about the Kennedy mystique and the medium of television? Enter your answers into the chart.

IMPORTANT DETAILS

↓

KEY IDEA

legacy. In contrast, millions of Americans still recall where they were when they heard that Kennedy had been shot. (I was attending history class at St. Rose High School in Belmar, N.J., when the principal came on the public-address system and, choking back tears, told us what had happened. Everyone marched to our nearby church, and we spent the next few hours praying for the president's survival and, a bit later, his soul.) **B**

We all seem to have vivid memories of his funeral, carried
30 on live television, with those unforgettable images of his grieving widow and his young son saluting smartly when his father's cortege passed by.

"Kennedy is frozen in our memory at age 46," says historian Robert Dallek, author of *An Unfinished Life: John F. Kennedy 1917–1963*. "People don't realize that this past May 29 he would have been 86 years of age."

Some deft PR by the White House helped to create his charismatic aura in the first place. He and his advisers quickly grasped the power of the new medium of television,
40 and the handsome, eloquent young leader quickly mastered it and went on to convey an image of optimism and charm that still surrounds him today. His performances at live press conferences are remembered as tours de force. His speeches are used as brilliant examples of political communication. And if his legislative record fell short, his ideas about ending the Cold War and achieving racial equality at home, at least under the law, eventually took root and became reality. **C**

Further, his glamorous wife, Jacqueline, reinforced the exciting image of Camelot, especially in contrast to his solid
50 but dull predecessor, Dwight Eisenhower. Ike had been the oldest man to serve as president up until that time; Kennedy was the youngest ever elected to the office. The White House never let anyone forget it.

"One of the things President Kennedy did was instill in the American people the idea they could make a difference," says Deborah Leff, director of the Kennedy Library and Museum. ". . . It was a time when you saw America striving to be its best."

For his part, Kennedy said in one of his famous speeches, at American University on June 10, 1963: "No problem of
60 human destiny is beyond human beings. Man's reason and spirit have often solved the seemingly unsolvable—and we believe they can do it again." **D**

The tragic Kennedy mythology was reinforced when his brother Robert was assassinated in 1968 and, later, when his son, John F. Kennedy Jr., died in a plane crash in 1999. All of this perpetuated the idea that the Kennedys, despite all their advantages, were not immune from life's calamities. This deepened their connection to the rest of us.

Yet Kennedy governed prior to the age of cynicism
70 brought on by the Vietnam War, the Watergate scandal, and the wrenching social changes of the past four decades (including, of course, his own assassination). Perhaps not even Kennedy could have emerged from this era unscathed had he lived and remained in public life.

"The sudden end to Kennedy's life and presidency has left us with tantalizing 'might have beens,'" Dallek writes. "Yet even setting these aside and acknowledging some missed opportunities and false steps, it must be acknowledged that the Kennedy thousand days spoke to the country's better
80 angels, inspired visions of a less divisive nation and world, and demonstrated that America was still the last best hope of mankind." It is a legacy any president would be proud of.

PAUSE & REFLECT

D CONTROLLING IDEA
How do the quotations in lines 54–62 support the controlling idea of the article?

_____

_____

_____

_____

_____

_____

_____

_____

_____

_____

PAUSE & REFLECT
How does this article add to your understanding of how the loss of President Kennedy affected the nation? Explain.

_____

_____

_____

_____

_____

_____

Practicing Your Skills

Now that you have read the magazine article, think about the author's style and purpose. First fill in the chart below and then use the chart to help you answer the question.

- Record three important quotations that you find in the article.

- Look back at the notes you took while you read. What point was the author trying to make by writing this article?

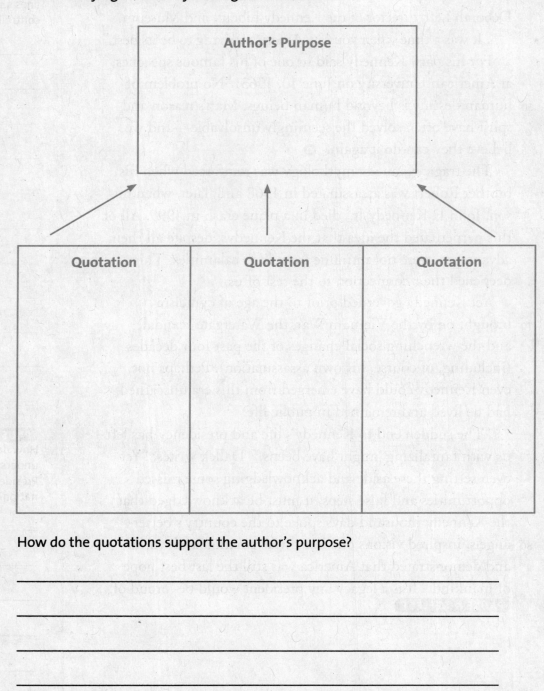

Author's Purpose

Quotation	Quotation	Quotation

How do the quotations support the author's purpose?

_____

_____

_____

_____

Academic Vocabulary in Writing

| contrast | environment | factor | incorporate | predominant |

According to the author, how are the other tragedies that befell the Kennedy family a **factor,** or influence, on people's feelings about President Kennedy and his family? Use at least one Academic Vocabulary word in your response. Definitions for these terms are listed on page 373.

_____

_____

_____

_____

Assessment Practice

DIRECTIONS Use "Special Report" to answer questions 1–4.

1 Many people who visited the John F. Kennedy Library after 9/11 were looking for —
  A information
  B someone to blame
  C reassurance
  D a safe place

2 In lines 20–21, the writer says that there was "no enduring sense of a lost legacy" after President McKinley's assassination in order to —
  A present a reminder that presidents are not always important
  B tell the reader that assassination is common in the United States
  C give the reader additional information about President McKinley
  D emphasize the sorrow of the people after Kennedy's assassination

3 In line 43, what does the writer's use of the expression "tours de force," meaning "feats of unusual skill," tell you about Kennedy's press conferences?
  A Kennedy toured the country for press conferences.
  B Kennedy used press conferences to speak French.
  C Kennedy handled press conferences skillfully.
  D Kennedy's press conferences were unappreciated.

4 What is the most important reason that the subject of President John F. Kennedy continues to attract people?
  A He represented America's enormous potential.
  B He was elected at a young age.
  C He was able to speak well on television.
  D He failed to encourage people to make a difference.

Be sure to read the Historical Background and the Text Analysis Workshop on pp. 1022–1033 in *Holt McDougal Literature*.

Academic Vocabulary for Unit 10

Preview the following Academic Vocabulary words. You will encounter these words as you work through this book and will use them as you write and talk about the selections in the unit.

characteristic (kăr´ək-tə-rĭs´tĭk) *n.* a feature that helps to identify, tell apart, or describe recognizably
Characteristics of his novels include high suspense and surprise endings.

critical (krĭt´ĭ-kəl) *n.* characterized by careful, exact evaluation and judgment
As a critical reader, you analyze various elements of the story.

influence (ĭn´floo-əns) *v.* to produce an effect on; sway
How did the timing of the announcement influence the audience's reaction?

motivate (mō´tə-vāt) *v.* to provide with an incentive; move to action
What would motivate the protagonist to change her mind?

resolve (rĭ-zŏlv´) *v.* to bring to a conclusion
How do you think the characters will resolve their conflict?

Think about a book or a movie that you recently enjoyed. Write a brief **critical** review describing your opinions about it. Use at least two Academic Vocabulary words in your response.

_____

_____

_____

_____

The Tragedy of Romeo and Juliet
Drama by **William Shakespeare**

Is **LOVE** stronger than **HATE?**

It sounds like a story ripped from the tabloids. Two teenagers fall in love. Then they learn that their parents hate each other. Murder and suffering follow, and by the end, a whole town is mourning. What love can—and cannot—overcome is at the heart of *Romeo and Juliet*, considered by many to be the greatest love story of all time.

DEBATE People say that love conquers all. Is this true? In a small group, talk about times when love has brought people together and when hate has driven them apart. At left, write your answer to the question *Is love stronger than hate?* and list some reasons for your opinion. Then form two teams and debate the question.

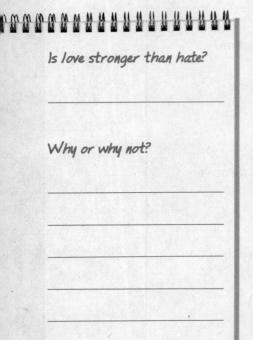

Is love stronger than hate?

_____

Why or why not?

_____

_____

_____

_____

_____

Text Analysis: Shakespearean Drama

You can probably guess that a **tragedy** isn't going to end with the words "and they all lived happily ever after." Shakespearean tragedies are dramas that end in disaster—most often death—for the main characters. The conflicts in a tragedy are caused by both the actions of the characters and by fate. As you read *Romeo and Juliet*, pay attention to the specific characteristics of Shakespearean drama.

CHARACTERISTICS OF SHAKESPEAREAN DRAMA
Soliloquy
• is a speech given by a character alone on stage
• lets the audience know what the character is thinking or feeling
Aside
• is a character's remark, either to the audience or to another character
• reveals the character's private thoughts
Dramatic Irony
• occurs when the audience knows more than the characters—for example, the chorus reveals Romeo and Juliet's tragic fate in the prologue
• helps build suspense

CHARACTERISTICS OF SHAKESPEAREAN DRAMA, *continued*

Allusion

- is an indirect reference to a famous person, place, event, or literary work

- adds an extra layer of meaning to certain passages

Blank Verse

- is unrhymed poetry written in **iambic pentameter:** each line has five pairs of syllables; an unstressed syllable is usually followed by a stressed syllable

- resembles the rhythm of natural speech

Figurative Language

- is language that communicates ideas beyond the ordinary, literal meaning of the words

- used to create effects, to emphasize ideas, and to evoke emotion

Reading Strategy: Reading Shakespearean Drama

Shakespeare's English is sometimes hard for modern readers to understand. Use the following strategies to help you read the excerpt from the play:

- Read the background notes and the summary notes set in italics to get important information about the structure and main conflict in the play.

- Use the footnotes to figure out the meanings of unfamiliar words, unusual grammatical structures, and allusions.

- As you read, use the prompts in the text to take note of the events that move the plot along. You may want to take notes about the order of events in a chart like the one below.

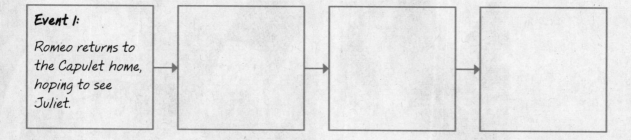

Event 1:

Romeo returns to the Capulet home, hoping to see Juliet.

SET A PURPOSE FOR READING

Read the Prologue to see how the tragedy is introduced to the audience. Then, read one of the most famous scenes in all of Shakespeare's works.

THE TRAGEDY OF

Romeo & Juliet

Prologue and Act 2, Scene 2

Drama by

WILLIAM SHAKESPEARE

BACKGROUND Although Shakespeare wrote *Romeo and Juliet* in the 1590s, its themes are still relevant today. This timeless drama tells the story of two teenagers who dare to risk everything for love. They live in a society torn apart by violence. In this tense setting, Shakespeare explores which force is stronger—love or hate.

TIME

The 14th century

PLACE

Verona (və-rō′nə) and Mantua (măn′choo-ə) in northern Italy

CAST

THE MONTAGUES

Lord Montague (mŏn′tə-gyoo′)

Lady Montague

Romeo, son of Montague

Benvolio (bĕn-vō′lē-ō), nephew of Montague and friend of Romeo

Balthasar (bäl′thə-sär′), servant to Romeo

Abram, servant to Montague

THE CAPULETS

Lord Capulet (kăp′yoo-lĕt′)

Lady Capulet

Juliet, daughter of Capulet

Tybalt (tĭb′əlt), nephew of Lady Capulet

Nurse to Juliet

Peter, servant to Juliet's nurse

Sampson, servant to Capulet

Gregory, servant to Capulet

An Old Man of the Capulet family

OTHERS

Prince Escalus (ĕs′kə-ləs), ruler of Verona

Mercutio (mĕr-kyoo′shē-ō), kinsman of the prince and friend of Romeo

Friar Laurence, a Franciscan priest

Friar John, another Franciscan priest

Count Paris, a young nobleman, kinsman of the prince

Apothecary (ə-pŏth′ĭ-kĕr′ē)

Page to Paris

Chief Watchman

Three Musicians

An Officer

Chorus

Citizens of Verona, **Gentlemen** and **Gentlewomen** of both houses, **Maskers, Torchbearers, Pages, Guards, Watchmen, Servants,** and **Attendants**

Prologue

The Chorus is one actor who serves as a narrator. He enters from the back of the stage to introduce and explain the theme of the play. His job is to "hook" the audience's interest by telling them just enough to quiet them down and make them eager for more. In this prologue, or preview, the narrator explains that the play will be about a feud between two families (the Capulets and the Montagues). In addition, the narrator says that the feud will end in tragedy. As you read the prologue, determine what the tragedy will be.

[*Enter* Chorus.]

Chorus. Two households, both alike in dignity,
In fair Verona, where we lay our scene,
From ancient grudge break to new mutiny,
Where civil blood makes civil hands unclean. [1]
5 From forth the fatal loins of these two foes,
A pair of star-crossed[2] lovers take their life,
Whose misadventured[3] piteous overthrows
Doth with their death bury their parents' strife.
The fearful passage of their death-marked love,
10 And the continuance of their parents' rage,
Which, but[4] their children's end, naught[5] could remove,
Is now the two hours' traffic of our stage,[6]
The which if you with patient ears attend,
What here shall miss, our toil shall strive to mend.[7]

[*Exit.*]   **PAUSE & REFLECT**

PAUSE & REFLECT

What does the chorus reveal about the fate of Romeo and Juliet?

_____

_____

_____

_____

_____

_____

_____

_____

_____

_____

---

1. **ancient . . . unclean:** A new outbreak of fighting (**mutiny**) between families has caused the citizens of Verona to have one another's blood on their hands.
2. **star-crossed:** doomed. The position of the stars when the lovers were born was not favorable. In Shakespeare's day, people took astrology very seriously.
3. **misadventured:** unlucky.
4. **but:** except for.
5. **naught:** nothing.
6. **the two hours' . . . stage:** what will be shown on the stage in the next two hours.
7. **what . . . mend:** The play will fill in the details not mentioned in the prologue.

BACKGROUND When we first meet Romeo, who is a Montague, he is pining for a girl named Rosaline, who does not return his affections. To distract Romeo, his friends Mercutio and Benvolio take him to a party at the home of the Capulets. It's a masquerade, so the boys wear masks. There, Romeo and Juliet, who is a Capulet, fall in love at first sight. Only after they talk and share their first kiss do they discover they have fallen in love with an enemy. Following the party, Romeo makes his way to Juliet's room, where he hides in the orchard, hoping to catch a glimpse of his new love. His friends have just left him. They have been teasing him for being in love—but they think he still loves Rosaline.

Act 2

SCENE 2 *Capulet's orchard.*

The following is one of the most famous scenes in all literature. The speeches contain some of the most beautiful poetry Shakespeare ever wrote.

Juliet appears on the balcony outside her room. She cannot see Romeo, who stands in the garden just below. At the beginning of the scene, both characters are speaking private thoughts to themselves. Romeo, however, can hear Juliet as she expresses her love for him despite his family name. Eventually, he speaks directly to her, and they declare their love for each other. Just before dawn Romeo leaves to make plans for their wedding.

[*Enter* Romeo.]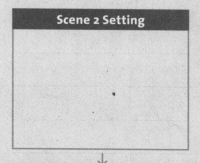

Romeo. He jests at scars that never felt a wound.[1]

[*Enter* Juliet *above at a window.*]

But soft! What light through yonder window breaks?
It is the East, and Juliet is the sun![2]
Arise, fair sun, and kill the envious moon,
5 Who is already sick and pale with grief
That thou her maid art far more fair than she.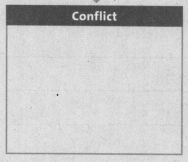

---

1. **He jests . . . wound:** Romeo has overheard Mercutio and comments that Mercutio makes fun of love because he has never been wounded by it.
2. **But soft . . . the sun:** Romeo sees Juliet at the window.

Ⓐ SHAKESPEAREAN DRAMA

Reread the background note and the summary of Scene 2. Underline the reason Romeo has gone to the Capulets' orchard. Then complete the organizer below.

Scene 2 Setting

↓

Conflict

Ⓑ SHAKESPEAREAN DRAMA

Reread lines 3–6. Circle what Romeo compares Juliet to. Why is the moon envious?

_____

_____

_____

Be not her maid, since she is envious;

Her vestal livery³ is but sick and green,⁴

And none but fools do wear it; cast it off.

10 It is my lady; O, it is my love!

O that she knew she were!

She speaks, yet she says nothing. What of that?

Her eye discourses;⁵ I will answer it.

I am too bold; 'tis not to me she speaks.

15 Two of the fairest stars in all the heaven,

Having some business, do entreat her eyes

To twinkle in their spheres till they return.

What if her eyes were there, they in her head?

The brightness of her cheek would shame those stars

20 As daylight doth a lamp; her eyes in heaven

Would through the airy region stream so bright

That birds would sing and think it were not night.

See how she leans her cheek upon her hand!

O that I were a glove upon that hand,

25 That I might touch that cheek! **C**

Juliet.   Ay me!

Romeo.   She speaks.

O, speak again, bright angel! for thou art

As glorious to this night, being o'er my head,

As is a winged messenger of heaven

Unto the white-upturned wond'ring eyes

30 Of mortals that fall back to gaze on him

When he bestrides the lazy-pacing clouds

And sails upon the bosom of the air.

Juliet. O Romeo, Romeo! wherefore⁶ art thou Romeo?

Deny thy father and refuse thy name!

35 Or, if thou wilt not, be but sworn my love,

And I'll no longer be a Capulet.

Romeo [*aside*]. Shall I hear more, or shall I speak at this? **D**

---

3. **vestal livery:** maidenly clothing.

4. **sick and green:** Unmarried girls supposedly had "greensickness," or anemia.

5. **discourses:** speaks.

6. **wherefore:** why. Juliet asks why Romeo is who he is—someone from her enemy's family.

C SHAKESPEAREAN DRAMA

Reread lines 10–23. Underline all the lines in which Romeo compares Juliet's eyes to stars. What does Romeo's opening soliloquy tells you about his thoughts?

_____

_____

_____

_____

_____

_____

_____

_____

_____

_____

D SHAKESPEAREAN DRAMA

An aside is a character's remark that others do not hear. Underline the aside in line 39. Why is Romeo unsure if he should speak?

_____

_____

_____

Juliet. 'Tis but thy name that is my enemy.
Thou art thyself, though not[7] a Montague.
40 What's Montague? It is nor hand, nor foot,
Nor arm, nor face, nor any other part
Belonging to a man. O, be some other name!
What's in a name? That which we call a rose
By any other name would smell as sweet.
45 So Romeo would, were he not Romeo called,
Retain that dear perfection which he owes
Without that title. Romeo, doff[8] thy name;
And for that name, which is no part of thee,
Take all myself. **PAUSE & REFLECT**

Romeo.   I take thee at thy word.
50 Call me but love, and I'll be new baptized;
Henceforth I never will be Romeo.

Juliet. What man art thou that, thus bescreened[9] in night,
So stumblest on my counsel?[10]

Romeo.   By a name
I know not how to tell thee who I am.
55 My name, dear saint, is hateful to myself,
Because it is an enemy to thee.
Had I it written, I would tear the word. **E**

Juliet. My ears have yet not drunk a hundred words
Of that tongue's utterance, yet I know the sound.
60 Art thou not Romeo, and a Montague?

Romeo. Neither, fair saint, if either thee dislike.

Juliet. How camest thou hither, tell me, and wherefore?
The orchard walls are high and hard to climb,
And the place death, considering who thou art,
65 If any of my kinsmen find thee here. **PAUSE & REFLECT**

---

7. **though not:** even if you were not.
8. **doff:** get rid of.
9. **bescreened:** hiding.
10. **counsel:** private thoughts.

PAUSE & REFLECT
Reread lines 40–41. Then restate
Juliet's lines in your own words.

_____

_____

_____

_____

_____

_____

E **SHAKESPEAREAN
DRAMA**
Why is Romeo's name "hateful"
to him?

_____

_____

_____

_____

PAUSE & REFLECT
Why does Juliet warn Romeo?

_____

_____

_____

F SHAKESPEAREAN DRAMA

Reread lines 71–73. Circle the phrase that tells how Romeo feels about the risk he has taken. What does this reveal about his character?

_____

_____

_____

_____

_____

_____

_____

PAUSE & REFLECT

Why is Juliet embarrassed that Romeo has overheard her?

_____

_____

_____

_____

_____

Romeo. With love's light wings did I o'erperch these walls;
For stony limits cannot hold love out,
And what love can do, that dares love attempt.
Therefore thy kinsmen are no let to me.[11]

70 **Juliet.** If they do see thee, they will murder thee.

Romeo. Alack, there lies more peril in thine eye
Than twenty of their swords! Look thou but sweet,
And I am proof against their enmity.[12]

Juliet. I would not for the world they saw thee here.

75 **Romeo.** I have night's cloak to hide me from their sight;
And but thou love me, let them find me here.
My life were better ended by their hate
Than death prorogued,[13] wanting of thy love. **F**

Juliet. By whose direction foundst thou out this place?

80 **Romeo.** By love, that first did prompt me to enquire.
He lent me counsel, and I lent him eyes.
I am no pilot, yet, wert thou as far
As that vast shore washed with the farthest sea,
I would adventure for such merchandise.

85 **Juliet.** Thou knowest the mask of night is on my face;
Else would a maiden blush bepaint my cheek
For that which thou hast heard me speak tonight.
Fain would I dwell on form—fain, fain deny
What I have spoke; but farewell compliment![14] **PAUSE & REFLECT**

90 Dost thou love me? I know thou wilt say "Ay";
And I will take thy word. Yet, if thou swearst,
Thou mayst prove false. At lovers' perjuries,

11. **With . . . me:** Love helped me climb (**o'perch**) the walls. Neither walls nor your relatives are a hindrance (**let**) to me.
12. **Look . . . enmity:** Smile on me, and I will be defended against my enemies' hatred (**enmity**).
13. **prorogued:** postponed.
14. **Thou . . . compliment:** Had I known you were listening, I would have gladly (**fain**) behaved more properly, but now it's too late for good manners (**farewell compliment**).

They say Jove[15] laughs. O gentle Romeo,
If thou dost love, pronounce it faithfully. **G**
95 Or if thou thinkst I am too quickly won,
I'll frown, and be perverse, and say thee nay,
So thou wilt woo; but else, not for the world.
In truth, fair Montague, I am too fond,
And therefore thou mayst think my 'havior light;
100 But trust me, gentleman, I'll prove more true
Than those that have more cunning to be strange.[16]
I should have been more strange, I must confess,
But that thou overheardst, ere I was ware,
My true love's passion. Therefore pardon me,
105 And not impute this yielding to light love,
Which the dark night hath so discovered.[17]

Romeo. Lady, by yonder blessed moon I swear,
That tips with silver all these fruit-tree tops—

Juliet. O, swear not by the moon, the inconstant moon,
110 That monthly changes in her circled orb,
Lest that thy love prove likewise variable. **H**

Romeo. What shall I swear by?

Juliet.   Do not swear at all;
Or if thou wilt, swear by thy gracious self,
Which is the god of my idolatry,
115 And I'll believe thee.

Romeo.   If my heart's dear love—

Juliet. Well, do not swear. Although I joy in thee,
I have no joy of this contract[18] tonight.
It is too rash, too unadvised, too sudden;
120 Too like the lightning, which doth cease to be
Ere one can say "It lightens." Sweet, good night!
This bud of love, by summer's ripening breath,
May prove a beauteous flow'r when next we meet.

---

15. **Jove:** Jupiter, Roman king of the gods.
16. **strange:** aloof or cold.
17. **discovered:** revealed.
18. **contract:** declaration of love.

G **SHAKESPEAREAN DRAMA**

An **allusion** is a passing reference to something else with which the audience would be familiar. Underline the allusion Juliet uses in lines 92–93. When does Jove laugh at lovers?

_____

_____

_____

_____

_____

H **SHAKESPEAREAN DRAMA**

Reread lines 107–111. Restate the dialogue between Romeo and Juliet in your own words.

Romeo

↓

Juliet

❶ SHAKESPEAREAN DRAMA

Reread lines 116–124. Circle words and phrases that show Juliet's attitude about her and Romeo's romance. Why does she seem uneasy about their relationship?

_____

_____

_____

_____

_____

_____

_____

❶ SHAKESPEAREAN DRAMA

Reread lines 142–148. Underline the couple's plans for tomorrow. Given what the audience learned in the Prologue, how is this an example of **dramatic irony**?

_____

_____

_____

_____

_____

_____

_____

Good night, good night! As sweet repose and rest
Come to thy heart as that within my breast! **❶**

125 **Romeo.** O, wilt thou leave me so unsatisfied?

Juliet. What satisfaction canst thou have tonight?

Romeo. The exchange of thy love's faithful vow for mine.

Juliet. I gave thee mine before thou didst request it;
And yet I would it were to give again.

130 **Romeo.** Wouldst thou withdraw it? For what purpose, love?

Juliet. But to be frank[19] and give it thee again.
And yet I wish but for the thing I have.
My bounty[20] is as boundless as the sea,
My love as deep; the more I give to thee,
135 The more I have, for both are infinite.
I hear some noise within. Dear love, adieu!

[*Nurse calls within.*]

Anon,[21] good nurse! Sweet Montague, be true.
Stay but a little, I will come again.

[*Exit.*]

Romeo. O blessed, blessed night! I am afeard,
140 Being in night, all this is but a dream,
Too flattering-sweet to be substantial.

[*Re-enter Juliet, above.*]

Juliet. Three words, dear Romeo, and good night indeed.
If that thy bent of love be honorable,
Thy purpose marriage, send me word tomorrow,
145 By one that I'll procure to come to thee,
Where and what time thou wilt perform the rite;[22]
And all my fortunes at thy foot I'll lay
And follow thee my lord throughout the world. **❶**

Nurse [*within*]. Madam!

---

19. **frank:** aloof or cold.
20. **bounty:** revealed.
21. **Anon:** right away.
22. **If that . . . rite:** I'll send a messenger to you tomorrow. If your intention is to marry me, tell the messenger where and when the ceremony will be.

Juliet. I come, anon.—But if thou meanst not well,
I do beseech thee—

Nurse [*within*].   Madam!

Juliet.   By-and-by I come.—
To cease thy suit and leave me to my grief.
Tomorrow will I send.

Romeo.   So thrive my soul—

Juliet. A thousand times good night!

[*Exit.*]

155 **Romeo.** A thousand times the worse, to want thy light!
Love goes toward love as schoolboys from their books;
But love from love, towards school with heavy looks.  **K**

[*Enter* Juliet *again, above.*]

Juliet. Hist! Romeo, hist! O for a falc'ner's voice²³
To lure this tassel-gentle²⁴ back again!
160 Bondage is hoarse²⁵ and may not speak aloud;
Else would I tear the cave where Echo²⁶ lies,
And make her airy tongue more hoarse than mine **L**
With repetition of my Romeo's name.
Romeo!

165 **Romeo.** It is my soul that calls upon my name.
How silver-sweet sound lovers' tongues by night,
Like softest music to attending ears!

Juliet. Romeo!

---

23. **falc'ner's:** A falconer is a person who hunts with falcons.
24. **tassel-gentle:** male falcon.
25. **Bondage is hoarse:** Juliet is in "bondage" to her parents and must whisper.
26. **Echo:** In Greek mythology, a girl who could only repeat others' words.

K **SHAKESPEAREAN DRAMA**
Reread lines 156–157. Describe the **figurative language** Romeo uses to describe lovers.

_____
_____
_____
_____
_____
_____

L **SHAKESPEAREAN DRAMA**
Reread lines 158–159. Falconry and Greek mythology were both popular during Shakespeare's time. Juliet uses a **metaphor** to describe how desperately she wants to call out Romeo's name. Restate her lines in your own words.

_____
_____
_____
_____
_____
_____
_____
_____

Romeo.   My sweet?

Juliet.   What o'clock tomorrow
Shall I send to thee?

Romeo.   By the hour of nine.

170 **Juliet.** I will not fail. 'Tis twenty years till then.
I have forgot why I did call thee back.

Romeo. Let me stand here till thou remember it.

Juliet. I shall forget, to have thee still stand there,
Rememb'ring how I love thy company.

175 **Romeo.** And I'll still stay, to have thee still forget,
Forgetting any other home but this.

Juliet. 'Tis almost morning. I would have thee gone—
And yet no farther than a wanton's bird,
That lets it hop a little from her hand,
180 Like a poor prisoner in his twisted gyves,
And with a silk thread plucks it back again,
So loving-jealous of his liberty.[27]

Romeo. I would I were thy bird.

Juliet.   Sweet, so would I.
Yet I should kill thee with much cherishing.
185 Good night, good night! Parting is such sweet sorrow,
That I shall say good night till it be morrow.

[*Exit.*]

Romeo. Sleep dwell upon thine eyes, peace in thy breast!
Would I were sleep and peace, so sweet to rest!
Hence will I to my ghostly father's[28] cell,
190 His help to crave and my dear hap[29] to tell. **PAUSE & REFLECT**

[*Exit.*]

---

27. **I would . . . liberty:** I know you must go, but I want you close to me like a pet bird that a thoughtless child (**wanton**) keeps on a string.
28. **ghostly father:** spiritual father or priest.
29. **dear hap:** good fortune.

Text Analysis: Shakespearean Drama

Shakespeare uses **soliloquies, dramatic irony, figurative language,** and **allusion** in this scene from Act Two. Complete the chart below by identifying passages that contain these elements. Identify who is speaking, describe the passage, and include line numbers.

Dramatic Convention	Example
Soliloquy	
Dramatic irony	
Figurative language	
Allusion	

Review your notes for *Romeo and Juliet* and your completed chart above. Which of these conventions helps you understand the tragedy of the play best? Explain.

_____

_____

_____

Reading Strategy: Reading Shakespearean Drama

Look back at the notes you made as you read. Complete the chart with the most important details from the selection.

Prologue
Scene 2
Romeo's Soliloquy:
Juliet's Soliloquy:
Dialogue Between Romeo and Juliet:

Is LOVE stronger than **HATE?**

What consequences can arise from hating someone?

_____

_____

_____

_____

_____

_____

Academic Vocabulary in Speaking

characteristic	critical	influence	motivate	resolve

TURN AND TALK How does the feud between Romeo's and Juliet's families **influence** their actions? Discuss their actions and what you think about them with a partner. Use at least one Academic Vocabulary word in your conversation. Definitions for these terms are listed on page 415.

Assessment Practice

DIRECTIONS Use *The Tragedy of Romeo and Juliet* to answer questions 1–4.

1 In lines 26–32, Romeo compares Juliet to —
- **A** a bird
- **B** the sun
- **C** an angel
- **D** the moon

2 In the aside in line 36, Romeo considers —
- **A** leaving the orchard
- **B** revealing his presence
- **C** giving up his family name
- **D** continuing his conversation

3 In line 133, when Juliet says, "My bounty is as boundless as the sea," she means —
- **A** her ability to love Romeo is endless
- **B** her father's fortune is vast like the ocean
- **C** her riches will keep them happy for eternity
- **D** her love for Romeo will cause incessant bloodshed

4 Romeo and Juliet's wedding plans are ironic because —
- **A** the audience knows they will die
- **B** the arrangements are made in secret
- **C** the scene begins with another celebration
- **D** the union will bring peace to their families

Great Movies: *Romeo and Juliet*

Critical Review by **Roger Ebert**

Background

Roger Ebert has been the film critic for the *Chicago Sun-Times* since 1967. He has also co-hosted a successful movie review television show. In this critical review, Roger Ebert compares several film versions of the play *Romeo and Juliet* and discusses their stagecraft.

Standards Focus: Analyze a Critical Review

A **critical review** is an essay in which the writer gives his or her opinions about a movie, a play, a book, a TV show, or another work. A critical review typically includes these elements:

- the name of the work and its creator
- a description of the work, often including some background information and a summary of the plot
- a clearly stated opinion of the work
- reasons that support the opinion
- examples or details that illustrate the reasons

The heart of a review is the writer's opinion and the reasons and examples used to back it up. Opinions that are **substantiated,** or supported, are more persuasive than those that are simply stated without appropriate support.

As you read, use a chart like the one shown to record Roger Ebert's opinion and the main reasons and examples he gives to support it.

Ebert's Opinion:	
Reason	*Supporting Examples or Details*
Reason 1:	
Reason 2:	
Reason 3:	

SECTION 5

GREAT MOVIES

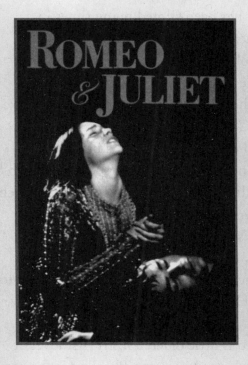

Romeo and Juliet

BY ROGER EBERT

SET A PURPOSE
FOR READING
Read to find out one movie
reviewer's opinion about
various film productions of the
play *Romeo and Juliet*.

"Romeo and Juliet" is always said to be the first romantic tragedy ever written, but it isn't really a tragedy at all. It's a tragic misunderstanding, scarcely fitting the ancient requirement of tragedy that the mighty fall through their own flaws. Romeo and Juliet have no flaws, and aren't old enough to be blamed if they did. They die because of the pigheaded quarrel of their families, the Montagues and the Capulets. By writing the play, Shakespeare began the shaping of modern drama, in which
10 the fates of ordinary people are as crucial as those of the great. The great tragedies of his time, including his own, involved kings, emperors, generals. Here, near the dawn of his career, perhaps remembering a sweet early romance before his forced marriage to Anne Hathaway, he writes about teenagers in love. Ⓐ

Ⓐ CRITICAL REVIEW
Reread lines 1–11. According to Roger Ebert, how did Shakespeare influence modern drama? Why does Ebert say *Romeo and Juliet* is not a tragedy?

_____

_____

_____

_____

_____

_____

"Romeo and Juliet" has been filmed many times in many ways; Norma Shearer and Leslie Howard starred in the beloved 1936 Hollywood version, and modern transformations include Robert Wise's "West Side Story" (1961), which applies the plot to Manhattan gang warfare; Abel Ferrara's "China Girl" (1987), about a forbidden romance between a girl of Chinatown and a boy of Little Italy; and Baz Luhrmann's "William Shakespeare's Romeo & Juliet" (1996), with California punk gangs on Verona Beach. But the favorite film version is likely to remain, for many years, Franco Zeffirelli's 1968 production. **B**

His crucial decision, in a film where almost everything went well, was to cast actors who were about the right age to play the characters (as Howard and Shearer were obviously not). As the play opens, Juliet "hath not seen the change of 14 years," and Romeo is little older. This is first love for Juliet, and Romeo's crush on the unseen Rosalind is forgotten the moment he sees Juliet at the masked ball: "I ne'er saw true beauty until this night." After a well-publicized international search, Zeffirelli cast Olivia Hussey, a 16-year-old from Argentina, and Leonard Whiting, a British 17-year-old. **C**

They didn't merely look their parts, they embodied them in the freshness of their personalities, and although neither was a trained actor, they were fully equal to Shakespeare's dialogue for them; Anthony Holden's new book *William Shakespeare: The Man Behind the Genius* contrasts "the beautiful simplicity with which the lovers speak at their moments of uncomplicated happiness," with "the ornate rhetorical flourishes which fuel so much else in the play"— flourishes that Zeffirelli severely pruned, trimming about half the play. He was roundly criticized for his edits, but much that

B CRITICAL REVIEW
Roger Ebert provides information about other film versions of the play in lines 16–26. Underline Ebert's opinion statement about Zeffirelli's film.

C CRITICAL REVIEW
In lines 27–36, what was Zeffirelli's "crucial decision"? Underline and then paraphrase the first reason Ebert gives to support his opinion of the movie.

_____

_____

_____

_____

_____

_____

_____

needs describing on the stage can simply be shown onscreen, as when Benvolio is shown witnessing Juliet's funeral and thus does not need to evoke it in a description to the exiled Romeo. Shakespeare, who took such wholesale liberties with his own sources, might have understood. **PAUSE & REFLECT**

What is left is what people love the play for-—the purity of the young lovers' passion, the earthiness of Juliet's nurse, the well-intentioned plans of Friar Laurence, the hot-blooded feud between the young men of the families, the cruel irony of the double deaths. And there is time, too, for many of the great speeches, including Mercutio's poetic evocation of Mab, the queen of dreams.

Hussey and Whiting were so good because they didn't know any better. Another year or two of experience, perhaps, and they would have been too intimidated to play the roles. It was my good fortune to visit the film set, in a small hill town an hour or so outside Rome, on the night when the balcony scene was filmed. I remember Hussey and Whiting upstairs in the old hillside villa, waiting for their call, unaffected, uncomplicated. And when the balcony scene was shot, I remember the heedless energy that Hussey threw into it, take after take, hurling herself almost off the balcony for hungry kisses. (Whiting, balanced in a tree, needed to watch his footing.) **D**

Between shots, in the overgrown garden, Zeffirelli strolled with the composer Nino Rota, who had written the music for most of Fellini's films and now simply hummed the film's central theme, as the director nodded. Pasqualino De Santis, who was to win an Oscar for his cinematography, directed

PAUSE & REFLECT
How did Zeffirelli show strength and conviction about his artistic vision for *Romeo and Juliet*? What is Ebert's opinion about Zeffirelli?

D CRITICAL REVIEW
Reread lines 59–70. Why does Ebert think Hussey and Whiting were so successful at bringing the star-crossed lovers to life? How does Ebert substantiate his opinion?

his crew quietly, urgently, trying to be ready for the freshness of the actors instead of making them wait for technical quibbles. At dawn, drinking strong coffee as cars pulled around to take his actors back to Rome, Zeffirelli said what

80 was obvious: That the whole movie depended on the balcony and the crypt scenes, and he felt now that his casting decision had proven itself, and that the film would succeed.

It did, beyond any precedent for a film based on Shakespeare, even though Shakespeare is the most filmed writer in history. The movie opened in the tumultuous year of 1968, a time of political upheaval around the world, and somehow the story of the star-crossed lovers caught the mood of rebellious young people who had wearied of their elders' wars. "This of all works of literature eternizes the ardor of

90 young love and youth's aggressive spirit," wrote Anthony Burgess. **E**

Zeffirelli, born in Florence in 1923, came early to the English language through prewar experiences hinted at in the loosely autobiographical "Tea with Mussolini" (1999). His crucial early artistic influence was Laurence Olivier's "Henry V" (1945), which inspired him to go into the theater; he has had parallel careers directing plays, films and operas. Before the great success of "Romeo and Juliet," he first visited Shakespeare for the shaky but high-spirited "Taming of the

100 Shrew" (1967), with Burton and Taylor. Later he directed Placido Domingo in "Otello" (1986), Verdi's opera, and directed Mel Gibson in "Hamlet" (1990).

"Romeo and Juliet" remains the magical high point of his career. To see it again is to luxuriate. It is intriguing that Zeffirelli in 1968 focused on love, while Baz Luhrmann's popular version of 1996 focused on violence; something fundamental has changed in films about and for young

E CRITICAL REVIEW
Why does Ebert think audiences—particularly young people—were so taken with the movie when it premiered in 1968?

people, and recent audiences seem shy of sex and love but eager for conflict and action. I wonder if a modern Friday night audience would snicker at the heart-baring sincerity of the lovers. . . .

The costumes by Danilo Donati won another Oscar for the film (it was also nominated for best picture and director), and they are crucial to its success; they are the avenue for color and richness to enter the frame, which is otherwise filled with gray and ochre stones and the colors of nature. The nurse (Pat Heywood) seems enveloped in a dry goods' sale of heavy fabrics, and Mercutio (John McEnery) comes flying a handkerchief that he uses as a banner, disguise and shroud. Hussey's dresses, with low bodices and simple patterns, set off her creamy skin and long hair; Whiting is able to inhabit his breeches, blouse and codpiece with the conviction that it is everyday clothing, not a costume. **F**

The costumes and everything else in the film—the photography, the music, above all Shakespeare's language—is so voluptuous, so sensuous. The stagecraft of the twinned death scenes is of course all contrivance; the friar's potion works with timing that is precisely wrong, and yet we forgive the manipulation because Shakespeare has been able to provide us with what is theoretically impossible, the experience of two young lovers each grieving the other's death. When the play was first staged in London, Holden writes, Shakespeare had the satisfaction "of seeing the groundlings moved to emotions far beyond anything before known in the theater." Why? Because of craft and art, yes, but also because Romeo and Juliet were not distant and august figures, not Caesars, Othellos or Macbeths, but a couple of kids in love, as everyone in the theater had known, and everyone in the theater had been. **PAUSE & REFLECT**

F CRITICAL REVIEW
Reread lines 112–123. Circle the words and phrases that convey the aspect of the film that Ebert praises in this paragraph. Explain why he found this element essential to the movie's success.

_____

_____

_____

_____

_____

_____

_____

PAUSE & REFLECT
Reread lines 137–139. Do you think Roger Ebert is right when he says that "everyone in the theater had been" a couple of kids in love? Why or why not?

_____

_____

_____

_____

Practicing Your Skills

Use the chart that you filled in as you read to write a brief summary of Roger Ebert's critical review. Remember, a **summary** is a brief retelling, in your own words, of the main ideas in a piece of writing.

Great Movies: *Romeo and Juliet*
MY SUMMARY:

What is your opinion of Ebert's review? Did Ebert do a good job of stating and supporting his opinion? Explain.

Academic Vocabulary in Speaking

| characteristic | critical | influence | motivate | resolve |

TURN AND TALK With a partner, discuss other **critical** reviews that you have read or heard. Are the reviews always positive? What **characteristics** do the reviews share? How do critical reviews **influence** you? Use at least one Academic Vocabulary word in your discussion. Definitions for these terms are listed on page 415.

Assessment Practice

DIRECTIONS Use "Great Movies: *Romeo and Juliet*" to answer questions 1–4.

1 Which statement best describes the opinion that Roger Ebert voices in "Great Movies: *Romeo and Juliet*"?

   A All of the filmmakers he mentions have failed to create a good *Romeo and Juliet*.

   B Franco Zeffirelli's 1968 *Romeo and Juliet* will long endure as a great movie.

   C Costuming is a small factor in a film version of *Romeo and Juliet*.

   D The 1936 Hollywood version of *Romeo and Juliet* is the most enjoyable.

2 How does the focus of the Zeffirelli version of *Romeo and Juliet* differ from the focus of the Baz Luhrmann version?

   A Zeffirelli focuses on violence while Luhrmann focuses on love.

   B Zeffirelli focuses on costuming while Luhrmann focuses on photography.

   C Zeffirelli focuses on older actors while Luhrmann focuses on younger actors.

   D Zeffirelli focuses on love while Luhrmann focuses on violence.

3 The author uses lines 71–78 and 124–126 to —

   A reveal how difficult it was to get the music and cinematography to work well together

   B contradict the importance of music and cinematography in the film's creation

   C explain the importance of music and cinematography to the film's success

   D describe the newest ideas about music and cinematography

4 Ebert believes audiences have been moved by the story of *Romeo and Juliet* ever since it was first staged because they —

   A identify with Romeo and Juliet because they represent something with which people are familiar—a young couple in love.

   B understand and appreciate the conflicts between families that cause innocent people to be hurt.

   C expect films to be focused on conflict and action.

   D find comfort in films that are based on age-old themes and plot lines.

UNIT 11

Epic Poetry
THE ODYSSEY

Be sure to read the Historical Background and the Text Analysis Workshop on pp. 1188–1201 in *Holt McDougal Literature*.

Academic Vocabulary for Unit 11

Preview the following Academic Vocabulary words. You will encounter these words as you work through this book and will use them as you write and talk about the selection in this unit.

---

demonstrate (dĕm'ən-strāt') *v.* to show clearly and purposefully

The character's actions demonstrate the beliefs and values of ancient Greek society.

•

emphasis (ĕm'fə-sĭs) *n.* a special stress on something—a word, phrase, idea, etc.—to make it stand out

The poet places special emphasis on the hero's cleverness.

•

ideology (ī'dē-ŏl'ə-jē) *n.* the beliefs or way of thinking of an individual or a group of people

What kind of political ideology requires people to obey a tyrant?

•

monitor (mŏn'ĭ-tər) *v.* to check in on, watch, regulate

When you read a challenging text, pause frequently to monitor your understanding of it.

•

undertake (ŭn'dər-tāk') *v.* to take on a task or assume a responsibility

Who will undertake the job of summarizing this story for the class?

Suppose you want to describe a favorite book or movie. Which parts would you give the greatest **emphasis**? Write your description on the lines below. Use at least one Academic Vocabulary word in your response.

_____

_____

_____

_____

The Cyclops

from the *Odyssey*

Epic Poem by **Homer**

Translated by **Robert Fitzgerald**

What is a **HERO**?

When you hear the word *hero*, who comes to mind? Do you think of someone with physical strength, unwavering courage, or rare talent? In Homer's *Odyssey*, you'll meet a classic hero of Western literature—Odysseus, a man with many heroic traits and some very human flaws.

DISCUSS Work with a small group to make a list of people—male and female—who are generally considered heroes. Record your list at left. Then discuss the heroic qualities of each person. Which qualities seem essential to every hero? List the qualities your group agrees on.

Text Analysis: Epic Hero

In literature, an **epic** is a long narrative poem that tells the story of an **epic hero,** a larger-than-life character who pursues long and dangerous adventures. The web below shows some typical traits of an epic hero.

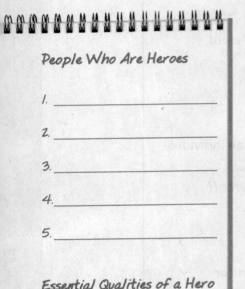

People Who Are Heroes

1. _____
2. _____
3. _____
4. _____
5. _____

Essential Qualities of a Hero

1. _____
2. _____
3. _____

possesses superhuman strength and craftiness

is both helped and harmed by interfering gods

Epic Hero

embodies ideals and values that a culture considers admirable

emerges victorious from perilous situations

In addition to the traits mentioned above, Odysseus has great courage, extreme self-confidence, and a tendency to ignore warnings. As you read "The Cyclops," consider how Odysseus faces various conflicts. What does this tell you about his character? What do his character traits tell you about what the ancient Greeks admired?

Reading Strategy: Reading an Epic Poem

The strategies for reading an epic are very similar to those for reading any narrative poem. As you read, apply these strategies:

- Keep track of the events and the order in which they happen.

- Visualize the **imagery,** or language that appeals to readers' senses.

- Notice how figurative language makes the story vivid and interesting. In particular, watch for Homer's use of the **epic simile**—a comparison using *like* or *as* that is developed over several lines.

- Look for repeated **epithets**—brief descriptive phrases used to characterize certain people and things. For example, Odysseus is known by the epithets "son of Laertes" and "raider of cities."

- Be aware of **allusions**—references to famous people, places, and things— that would have been meaningful to Homer's audience.

- Read difficult passages more than once. Use the footnotes for help.

- Read the poem aloud, as it was originally performed.

Vocabulary in Context

Note: Words are listed in the order in which they appear in the poem.

appalled (ə-pôld′) *adj.* filled with dismay; horrified
 *The men were **appalled** at the size of the Cyclops.*

ponderous (pŏn′dər-əs) *adj.* heavy in a clumsy way; bulky
 *The sheep moved awkwardly due to the **ponderous** weight on its back.*

profusion (prə-fyo͞o′zhən) *n.* abundance
 *The neglected garden was covered in a **profusion** of weeds.*

meditation (mĕd′ĭ-tā′shən) *n.* the act of being in serious, reflective thought
 *After a period of **meditation,** he found a solution to the problem.*

adversary (ăd′vər-sĕr′ē) *n.* an opponent; enemy
 *He glared at his **adversary** and threatened to take him down.*

Vocabulary Practice

Review the vocabulary words and their meanings. Then think about the conflicts or challenges an epic hero might encounter. Write a sentence or two describing a heroic adventure, using at least two of the vocabulary words.

_____

_____

_____

**SET A PURPOSE
FOR READING**

Read to learn about the epic hero Odysseus and his adventure with the Cyclops.

THE CYCLOPS
from the
ODYSSEY

Epic Poem by
HOMER
Translated by
**ROBERT
FITZGERALD**

BACKGROUND The *Odyssey*, an epic from ancient Greece, tells of the many adventures of a soldier named Odysseus on his ten-year journey home from the Trojan War. The *Odyssey* is composed of many different stories, or episodes, in which the hero Odysseus faces all sorts of challenges.

In this adventure, Odysseus describes his encounter with a Cyclops named Polyphemus, the giant one-eyed monster son of Poseidon. It is Odysseus' famed curiosity that leads him to the Cyclops' cave and that makes him insist on waiting for the giant.

In the next land we found were Cyclops,[1]
giants, louts, without a law to bless them.
In ignorance leaving the fruitage of the earth in mystery
to the immortal gods, they neither plow
5 nor sow by hand, nor till the ground, though grain—
wild wheat and barley—grows untended, and
wine-grapes, in clusters, ripen in heaven's rain.
Cyclopes have no muster and no meeting,

---

1. **Cyclopes** (sī-klō'pēz): refers to the creatures in plural; *Cyclops* is singular.

no consultation or old tribal ways,
10 but each one dwells in his own mountain cave
dealing out rough justice to wife and child,
indifferent to what the others do. . . ." **Ⓐ**

*Across the bay from the land of the Cyclopes was a lush, deserted
island. Odysseus and his crew landed on the island in a dense fog
and spent days feasting on wine and wild goats and observing the
mainland, where the Cyclopes lived. On the third day, Odysseus
and his company of men set out to learn if the Cyclopes were
friends or foes.*

"When the young Dawn with finger tips of rose
came in the east, I called my men together
15 and made a speech to them: **Ⓑ**

                          'Old shipmates, friends,
the rest of you stand by; I'll make the crossing
in my own ship, with my own company,
and find out what the mainland natives are—
for they may be wild savages, and lawless,
20 or hospitable and god fearing men.'

At this I went aboard, and gave the word
to cast off by the stern.[2] My oarsmen followed,
filing in to their benches by the rowlocks,
and all in line dipped oars in the gray sea.

25 As we rowed on, and nearer to the mainland,
at one end of the bay, we saw a cavern
yawning above the water, screened with laurel,[3]
and many rams and goats about the place
inside a sheepfold—made from slabs of stone

---

2. **stern:** the rear end of a ship.
3. **screened with laurel:** partially hidden by laurel trees.

Ⓐ EPIC HERO
In lines 1–12, Odysseus explains why he has no respect for the Cyclopes. Assuming he expresses the values of his culture, what kind of society did the ancient Greeks admire?

_____

_____

_____

_____

Ⓑ READING AN EPIC POEM
An **epithet** is a short descriptive phrase used to characterize a particular person or thing. Circle the epithet Homer uses to characterize the dawn. What does this description tell you about the dawn?

_____

_____

_____

_____

_____

_____

_____

_____

C **READING AN EPIC POEM**
Reread lines 32–38. Underline the
Imagery that helps you visualize
the Cyclops. On the lines below,
briefly describe how you picture
this creature.

_____

_____

_____

_____

_____

_____

_____

_____

_____

_____

_____

_____

_____

_____

_____

_____

_____

30   earthfast between tall trunks of pine and rugged
      towering oak trees.

                                      A prodigious man

      slept in this cave alone, and took his flocks
      to graze afield—remote from all companions,
      knowing none but savage ways, a brute
35   so huge, he seemed no man at all of those
      who eat good wheaten bread; but he seemed rather
      a shaggy mountain reared in solitude. **C**
      We beached there, and I told the crew
      to stand by and keep watch over the ship;
40   as for myself I took my twelve best fighters
      and went ahead. I had a goatskin full
      of that sweet liquor that Euanthes' son,
      Maron,[4] had given me. He kept Apollo's
      holy grove at Ismarus; for kindness
45   we showed him there, and showed his wife and child,
      he gave me seven shining golden talents[5]
      perfectly formed, a solid silver winebowl,
      and then this liquor—twelve two-handled jars
      of brandy, pure and fiery. Not a slave
50   in Maron's household knew this drink; only
      he, his wife and the storeroom mistress knew;
      and they would put one cupful—ruby-colored,
      honey-smooth—in twenty more of water,
      but still the sweet scent hovered like a fume
55   over the winebowl. No man turned away
      when cups of this came round.

                                      A wineskin full

      I brought along, and victuals[6] in a bag,
      for in my bones I knew some towering brute

---

4. **Euanthes** (yōō-ăn′thēz); **Maron** (mâr′ŏn′).

5. **talents:** bars of gold or silver of a specified weight, used as money in ancient
   Greece.

6. **victuals** (vĭt′lz): food.

would be upon us soon—all outward power,
60 a wild man, ignorant of civility.

We climbed, then, briskly to the cave. But Cyclops
had gone afield, to pasture his fat sheep,
so we looked round at everything inside:
a drying rack that sagged with cheeses, pens
65 crowded with lambs and kids, each in its class:
firstlings apart from middlings, and the 'dewdrops,'
or newborn lambkins, penned apart from both.[7]
And vessels full of whey[8] were brimming there—
bowls of earthenware and pails for milking.
70 My men came pressing round me, pleading:

                                        'Why not
take these cheeses, get them stowed, come back,
throw open all the pens, and make a run for it?
We'll drive the kids and lambs aboard. We say
put out again on good salt water!'[9]

                              Ah,
75 how sound that was! Yet I refused. I wished
to see the caveman, what he had to offer—
no pretty sight, it turned out, for my friends. **PAUSE & REFLECT**

We lit a fire, burnt an offering,[10]
and took some cheese to eat; then sat in silence
80 around the embers, waiting. When he came
he had a load of dry boughs on his shoulder
to stoke his fire at suppertime. He dumped it

PAUSE & REFLECT
Underline the "sound" request that Odysseus' men make. Why do you think Odysseus refuses their request?

_____

_____

_____

_____

_____

_____

_____

_____

_____

_____

---

7. **firstlings apart . . . from both:** The Cyclops has separated his lambs into three age groups.
8. **whey:** the watery part of milk, which separates from the curds, or solid part, during the making of cheese.
9. **good salt water:** the open sea.
10. **burnt an offering:** burned a portion of the food as an offering to secure the gods' goodwill. (Such offerings were frequently performed by Greek sailors during difficult journeys.)

with a great crash into that hollow cave,
and we all scattered fast to the far wall.
85 Then over the broad cavern floor he ushered
the ewes he meant to milk. He left his rams
and he-goats in the yard outside, and swung
high overhead a slab of solid rock
to close the cave. Two dozen four-wheeled wagons,
90 with heaving wagon teams, could not have stirred
the tonnage of that rock from where he wedged it
over the doorsill. Next he took his seat
and milked his bleating ewes. A practiced job
he made of it, giving each ewe her suckling;
95 thickened his milk, then, into curds and whey,
sieved out the curds to drip in withy baskets,[11]
and poured the whey to stand in bowls
cooling until he drank it for his supper.
When all these chores were done, he poked the fire,
100 heaping on brushwood. In the glare he saw us.

PAUSE & REFLECT

'Strangers,' he said, 'who are you? And where from?
What brings you here by sea ways—a fair traffic?[12]
Or are you wandering rogues, who cast your lives
like dice, and ravage other folk by sea?'

105 We felt a pressure on our hearts, in dread
of that deep rumble and that mighty man.
But all the same I spoke up in reply:

'We are from Troy, Achaeans, blown off course
by shifting gales on the Great South Sea;
110 homeward bound, but taking routes and ways
uncommon; so the will of Zeus would have it.
We served under Agamemnon, son of Atreus—

---

11. **withy baskets:** baskets made from twigs.
12. **fair traffic:** honest trading.

PAUSE & REFLECT
Reread lines 78–100. What is the
Cyclops like?

the whole world knows what city
he laid waste, what armies he destroyed. **D**
115 It was our luck to come here; here we stand,
beholden for your help, or any gifts
you give—as custom is to honor strangers.
We would entreat you, great Sir, have a care
for the gods' courtesy; Zeus will avenge
120 the unoffending guest.'¹³

He answered this
from his brute chest, unmoved:

'You are a ninny,
or else you come from the other end of nowhere,
telling me, mind the gods! We Cyclopes
care not a whistle for your thundering Zeus
125 or all the gods in bliss; we have more force by far.
I would not let you go for fear of Zeus—
you or your friends—unless I had a whim to.
Tell me, where was it, now, you left your ship—
around the point, or down the shore, I wonder?'

130 He thought he'd find out, but I saw through this,
and answered with a ready lie:

'My ship?
Poseidon Lord, who sets the earth a-tremble,
broke it up on the rocks at your land's end.
A wind from seaward served him, drove us there.
135 We are survivors, these good men and I.' **E**

Neither reply nor pity came from him,
but in one stride he clutched at my companions

---

13. **as custom is . . . unoffending guest:** It was a sacred Greek custom to honor
strangers with food and gifts. Odysseus is reminding the Cyclops that Zeus
will punish anyone who mistreats a guest.

D **READING AN EPIC POEM**
Reread lines 108–114 and
underline the **allusion** to the
Trojan War. Agamemnon is
the Greek king who led the
successful war against the city
of Troy. What point is Odysseus
making about himself through
this connection?

_____
_____
_____
_____
_____
_____
_____

E **EPIC HERO**
Reread lines 130–135. Why does
Odysseus lie to the Cyclops
about his ship?

_____
_____
_____
_____
_____

and caught two in his hands like squirming puppies
to beat their brains out, spattering the floor.
140 Then he dismembered them and made his meal,
gaping and crunching like a mountain lion—
everything: innards, flesh, and marrow bones.
We cried aloud, lifting our hands to Zeus,
powerless, looking on at this, **appalled**;
145 but Cyclops went on filling up his belly
with manflesh and great gulps of whey,
then lay down like a mast among his sheep.
My heart beat high now at the chance of action,
and drawing the sharp sword from my hip I went
150 along his flank to stab him where the midriff
holds the liver. I had touched the spot
when sudden fear stayed me: if I killed him
we perished there as well, for we could never
move his **ponderous** doorway slab aside.
155 So we were left to groan and wait for morning.

When the young Dawn with fingertips of rose
lit up the world, the Cyclops built a fire
and milked his handsome ewes, all in due order,
putting the sucklings to the mothers. Then,
160 his chores being all dispatched, he caught
another brace[14] of men to make his breakfast,
and whisked away his great door slab
to let his sheep go through—but he, behind,
reset the stone as one would cap a quiver.[15]
165 There was a din of whistling as the Cyclops
rounded his flock to higher ground, then stillness.
And now I pondered how to hurt him worst,
if but Athena granted what I prayed for.

appalled (ə-pôld´) *adj.* filled with dismay; horrified

ponderous (pŏn´dər-əs) *adj.* heavy in a clumsy way; bulky

How does the **ponderous** rock present a problem for Odysseus?

_____

_____

_____

_____

F READING AN EPIC POEM
Circle the epithet that is repeated in lines 156–157. As you continue reading, look for more repetitions like this one.

---

14. **brace:** pair.
15. **but he . . . a quiver:** The Cyclops reseals the cave with the massive rock as easily as an ordinary human places the cap on a container of arrows.

Here are the means I thought would serve my turn:

170 a club, or staff, lay there along the fold—
an olive tree, felled green and left to season[16]
for Cyclops' hand. And it was like a mast
a lugger[17] of twenty oars, broad in the beam—
a deep-sea-going craft—might carry:
175 so long, so big around, it seemed. Now I
chopped out a six foot section of this pole
and set it down before my men, who scraped it;
and when they had it smooth, I hewed again
to make a stake with pointed end. I held this
180 in the fire's heart and turned it, toughening it,
then hid it, well back in the cavern, under
one of the dung piles in **profusion** there.
Now came the time to toss for it: who ventured
along with me? whose hand could bear to thrust
185 and grind that spike in Cyclops' eye, when mild
sleep had mastered him? As luck would have it,
the men I would have chosen won the toss—
four strong men, and I made five as captain. **G**

At evening came the shepherd with his flock,
190 his woolly flock. The rams as well, this time,
entered the cave: by some sheep-herding whim—
or a god's bidding—none were left outside.
He hefted his great boulder into place
and sat him down to milk the bleating ewes
195 in proper order, put the lambs to suck,
and swiftly ran through all his evening chores.
Then he caught two more men and feasted on them.
My moment was at hand, and I went forward

profusion (prə-fyo͞o′zhən) *n.*
abundance

G EPIC HERO
What is Odysseus planning
to do to the Cyclops? How
do Odysseus' actions in
lines 167–188 show the qualities
of an **epic hero**? Underline
key passages in the text and
summarize your answer below.

_____

_____

_____

_____

_____

_____

_____

---

16. **left to season:** left to dry out and harden.
17. **lugger:** a small, wide sailing ship.

holding an ivy bowl of my dark drink,
200 looking up, saying:

                                    'Cyclops, try some wine.
Here's liquor to wash down your scraps of men.
Taste it, and see the kind of drink we carried
under our planks. I meant it for an offering
if you would help us home. But you are mad,
205 unbearable, a bloody monster! After this,
will any other traveller come to see you?'

He seized and drained the bowl, and it went down
so fiery and smooth he called for more:

'Give me another, thank you kindly. Tell me,
210 how are you called? I'll make a gift will please you.
Even Cyclopes know the wine-grapes grow
out of grassland and loam in heaven's rain,
but here's a bit of nectar and ambrosia!'[18]

Three bowls I brought him, and he poured them down.
215 I saw the fuddle and flush[19] come over him,
then I sang out in cordial tones:

                                    'Cyclops,
you ask my honorable name? Remember
the gift you promised me, and I shall tell you.
My name is Nohbdy: mother, father, and friends,
220 everyone calls me Nohbdy.'

                                    And he said:
'Nohbdy's my meat, then, after I eat his friends.
Others come first. There's a noble gift, now.'

EPIC HERO
Say the name *Nohbdy* out loud and listen to what it sounds like. What might Odysseus be planning?

_____

_____

_____

_____

---

18. **nectar** (nĕk′tər) **and ambrosia** (ăm-brō′zhə): the drink and food of the gods.

19. **fuddle and flush:** the state of confusion and redness of the face caused by drinking alcohol.

Even as he spoke, he reeled and tumbled backward,
his great head lolling to one side: and sleep
225 took him like any creature. Drunk, hiccupping,
he dribbled streams of liquor and bits of men.

Now, by the gods, I drove my big hand spike
deep in the embers, charring it again,
and cheered my men along with battle talk
230 to keep their courage up: no quitting now.
The pike[20] of olive, green though it had been,
reddened and glowed as if about to catch.
I drew it from the coals and my four fellows
gave me a hand, lugging it near the Cyclops
235 as more than natural force nerved them; straight
forward they sprinted, lifted it, and rammed it
deep in his crater eye, and I leaned on it
turning it as a shipwright turns a drill
in planking, having men below to swing
240 the two-handled strap that spins it in the groove.
So with our brand we bored that great eye socket
while blood ran out around the red hot bar.
Eyelid and lash were seared; the pierced ball
hissed broiling, and the roots popped.

                            In a smithy[21]
245 one sees a white-hot axehead or an adze[22]
plunged and wrung in a cold tub, screeching steam—
the way they make soft iron hale and hard—:
just so that eyeball hissed around the spike. ❶
The Cyclops bellowed and the rock roared round him,
250 and we fell back in fear. Clawing his face
he tugged the bloody spike out of his eye,

---

20. **the pike:** the pointed stake.
21. **smithy:** blacksmith's shop.
22. **adze** (ădz): an axlike tool with a curved blade.

❶ **READING AN EPIC POEM**
Reread lines 237–248 and
underline the two **epic similes**
you find there. In the chart
below, write the two things
being compared in each simile.

Simile #1
Event from Poem:
Compared to:

Simile #2
Event from Poem:
Compared to:

threw it away, and his wild hands went groping;
then he set up a howl for Cyclopes
who lived in caves on windy peaks nearby.
255 Some heard him; and they came by divers[23] ways
to clump around outside and call:

                        'What ails you,

Polyphemus?[24] Why do you cry so sore
in the starry night? You will not let us sleep.
260 Sure no man's driving off your flock? No man
has tricked you, ruined you?'

                    Out of the cave

the mammoth Polyphemus roared in answer:

'Nohbdy, Nohbdy's tricked me, Nohbdy's ruined me!'

To this rough shout they made a sage[25] reply:

'Ah well, if nobody has played you foul
there in your lonely bed, we are no use in pain
265 given by great Zeus. Let it be your father,
Poseidon Lord, to whom you pray.' J

                    So saying

they trailed away. And I was filled with laughter
to see how like a charm the name deceived them.
270 Now Cyclops, wheezing as the pain came on him,
fumbled to wrench away the great doorstone
and squatted in the breach[26] with arms thrown wide
for any silly beast or man who bolted—
hoping somehow I might be such a fool.

J READING AN EPIC POEM
Circle the allusion in lines 266–267.
What do you learn about
Polyphemus from this allusion?

_____

_____

_____

_____

_____

_____

_____

---

23. **divers:** various.
24. **Polyphemus** (pŏl′ə-fē′məs): the name of the Cyclops.
25. **sage:** wise.
26. **breach:** opening.

275 But I kept thinking how to win the game:
    death sat there huge; how could we slip away?
    I drew on all my wits, and ran through tactics,
    reasoning as a man will for dear life,
    until a trick came—and it pleased me well.
280 The Cyclops' rams were handsome, fat, with heavy
    fleeces, a dark violet.

                                        Three abreast

    I tied them silently together, twining
    cords of willow from the ogre's bed;
    then slung a man under each middle one
285 to ride there safely, shielded left and right.
    So three sheep could convey each man. I took
    the woolliest ram, the choicest of the flock,
    and hung myself under his kinky belly,
    pulled up tight, with fingers twisted deep
290 in sheepskin ringlets for an iron grip.
    So, breathing hard, we waited until morning. **PAUSE & REFLECT**

    When Dawn spread out her finger tips of rose
    the rams began to stir, moving for pasture,
    and peals of bleating echoed round the pens
295 where dams with udders full called for a milking.
    Blinded, and sick with pain from his head wound,

K EPIC HERO
During the Trojan War, Odysseus had the idea for Greek soldiers to hide inside a wooden horse, which the Trojans accepted as a gift and brought into their city. The Greeks then jumped out and destroyed the city. Keep this in mind as you reread lines 275–281. What trait does Odysseus reveal in both situations?

PAUSE & REFLECT
How does Odysseus plan to escape from the Cyclops' cave?

THE CYCLOPS   **455**

meditation (mĕd'ĭ-tā'shən)
n. the act of being in serious, reflective thought

What meditations might be weighing on Odysseus' mind?

_____

_____

_____

_____

_____

_____

_____

● **EPIC HERO**
What character traits has Odysseus revealed in his dealings with Polyphemus? Consider both positive and negative qualities.

_____

_____

_____

_____

the master stroked each ram, then let it pass,
but my men riding on the pectoral fleece[27]
the giant's blind hands blundering never found.
300 Last of them all my ram, the leader, came,
weighted by wool and me with my **meditations**.
The Cyclops patted him, and then he said:

'Sweet cousin ram, why lag behind the rest
in the night cave? You never linger so,
305 but graze before them all, and go afar
to crop sweet grass, and take your stately way
leading along the streams, until at evening
you run to be the first one in the fold.
Why, now, so far behind? Can you be grieving
310 over your Master's eye? That carrion rogue
and his accurst companions burnt it out
when he had conquered all my wits with wine.
Nohbdy will not get out alive, I swear.
Oh, had you brain and voice to tell
315 where he may be now, dodging all my fury!
Bashed by this hand and bashed on this rock wall
his brains would strew the floor, and I should have
rest from the outrage Nohbdy worked upon me.'

He sent us into the open, then. Close by,
320 I dropped and rolled clear of the ram's belly,
going this way and that to untie the men.
With many glances back, we rounded up
his fat, stiff-legged sheep to take aboard,
and drove them down to where the good ship lay. ●
325 We saw, as we came near, our fellows' faces
shining; then we saw them turn to grief
tallying those who had not fled from death.
I hushed them, jerking head and eyebrows up,

---

27. **pectoral fleece:** the wool covering a sheep's chest.

and in a low voice told them: 'Load this herd;
330 move fast, and put the ship's head toward the breakers.'[28]
They all pitched in at loading, then embarked
and struck their oars into the sea. Far out,
as far off shore as shouted words would carry,
I sent a few back to the **adversary**:

335 'O Cyclops! Would you feast on my companions?
Puny, am I, in a Caveman's hands?
How do you like the beating that we gave you,
you damned cannibal? Eater of guests
under your roof! Zeus and the gods have paid you!'[29]

340 The blind thing in his doubled fury broke
a hilltop in his hands and heaved it after us.
Ahead of our black prow it struck and sank
whelmed in a spuming geyser, a giant wave
that washed the ship stern foremost back to shore.
345 I got the longest boathook out and stood
fending us off, with furious nods to all
to put their backs into a racing stroke—
row, row, or perish.[30] So the long oars bent
kicking the foam sternward, making head
350 until we drew away, and twice as far.
Now when I cupped my hands[31] I heard the crew
in low voices protesting:

                                    'Godsake, Captain!
Why bait the beast again? Let him alone!'

---

28. **put . . . the breakers:** turn the ship around so that it is heading toward the open sea.

29. **O Cyclops! . . . paid you!:** Odysseus assumes that the gods are on his side.

30. **The blind thing . . . or perish:** The hilltop thrown by Polyphemus lands in front of the ship, causing a huge wave that carries the ship back to the shore. Odysseus uses a long pole to push the boat away from the land.

31. **cupped my hands:** put his hands on either side of his mouth in order to magnify his voice.

adversary (ăd′vər-sĕr′ē) *n.* an opponent; enemy

'That tidal wave he made on the first throw
355 all but beached us.'

                                        'All but stove us in!'

'Give him our bearing with your trumpeting,
he'll get the range and lob a boulder.'

                                            'Aye
He'll smash our timbers and our heads together!'

I would not heed them in my glorying spirit,
360 but let my anger flare and yelled: **PAUSE & REFLECT**

                                          'Cyclops,
if ever mortal man inquire
how you were put to shame and blinded, tell him
Odysseus, raider of cities, took your eye:
Laertes' son, whose home's on Ithaca!' 

365 At this he gave a mighty sob and rumbled:

'Now comes the weird upon me, spoken of old.[32]
A wizard, grand and wondrous, lived here—Telemus,
a son of Eurymus; great length of days
he had in wizardry among the Cyclopes,
370 and these things he foretold for time to come:
my great eye lost, and at Odysseus' hands.
Always I had in mind some giant, armed
in giant force, would come against me here.
But this, but you—small, pitiful and twiggy—
375 you put me down with wine, you blinded me.[33]

---

32. **Now comes . . . of old:** Now I recall the destiny predicted long ago.

33. **Now comes . . . you blinded me:** Polyphemus tells of a prophecy made long ago by Telemus, a prophet who predicted that Polyphemus would lose his eye at the hands of Odysseus.

PAUSE & REFLECT
Odysseus taunts the Cyclops as he and his men are trying to escape. How do the men react to Odysseus' behavior, and why?

ⓜ EPIC HERO
Circle the epithets Odysseus uses to refer to himself in lines 366–369. What traits does Odysseus show in revealing so much about himself?

Come back, Odysseus, and I'll treat you well,
praying the god of earthquake[34] to befriend you—
his son I am, for he by his avowal[35]
fathered me, and, if he will, he may
380 heal me of this black wound—he and no other
of all the happy gods or mortal men.'

Few words I shouted in reply to him:
'If I could take your life I would and take
your time away, and hurl you down to hell!
385 The god of earthquake could not heal you there!'

At this he stretched his hands out in his darkness
toward the sky of stars, and prayed Poseidon:

'O hear me, lord, blue girdler of the islands,
if I am thine indeed, and thou art father:
390 grant that Odysseus, raider of cities, never
see his home: Laertes' son, I mean,
who kept his hall on Ithaca. Should destiny
intend that he shall see his roof again
among his family in his father land,
395 far be that day, and dark the years between.
Let him lose all companions, and return
under strange sail to bitter days at home.' **PAUSE & REFLECT**

In these words he prayed, and the god heard him.
Now he laid hands upon a bigger stone
400 and wheeled around, titanic for the cast,[36]
to let it fly in the black-prowed vessel's track.
But it fell short, just aft[37] the steering oar,

PAUSE & REFLECT

Summarize Polyphemus' curse in lines 408–417. How has Odysseus brought this curse upon himself?

---

34. **the god of earthquake:** Poseidon.
35. **avowal:** honest admission.
36. **titanic for the cast:** drawing on all his enormous strength in preparing to throw.
37. **aft:** behind.

and whelming seas rose giant above the stone
to bear us onward toward the island.[38]

                                           There

405 as we ran in we saw the squadron waiting,
the trim ships drawn up side by side, and all
our troubled friends who waited, looking seaward.
We beached her, grinding keel in the soft sand,
and waded in, ourselves, on the sandy beach.
410 Then we unloaded all the Cyclops' flock
to make division, share and share alike,
only my fighters voted that my ram,
the prize of all, should go to me. I slew him
by the sea side and burnt his long thighbones
415 to Zeus beyond the stormcloud, Cronus' son,[39]
who rules the world. But Zeus disdained my offering;
destruction for my ships he had in store
and death for those who sailed them, my companions.

Now all day long until the sun went down
420 we made our feast on mutton and sweet wine,
till after sunset in the gathering dark
we went to sleep above the wash of ripples.

When the young Dawn with finger tips of rose
touched the world, I roused the men, gave orders
425 to man the ships, cast off the mooring lines;
and filing in to sit beside the rowlocks
oarsmen in line dipped oars in the gray sea.
So we moved out, sad in the vast offing,[40]
having our precious lives, but not our friends." **PAUSE & REFLECT**

PAUSE & REFLECT
Why do Odysseus and his men
have mixed feelings as they
leave the land of the Cyclopes?

_____

_____

_____

_____

_____

_____

_____

_____

---

38. **the island:** the deserted island where most of Odysseus' men had stayed behind.
39. **Cronus' son:** Zeus' father, Cronus, was a Titan, one of an earlier race of gods.
40. **offing:** the part of the deep sea visible from the shore.

Text Analysis: Epic Hero

How does Odysseus embody the traits of an epic hero? For each trait in the chart below, provide an example of Odysseus' actions or words from his adventure with the Cyclops.

ODYSSEUS	
Traits of an Epic Hero	**Examples from "The Cyclops"**
Possesses superhuman strength and craftiness	
Is both helped and harmed by interfering gods	
Embodies ideals and values that a culture considers admirable	
Emerges victorious from perilous situations	

Odysseus has many admirable qualities, but he's not perfect. What weaknesses or faults does he reveal in the story?

_____

_____

_____

_____

_____

Reading Strategy: Reading an Epic Poem

Homer uses epic similes to describe certain events in the story very vividly. Use the chart below to analyze how another epic simile affected you as a reader.

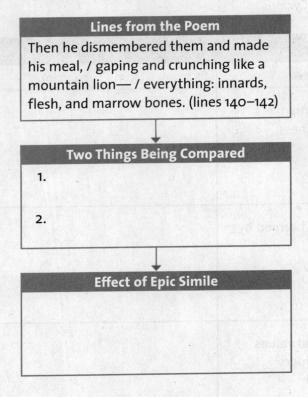

Lines from the Poem
Then he dismembered them and made his meal, / gaping and crunching like a mountain lion— / everything: innards, flesh, and marrow bones. (lines 140–142)

↓

Two Things Being Compared
1.
2.

↓

Effect of Epic Simile

What is a HERO?

What heroes like Odysseus have you encountered in modern literature, movies, or television programs? Tell what traits they have in common with Odysseus.

_____

_____

Vocabulary Practice

Decide whether the words in each pair are synonyms or antonyms. Write **A** if they are antonyms or **S** if they are synonyms.

_____ **1.** appalled/dismayed

_____ **2.** profusion/shortage

_____ **3.** adversary/friend

_____ **4.** ponderous/awkward

_____ **5.** meditation/contemplation

Academic Vocabulary in Writing

demonstrate	emphasis	ideology	monitor	undertake

Select one of the epithets used for Odysseus in "The Cyclops," or invent a new one that captures an important quality or accomplishment of his. Then, write a few sentences explain what the epithet **demonstrates** about Odysseus' character. Use at least one Academic Vocabulary word. Definitions for these terms are listed on page 441.

_____

_____

_____

Assessment Practice

DIRECTIONS Use "The Cyclops" to answer questions 1–6.

1 The *Odyssey* is an epic poem because it —
- **A** has a main character who is strong and brave
- **B** is a long narrative poem about the deeds of a hero
- **C** features a monster that eats human beings
- **D** was performed orally before it was written down

2 When he first speaks to the Cyclops, Odysseus warns him that —
- **A** the Greeks will kill him
- **B** the Greeks want his land
- **C** Zeus will avenge the Greeks if the Cyclops is not courteous
- **D** Zeus will kill the Cyclops if he doesn't give the Greeks money

3 Which of the following is part of an epic simile?
- **A** "young Dawn with finger tips of rose" (line 13)
- **B** "a shaggy mountain reared in solitude" (line 37)
- **C** "caught two in his hands like squirming puppies" (line 138)
- **D** "mother, father, and friends, / everyone calls me Nohbdy" (lines 219–220)

4 Why doesn't Odysseus kill the Cyclops after the monster eats the first two men?
- **A** He respects the customs of the Cyclopes.
- **B** The Cyclops is protected by his father, Poseidon.
- **C** Athena advises Odysseus to try a different tactic.
- **D** The Greeks would be trapped in the Cyclops' cave.

5 Which character trait is revealed in Odysseus' plan to escape the Cyclops?
- **A** cleverness
- **B** arrogance
- **C** respect for the gods
- **D** courtesy toward strangers

6 Odysseus gets out of the Cyclops' cave by —
- **A** using a pole to move the heavy slab
- **B** clinging to the belly of a ram
- **C** plunging a spike into the Cyclops' eye
- **D** making an offering to Zeus

Resources

The Glossary of Academic Vocabulary in this section is an alphabetical list of the Academic Vocabulary words found in this textbook. Use this glossary just as you would use a dictionary—to find out the meanings of words used in your literature class, to talk about and write about literary and informational texts, and to talk about and write about concepts and topics in your other academic classes.

For each word, the glossary includes the pronunciation, syllabication, part of speech, and meaning. A Spanish version of each word and definition follows the English version. For more information about the words in this glossary, please consult a dictionary.

accurate (ăk′yər-ĭt) *adj.* correct; free from errors
　preciso *adj.* correcto; sin errores

analyze (ăn′ə-līz′) *v.* to separate or break into parts and examine
　analizar *v.* separar o dividir en partes y examinar

appreciate (ə-prē′shē-āt′) *v.* to think highly of; to recognize favorably the quality or value of
　apreciar *v.* tener una buena opinión de algo o alguien; reconocer de manera favorable la calidad o el valor de algo o alguien

aspect (ăs′pĕkt) *n.* a quality, part, or element
　aspecto *sust.* cualidad, parte o elemento

attribute (ăt′rə-byo͞ot′) *n.* a quality thought of as a natural part of someone or something
　atributo *sust.* cualidad considerada como parte natural de alguien o algo

characteristic (kăr′ək-tə-rĭs′tĭk) *n.* a feature that helps to identify, tell apart, or describe recognizably
　característica *s.* rasgos o cualidades que ayudan a identificar, describir o reconocer algo

circumstance (sûr′kem-stăns′) *n.* a happening, event, or fact occurring near or in company with another
　circunstancia *sust.* suceso, evento o hecho que ocurre cerca a otro o junto a otro

cite (sīt) *v.* to refer to as example or proof
　citar *v.* hacer referencia a un ejemplo o prueba

coherent (kō-hîr′ənt) *adj.* logical, consistent, or connected
　coherente *adj.* lógico, constante o relacionado

complex (kəm-plĕks′) *adj.* made up of two or more parts; hard to understand or analyze
　complejo *adj.* compuesto por dos o más partes; difícil de comprender o analizar

conclude (kən-ko͞od′) *v.* to decide or infer by reasoning
　concluir *v.* decidir o inferir por medio del razonamiento

construct (kən-strŭkt′) *v.* to systematically create or build
　construir *v.* crear o edificar de manera sistemática

context (kŏn′tĕkst′) *n.* the words that surround a particular word or passage and make the meaning of that word or passage clear; the circumstances in which an event occurs
　contexto *sust.* palabras que rodean una palabra o un pasaje en particular y aclaran el significado de esa palabra o pasaje; circunstancias en las que ocurre un evento

contrast (kən-trăst′) *v.* to show differences
　contrastar *v.* mostrar las diferencias

contribute (kən-trĭb′yo͞ot) *v.* to provide or give ideas, knowledge, material goods, etc.
　contribuir *v.* dar u ofrecer ideas, conocimientos, bienes materiales, etc.

conventional (kən-vĕn′shə-nəl) *adj.* conforming to traditional standards

    convencional *adj.* mantener las ideas o las costumbres

critical (krĭt′ĭ-kəl) *n.* characterized by careful, exact evaluation and judgment

    critico *n.* relacionado con realizar juicios basándose en lot puntos fuertes y débiles

demonstrate (dĕm′ən-strāt′) *v.* to show clearly and purposefully

    demostrar *v.* mostrar en forma clara y con determinación

device (dĭ-vīs′) *n.* a thing created; a mechanical invention or creation

    dispositivo *sust.* algo creado; invento o creación mecánica

differentiate (dĭf′ə-rĕn′shē-āt′) *v.* to perceive or create a difference between

    diferenciar *v.* percibir o crear una diferencia

distinct (dĭ-stĭngkt′) *adj.* separate or different; defined clearly

    distinto *adj.* individual o diferente; definido con claridad

effect (ĭ-fĕkt′) *n.* something brought about by a cause; result

    efecto *sust.* un sustantivo que significa resultado de un evento o una acción llevada a cabo por alguien

element (ĕl′ə-mənt) *n.* one necessary or basic part of a whole

    elemento *sust.* parte necesaria o básica de un todo

emphasis (ĕm′fə-sĭs) *n.* special stress on something—a word, phrase, idea, etc.— to make it stand out

    énfasis *sust.* hincapié que se hace en algo (palabra, frase, idea, etc.) para destacarlo

environment (ĕn-vī′rən-mənt) *n.* surroundings; the land, water, climate, plants, and animals of an area

    ambiente *sust.* entorno; tierra, agua, clima, plantas y animales de un área

evaluate (ĭ-văl′yoo-āt′) *v.* to find out the value or worth of something; to judge or examine

    evaluar *v.* hallar el valor o el precio; juzgar o examinar

evident (ĕv′ĭ-dənt) *adj.* obvious, easy to see or understand

    evidente *adj.* obvio, fácil de ver o comprender

evoke (ĭ-vōk′) *v.* to call to mind

    factor *sust.* elementos o condiciones que hacen que algo exista o produzca un resultado.

factor (făk′tər) *n.* elements or conditions that make something what it is or create a result

    factor *sust.* elementos o condiciones que hacen que algo exista o produzca un resultado

form (fôrm) *n.* the structure of something

    forma *sust.* en forma de

ideology (ī′dē-ŏl′ə-jē) *n.* the beliefs or way of thinking—especially political, economic, or social beliefs and ways of thinking—of an individual or group of people

    ideología *sust.* creencias o maneras de pensar, especialmente políticas, económicas o sociales, de una persona o un grupo de personas

implicit (ĭm-plĭs′ĭt) *adj.* not plainly obvious or exhibited; suggested or implied

    implícito *adj.* que no es obvio o se muestra; sugerido o tácito

incorporate (ĭn-kôr′pə-rāt′) *v.* to join or combine into a single whole

    incorporar *v.* unir o combinar en un todo

indicate (ĭn′dĭ-kāt′) *v.* to point out or show

    indicar *v.* señalar o mostrar

Glossary of Academic Vocabulary in English & Spanish

infer (ĭn-fûr') *v.* to decide based on evidence or knowledge; to draw a conclusion
　inferir *v.* decidir a partir de pruebas o del conocimiento; sacar una conclusión

influence (ĭn'flōō-əns) *v.* to produce an effect on; sway
　influenciar *v.* producir efecto en

interact (ĭn'tər-ăkt') *v.* to act or work with someone or something; to act with one another
　interactuar *v.* actuar o trabajar con alguien o algo; actuar en forma conjunta

interpret (ĭn-tûr'prət) *v.* to explain the meaning of or translate
　interpretar *v.* explicar el significado o traducir

investigate (ĭn-vĕs'tĭ-gāt') *v.* to search carefully, as to acquire or verify facts
　investigar *v.* buscar en detalle para obtener o verificar datos

monitor (mŏn'ĭ-tər) *v.* to check in on, watch, regulate
　supervisar *v.* controlar, observar, regular

motivate (mō'tə-vāt) *v.* to provide with an incentive; move to action
　motivar *v.* incitar a alguien para que realice una acción.

perceive (pər-sēv') *v.* to observe or become aware of
　percibir *v.* observar o tomar conciencia de algo

perspective (pər-spĕk'tĭv) *n.* point of view or mental view
　perspectiva *sust.* punto de vista u opinión

predominant (prĭ-dăm'ə-nənt) *adj.* the most frequent or the most important
　predominante *adj.* el más frecuente o el más importante

primary (prī'mĕr-ē) *adj.* highest in rank or first in importance
　primario *adj.* de categoría superior o primero en importancia

refer (rĭ-fûr') *v.* to pertain or concern
　referirse *v.* concernir a, pertenecer a

relevant (rĕl'ə-vənt) *adj.* related or pertinent to the matter at hand
　relevante *adj.* relacionado con el tema en cuestión o pertinente

resolve (rĭ-zŏlv') *v.* to bring to a conclusion
　resolver *v.* concluir, llegar a una conclusión

reveal (rĭ-vēl') *v.* to show, make known, or expose
　revelar *v.* mostrar, dar a conocer o exponer

sequence (sē'kwəns) *n.* the chronological, causal, or logical order in which one thing follows another
　secuencia *sust.* orden cronológico, causal o lógico en el que una cosa sigue a otra

significant (sĭg-nĭf'ĭ-kənt) *adj.* having meaning; important
　significativo *adj.* que tiene sentido; importante

source (sôrs) *n.* a book, document, person, etc., that supplies information
　fuente *sust.* libro, documento, persona, etc., que proporciona información

specific (spĭ-sĭf'ĭk) *adj.* definite; of a special sort
　específico *adj.* definitivo; de una clase en especial

structure (strŭk'chər) *n.* something constructed or built, such as a building
　estructura *sust.* algo que se construye, como un edificio

synthesize (sĭn′thĭ-sīz′) *v.* to combine separate elements into a whole

  sintetizar *v.* combinar elementos individuales para formar un todo

technique (tĕk-nēk′) *n.* a method of procedure or a manner of doing something

  técnica *sust.* método para proceder o manera de hacer algo

tradition (trə-dĭsh′ən) *n.* a practice passed down from generation to generation

  tradición *sust.* práctica que se transmite de generación en generación

undertake (ŭn′dər-tāk′) *v.* to take on a task or assume a responsibility

  asumir *v.* aceptar una tarea o contraer una responsabilidad

unique (yōō-nēk′) *adj.* the only one; having no equal

  único *adj.* exclusivo; sin igual

vary (vâr′ē) *v.* to modify or alter; to change the characteristics of something

  variar *v.* modificar o alterar; cambiar las características de algo

Pronunciation Key

Symbol	Examples	Symbol	Examples	Symbol	Examples
ă	at, gas	m	man, seem	v	van, save
ā	ape, day	n	night, mitten	w	web, twice
ä	father, barn	ng	sing, hanger	y	yard, lawyer
âr	fair, dare	ŏ	odd, not	z	zoo, reason
b	bell, table	ō	open, road, grow	zh	treasure, garage
ch	chin, lunch	ô	awful, bought, horse	ə	awake, even, pencil,
d	dig, bored	oi	coin, boy		pilot, focus
ĕ	egg, ten	ŏŏ	look, full	ər	perform, letter
ē	evil, see, meal	ōō	root, glue, through		
f	fall, laugh, phrase	ou	out, cow	**Sounds in Foreign Words**	
g	gold, big	p	pig, cap	KH	*German* i**ch**, au**ch**;
h	hit, inhale	r	rose, star		*Scottish* lo**ch**
hw	white, everywhere	s	sit, face	N	*French* e**n**tre, bo**n**, fi**n**
ĭ	inch, fit	sh	she, mash	œ	*French* f**eu**, c**œu**r;
ī	idle, my, tried	t	tap, hopped		*German* sch**ö**n
îr	dear, here	th	thing, with	ü	*French* **u**tile, r**u**e;
j	jar, gem, badge	*th*	then, other		*German* gr**ü**n
k	keep, cat, luck	ŭ	up, nut		
l	load, rattle	ûr	fur, earn, bird, worm		

Stress Marks

′ This mark indicates that the preceding syllable receives the primary stress. For example, in the word *language*, the first syllable is stressed: lăng′gwĭj.

′ This mark is used only in words in which more than one syllable is stressed. It indicates that the preceding syllable is stressed, but somewhat more weakly than the syllable receiving the primary stress. In the word *literature*, for example, the first syllable receives the primary stress, and the last syllable receives a weaker stress: lĭt′ər-ə-chŏŏr′.

High-Frequency Word List

Would you like to build your word knowledge? If so, the word lists on the next six pages can help you. These lists contain the 600 most common words in the English language. The most common words are on the First Hundred Words list; the next most common are on the Second Hundred Words list; and so on.

Study tip: Read through these lists starting with the First Hundred Words list. For each word you don't know, make a flash card. Work through the flash cards until you can read each word quickly.

FIRST HUNDRED WORDS

the	he	go	who
a	I	see	an
is	they	then	their
you	one	us	she
to	good	no	new
and	me	him	said
we	about	by	did
that	had	was	boy
in	if	come	three
not	some	get	down
for	up	or	work
at	her	two	put
with	do	man	were
it	when	little	before
on	so	has	just
can	my	them	long
will	very	how	here
are	all	like	other
of	would	our	old
this	any	what	take
your	been	know	cat
as	out	make	again
but	there	which	give
be	from	much	after
have	day	his	many

SECOND HUNDRED WORDS

saw	big	may	fan
home	where	let	five
soon	am	use	read
stand	ball	these	over
box	morning	right	such
upon	live	present	way
first	four	tell	too
came	last	next	shall
girl	color	please	own
house	away	leave	most
find	red	hand	sure
because	friend	more	thing
made	pretty	why	only
could	eat	better	near
book	want	under	than
look	year	while	open
mother	white	should	kind
run	got	never	must
school	play	each	high
people	found	best	far
night	left	another	both
into	men	seem	end
say	bring	tree	also
think	wish	name	until
back	black	dear	call

THIRD HUNDRED WORDS

ask	hat	off	fire
small	car	sister	ten
yellow	write	happy	order
show	try	once	part
goes	myself	didn't	early
clean	longer	set	fat
buy	those	round	third
thank	hold	dress	same
sleep	full	tell	love
letter	carry	wash	hear
jump	eight	start	eyes
help	sing	always	door
fly	warm	anything	clothes
don't	sit	around	through
fast	dog	close	o'clock
cold	ride	walk	second
today	hot	money	water
does	grow	turn	town
face	cut	might	took
green	seven	hard	pair
every	woman	along	now
brown	funny	bed	keep
coat	yes	fine	head
six	ate	sat	food
gave	stop	hope	yesterday

FOURTH HUNDRED WORDS

told	yet	word	airplane
Miss	true	almost	without
father	above	thought	wear
children	still	send	Mr.
land	meet	receive	side
interest	since	pay	poor
feet	number	nothing	lost
garden	state	need	wind
done	matter	mean	Mrs.
country	line	late	learn
different	large	half	held
bad	few	fight	front
across	hit	enough	built
yard	cover	feet	family
winter	window	during	began
table	even	gone	air
story	city	hundred	young
I'm	together	week	ago
tried	sun	between	world
horse	life	change	kill
brought	street	being	ready
shoes	party	care	stay
government	suit	answer	won't
sometimes	remember	course	paper
time	something	against	outside

FIFTH HUNDRED WORDS

hour	grade	egg	spell
glad	brother	ground	beautiful
follow	remain	afternoon	sick
company	milk	feed	became
believe	several	boat	cry
begin	war	plan	finish
mind	able	question	catch
pass	charge	fish	floor
reach	either	return	stick
month	less	sir	great
point	train	fell	guess
rest	cost	fill	bridge
sent	evening	wood	church
talk	note	add	lady
went	past	ice	tomorrow
bank	room	chair	snow
ship	flew	watch	whom
business	office	alone	women
whole	cow	low	among
short	visit	arm	road
certain	wait	dinner	farm
fair	teacher	hair	cousin
reason	spring	service	bread
summer	picture	class	wrong
fill	bird	quite	age

SIXTH HUNDRED WORDS

become	themselves	thousand	wife
body	herself	demand	condition
chance	idea	however	aunt
act	drop	figure	system
die	river	case	line
real	smile	increase	cause
speak	son	enjoy	marry
already	bat	rather	possible
doctor	fact	sound	supply
step	sort	eleven	pen
itself	king	music	perhaps
nine	dark	human	produce
baby	whose	court	twelve
minute	study	force	rode
ring	fear	plant	uncle
wrote	move	suppose	labor
happen	stood	law	public
appear	himself	husband	consider
heart	strong	moment	thus
swim	knew	person	least
felt	often	result	power
fourth	toward	continue	mark
I'll	wonder	price	voice
kept	twenty	serve	whether
well	important	national	president

Brandt & Hochman Literary Agents: "The Most Dangerous Game" by Richard Connell. Copyright © 1924 by Richard Connell. Copyright renewed © 1952 by Louise Fox Connell. Reprinted by permission of Brandt & Hochman Literary Agents, Inc.

Laura Hillenbrand: "Four Good Legs Between Us," from *American Heritage,* July/August 1998, by Laura Hillenbrand. Copyright © 1998 by Laura Hillenbrand. Reprinted by permission of the author.

WGBH/Boston: Excerpt from "Timeline: Seabiscuit" from the American Experience/WGBH Educational Foundation © 2009 WGBH/Boston. Used by permission of WGBH/Boston.

NBC News Archives: Excerpt from the radio broadcast "Santa Anita Handicap" by Clem McCarthy and Buddy Twist. Copyright © 1937 by NBC News Archives. Reprinted by permission of NBC News Archives.

Alfred A. Knopf: "Incident in a Rose Garden," from *Collected Poems* by Donald Justice. Copyright © 2004 by Donald Justice. Reprinted by permission of Alfred A. Knopf, a division of Random House, Inc.

Houghton Mifflin Harcourt: "The Necklace" by Guy de Maupassant from *Adventures in Reading,* Laureate Edition, Grade 9. Copyright © 1963 by Harcourt, Inc., and renewed 1991. Reprinted by permission of the publisher. This material may not be reproduced in any form or by any means without prior written permission of the publisher.

Random House: Excerpt from "Sister Flowers," from *I Know Why the Caged Bird Sings* by Maya Angelou. Copyright © 1969 and renewed © 1997 by Maya Angelou. Used by permission of Random House, Inc.

Penguin Group (USA): Excerpt from "The Bus Boycott" from *Rosa Parks* by Douglas Brinkley. Copyright © 2000 by Douglas Brinkley. Used by permission of Viking Penguin, a division of Penguin Group (USA) Inc.

Rita Dove: "Rosa" by Rita Dove was first published in the *Georgia Review,* Winter 1998, and subsequently in *On the Bus with Rosa Parks,* published by W.W. Norton. Copyright © 1999 by Rita Dove. Reprinted by permission of the author.

Random House: "A Christmas Memory" by Truman Capote. Copyright © 1956 by Truman Capote. Used by permission of Random House, Inc.

HarperCollins Publishers and Jonathan Clowes: "Through the Tunnel," from *The Habit of Loving* by Doris Lessing. Copyright © 1954, 1955 by Doris Lessing, originally appeared in the *New Yorker.* Reprinted by permission of HarperCollins Publishers Inc. and the kind permission of Jonathan Clowes Ltd., London, on behalf of Doris Lessing.

Broadway Books and Doubleday Canada: Excerpt from *A Walk in the Woods* by Bill Bryson. Copyright © 1997 by Bill Bryson. Used by the permission of Broadway Books, a division of Random House, Inc., and Doubleday Canada, a division of Random House of Canada Limited.

Doubleday: "Wilderness Letter," from *The Sound of Mountain Water* by Wallace Stegner. Copyright © 1969 by Wallace Stegner. Used by permission of Doubleday, a division of Random House, Inc.

James Hurst: "The Scarlet Ibis" by James Hurst. Copyright © 1960 by the *Atlantic Monthly* and renewed 1988 by James Hurst. Reprinted by permission of James Hurst.

Thames & Hudson: "Poem on Returning to Dwell in the Country," from *T'ao the Hermit: Sixty Poems by Tao Chien by Tao Ch'ien,* translated by William Acker. Copyright © 1952 by William Acker. Reprinted by kind permission of Thames & Hudson Ltd., London.

Beacon Press: "The Sun," from *New and Selected Poems* by Mary Oliver. Copyright © 1992 by Mary Oliver. Reprinted by permission of Beacon Press, Boston.

G. P. Putnam's and Sons: "Two Kinds," from *The Joy Luck Club* by Amy Tan. Copyright © 1989 by Amy Tan. Used by permission of G. P. Putnam's and Sons, a division of Penguin Group (USA) Inc.

Diane Mei Lin Mark: "Rice and Rose Bowl Blues" by Diane Mei Lin Mark. Copyright © by Diane Mei Lin Mark. Reprinted by permission of the author.

National Geographic Society: "Who Killed the Iceman?" *National Geographic,* February 2002. Copyright © 2002 by National Geographic Society. Reprinted by permission of National Geographic Society.

Little, Brown and Company: Excerpt from "Skeletal Sculptures" from *The Bone Detectives* by Donna M. Jackson and Illustrated by Charlie Fellenbaum. Copyright © 1996 by Donna M. Jackson. Photographs copyright © 1996 by Charlie Fellenbaum. By permission of Little, Brown & Company.

Scholastic: "The Lost Boys" by Sara Corbett, *New York Times Upfront,* September 3, 2001. Copyright © 2001 by Scholastic Inc. Used by permission.

Writers House: "I Have a Dream" speech by Martin Luther King Jr. Copyright © 1963 Martin Luther King Jr., copyright renewed 1991 Coretta Scott King. Reprinted by arrangement with The Heirs to the Estate of Martin Luther King Jr., c/o Writers House as agent for the proprietor, New York, NY.

Andrea Rock: "How Private Is Your Private Life?" by Andrea Rock, *Ladies Home Journal,* October 2000. Copyright © 2000 by Andrea Rock. Reprinted with the permission of the author.

Acknowledgments

Arthur M. Ahalt: "The Privacy Debate: One Size Doesn't Fit All" by Arthur M. Ahalt from *The Daily Record,* June 20, 2003. Copyright © 2003 by Arthur M. Ahalt. Reprinted by permission of the author.

Liveright Publishing Corporation: "Spring is like a perhaps hand," from *Complete Poems: 1904–1962* by E. E. Cummings, edited by George J. Firmage. Copyright 1923, 1925, 1951, 1953, © 1991 by the Trustees for the E. E. Cummings Trust. Copyright © 1976 by George James Firmage. Used by permission of Liveright Publishing Corporation.

Houghton Mifflin Harcourt and Larmore Literary Agency: "Elegy for the Giant Tortoises," *Selected Poems 1965–1975* by Margaret Atwood. Copyright © 1976 by Margaret Atwood. Reprinted by permission of Houghton Mifflin Harcourt Publishing Company and Larmore Literary Agency. All rights reserved.

Random House: "Today," by Billy Collins from *Nine Horses.* Copyright © 2002 by Billy Collins. Used by permission of Random House, Inc.

Tim O'Brien: "Where Have You Gone, Charming Billy?" by Tim O'Brien, from *Redbook,* May 1975. Copyright © 1975 by Tim O'Brien. Reprinted by permission of the author.

Scissor Press: Interview with Tim O'Brien by Douglas Novielli, Chris Connal, and Jackson Ellis. From *Verbicide,* Issue 8. Copyright © 2003 by Scissor Press. Reprinted by permission of Scissor Press.

Houghton Mifflin Harcourt: "A Few Words," from *Blue Pastures* by Mary Oliver. Copyright © 1995, 1992, 1991 by Mary Oliver. Reprinted by permission of Houghton Mifflin Harcourt Publishing Company. All rights reserved.

Gary N. DaSilva: "The Sneeze" from *The Good Doctor,* by Neil Simon. Copyright © 1974 by Neil Simon, copyright renewed 2004 by Neil Simon. Professionals and amateurs are hereby warned that *The Good Doctor* is fully protected under the Berne Convention and the Universal Copyright Convention and is subject to royalty. All rights, including without limitation professional, amateur, motion picture, television, radio, recitation, lecturing, public reading and foreign translation rights, computer media rights and the right of reproduction, and electronic storage or retrieval, in whole or in part and in any form, are strictly reserved and none of these rights can be exercised or used without written permission from the copyright owner. Inquiries for stock and amateur performances should be addressed to Samuel French, Inc., 45 West 25th Street, New York, NY 10010. All other inquiries should be addressed to Gary N. DaSilva, 111 N. Sepulveda Blvd., Manhattan Beach, CA, 90266-6850.

Simon & Schuster: Excerpt from *Angela's Ashes* by Frank McCourt. Copyright © 1996 by Frank McCourt. Reprinted with the permission of Scribner, an imprint of Simon & Schuster Adult Publishing Group.

University of Georgia Press: "American History," from *The Latin Deli: Prose & Poetry* by Judith Ortiz Cofer. Copyright © 1992 by Judith Ortiz Cofer. Reprinted by permission of the University of Georgia Press.

U.S. News & World Report: "Dark Day" by Kenneth T. Walsh from *U.S. News & World Report,* November 24, 2003. Copyright © 2003 by U.S. News & World Report. Reprinted by permission of U.S. News & World Report.

Universal Press Syndicate: Excerpt from "Romeo and Juliet" by Roger Ebert, from the *Chicago Sun-Times,* September 17, 2000. Copyright © 2000 by The Ebert Company. Reprinted with permission. All rights reserved.

Farrar, Straus and Giroux: Excerpts from *The Odyssey* by Homer, translated by Robert Fitzgerald. Translation copyright © 1961, 1963 renewed 1989 by Benedict R. C. Fitzgerald on behalf of the Fitzgerald children. This edition © 1998 by Farrar, Straus & Giroux, LLC. Reprinted by permission of Farrar, Straus and Giroux, LLC.

McGraw-Hill Companies: From *Elementary Reading Instruction* by Edward Fry. Copyright © 1977 by McGraw-Hill Companies, Inc. All rights reserved. Reprinted by permission of the publisher.

COVER

(tc) Sea World of California/Corbis; (tr) Odysseus Slaying the Suitors (400's B.C.), Penelope Painter. Attic red figure painting on kylix. Height 20 cm. Inv F 2588. Antikensammlung, Staatliche Museen zu Berlin, Berlin. Photo by Juergen Liepe. © Bildarchiv Preussischer Kulturbesitz/Art Resource, New York; (bc) Colin Anderdson/Getty Images; (b) Portrait of William Shakespeare (about 1610), John Taylor. Oil on canvas. National Portrait Gallery, London. © Bridgeman Art Library; (bkgd) © Walter Geiersperger/Corbis; (bl) Ken Kinzie/HMH Publishers.

HOW TO USE THIS BOOK

xiii *top* © photostogo.com; *bottom* Detail of *Woman at Her Toilette*, Edgar Degas. Pastel on cardboard. State Hermitage Museum, St. Petersburg, Russia. © SuperStock/SuperStock; **xvi** © photostogo.com.

UNIT 1

2 © Firefly Productions/Corbis; **6–30** © AbleStock.com/Jupiterimages Corporation; **6** © Comstock Images/Jupiterimages Corporation; **11** © Gordan/ShutterStock; **27** © Comstock Images/Jupiterimages Corporation; **36–42** © photostogo.com; **36** Detail of *Woman at Her Toilette,* Edgar Degas. Pastel on cardboard. State Hermitage Museum, St. Petersburg, Russia. © SuperStock/SuperStock; **47** © Hulton Archive/Getty Images; **51** *left* © Bettmann/Corbis; *right* © Keystone/Hulton Archive/Getty Images; **58–65** © George Burba/ShutterStock; **58** © IT Stock Free/Jupiterimages Corporation; **64** © Leonid Kashtalian/istockphoto.com.

UNIT 2

68 © Design Pics/Punchstock; **72–82** © photostogo.com; **72, 77** © DAJ/PunchStock; **88–96** © Digital Vision/PunchStock; **88** © Solus-Veer/Corbis; **102–106** © Feng Yu/ShutterStock; **102** © Bettmann/Corbis.

UNIT 3

110 © Heidi Hart/ShutterStock; **114–128** © Comstock Images/Jupiterimages Corporation; **114** © Edward Charles Le Grice/Hulton Archive/Getty Images; **134–144** © Comstock Images/Jupiterimages Corporation; **134** © Nathan B. Dappen/ShutterStock; **148** © The Kobal Collection; **150–158** © Digital Archive Japan/PunchStock; **150** San Gennaro Catacombs, Naples, Italy. Photo © Gianni Dagli Orti/The Art Archive; **164–172** © David Raboin/istockphoto.com; **164** © Comstock Images/Jupiterimages Corporation; **177** © Photos.com/Jupiterimages Corporation.

UNIT 4

186 © Design Pics/PunchStock; **190–204** © photostogo.com; **190, 201** © Comstock Images/Jupiterimages Corporation; **210–214** © istockphoto.com; **210** © redchopsticks/PunchStock; **212** © Bill Binzen/Corbis; **213** © EvGraf/ShutterStock; **220–235** © Loke Yek Mang/ShutterStock; **220, 231** © Renars Jurkovskis/ShutterStock; **234** © Noam Armonn/ShutterStock.

UNIT 5

238 © Lara Jo Regan/Liaison/Getty Images; **242** © Reuters/Corbis; **243** © Regional Hospital of Bolzano/South Tyrol Museum of Archaeology www.iceman.it; **245** top © GeoNova LLC; *bottom* © Copper Age/The Bridgeman Art Library/Getty Images; **247–252** © Comstock Images/Jupiterimages Corporation; **248–252** Photos from *The Bone Detective* © Charles Fellenbaum, Boulder, Colorado; **258–263** © Rob Broek/istockphoto.com; **258** © Miroslava Vilimova/Alamy Ltd.

UNIT 6

276 Andrew Rullestad/The Ames Tribune/AP/Wide World Photos; **280–284** © Digital Vision/PunchStock; **280** Library of Congress, Prints and Photographs Division [LC-DIG-ppmsc-01269]; **291** © Ron Sachs/CNP/Sygma/Corbis; **292, 295** © Jonathan Larsen/istockphoto.com; **302** © Digital Vision/PunchStock; **308, 311** © istockphoto.com.

UNIT 7

316 © Saniphoto/ShutterStock; **320–325** © Photos.com/Jupiterimages Corporation; **320** © PhotoDisc/Getty Images; **322** © PhotoObjects.net/Jupiterimages Corporation; **324** © Comstock Images/Jupiterimages Corporation.

UNIT 8

328 Detail of *Self Portrait* (1889–1890), Vincent Van Gogh. Oil on canvas. Musée d'Orsay, Paris. © SuperStock/SuperStock; **332–341** © Grant Terry/ShutterStock; **332, 342** © Lukasz Janicki/ShutterStock; **350–352** © Karel Broz/ShutterStock; **350** © PhotoDisc/Getty Images; **358–368** © Comstock Images/Jupiterimages Corporation; **358** The Granger Collection, New York.

UNIT 9

372 © John Leung/ShutterStock; **376–388** © AbleStock.com/Jupiterimages Corporation; **376** © Corbis Sygma; **394–404** © photostogo.com; **394, 401** © dubassy/ShutterStock; **409** © photostogo.com.

UNIT 10

414 © Mary Evans Picture Library; **418–428** © Comstock Images/Jupiterimages Corporation; **418** *Romeo and Juliet,* 1996. Leonardo Di Caprio and Claire Danes. © 20th Century Fox/Courtesy Everett Collection; **433** Courtesy Everett Collection.

UNIT 11

440 © Ruggero Vanni/Corbis; **444–460** © Corbis; **444** © Mary Evans Picture Library.

Index of Authors and Titles